Personnel and Human Resource Management

Personnel and Human Resource Management: Theory and Practice in Ireland

Patrick Gunnigle, Noreen Heraty
and
Michael Morley

GILL & MACMILLAN

Gill & Macmillan Ltd
Hume Avenue, Park West
Dublin 12
with associated companies throughout the world
www.gillmacmillan.ie

Index compiled by
Helen Litton

Design and print origination in Ireland by
O'K Graphic Design, Dublin

The paper used in this book is made from the wood pulp of managed forests. For every tree felled, at least one tree is planted, thereby renewing natural resources.

Contents

Preface

In a previous text published in 1990 on personnel management in Ireland, a key backdrop to the analysis of developments in Irish personnel/human resource (HR) management was the significant changes that occurred in the business environment during the 1980s. Economic depression, spiralling unemployment and emigration, 'downsizing' and falling union density were some of the key factors that impacted on developments in personnel management. It is clear that so far the 1990s have provided a context of equally rapid change but of a somewhat differing nature: most indicators of macro-economic performance provide a positive and optimistic picture for the Irish economy, while the international business environment is characterised by increasing pressures of change and adaptation in HRM.

This text seeks to provide a new and comprehensive analysis of the implications of such contemporary developments for personnel management in Ireland. Particular emphasis is placed on addressing current debates in the literature in the context of Irish research evidence and case study 'vignettes'. Novel aspects of this text include (i) a strong strategy dimension, incorporating material on linking business and personnel/HR strategies and on the development and diffusion of 'human resource management'; (ii) an extensive labour market focus, with particular emphasis on the nature of the Irish labour market; (iii) a comprehensive review of the full range of personnel activity areas, with particular emphasis on areas of current focus such as employee relations and employee development; and (iv) an overview of employment legislation and its implications for personnel/HR management in Ireland.

A number of people have contributed to this text in a variety of different ways and we take this opportunity to place on record our thanks to them.

Both Catherine Horgan and Noreen Clifford from the University of Limerick provided particular help and assistance.

Professor Shaun Tyson and Professor Chris Brewster, both of Cranfield School of Management, Dr Gerry McMahon of the Dublin Institute of Technology, Professor Bill Roche, Professor Aidan Kelly and Juliet MacMahon of University College, Dublin, Dr Jim Walsh of University College, Cork, Dr Kathy Monks of Dublin City University, Professor Phil Beaumont of the University of Glasgow, Seán Healy of the Labour Relations Commission and Martin Territt, Pádraic Cullinane, Ronald Long and Joe McLoughlin of the Department of Enterprise and Employment have all assisted us in many different ways in recent years.

Colleagues at the University of Limerick, in particular Tom Turner, Sarah Moore, Daryl D'Art, Tom Garavan, Joe Wallace, Patrick Flood, Ger Fitzgerald, Geraldine Floyd,

Bernard Delaney, Sarah MacCurtain, Siobhán Tiernan, Noel Whelan, Donal Dineen, Bernadette Andreosso and Stuart Hampshire are thanked for their on-going support and encouragement.

We are also grateful to Mike McDonnell, Tom Kennedy and Frank Brennan of the Institute of Personnel and Development and Kiernan Mulvey of the Labour Relations Commission.

Finally, Hubert Mahony, Ailbhe O'Reilly, Gabrielle Noble and all the production team at Gill & Macmillan have been a constant source of support.

1

Personnel Management: an Introduction

People are the lifeblood of organisations. A company's work-force represents one of its most potent and valuable resources. Consequently, the extent to which a work-force is managed effectively is a critical element in improving and sustaining organisational performance.

It is widely argued that effective work-force management is one of the pivotal characteristics of high-performing companies (Hanna 1988; Buchanan and McCalman 1989; Tiernan, Morley, and Foley 1996). However, the challenge is also great. Managing people is one of the most difficult aspects of organisational management; this difficulty largely stems from the fact that people are inherently different. Managing an organisation's work-force therefore means dealing with people who differ physically and psychologically. This is the essence of personnel management: that aspect of organisational management concerned with the management of an organisation's work-force.

This chapter provides an overview of the field of personnel management. It explores the nature of personnel management and identifies key personnel activities within companies. The objective of this chapter is to place personnel management in Ireland within a national and international context and so facilitate an analysis of Irish developments in the context of broader contemporary developments in the field. This chapter places a particular focus on the issue of *personnel policy choice* in an attempt to explain the considerable variation in approaches to personnel management between organisations.

However, before engaging the debate on the nature and role of personnel management it is useful to consider the historical background of personnel management.

THE HISTORICAL DEVELOPMENT OF PERSONNEL MANAGEMENT
The origins of contemporary personnel management lie in the dramatic changes brought about by the Industrial Revolution in England (see Niven 1967). A central component of this was the growth of the 'factory system', where owners of capital employed large numbers of wage labourers to produce goods for large markets. These

developments had dramatic effects on the organisation of work. From the owner's perspective, the new factory employees required direction, equipment had to be maintained, production controlled, and goods distributed and sold. Here we have the origins of modern management: the need to plan, organise, direct and control the use of equipment, capital, materials and labour within organisations. These early stages were characterised by extremely poor working conditions for the bulk of the new factory labour. Workers could do little about this situation, since they had little economic or political power. It was not until the growth of organised labour through the trade union movement that the concerns of workers could command the attention and action of employers.

Two important developments emerged in the late nineteenth and early twentieth century that represent the first significant influences on the evolution of personnel management and, particularly, the specialist personnel function. These were (a) the welfare tradition and (b) scientific management (see Niven 1967; Foley and Gunnigle 1994).

The welfare tradition

The origins of modern personnel management are generally traced back to what has become known as the welfare tradition, which developed in a few large companies in Britain during the late nineteenth and early twentieth century. In the early stages of industrialisation many factory owners regarded their labour force in largely instrumental terms. Working conditions were poor, and workers enjoyed few of the benefits we now associate with employment, such as sickness pay, pensions, and basic welfare provisions (Niven 1967). The welfare tradition refers to a series of voluntary initiatives undertaken in certain companies to improve the conditions of factory workers, particularly in relation to pay, working hours, and health and safety provisions.

This phase is particularly important in the development of personnel management, as it was characterised by the appointment of welfare officers, who are seen as the forerunners of the modern personnel practitioner. Welfare officers first emerged in the mainly Quaker-owned firms in the food and confectionery industries in Britain in the late eighteen-nineties. Prominent Irish examples are those of Jacob's and of Maguire and Paterson in Dublin (Byrne 1988).

The First World War added some impetus to the welfare movement in Britain, because of the need to accelerate factory production. However, large-scale unemployment and depression in the postwar period meant that developments in welfare and personnel work were abandoned in many companies. In 1919 the Welfare Workers' Institute, founded in Britain in 1913 as the Welfare Workers' Association, had a membership of 700. By 1927, when it had been renamed the Institute of Industrial Welfare Workers, its membership had fallen to 420 (Farnham 1984).

The impact of the welfare approach is still very apparent in contemporary personnel practice. Welfare has been inextricably linked with a 'caring' approach to employees, dealing with issues such as health, working conditions, and personal problems. This is very much in evidence in modern personnel management in areas such as counselling, sickness benefits, and employee assistance programmes. On a rather different level the welfare tradition has been a source of some confusion about the position of the personnel practitioner in the managerial hierarchy. Welfare officers occupied a semi-independent position in the factory system, with employees the main beneficiaries of their work. This led to the so-called 'middle man' perception of the welfare role, with employees seeing them as the representatives of workers' interests. However, it is clear that modern personnel practitioners operate as an integral part of the management team and primarily represent employer rather than worker interests.

Scientific management

Another important early influence on the emergence of personnel management was the advent of 'scientific management' and what became known as 'Taylorism'. As the welfare tradition succumbed in the face of economic depression, Taylorism and its associated notions of labour efficiency became an increasingly popular alternative. By the early years of the twentieth century improvements in technology coupled with increases in company size and complexity forced employers to investigate new ways of improving organisation performance. In the United States, F. W. Taylor led the way by pointing to the efficiency and profitability benefits to be gained through greater standardisation of work systems and methods.

Based on his work at the Bethlehem Steel Company (1900–11), Taylor encouraged employers to adopt a more systematic approach to job design, employment, and payment systems (Taylor 1947). Such scientific management approaches were widely adopted in both the United States and Britain in the inter-war years. Particular emphasis was placed on job analysis, time and motion studies, and the creation of incentive bonus schemes, thereby extending the work of the emerging personnel function. Scientific management led to a shift in the emphasis of personnel away from the employee-oriented 'caring' or 'do-gooding' agenda of the welfare tradition and towards the managerial 'efficiency-profitability' agenda of the work study officer. From the personnel management perspective, the spread of scientific management placed greater weight on the careful selection and systematic training of employees. Associated with this trend was increased attention to job design, working conditions, and payment systems. Personnel also took responsibility for much of the research and administration required to underpin such initiatives.

Despite extensive criticism, the principles of Taylorism had, and continue to have, a profound impact on management practice. Probably its most significant legacy is the notion that work *planning* (seen as a management task) should be separated from work *doing* (seen as a worker task). This separation delineated the primary role of management as that of establishing work standards, procedures, and methods. Such approaches to work organisation were dominated by a desire to maximise the productive efficiency of the company's technical resources. Management's role was to ensure that other organisational resources, including employees, were organised in such a way as to facilitate the optimal use of the technical system.

This efficiency approach, based on Taylorist principles, has been a characteristic of employer approaches to job design since the early years of the twentieth century. Jobs were broken down into simple, repetitive, measurable tasks requiring skills that could be easily acquired through systematic job training. Taylorism helped to improve efficiency and promoted a systematic approach to selection, training, work measurement, and payment. However, it is also seen as the source of many of the problems associated with industrial work, such as high levels of turnover and absenteeism and low motivation (see, for example, Mowday, Porter, and Steers 1982; Steers and Mowday 1987). Indeed the growth of the behavioural science movement (discussed below) can be traced to criticisms of Taylorism and to suggestions that improvements in organisational effectiveness could be achieved through greater attention to workers' needs and, particularly, by providing workers with more challenging jobs and an improved working environment.

The behavioural science movement

The emergence of the behavioural sciences gave a huge impetus to personnel management by establishing a body of knowledge to underpin many aspects of personnel work, such as selection, training, motivation, industrial relations, and payment systems. It also served to focus attention on some of the problems created by work organisation in the large factories of the new industrial era, such as monotony and low morale.

The emergence of the behavioural science movement is most commonly associated with the work of Elton Mayo and of Roethlisberger and Dickson (see Roethlisberger and Dickson 1939). Based on their studies of worker productivity it was suggested that employees' behaviour and performance was influenced by motivation and needs as well as by working conditions and payment practices. This research highlighted the importance of issues such as social factors, group dynamics and employee motivation in affecting both individual performance and organisational effectiveness.

Although the work of the human relations school has been the subject of methodological criticisms (see Carey 1967), it has had an important influence on management practice, particularly in the sphere of personnel management. Possibly its principal contribution was in initiating interest in applying behavioural science principles to the study of organisational and worker behaviour. Much of this research involved investigating sources of employees' motivation and attempting to reconcile employers' and workers' needs through appropriate organisational structures, work systems, and managerial styles.

Industrial relations as a key personnel activity

A particularly important development affecting the nature of personnel management and the role of the emerging personnel function was the growing significance of industrial relations. The growth of an industrial relations emphasis in personnel work was a direct result of the increasing influence of trade unions. In Ireland the trade union movement had become well established in the early years of the twentieth century in industries in Dublin, Belfast, and Cork (McNamara et al. 1988). A particularly important development was the emergence of the 'new unionism', involving the organisation of unskilled or 'general' workers. In Britain economic depression after the First World War saw the re-emergence of autocratic management styles. A combination of factors, particularly low pay and poor working conditions, contributed to high levels of industrial conflict, which culminated in the General Strike of 1926. During this period workers and their trade unions became increasingly suspicious of management motives in introducing welfare initiatives in the work-place. Indeed trade unions became quite anti-welfare, viewing this as an employer strategy to prevent worker organisation.

In Ireland the 'new unionism' also began to take hold, led by Jim Larkin's Irish Transport and General Workers' Union. A period of conflict between employer and worker interests came to a head in the Dublin lock-out of 1913. An important result of this turbulent period was that it served to accelerate the organisation of employees into trade unions and employers into employer associations and thus placed an ever-increasing emphasis on industrial relations as a critical aspect of work-force management.

Opposition to trade unions slowly gave way to reluctant acceptance of their role and legitimacy. Trade union membership increased steadily from the early nineteen-thirties. Employers were forced to accommodate the reality of organised labour and responded through multi-employer bargaining via employers' associations and in the employment of 'labour relations officers' to deal with personnel and industrial relations matters at organisation level.

A related and important factor contributing to the growth in the significance of industrial relations was the nature of pay bargaining. During the Second World War wages were controlled under the Emergency Powers Orders. The rescinding of these in 1946 marked the start of a new era in industrial relations with the establishment of the Labour Court: the removal of the Emergency Powers Orders and the general pay increase for unionised employees became known as the first *wage round* (Nevin 1963; McCarthy et al. 1975; O'Brien 1989). A wage round was essentially a period of intensive collective bargaining between employers and trade unions occurring at regular intervals and resulting in a similar general wage increase for unionised employees (Gunnigle et al. 1995).

The nature of collective bargaining in the immediate postwar period had important implications for the development of personnel management in Ireland. Growth in company size and complexity demanded greater specialisation and knowledge in work-force management, particularly in the area of industrial relations. In the public sector and among some larger private companies these needs were achieved through the establishment of specialist personnel departments, whose key activity was industrial relations (O'Mahony 1958). By the nineteen-sixties levels of unionisation among manual workers had increased significantly, and the *shop steward movement* began to emerge as a significant factor in establishing plant-level bargaining as a central component of work-force management (Roche and Larragy 1989; Marsh 1973). This situation was accentuated by the growth in white-collar trade unionisation from the nineteen-sixties (Bain 1970; Kelly 1975).

A further development contributing to the increasing significance of industrial relations as a critical concern in personnel management was the onset of the 'national wage agreement era' (1970–82). The negotiation of the first national wage agreement marked a transformation from the rather unclear system of wage rounds that had existed since the end of the war. A key effect of national wage agreements was to move major pay bargaining issues away from the level of the enterprise. This development was at first seen as freeing the management from complex negotiations with trade unions and giving them more certainty in corporate planning. However, the reality was somewhat different. At a time of relative economic prosperity and substantial growth in union membership, the key work-place role for trade unions, namely pay bargaining, was removed. With the expectation that pay increases would be obtained by means of national agreements, trade unions increasingly focused their attention on matters that could be negotiated at local level, such as employment conditions, pay anomalies, and productivity deals. Indeed, far from eliminating enterprise-level bargaining, national agreements merely changed the focus, and the period saw the negotiation of various types of productivity deals. These became an important means by which trade unions could gain pay increases above the stated maximum in national wage agreements. The emphasis on industrial relations therefore continued to expand during the national wage agreement era.

For the personnel function, industrial relations remained a priority, with personnel practitioners heavily involved in work-place bargaining with trade unions. Industrial harmony was the objective, and industrial relations specialists, through their negotiating, interpersonal and procedural skills, had the responsibility for its achievement. Increased industrial unrest from the mid-sixties to the end of the seventies served to confirm industrial relations as a key concern of employers. It gave the emerging personnel function a central management role. Personnel departments whose major responsibility was industrial relations became established in most medium-sized and larger companies. The Donovan Report (1968) in Britain was also influential in encouraging collective bargaining, the adoption of comprehensive procedures, and greater specialisation in industrial relations management.

Increased Government intervention in the management sphere since the seventies has also had a significant influence on the personnel function. As discussed above, this was particularly evident in the area of centralised pay bargaining. The early seventies also witnessed an unprecedented wave of employment legislation. This legislation primarily focused on extending the individual employment rights of workers in areas such as dismissals and equality. Key legislation passed in this period was the Unfair Dismissals Act, 1977, the Anti-Discrimination (Pay) Act, 1974, the Employment Equality Act, 1977, and a number of Redundancy Acts. Organisations had to come to grips with the application of such legislation, and much of this responsibility was assumed by the emerging personnel function. Personnel practitioners were expected to provide expert advice and guidance on the new legislation and to oversee its implementation at the work-place level.

Other factors: multinationals and personnel management education

Two other important factors facilitating the growth and expansion of the personnel role were the increasing emphasis on the professional education of personnel practitioners since the nineteen-seventies and the impact of multinational corporations in contributing to increased knowledge of personnel techniques and greater sophistication in the execution of the personnel role.

Ireland has a heavy presence of *multinational companies* (MNCs). Direct foreign investment in industry in the Republic comprises over a thousand overseas firms employing over 100,000 people (Gunnigle 1993). These foreign-owned firms account for 50 per cent of manufactured output and three-quarters of industrial exports. The main sources of direct foreign investment are the United States, Britain, and Germany (see table 1.2).

Given the significance of multinational companies it is hardly surprising that they have had an important impact on the development of personnel management. MNCs have been to the fore in developing more comprehensive policies and procedures in personnel management and in giving a greater impetus to the role of the specialist personnel function (personnel department).

An important legacy of MNC investment has been the diffusion of new personnel techniques. In areas such as selection testing, training methods, reward systems and communications MNCs have been to the fore in introducing new developments and methods.

On a general level the effect of MNCs has been to contribute to establishing personnel management as a more central component of the management process.

Increasing specialisation in the personnel sphere required commensurate growth in the *education and training* of personnel specialists. Many of the newer multinational and larger indigenous companies emphasised the appointment of qualified and experienced personnel practitioners. While personnel management education in Ireland can be traced back to the nineteen-forties, the most significant developments have taken place since the sixties. The establishment of AnCO in 1967 added impetus to the development of the personnel role through increased emphasis on training and development. In the seventies the first courses leading to membership of the Institute of Personnel Management (IPM) were offered in Dublin, Limerick, and Galway; since then full-time and part-time undergraduate and postgraduate courses have been developed at most universities and a number of other colleges of higher education.

CONTEMPORARY DEVELOPMENTS

In evaluating the development of personnel management in Ireland it appears that growth in industrialisation, direct foreign investment and state-sponsored activity since the sixties have contributed to the establishment of personnel as a discrete management function. By the late seventies the personnel management role was firmly established in most larger companies. Personnel departments operated as a distinct management function, with responsibility for a well-defined range of personnel activities. Industrial relations was the key activity area, with the greatest emphasis on collective bargaining.

However, the nineteen-eighties heralded a period of considerable change for personnel management. A depressed economic climate together with increased competitive pressures led to a slump in business activity for most of the decade. These developments helped to change both the focus of personnel management and the nature of personnel activities. Competitive pressures combined to set new priorities, forcing the personnel function to act under tighter cost controls and to undertake a wider range of activities (Berridge 1992; Tyson 1987; Foley and Gunnigle 1994). The recessionary climate reduced the need for many hitherto core activities, particularly recruitment and industrial relations.

The harsh economic climate of the nineteen-eighties, characterised by widespread redundancies and high unemployment, dramatically changed the industrial relations environment, with adverse consequences for trade unions. Increasingly employers sought to address issues such as payment structures and levels of wage increases, the extent of demarcation and restrictive work practices, and, ultimately, the erosion of managerial prerogative by trade unions. Restrictive trade union legislation in Britain and hard-line management approaches in many firms indicated a more offensive approach to dealings with trade unions. This was reflected in the adverse outcomes for trade unions of strikes by miners in Britain and of air traffic controllers in the United States in the early eighties. Trade unions were apparently in retreat, and membership began to fall in many countries. In Ireland union membership fell significantly in the period 1980–87, and industrial unrest also declined significantly over the decade.

At the same time increased market competition forced many companies to seek ways of establishing competitive advantage. One apparent source of such improvements was the better use of human resources. Some companies began to investigate different approaches to work-force management, particularly in areas such as work organisation and job design, reward systems, and employee development. However, the most widely debated development over the period was the emergence of *human resource management* (HRM). This essentially means the development of a more integrated and strategic corporate approach to work-force management. It has its roots in the United States, which has been receptive to the application of organisational psychology and behavioural science principles as a means of improving organisational performance (Beaumont 1992).

The nature and implications of HRM are considered in some detail in chapter 2. However, we now move beyond our historical review to consider personnel management practice in organisations.

THE NATURE OF PERSONNEL MANAGEMENT

During discussions with a recent class of mature students taking an introductory personnel management course, a number of class members suggested that 'personnel' did not really operate in their companies, since they had 'no personnel department.' This interpretation of personnel management as being the responsibility of personnel specialists is a common, if flawed, conception. Personnel management is concerned with the management of an organisation's work-force. Thus conceived, it is a generalist responsibility that constitutes an important aspect of the job of everyone with managerial responsibilities. It incorporates all policies and practices involving work-force management and is therefore an inherent aspect of the management process. All organisations have important personnel management responsibilities, with the deployment, development and motivation of employees as core personnel activities.

However, personnel management may also be seen as a specialist management function. Personnel specialists have particular responsibility for developing and monitoring their organisations' personnel management strategies, policies, and practices. Even where a specialist function exists, line management continue to play a central role in operational, day-to-day personnel activities, such as recruitment and on-the-job training. The key role of the specialist personnel function is to provide adequate assistance, advice and administrative support. However, it may also play a more executive role by taking direct responsibility for certain activities. Common examples here might include collective bargaining with trade unions or approving promotion decisions.

This conception of personnel management in generalist and specialist terms is important. Firstly, it recognises that personnel management is a key responsibility of all managers. It also recognises that in some, particularly large organisations, personnel specialists are employed to undertake particular aspects of the personnel management role. Thus, although personnel involves managers at all levels in the company's hierarchy, it is useful to consider the roles of three critical layers, namely top management, line management, and the specialist personnel function.

At the highest level of organisational decision-making, personnel management involves the senior management developing the company's overall personnel policy and strategy. The senior management might comprise the owner-manager of a small shop or the corporate board of directors of a multinational corporation. At the operational level personnel management primarily involves the line management undertaking the day-to-day operational activities of personnel management: communicating with employees, monitoring performance, handling employees' grievances, etc. In most larger organisations one generally finds a specialist personnel function. This involves the employment of one or more personnel specialists who together constitute a personnel department. The primary role of the specialist function is to help devise and execute the company's personnel management strategies and policies (Cole 1988). It also undertakes specialist tasks and acts as a source of expert advice and guidance to line and top management.

Personnel management activities

If we accept that personnel management is concerned with the management of an organisation's work-force, it is clear that the range of personnel activities that may be undertaken by a company is extensive. Many of these are basic activities common to all types of organisation, such as recruiting and rewarding workers. Certain personnel activities may only be appropriate in particular organisational contexts and may require more specialist skills; examples here would include the administration of job evaluation schemes or negotiating collective agreements with trade unions. Other personnel activities may be more optional in character and their incidence related to preferred managerial approaches or styles; examples of these might include the operation of profit-sharing schemes or the establishment of quality circles. Therefore, since there is a wide range of personnel activities that may be undertaken, it is clear that the nature of personnel management may differ considerably between organisations.

At a general level it is possible to identify critical personnel management activities that are shared by all types of organisations. Possibly the most comprehensive attempt to chart these activities was that undertaken by the Personnel Standards Lead Body (1993) in Britain, which identified the following core activities:

1. **Strategy and organisation**
   Contributing to organisational strategy, organisation structure and processes; influencing culture and values, and developing personnel strategies and policies.
2. **Employee resourcing**
   Incorporating human resource planning, recruitment, and selection; deployment and termination of employment.
3. **Employee development**
   Incorporating training and development, management development, career development, and performance management.
4. **Reward management**
   Incorporating the selection of reward strategies and the administration of payment and benefit systems.
5. **Employee relations**
   Incorporating industrial relations, employee involvement and participation, communications, health, safety and welfare, and employee services.
6. **Employment and personnel administration**
   Incorporating the administration of employee records, employment policies and practices, working conditions, and personnel information systems.

The impact of organisation size

A useful approach in considering the nature of personnel management is to reflect on the extent and variation of personnel management activities as the size of the organisation increases. In smaller companies one finds that the responsibility for all personnel matters normally rests with the line management (Gunnigle and Brady 1984); for obvious financial and structural reasons, such organisations would not normally employ a personnel specialist. Nevertheless, effective personnel management remains a vital consideration. Since pay is often the largest continuing cost in many small firms, performance and profitability can often be increased by better use of human resources (Gunnigle 1989; McMahon 1994). Indeed poor recruitment, inadequate training or confrontational employee relations can have a proportionately more serious effect in smaller companies than in their larger counterparts.

Of course the nature of personnel management is made potentially simpler in small organisations because of the scale of operations, which eases the burden of communication and reduces the level of administrative support required. In the majority of small companies, personnel management will be concerned with basic activities essential to the effective running of the firm. For such companies, key personnel activities incorporate human resource planning, recruitment and selection, training and development, reward management, employee relations, health, safety and welfare, and administrative support.

When we consider larger organisations we find that increases in size normally make the personnel management process more complex. It expands the scale of personnel management activities, administration, and employee relations. Normally there is also greater formality and sophistication of personnel policies and procedures. However, such changes simply affect the nature of the personnel management process, while the basic objectives and activities remain the same.

A common response of most larger organisations is to have a specialist personnel department, which co-ordinates personnel activities and carries out much of the administrative work (Shivanath 1987; Foley and Gunnigle 1994; Monks 1992). Such specialist departments may comprise one or two people with general responsibility for personnel matters. Alternatively, very large companies may employ an extensive personnel department, characterised by a high degree of task specialisation, as outlined in fig. 1.1.

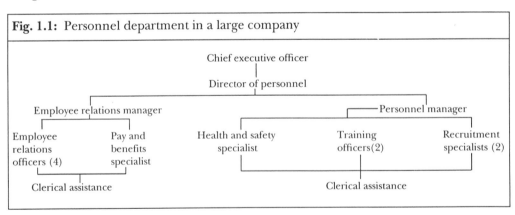

Fig. 1.1: Personnel department in a large company

It is apparent that increases in company size and complexity result in specialisation and formalisation in the conduct of personnel activities. One also finds that the specialist personnel function takes responsibility for a larger range of activities. However, the key role of the top management in deciding on the corporate personnel approach, and of the line management in undertaking a range of operational personnel tasks, should remain intact. The specialist personnel function normally operates in a staff capacity, which means that its primary role is to help and advise the line management (at all levels) in undertaking their personnel responsibilities.

STRATEGY, POLICY AND PRACTICE IN PERSONNEL MANAGEMENT
The study of *business strategy* has achieved increasing prominence as companies seek to

adapt to a changing business environment. Business strategy is concerned with policy decisions affecting the entire organisation, the overall objective being to best position it to deal effectively with its environment. Strategic decisions are long-term in nature, affect the future of the company, and serve to guide subsequent decision-making at lower levels.

In recent years the personnel management literature has placed an ever increasing emphasis on the need to *align personnel strategies and policies with overall business strategy* (Beer et al. 1984; Fombrun et al. 1984; Schuler 1987, 1998, 1992; Schuler and Jackson 1987a, 1987b). It is suggested that personnel management activities should be guided by the overall business strategy and related personnel management strategies. Therefore it is argued that the role of personnel strategy, policies and activities is to contribute to the company's primary business goals (Fombrun et al. 1984). This link between business strategy, personnel management strategies and personnel management activities is illustrated in fig. 1.2.

Fig. 1.2: Business strategy and personnel management

Business strategy
(incorporating marketing and product development strategies)

Personnel management strategy
(incorporating the company's desired approach to personnel management and its key personnel management objectives)

Personnel management policies and procedures
(incorporating key polices in areas of employment, rewards, and employee relations)

Strategy & organisation	Employee resourcing	Employee development	Reward management	Employee relations
Organisation strategy and structure; personnel strategy	Human resource planning; recruitment; selection; socialisation; deployment	Training; development; performance management	Pay systems; benefits; employment conditions	Industrial relations; communications; employee involvement; health and safety; employee services

Personnel information systems and support

Personnel and HR strategy

A personnel management strategy incorporates a company's basic policy and long-term objectives in managing human resources. It involves identifying the company's beliefs and values about how employees should be managed and forms the basis for the subsequent development of more explicit personnel policies in critical areas of work-force management, such as employee selection and reward management. The responsibility for developing personnel strategy rests primarily with the top management, aided, as appropriate, by the specialist personnel function. Personnel strategies are normally designed to complement the overall business strategy and may often be expressed in the form of general statements outlining key organisational values or beliefs concerning personnel management. Table 1.1 outlines examples of such statements from two companies.

Table 1.1: Statements of corporate beliefs in personnel management

Company 1: 'Key beliefs in managing people'
- To treat each employee with dignity as an individual.
- To maintain an open atmosphere where direct communication with employees affords the opportunity to contribute to the maximum of their potential and fosters unity of purpose.
- To provide personal opportunities for training and development to ensure the most capable and most efficient work-force.
- To respect senior service.
- To reward fairly by salary, benefits, and incentives.
- To promote on the basis of capability.

Company 2: 'Core values and beliefs about how employees should be managed' (selection)
- **Employment**: Employees are recruited and promoted on merit, and we believe in maximum openness in competition and appointments. We respect our employees and value each as an individual. All employees have equal opportunity for development and advancement according to their qualifications and abilities and the needs of the business. We seek to use individual talents and skills to the best advantage of the person and the company.
- **Pay and conditions**: We have pay and conditions of employment designed to attract the right people, motivate employees, stimulate quality work, and reflect performance, while taking account of national economic circumstances and policy. We try always to be fair and equitable in the treatment of individuals and in responding to their needs.

The examples in table 1.1 are explicit indications of particular espoused organisational strategies in personnel management. However, in practice one finds that a majority of companies do not have such explicit statements. Data generated from the Price Waterhouse Cranfield survey of human resource management in Irish companies found that only 29 per cent of firms had a written personnel or HR strategy (Gunnigle et al. 1994). This was particularly the case in smaller companies. Does this imply that such companies do not a have personnel strategy? Generally not. Virtually all organisations have a policy in relation to how they view and manage their work-force. While this may not always be written, it can be inferred from how employees are treated and rewarded within the organisation. In such situations the organisation's personnel policy is implicit rather than explicit in nature. This approach may sometimes reflect a lack of strategic awareness of personnel management considerations on the part of the organisation.

Personnel and HR policies
Of course broad personnel strategies and related personnel policy statements expressing corporate beliefs and values are ineffective unless they are implemented in the day-to-day practice of personnel management. To effectively bridge the gap between espoused beliefs and work-place practice, companies normally develop a set of personnel policies in key areas such as recruitment, rewards, and employee relations. The primary role of such policies is to guide managers in the execution of their personnel management responsibilities. They also act as an important yardstick for workers in outlining the standards and approaches they should expect from the company and also the norms the company expects from its work-force. Examples of personnel policy statements are outlined in table 1.2.

Table 1.2: Personnel policy statements (indicative)

Company 1: Policy statement on promotion and development
This company encourages everyone to prepare for career enhancement through its educational assistance and training programmes. It is our policy to promote from within whenever suitable and experienced candidates are available.

Company 2: Policy statement on employment equality
It is our policy to ensure that all employees are afforded equal treatment, irrespective of their sex, marital or parental status, race, or religion. This company ensures equal access to employment, training, development and promotion solely on the basis of essential job requirements and the individual's ability and fitness for work.

Company 3: Policy statement on pay and employment conditions
It is our policy to provide pay and terms of employment that are competitive with the top quartile of comparable firms in our industrial segment.

Company 4: Policy statement on employee relations
We seek to develop good relations with employees and their trade unions. Where difficulties arise the company will seek to resolve these quickly and as close to the work-place as possible. The company is committed to adherence to agreed procedures in the resolution of employee relations difficulties.

Personnel and HR procedures

Policy statements, therefore, establish the parameters within which managers and supervisors execute their various operational personnel management responsibilities. To further aid this process, companies may develop a set of personnel management procedures, which are detailed statements to guide managers and workers in the effective implementation of policies. These procedures normally embrace detailed statements covering a range of operational personnel activities, such as recruitment, promotion, performance management, and industrial relations. Examples of such personnel procedures are outlined in table 1.3. The specialist personnel function normally plays a key role in developing personnel management policies and procedures. It also provides support and direction to line managers in the implementation of procedures through advice, guidance, and administrative assistance (Tyson and Fell 1986).

Table 1.3: Personnel procedures (indicative)

Company 1: Procedure on educational assistance
To help with personal development and maintain the company's competitive position, all relevant educational courses or parts thereof that have been successfully completed and are appropriate to your career will be paid for by the company. All such courses must be approved before the beginning of the course by your department manager and the human resource manager in order to be considered for reimbursement. Application forms are available from the Human Resource Department.

Company 2: Procedure on probationary period
The first six months of your employment will be considered a probationary period. During this time your supervisor will assess your suitability for the job. He or she will sit down with you and discuss your performance after one month, after three months, and again after six months' service. You will be given every opportunity and assistance in making a success of your new position. Within this time the company will have the sole and absolute right of deciding on your suitability for continued employment. Your employment may be terminated by the company at any time during this period without recourse to the disciplinary or grievance procedure.

PERSONNEL POLICY CHOICE: EXPLAINING VARIATIONS IN STRATEGY, POLICY AND PRACTICE IN PERSONNEL MANAGEMENT

The preceding discussion has alluded to the fact that, in practice, one finds immense variation between companies in their approach to work-force management. This is manifested in differing personnel management strategies, policies and procedures and may be attributed to the differential impact of factors in the external or internal environment of organisations. Purcell (1987) notes the tendency to identify and contrast prominent companies according to their 'employment policies and practices'. While many of these differences are due to external environmental factors, such as product market performance, Purcell also identifies *strategic choice* (exercised by the senior management) as a key factor explaining differences in organisational approaches to personnel management (see also Beer et al. 1984; Kochan et al. 1986).

Strategic choice addresses the extent to which the management (*a*) possess and (*b*) exercise choice in developing their personnel management strategies, policies, and procedures. This implies that senior managements possess some room for manoeuvre, and while environmental factors may constrain the range of choice, they retain considerable power in making decisions on 'appropriate' styles and policies. The senior management can therefore use their resources and power to make strategic choices that both influence environmental factors and affect particular management styles. Organisational approaches to personnel management should therefore be evaluated according to the interplay between environmental factors, managerial ideology or values, and strategic choice. As Marchington and Parker (1990, 99) state,

> choice should be viewed as both a cause and a consequence of environmental influences, that is, managements have some influence over the kind of markets in which they choose to operate, and in some cases over the structure of the market itself, as well as having some choice over the way in which they respond to environmental pressures.

The interplay of such factors will clearly lead to consequential variations in patterns of personnel management. Such disparity will become manifest in a huge range of personnel management activities, such as recruitment and selection, reward systems, and employee development.

The context for choice: explaining variation in organisational approaches to personnel management

To identify and explain variations in organisational approaches to personnel management it is necessary to examine the interplay between a diverse range of external and internal factors that influence and constrain managerial choice and practice in the sphere of work-force management. A particular focus of such analysis is the external environment (such as product and labour markets), management values, business strategy and historical factors as key triggers affecting organisational approaches to personnel management (Kochan et al. 1986). It is argued that changes in environmental conditions affect decisions on business strategy and ultimately personnel management. Such decisions will be conditioned by managerial values and constrained by historical factors and current practice in personnel management. Fig. 1.3 presents a framework for evaluating variation in organisational approaches to personnel management. This framework is further discussed below.

Fig. 1.3: Personnel policy choice: context and variation

External environment

Labour market	Product market	Public policy	Technology	Social/ economic

Internal environment

Management values	Competitive strategy	Work-force characteristics	Established personnel/IR practices	Company size structure

Personnel policy choice

Work system	Employee relations	Reward system	Recruitment/ internal flow practices	Role of personnel function

The external environment

The external environment is a major influence on organisational decision-making. Trends in the external environment, such as levels of economic performance, public policy and cultural or social values will affect business strategy and management practice.

Economic performance and public policy, as manifested in areas such as levels of economic activity, state intervention and control and approaches to organised labour, clearly have a general impact on personnel management (Gunnigle, McMahon and Fitzgerald 1995). Levels of economic activity in Ireland remained depressed for much of the nineteen-eighties but recovered considerably in the period since 1987. However, the impact of such recovery was severely curtailed by the international recession, which particularly affected Ireland's largest export market, Britain. These product market conditions meant that many companies were operating under high levels of market pressure and so may have had considerably reduced scope for choice in personnel management policies, so that the traditional emphasis on cost and labour control may have been more appropriate. Broader social changes in areas such as education, living standards and class mobility also exert a significant influence on organisational approaches to work-force management.

Developments in technology are a key external environmental factor affecting organisational approaches to personnel management. Technology, seen in generic terms as the equipment used to perform particular tasks and the way in which it is organised, has a significant influence on approaches to work-force management (Beer et al. 1984). Guest (1987) identifies technological and production feasibility as a requisite condition for the successful implementation of more strategic human resource management (HRM) and suggests that large-scale investment in short-cycle, repetitive, assembly-line technology mitigates against the job design principles and autonomous team-working characteristic of 'strategic' HRM. Technology also affects cost structure and consequently affects key aspects of personnel management, such as reward systems. Marchington (1982) suggests that in labour-intensive sectors, where wage costs are high, companies may be more constrained in developing employee-oriented management styles. However, in capital-intensive sectors, where labour constitutes a small proportion of total costs, companies may have greater scope to adopt 'softer' personnel management approaches, incorporating, for example, attractive reward and employee development policies. The labour market has exerted possibly the most profound influence on personnel management, especially in the areas of recruitment, training, and reward systems. The most notable developments in the Irish labour market include the progressive decline of agricultural employment and the growth of the service sector. The Irish labour market is characterised by extremely high levels of unemployment, largely concentrated in the younger age categories (Leddin and Walsh 1994). Consequently, several categories of labour are in oversupply, with the result that 'dipping' into the external labour market is a ready option for employers. Such conditions tend to reduce the onus on companies to establish comprehensive training and development policies, as might be the case in less buoyant labour markets. High unemployment also tends to place a premium on job security. It exerts a downward pressure on wages and affects other aspects of personnel management, such as labour turnover and power relations in collective bargaining. Other notable developments in employment structure are the increased feminisation of the work-force and the growth of 'atypical' employment forms—defined as any form of employment that deviates from the full-time, permanent format—including self-employment and temporary and part-time work.

Product market performance is also a significant influence on strategic decision-making and organisational approaches to personnel management. It is clear that favourable market conditions, such as high market share, allow companies greater scope to adopt more benign personnel management practices, such as attractive reward systems. For example, Poole (1986) identifies the existence of a mature market and the will to compete throughout all segments as leading to a shift in work-force management emphasis 'away from maintaining labour peace ... to one of controlling labour costs, streamlining work roles and increasing productivity in order to meet growing price competition.' He suggests that highly competitive product markets lead to more 'directive managerial styles, the abandonment of constitutionalism and the focus on individual employees at the expense of trade union representatives.' The characteristics of a company's product market will be influenced by a variety of factors, such as the cost of entry, nature of competition, technology, and the customer base. (The impact of product market conditions on organisational approaches to personnel or human resource management is considered further in chapter 2.)

A number of important aspects of *public policy* have an impact on personnel management. This is most significant in the areas of industrial relations and employment law. In the industrial relations area the traditional approach of successive Governments has been grounded in the 'voluntarist' tradition, whereby employers and employees or their representative bodies are largely free to regulate the substantive and procedural terms of their relationship (Hillery 1994). However, this approach has been considerably diluted in recent years, with greater state intervention in industrial relations (Roche 1989, 1994a). Recent Governments have been strong advocates of centralised agreements on pay and other aspects of social and economic policy, involving negotiations with the main employer and trade union federations. A more established aspect of public policy is the constitutional guarantee of freedom of association, which gives people the right to join trade unions. However, there is no corresponding onus on the employer to recognise a trade union, which has become an important issue in recent years, as some companies choose to pursue a non-union strategy. In general, Governments have been supportive of trade unions and a consensus approach to labour relations.

An obvious manifestation of the influence of public policy on personnel management is in the area of labour legislation. The period since the nineteen-seventies has witnessed the passing of several important acts, particularly in the area of individual employment rights, such as dismissals and employment equality. A particularly important influence in the area of employment legislation is the impact of membership of the European Union. The Single European Act, 1987, aimed at strengthening economic cohesion, places a strong emphasis on the integrating of social policy throughout the EU (Hourihan 1994). In 1989 a Charter of Fundamental Social Rights of Workers—the 'Social Charter'—was signed by all member-states except Britain. The Social Charter (subsequently renamed the Social Chapter) and attendant Social Action Programme comprise forty-nine legally binding directives and recommendations designed to realise the aims of the Social Charter.

A final important aspect of public policy relates to approaches to industrial development. Since the middle nineteen-sixties Government policy has been to actively encourage foreign investment. There are now over a thousand overseas companies operating in Ireland, with a particular emphasis on engineering (including electronics) and chemicals. It is clear that multinational companies have been a source of innovation in personnel management in Ireland, particularly in the application of new personnel approaches and in expanding the role of the specialist personnel or HR function. However, it would also seem that MNCs pose particular and unique challenges in the employee relations sphere, particularly in their ability to switch the location of production and the recent and increasing trend of union avoidance (Kelly and Brannick 1988; McGovern 1988, 1989a, 1989b; Gunnigle 1995a, 1995b).

The internal environment

The *internal environment* of an organisation helps to determine unique responses to external factors. Such factors include the characteristics of the current work-force and established personnel management practices.

Company structure and size are important factors affecting personnel management. Irish companies are generally smaller in scale than most industrialised EU member-states. Numerous studies have noted that trade union recognition and greater specialisation in personnel management are positively correlated with company size (Brown et al. 1981; Purcell and Sisson 1983; Thomason 1984). In Ireland, Gunnigle and Brady (1984) found that managements in smaller companies veer towards a unitarist frame of reference and adopt less formality in employee relations than their counterparts in larger companies. In relation to company structure, Purcell (1990) argues that senior managements in highly diversified companies are primarily concerned with financial issues, with a consequence that personnel management considerations are not a concern in corporate decision-making but rather an operational concern of the management at the business unit level. A corollary of this is that 'core business' companies, whose operation relies on a narrow product range, are more likely to integrate personnel management issues into strategic planning, whereas highly diversified companies are more likely to adopt differing personnel policies suited to the needs of different constituent divisions and establishments (Gunnigle, McMahon and Fitzgerald 1995). Several writers identify the location of personnel strategy formulation as a key issue in influencing the nature of establishment-level personnel management (Purcell and Sisson 1983; Kochan et al. 1984, 1986; Poole 1986). For example, Poole (1986) argues that in the employee relations sphere the growth of large multinational enterprises presents managements with the opportunity to develop policies at corporate level 'where they are relatively unrestricted by intervention by government or plant-level agreements with labour.'

Managerial values or ideology are also seen as having a significant influence on variations in organisational approaches to personnel management. Management values incorporate the deeply held beliefs of the senior management, which guide decisions on various aspects of work-force management (Purcell 1987; Gunnigle 1995a). They are particularly important in interpreting developments in the external and internal environment and in making decisions on the company's overall approach to work-force management. Clearly all companies are characterised by particular values and policies on work-force management and employee relations. As discussed earlier, such values or ideology may be explicit in some companies, as demonstrated in statements of corporate 'mission' or 'philosophy'; in others they may be implicit and must therefore be inferred from management practice in areas such as supervisory style, reward systems, and communications.

Gunnigle (1995a) points to a particular example of the impact of managerial values on variations in organisational approaches to personnel management by highlighting the notion that managerial ideology is related to broader ethnic and cultural values (also see Poole 1986). A traditional criticism of business culture in Ireland is that it has not always encouraged enterprise and innovation. This trait was attributed to Ireland's relatively late independence, which created what some have termed a 'dependence mentality'. However, this culture would seem to have been effectively laid to rest over recent decades. Levels of productivity and export performance have increased dramatically and compare very favourably with international standards. Recent studies have noted the flexibility of the Irish work-force and the relevance of coherent and strong corporate culture formation (Kakabadse 1990).

It also appears that managerial opposition to pluralism, particularly to trade union recognition, is a characteristic of the value system of American managers. HRM-type approaches, which emphasise individual freedom and initiative, direct communications, and merit-based rewards, are very much in line with this value system (Bendix 1956; Kochan et al. 1986). This interpretation is very significant in Ireland, where our economy is heavily dependent on foreign investment and where the bulk of such investment is American.

Another major internal factor affecting employee relations style is business or competitive strategy. Such strategies are developed at the level of the individual business unit and are concerned with achieving sustainable competitive advantage in a particular industry or segment. It is argued that different business strategies require particular personnel management strategies, policies, and practices (Schuler and Jackson 1987). Porter (1987) identifies generic strategies for the achievement of competitiveness, with particular emphasis on two distinctive routes to competitive advantage, namely *cost leadership* and *product differentiation*. Porter maintains that the company's choice of generic strategy specifies the fundamental approach to competitive advantage that the firm seeks to secure. Similarly this provides the context for policies and actions in each key functional area, including personnel management. Business strategy is therefore seen as having a significant influence on management approaches to personnel and human resource management. (The issue of business strategy and the links between strategy and personnel management are explored in considerable detail in chapter 2.)

Other important factors that affect organisational approaches to personnel management are characteristics of the current work-force and established personnel management practice. These factors will be particularly important in their effect on the efficacy of change initiatives in areas such as employee involvement or job redesign (Gunnigle, McMahon and Fitzgerald 1995). For example, Hackman and Oldham's (1980) job enrichment approach acknowledges that all employees may not react favourably to proposals for enriching jobs and the quality of work life: rather it is suggested that only those employees characterised by a strong desire for achievement, responsibility and autonomy will be motivated by such initiatives. Such employee characteristics may in turn have been conditioned by traditional personnel practices. For example, if internal mobility and individual initiative have traditionally been discouraged it may be difficult to effectively implement a comprehensive internal promotion and development policy.

Key areas of personnel management policy choice

The above discussions have outlined the major influences on variations in organisational approaches to personnel management. The manifestations of such variation will be evident in key areas of personnel policy choice, particularly the work system, employee relations, rewards, recruitment and internal flow policies, and the role of the personnel function.

The *work system* incorporates the way various organisational tasks are structured and affects issues such as organisational structure and job design. The past decade has seen an increased emphasis on improving competitiveness in many companies. This is often manifested in work redesign initiatives aimed at restructuring work systems to facilitate greater flexibility and improve performance and quality levels. Decisions on the work system are primarily a managerial responsibility. The approach chosen is a valuable indicator of management beliefs regarding personnel management. Traditional approaches to the organisation of work have been dominated by a desire to maintain control over the work process while maximising the productive efficiency of the company's technical resources. Choices on the organisation of work and the design of jobs were seen as primarily determined by the technical system; the management's role was to ensure that other resources, including employees, were organised in such a way as to facilitate the optimal use of the technical system. This approach often resulted in bureaucratic structures, elaborate procedures and systems, and top-down supervisory control with minimal employee involvement. It also encouraged the fragmentation of jobs into simple, repetitive, measurable tasks that gave post-holders little autonomy.

In contrast it is suggested that an increased emphasis on improving quality, service and overall competitiveness has led to work redesign initiatives aimed at restructuring work systems to increase employee autonomy, motivation, and performance (Beer 1984; Walton 1985; Guest 1989). Much of this focus has been on restructuring organisations and jobs to incorporate greater scope for intrinsic motivation and to facilitate greater involvement by employees. The consequent management emphasis was on developing broadly defined, challenging jobs within a more organic, flexible organisation structure. At the same time there is also evidence of the adoption of 'harder' approaches, as evidenced by job or work design initiatives that seek to tightly prescribe performance targets or objectives, accelerate the pace of work, and closely monitor individual employee performance (Gunnigle 1995b). These contrasting work systems are an important indicator of preferred organisational approaches to work-force management.

A second important area of personnel policy choice is *employee relations*. This incorporates all aspects of employer-employee relations, both individual and collective, and involves issues such as industrial relations, communications, health, safety and welfare, and employee services. Traditionally there has been an emphasis on 'industrial relations', with collective bargaining as the central activity. However, in recent years the term 'employee relations' has become synonymous with a more individual approach to work-force management and the pursuit of a non-union strategy. Differences in management approaches to this aspect of personnel policy tend to focus on the range of communications mechanisms used and the level of senior management involvement in and commitment to these mechanisms. An emerging development in personnel management practice is an increasing focus on direct communications with employees (Gunnigle 1991, 1995a; Gunnigle, McMahon and Fitzgerald 1995). The Price Waterhouse Cranfield Survey on HRM practice in Ireland found that there had been a significant increase in verbal and written communication with employees (Gunnigle et al. 1994; Brewster and Hegewisch 1994).

A company's *reward system* is a critical indicator of organisational approaches to personnel management. Basic wage rates, the level and basis of wage increases and the range of fringe benefits provide valuable insights into the corporate approach to work-force management. Significant considerations in the design of reward systems are the role of pay, the degree to which pay increases are based on measures of employee performance, and the compatibility of the reward system with business goals and other personnel policies. In Ireland basic pay has traditionally been based on the 'going rate' for similar jobs in other companies or sectors. Pay increases in recent years have in most instances been determined at national level through centralised agreements. These apply to all unionised employees but also have 'knock-on' effects for some non-union employees. Increases for managerial and other professional or technical categories are generally agreed at the enterprise level. This may normally occur as a result of annual performance reviews based on a range of criteria such as individual performance, section or company performance, and comparisons with pay increases in other companies. An interesting trend is the growing incidence of performance-related pay (PRP). PRP based on formal performance appraisals for *all* employee grades is seen as a significant indicator of a preference for a more individualist (as opposed to collectivist) approach to employee relations. A study of recently established companies found that the incidence of PRP for *all* employee categories seems to be strongly linked to union recognition and company ownership (Gunnigle 1995a, 1995b). Most companies that used PRP for all employees were non-union and American-owned.

Another important area of personnel policy choice is *recruitment and internal flow practices*. This incorporates policies in the area of human resource planning, recruitment and selection, training and development, performance appraisal, and termination of employment. There are a number of significant developments in Ireland. Firstly, large-scale unemployment together with the young age profile and high education levels of the Irish labour force mean that many company vacancies are oversubscribed by well-qualified applicants. Another element has been an increase in the

20

use of performance management techniques, particularly performance appraisal. An important issue for companies is the relative emphasis placed on internal or external labour markets. This concerns the degree to which the management seeks to fill vacancies from within their current pool of employees or, alternatively, to rely on the external labour market. It seems that in some companies there is an increased desire to focus on the internal rather than the external labour market as a means of filling vacancies. Such an internal labour market emphasis is in line with 'softer' HRM approaches and is often linked to a range of supportive personnel policies in areas such as employee development, appraisal, and career counselling. In contrast, a preference for using the external labour market implies less internal mobility and demands less sophisticated employee development practices. Recent research evidence identifies an increased incidence of 'harder' HRM approaches and particularly a greater emphasis on sub-contracted labour and the use of other 'atypical' employment forms, such as temporary and part-time employees. (This issue is discussed further in chapter 2.)

The specialist personnel management function

A particularly significant aspect of personnel policy choice is the role of the specialist personnel management function. Organisational approaches to work-force management influence the role of the personnel function. For example, it is suggested that a key feature of the so-called 'strategic' HRM approach is that the main responsibility for personnel management be assumed by line managers. However, Guest (1987) notes 'the well established "professional" structure of personnel management' in Britain, where 'professional' personnel specialists undertake responsibility for a range of human resource issues and possess valued expertise in 'core' personnel management areas such as selection, training, pay, and employee relations. It would seem that the question of whether personnel issues are best managed by the specialist personnel function or by line managers is one of emphasis, since in most larger companies both will be involved in various aspects of personnel management practice. For example, the 'professional' personnel management model involves a major role for the personnel function in handling personnel activities, with a heavy reliance on systems and procedures and a strong emphasis on employee relations. Guest feels that this approach is most appropriate in stable, bureaucratic organisations. On the other hand, HRM-type approaches emphasise the primary role of the line management in personnel activities, high levels of individualism, and greater integration of personnel management considerations in strategic decision-making (Guest 1987, 1989). Recognising such variations in the organisational role of the personnel function, Tyson (1985, 1987) identifies three alternative role models of the personnel function, as outlined in table 1.4.

Table 1.4: Role models of the specialist personnel function

1. Administrative/support role: Within this model personnel management is a low-level activity operating in a clerical support mode to the line management. It is responsible for basic administration and welfare provision.

2. Systems/reactive role: Within this model personnel management is a high-level function with a key role in handling industrial relations and in developing policies and procedures in other core areas. The role is largely reactive, dealing with the personnel management implications of business decisions. This model incorporates a strong 'policing' component, where the personnel department is concerned with securing adherence to agreed systems and procedures.

3. Business manager role: Within this model personnel management is a top-level management function involved in establishing and adjusting corporate objectives and developing strategic personnel policies designed to facilitate the achievement of long-term business goals. Personnel management considerations are recognised as an integral component of corporate success, with the personnel director optimally placed to assess how the company's human resources can best contribute to this goal. Routine personnel activities are delegated, allowing senior practitioners to adopt a broad strategic outlook.

A study by Shivanath (1987) considered the relevance of Tyson's role models for personnel management practice in a cross-section of large companies in Ireland. In relation to the 'administrative/support model' the survey evidence found that the great majority of Irish practitioners were not limited to this role. While personnel departments were, of necessity, concerned with routine clerical and administrative tasks, these were generally delegated, allowing senior practitioners to deal with more strategic matters. The description of the personnel practitioner within the 'systems/reactive' model seemed to most accurately reflect the role of the majority of practitioners. Industrial relations was identified by the bulk of respondents as the most crucial area of their work. The study also found that the 'business manager model' was prominent in a number of companies.

In a similar vein but using a two-dimensional model, Storey (1992) categorises the personnel function along (*a*) strategic/tactical and (*b*) interventionary/non-interventionary continuums, as outlined in fig. 1.4. The tactical/strategic dimension measures the level at which the personnel function operates in making decisions or providing support in companies. This provides a useful addition to the Tyson model, as it points out that personnel may act at a strategic level but in an advisory capacity and thus may exhibit the strategic input of the business manager model but with the discretion of an administrative/support model.

Fig. 1.4: Storey's matrix of personnel types

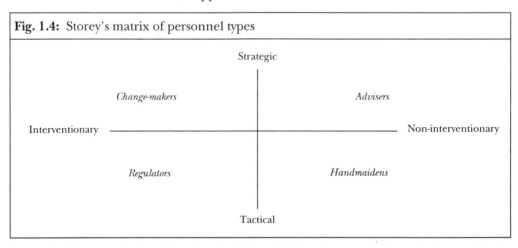

Source: Storey (1992)

The interventionary/non-interventionary dimension raises a key issue in the personnel and human resource management literature in recent times, namely the suggestion that the personnel function is adopting a less 'hands-on' approach in the management of the employment relationship (Mackay and Torrington 1986). Whether or not this approach is a result of a conscious policy decision there is certainly an evident trend towards reassessing the level of intervention that personnel and HR departments engage in. Consequently, this dimension represents an informative measure of the role of the personnel or HR function in companies.

Storey (1992) uses this two-dimensional model to produce a categorisation of four personnel function types:

(1) advisers
(2) handmaidens
(3) regulators
(4) change-makers.

'Advisers' essentially provide support to line and general management. While this function is carried out at a strategic level it is reactive and non-interventionist, providing specialist skills but in a consultancy capacity. 'Handmaidens' represent a 'subservient, attendant relationship', with personnel operating in a low-level and non-interventionist capacity, reacting to the needs of line managers in response to day-to-day operational problems. Storey suggests that this personnel type is indicative of a clerical and welfare role and was characteristic of subsidiaries where the personnel presence had been depleted or reduced. 'Regulators' operate in an interventionist mode but rarely at the level of strategy formulation. This approach is representative of a traditional industrial relations orientation, with the senior personnel practitioner responsible for devising and negotiating policies and procedures to ensure the smooth operation of the company. This has many similarities with the systems/reactive model. The rationale behind this category is that even where line managers wish to undertake this role many are not competent to do so or are not trained adequately. In this model the personnel contribution is significant at an operational level (in ensuring the smooth running of the company) rather than at a strategic level. In contrast, 'change-makers' act as specialists and are highly interventionist and strategic in perspective. This represents the highest level of operation of the personnel function and has marked similarities with Tyson's 'business manager' typology. In this model senior personnel practitioners are aware of both the 'soft' and 'hard' elements of personnel and employee relations practice. The two roles may exist in part side by side, the calculated, quantitative, rational approach of the business-oriented specialist and the 'softer' approach of realising the full potential of the 'human' side of the company.

CONTEMPORARY DEVELOPMENTS AFFECTING PERSONNEL MANAGEMENT

In assessing contemporary developments, the last decade may be typified as a period of both 'continuity and change' for the specialist personnel function in Ireland (see Monks 1992; Foley and Gunnigle 1994, 1995). The continuity dimension is manifested in the widespread presence of a specialist personnel function in organisations and a continuing emphasis on employee relations as a key aspect of the personnel role. The Price Waterhouse Cranfield study found that over 80 per cent of companies employing more than two hundred employees had a specialist personnel function (Gunnigle et al. 1994). However, this literature also identifies areas of important change, such as greater strategic integration of the personnel or HR function, some movement away from traditional industrial relations and collective bargaining to a more individual approach, a growth in atypical forms of employment, and greater emphasis on other aspects of personnel activity, particularly training and development.

Looking firstly at the area of strategic integration, Foley and Gunnigle (1994, 1995) identify some movement towards a 'strategic business manager' model. In some companies it appears that personnel or HR practitioners are adopting a more strategic role, devolving operational activities to line and staff managers. This trend is illustrated in the findings of the Price Waterhouse Cranfield survey: 45 per cent of respondents indicate that the HR manager had a seat on the board of directors, and 60 per cent of practitioners indicate that they are involved in formulating overall business strategy, 'either from the outset or on a consultative basis.' However, it is necessary to qualify this development by noting that it has occurred in a largely ad hoc fashion. Associated activities do not seem to have received the same level of attention. For example, although over 80 per cent of companies conduct manpower planning, 'such planning cannot be considered strategic, as in many cases it fails to consider environmental trends and is predominantly short-term in nature.' Therefore, although the personnel role appears to have achieved a higher status, the extent of strategic integration remains unclear and in many companies an aspiration.

Overall, it appears that there has been some general shift in the focus of the specialist personnel function. As noted earlier, personnel management in Ireland has traditionally been associated with a collectivist, industrial relations emphasis. It has already been mentioned that at present there seems to be a greater emphasis on direct communications, augmenting, if not replacing, traditional collective bargaining. Many commentators have noted an increasing opposition to trade union recognition (McGovern 1988, 1989a, 1989b; Gunnigle 1995a, 1995b). Foley and Gunnigle (1994, 1995) suggest that there is evidence of a more individual approach to work-force management, replacing traditional pluralism, particularly among newer companies. (This issue is considered further in chapter 11.) Recent research also identifies training and development as an increasingly important area in the work of the personnel function (Heraty et al. 1994). An additional area of change has been the growth in 'atypical' employment forms. (The development of atypical employment and its implications for personnel management is considered in chapter 3.)

This section has highlighted the extent of variation in the role of the specialist personnel function. The role adopted by the personnel function in a particular company will, like the other key areas of personnel policy choice discussed earlier, be influenced by factors in that company's internal and external context. The particular model adopted provides a rationale and driving force for the activities and operation of the personnel function. In recent years it has become common to contrast what has become labelled as 'traditional personnel management' with what has come to be termed 'human resource management' (HRM). This debate is addressed in the next chapter, which considers the development of HRM and the establishment of links between business strategy and personnel or HR management.

2

Business Strategy, Personnel Management, and Human Resource Management

One of the most notable characteristics of the management literature over the past decade has been the increased interest in achieving a closer alignment between business strategy and personnel management (see for example Fombrun 1984; Schuler 1987, 1992; Guest 1992; Salamon 1992; Tyson 1992). Emerging from this debate, the concept of 'strategic human resource management (HRM)' refers to the development of a strategic corporate approach to work-force management. In this approach, it is argued, personnel considerations become integral to strategic decision-making, and companies seek to establish a corporate personnel or human resource policy that complements their business strategy (Fombrun, Tichy and Devanna 1984; Buller and Napier 1993; Guest 1987; Purcell 1989).

Storey (1992) notes that an important emergent theme in the personnel management literature is a desire to address what he terms the 'dilemmas' in work-force management. Essentially this is reflected in a shift away from the tendency to prescribe the 'how to' in managing employees to an approach that takes a more contingent view of the personnel management practices considered suitable for particular organisations. He cites Schuler (1989), who advances the proposal that the key contingency affecting a company's work-force practices is its business strategy. It seems likely that this strategic focus will continue, since work-force management considerations have been a neglected area within strategic management thinking generally (Beer et al. 1984; Fombrun, Tichy, and Devanna 1984).

However, despite the extensive literature addressing the concept of strategy and 'strategic HRM', there appears to be little agreement on the substance, nature and meaning of these concepts. The methodological problems of addressing links between business strategy and personnel management include the differences in meaning associated with such terms as 'business strategy', 'personnel (or human resource) strategy', 'human resource management', and 'integration' (Tyson, Witcher, and Doherty 1994; Tyson 1992; Blyton and Turnbull 1992, 1994; Gunnigle et al. 1994).

This chapter considers the debate on linking decisions in the personnel management sphere with broader decisions on business strategy. It examines the nature of strategic management, with particular emphasis on competitive strategy at the level of the business unit. It also explores the impact of product market conditions on personnel management. Finally, it considers the emergence of HRM and assesses its relevance for personnel management practice in Ireland.

The concept of strategic management

There is an extensive literature on the concept of business strategy. Numerous writers dealing with managerial and business decision-making have used the term 'strategy' to describe a particular set of choices taken over a period to achieve given business objectives. *Strategic management*, therefore, is concerned with long-term policy decisions affecting the entire organisation and involving major decisions on resource allocation, the overall objective being to position the organisation to deal effectively with its environment.

More recent evaluations have attempted to identify the various components of the strategy concept and the levels and types of strategy that may occur. Hofer and Schendel (1978) found it useful to distinguish between strategy process and content. *Strategy process* concerns the activities involved in the formation of a strategy, such as analysing competitors and scanning the environment to identify threats and opportunities. *Strategy content*, on the other hand, refers to the actual policies chosen by a company and the methods used to implement these.

In addition, Hofer and Schendel (1978) identify three levels of strategy: the corporate, business and functional levels. *Corporate-level strategy* is essentially concerned with the question 'What business should we be in?' *Business-level (competitive) strategy* deals with the question 'How do we compete in this business?' Finally, *functional-level strategy* focuses on how the activities of particular functions (such as personnel management) come together to support business-level strategy. These differing strategy levels are illustrated in fig. 2.1. This conception of strategic management implies that in an organisational setting there is a hierarchy of decision choices and that key decisions on business strategy will steer more specific operational decisions on short-term problems and issues (Thurley and Wood 1983).

Fig. 2.1: Levels of strategic decision-making

Corporate strategy (What business should we be in?)	Multi-business
Business/competitive strategy (How to establish competitive advantage)	Single/related business(es)
Functional strategy (Role of component parts)	

Production/Marketing operations	Finance	Personnel management

Source: Gunnigle, McMahon and Fitzgerald (1995).

While these distinctions help to clarify the concept of strategic management, there remains some difficulty in relation to implementing it in such a way that it reflects the reality of organisational life. For example, there is an inherent assumption that a company's strategy is formed after key managers have analysed all relevant information, developed a number of possible options, and rationally chosen the option that maximises organisational performance. In addition, it is often assumed that implementing these strategic policies is not problematic, because there is goal congruity between the parties. Consequently decisions made by top managers will be followed by individuals and groups at lower levels with little resistance. Clearly such assumptions run contrary to evidence on the practice of organisational decision-making and implementation.

Recognising these difficulties, Mintzberg (1978, 1988) distinguished between 'realised' and 'unrealised' strategies and between 'intended' and 'emergent' strategies. 'Deliberate' strategies are those that are both intended and realised in the company. This is the concept of business strategy that appears most frequently in the literature. In addition to deliberate strategies there are 'unrealised' strategies, which may be intended but for some reason are never implemented. Finally, according to Mintzberg, realised strategies (patterns of decisions) may emerge without the conscious intentions of the strategists. These are termed 'emergent' strategies.

Mintzberg's categorisation goes beyond that of a deliberate strategy, in the sense of the traditional planning-oriented view of the term, to that of an emergent strategy, which is conceived as patterned responses that may not have been planned by the actors and may develop in an incremental and opportunistic manner. Strategies can therefore develop in a company without being consciously intended: indeed Mintzberg suggests that it would be a 'tall order' for a strategy to be realised exactly as intended.

Strategic decision-making and personnel management

The preceding discussion has highlighted the increasing emphasis on strategic management as companies strive to accommodate to an increasingly turbulent and competitive business environment. As we have already mentioned, decisions at higher levels, such as those at corporate or business unit level, will guide subsequent decisions on functional strategy. Purcell (1989) emphasises this point by differentiating between 'upstream' and 'downstream' strategic decisions. Upstream or first-order decisions concern the long-term direction and nature of the company. Downstream decisions deal with the implications of first-order decisions for organisational structure.

Purcell argues that personnel policy choices are made in the context of downstream strategic decisions on organisation structure. Although strategic in nature—they establish the company's basic approach to work-force management—Purcell suggests that personnel policy choices are third-order strategic decisions, since they will be heavily influenced by first and second-order decisions and broader environmental factors (see fig. 2.2).

Using British data, Purcell examined how trends in first and second-order strategies, particularly diversification and decentralisation, affect management decision-making. His analysis raises an important contrast between highly diversified companies operating in a variety of business sectors and 'critical function' companies, whose main activities are restricted to a core industry or sector. Purcell identified the growth in size and influence of the diversified firm as giving greater prominence to decision-making at the corporate level. Within this business form, portfolio planning is commonly used to

- evaluate the performance of constituent business units
- aid resource allocation and investment and divestment decisions.

The portfolio planning approach views the organisation as a collection of different businesses that should pursue various strategies to suit particular market conditions. This implies that different functional strategies, including personnel management, need to be applied at the business unit level to suit specific business strategies. Key decisions on the allocation of resources (first-order decisions) are taken at the corporate level, and it is the responsibility of business unit managers to deal with the implications of these and to make appropriate operational decisions to satisfy corporate requirements.

First-order decisions, therefore, while not necessarily incorporating personnel management considerations, significantly affect personnel policy and practice within particular business units.

Second-order decisions concern areas such as organisation structure, operating procedures, and the control of business unit performance. Purcell (1989) notes that diversified companies tend to prefer decentralised structures with a clear differentiation between strategic and operational responsibilities. He also notes that such companies normally view personnel management decisions as an operational responsibility at the business unit level. This implies that multi-business (diversified) companies are likely to have considerable variation in personnel or HR policies to fit with their different business conditions and strategies.

Fig. 2.2: Upstream and downstream strategic decision-making

Upstream

First-order	Long-term direction of the firm	
	Scope of activities, markets, location	
Second-order	Internal operating procedures	Environment
	Relationships between parts of the organisation	
Third-order	(e.g.) strategic choice in personnel management	

Downstream

Source: Purcell (1989).

The impact of competitive strategy

A key factor influencing the upsurge of interest in linking business strategies and personnel or human resource policies is the quest for competitive advantage. The idea of *competitive advantage* has been championed by Porter (1980, 1985, 1987) and can be described as any factors that allow a company to differentiate its product or service from its competitors to increase market share.

In contrast to the prominence given by Purcell to corporate decision-making, Porter argues that corporate strategy has failed 'dismally' and suggests that the focus of strategic decision-making should be on developing appropriate competitive strategies at the level of individual business units. *Competitive strategy* is concerned with achieving sustainable competitive advantage in particular industries or industry segments. Price and quality are common mechanisms by which companies attempt to achieve competitive advantage.

Porter identifies three generic competitive strategies:

1. *Cost leadership* (sometimes called *cost reduction*) involves positioning the company as a low-cost producer of a standard 'no-frills' product for either a broad or a focused market. To succeed with a cost leadership strategy it is suggested that the firm must become *the* cost leader and not one of several firms pursuing this strategy. Cost leadership requires an emphasis on tight managerial controls, low overheads, economies of scale, and a dedication to achieving productive efficiency.

2. *Product differentiation*, (sometimes called *product innovation*) on the other hand requires that a company's product or service become unique on some dimension that is valued by the buyer, to the extent that the buyer is willing to pay a premium price. The basis for a differentiation may be the product or service itself or other aspects, such as delivery or after-sales service.

3. A *focus strategy* involves choosing a narrow market segment and serving this either through a low-cost or a differentiation focus.

Another commonly used competitive strategy typology is that of Miles and Snow (1978, 1984), who advance three generic strategy types: 'defenders', 'prospectors', and 'analysers'. *Defenders* seek stability by producing only a limited set of products directed at a narrow segment of the total potential market. Within this niche, defenders strive to prevent competitors from entering the market through standard economic actions such as competitive pricing or the production of high-quality products. *Prospectors* are almost the opposite of defenders: their strength is in finding and exploiting new product and market opportunities. Innovation may be more important than high profitability. Success depends on developing and maintaining the capacity to survey a wide range of environmental conditions, trends and events and maintaining a high degree of flexibility. *Analysers* try to capitalise on the best of both the preceding types. They seek to minimise risk and maximise opportunity for profit. The strategy here is to move into new products or markets only after viability has been proved by prospectors.

A company's choice of generic strategy specifies its fundamental approach to achieving competitive advantage and provides the context for policies and actions in each key functional area, including personnel management. While there are criticisms of generic strategies, there is no doubt that such typologies help to clarify the nature of some of the basic strategies that are available to companies, given varying external factors.

Linking competitive strategy and personnel policy choice

It is suggested that different competitive strategies warrant different personnel strategies, policies, and practices. Of particular significance is the argued need to match personnel selection, work-force profile and employee relations practices with the desired competitive strategy (Schuler and Jackson 1987a). Porter (1987) further contends that different organisational cultures are implied in each strategy and that personnel policy choice is a key influence in establishing and maintaining 'appropriate' corporate cultures. It is argued that the personnel or HR function has an important role to play in managing the strategy process; Johnson and Scholes (1993) comment: 'Organisations which successfully manage change are those who have integrated their human resource management policies with their strategies and the strategic change process.' In the differentiation strategy it is suggested that culture might serve to encourage innovation, individuality, and risk-taking, whereas in cost leadership it might encourage frugality, discipline, and attention to detail. Porter argues that there is no such thing as a good or a bad culture: rather, he suggests that culture is a means of achieving competitive advantage and should match the company's business strategy.

Turning to the specific links between business strategy and personnel policies, it is argued that companies will experience severe problems in the implementation of strategy if it is not effectively linked with appropriate personnel policy choices (Galbraith and Nathanson 1978; Fombrun, Tichy, and Devanna 1984; Fombrun 1986). Alexander (1985) identifies personnel and human resource considerations as the critical aspect of successful strategy implementation: 'Implementation is that which addresses the issue of how to put a formulated strategy into effect—with the constraints of time, a firm's financial and human resources and its capabilities.'

Fombrun, Tichy and Devanna (1984) suggest that strategic management involves the consideration of three key issues:

Mission and strategy: Identification of a company's purpose, and plans for how this can be achieved.
Formal structure: For the organisation of people and tasks to achieve mission and strategy.
Personnel systems: Recruitment, development, evaluation and reward of employees.

This framework is represented in fig. 2.3 and is seen to differ from traditional approaches to strategic management by incorporating personnel management considerations as an integral component of strategic decision-making.

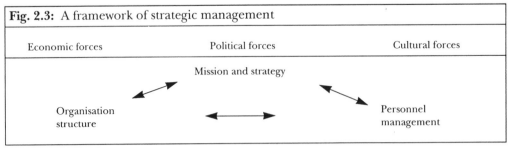

Fig. 2.3: A framework of strategic management

| Economic forces | Political forces | Cultural forces |

Mission and strategy

Organisation structure

Personnel management

Source: Adapted from Fombrun, Tichy, and Devanna (1984).

Fombrun, Tichy and Devanna (1984) suggest that a company's personnel policies and practices characterise managerial assumptions about employees and 'appropriate' work-force management practices. Fombrun (1986) identifies four key aspects of organisational approaches to work-force management:
(1) Nature of psychological contract: This may vary from, at one extreme, a managerial perspective that views employees in instrumental terms and emphasises high levels of

control both of employees and the work environment to, at the other extreme, an approach that sees employees as intelligent and committed beings who should be afforded challenging and meaningful work.

(2) **Level of employee involvement:** Here organisational approaches may vary from those with high levels of involvement by employees in decision-making to those where decisions are solely a management prerogative.

(3) **Internal v. external labour market:** This addresses the relative emphasis on internal versus external recruitment and related differences in emphasis on employee development.

(4) **Performance evaluation:** This factor addresses the relevant managerial emphasis on group versus individual performance evaluation.

Models of links between business strategy and personnel policy

Numerous writers have identified models of suggested links between business strategy and personnel policy (Miles and Snow 1984; Fombrun, Tichy, and Devanna 1984; Schuler, Galante, and Jackson 1987; Porter 1987). These models are based on the view that companies need to achieve a 'fit' between their business strategy, product market position, and internal personnel management strategy and polices (Beaumont 1993). They are predominantly American, and two of the more prominent models are reviewed below.

1. 'BUSINESS STRATEGY-EMPLOYEE BEHAVIOUR FIT' MODEL

Possibly the most extensive work on linking business strategy and personnel management has been conducted by Randall Schuler in the United States. He suggests that business strategies are most effective when 'systematically co-ordinated with human resources management practices' (Schuler 1987, 1989; Schuler and Jackson 1987a, 1987b; Schuler, Galante, and Jackson 1987). He further argues that a key objective in personnel policy choice is to develop employee behaviour that 'fits' the company's particular strategy. Schuler identifies three strategic types: 'cost reduction', 'differentiation' and 'focus strategy'. These are largely based on Porter's generic strategies discussed earlier. He proposes that for these strategies to be successful they have to be supported by particular patterns of employee behaviour, which in turn are shaped by the personnel or human resources strategies, policies and practices of the company. He identifies three alternative strategies designed to develop employee behaviour patterns that facilitate the achievement of the desired business strategy: 'accumulation', 'utilisation', and 'facilitation'.

Schuler argues that companies following a 'focus' competitive strategy require an *accumulation* personnel or human resources (P/HR) strategy. This emphasises careful selection based on personality rather than technical fit. Training, pay egalitarianism and lifetime employment are central. A *utilisation* P/HR strategy would be more appropriate for companies applying a 'cost-reduction' business strategy. Utilisation involves selecting people mainly on the basis of technical ability, and cost minimisation in the areas of training etc. Companies pursuing a 'differentiation' business strategy require a *facilitation* P/HR strategy. This focuses on the ability of people to work together in a reciprocal relationship. Cross-functional work teams are frequently used, while job rotation and broader career paths help to foster a collaborative work climate. This model is outlined in table 2.1.

31

Table 2.1: Linking business strategy and personnel management

Business strategy	Personnel/HR strategy	Desired employee behaviour		Personnel policy and activity focus
Cost reduction	Utilisation	Relatively repetitive and predictable behaviour	Recruitment	Explicit job analysis Mostly internal recruitment/labour market focus
		Mostly short-term focus High concern for quantity criteria; results-oriented criteria	Appraisal	Short-term focus; individual
		Moderate concern for quality	Rewards	Hierarchical pay, few incentives
		Major emphasis on results	Training and development	Narrow career paths; limited training
		Comfortable with stability	Employee relations	Little employment security; low employee participation; traditional industrial relations
Differentiation	Facilitation	Long-term focus	Recruitment	Implicit job analysis; external recruitment/labour market focus
		Creative job behaviour High level of independent co-operative behaviour criteria	Appraisal	Long-term focus; process and results criteria; some group
		Moderate concern for quality	Rewards	Egalitarian pay; numerous incentives
		Moderate concern for quantity	Training and development	Broad career paths; extensive training
		Equal concern for focus and results		

Focus	Behaviours	HRM practice	Practice description
	Tolerance of ambiguity	Employee relations	High employee participation; co-operative labour-management relations; some employment security
	Relatively predictable and repetitive behaviour	Recruitment	Explicit job analysis; some external recruitment
	Long/medium-term focus	Appraisal	Long-term focus; process and results criteria; some group criteria
Accumulation	High concern for quality	Rewards	Egalitarian pay; numerous incentives
	Moderate concern for quantity	Training and development	Broad career paths; extensive training
	Concern for process and results	Employee relations	High employee participation; co-operative labour management relations; some employment security
	Commitment to organisation goals		

Source: Adapted from Schuler (1987, 1989), Schuler and Jackson (1987a, 1987b).

2. 'DEFENDERS, PROSPECTORS, ANALYSERS' MODEL

Miles and Snow suggest that successful organisations possess a consistent strategy that is aligned with and supported by complementary organisation structures and management practices. They also suggest that organisations that do not possess this environment-strategy-structure alignment (i.e. 'reactors') are not as successful as the other three categories (see below). Difficulties in developing appropriate personnel management policies are seen as a barrier to the effective implementation of business strategies and structures.

Miles and Snow (1984) argue that these three basic types of strategic behaviour can be associated with particular personnel policy configurations, as outlined in fig. 2.4. To emphasise the need to align personnel policy choice and business strategy, they identify companies in each of the three strategic categorisations—Lincoln Electric ('defenders'), Hewlett-Packard ('prospectors'), and Texas Instruments ('analysers')—and suggest relevant personnel policy configurations for each strategy.

Fig. 2.4: Linking business strategy and personnel/ER policy

	STRATEGIC TYPE		
	Defender	*Prospector*	*Analyser*
Product and market strategy	Limited, stable product line; predictable markets	Broad, changing product line; changing markets	Stable and changing product line: predictable and changing markets
Research and development	Narrow; product improvement	Broad; new product development	Focused; 'second to market'
Marketing	Sales emphasis	Market research emphasis	Extensive marketing campaigns
Personnel/HR strategy	Maintenance	Entrepreneurial	Co-ordination
Recruitment and selection	'Make'; internal	'Buy'; external	'Make and buy'; mixed
Manpower planning	Formal, extensive	Informal, limited	Formal, extensive
Training and development	Extensive; skill building	Limited; skill acquisition	Extensive; skill building
Appraisal	Process-oriented; identify training needs; individual/ group performance evaluation	Results-oriented; identify staffing needs; corporate/ division performance evaluation	Process-oriented; identify training and staffing needs; individual/group/ divisional performance evaluation
Rewards	Based on level in hierarchy; internal equity; pay-oriented	Based on performance; external equity; incentive-oriented	Mostly based on level in hierarchy; internal and external comparisons; pay and incentive-oriented

Source: Adapted from Miles and Snow (1984).

'Defender' companies are characterised as lean and hard-working and demand predictable, planned and regularly maintained personnel policies. The emphasis is on building the company's own human resources through recruitment at entry level and promotion through the ranks. Selection, placement, training and development, appraisal and ensuring a fit between the reward system and job design are the key personnel activities.

'Prospector' companies experience rapid change, demanding considerable human resource redeployment. The main emphasis is on obtaining and deploying high-quality human resources. The personnel management objective is entrepreneurial, acquiring and developing critical staff. There is little opportunity for long-term planning or sophisticated personnel techniques.

In 'analyser' companies the focus is on developing the appropriate organisational structures and management approach, with personnel co-ordinating policies and allocating human resources throughout the company.

Strategy and personnel management: some evidence from Ireland

The preceding discussion suggests that personnel management represents an important area of strategic choice for companies. Such personnel policy choices have an important impact on competitive advantage (Porter 1987), organisation structure (Chandler 1962), and culture (Peters and Waterman 1982). However, the evidence from studies of personnel and HR practice in Irish companies presents quite a mixed picture. Gunnigle and Moore (1994) examined the level of integration between business strategy and personnel and HR policies using data generated by the Price Waterhouse Cranfield survey. The main areas of analysis were the incidence of formal personnel or HR strategies and the extent of involvement of the personnel or HR function in the formulation of strategy. This study found that less than half of the respondent companies had a written 'mission statement' (49.8 per cent) or corporate strategy (47.6 per cent), while 29 per cent had a written personnel or HR strategy. It was felt that the greater the amount of change and uncertainty the greater the likelihood of a written strategy. In assessing the contribution of the personnel function to the formulation of strategy, the results were quite positive (see fig. 2.5). It was found that in general, HR involvement in strategic areas has increased in recent years. Over half the firms surveyed reported personnel or HR involvement in strategy formulation from the outset. However, although personnel involvement has increased, some concerns have been expressed that there has simply been greater participation at a strategic level, without a corresponding increase in the all-important area of influence.

Fig. 2.5: Personnel/HR involvement in corporate strategy

	%
From the outset	52.6
Consultative	24.7
Implementation	11.9
Not consulted	10.8
n = 194.	

Source: University of Limerick (1992).

35

In evaluating the available research evidence it would appear that while some companies appear to be successfully aligning HR policies and business strategy, this development does not seem widespread.

THE IMPACT OF PRODUCT MARKETS

In the preceding chapter a company's product market was identified as a key influence in strategic decision-making, with important knock-on implications for personnel management and personnel policy choice. Indeed Kochan, Katz and McKersie (1986) identify increased product market competition as a critical factor in instigating significant changes in both competitive strategy and organisational approaches to work-force management. A company's product market incorporates the nature of the market to which it supplies its products or services and the company's competitive position within that market. It is commonly measured on the twin criteria of market share and market growth. Product market position will be influenced by a variety of factors, such as the cost of entry, nature of competition, technology, and the customer base.

A company's business strategy will be developed within the context of a particular product market. Thurley and Wood (1983) argue that broad strategy objectives can be linked to product market objectives, the enterprise's position in the market, the organisational characteristics, and the political, social and economic influences in the community where the enterprise operates (expressed through government policy and legislation and interest-group pressures). These factors will affect personnel management strategies and policies within the company. Kochan, Katz and McKersie (1986) identify product market changes as leading to a variety of strategic decisions that can profoundly affect personnel management policies and practices. This work seeks to explain how changes in the external environmental and, particularly, product market conditions lead to critical strategic choice decisions on a number of different levels, namely

- long-term strategy formulation at the top
- personnel, human resource and employee relations policy at the middle
- work-place and individual-organisation relationships at the shop floor level.

In reviewing the specific impact of product market developments on personnel or HR management, Marchington (1990) identifies two useful dimensions for evaluating a company's product market position: (a) monopoly power and (b) monopsony power (see also Marchington and Parker 1990). Monopoly power refers to the degree to which a company has the power to dictate market terms to customers. High monopoly power may be the result of factors such as cartel arrangements, regulated (e.g. state) monopolies, high barriers to entry, or unique product or technology. In such situations companies have considerable power to dictate terms, particularly price, and therefore tend to act as price makers. In contrast, monopsony power refers to the extent to which customers exert power over the company. High monopsony power may occur as a result of high levels of market competition (numerous competitors) or because of the existence of powerful customers who can exert considerable control over price and other factors (e.g. credit terms or service). In such situations, supplying companies may be forced to accept the market terms, particularly price, dictated by customers, i.e. to become price takers. These relationships are illustrated in fig. 2.6.

Marchington argues that the relative levels of monopoly and monopsony power a company experiences influence the extent of management discretion in making strategic policy decisions in all functional areas, including personnel management. Where monopoly power is high, the senior management will have considerable freedom to make broad personnel policy choices. Such favourable market conditions (high market share, growing market, stable demand) allow companies greater scope to adopt 'investment-oriented styles' and are more conducive to the application of benign personnel management practices, such as comprehensive employee development policies, tenure commitments, and gain-sharing.

Fig. 2.6: Product market conditions and personnel policy choice

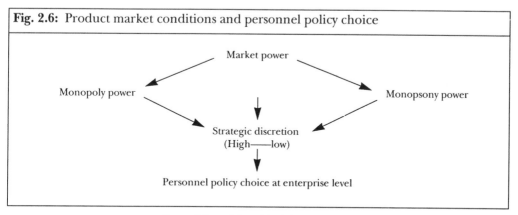

Source: Adapted from Marchington (1990).

This does not imply that employers will always adopt 'resource-type' policies in favourable product market conditions. Rather, such conditions provide the management with greater scope to choose from a range of personnel management policy choices: the actual choice will be further influenced by factors internal to the company, particularly management values and competitive strategy. On the other hand, companies operating under high levels of market pressure (high monopsony power) may have considerably less scope for choice, and a more traditional cost and labour control approach may be more appropriate.

Schuler and Jackson (1987a) are more prescriptive in suggesting that different market and cost considerations influence the appropriateness of various personnel policy choices. They use product life-cycle phases to evaluate product market influences on both business strategy and personnel policy choice.

In the **growth phase** the attraction of high-calibre employees is seen as the main priority. The key organisational need is for technical talent, to transform ideas into salable products or services. The main source of human resources is the external labour market. The company attracts employees by differentiating itself, using innovative personnel policies such as employment tenure and high levels of employee participation. Various categories of part-time, temporary or sub-contract labour may be used to buffer full-time employees during economic downturns. Employee relations issues are handled through various communications and participatory mechanisms. Wages are normally high and tied to profitability and/or employee skills.

In the **maturity phase** the company has a large internal labour market and the emphasis is on human resource retention. Jobs tend to be more narrowly defined, and wages tend to be based more on grade definitions than on profitability or skill. There is less employee participation, and downturns in profitability may result in dismissals. Employee relations issues are handled through collective bargaining.

In the *decline phase* the company needs cuts in both costs and employee numbers. There is downward pressure on wages and a need to agree criteria on which to base redundancy decisions.

Schuler and Jackson (1987a) then examined policy-choice decisions in four specific areas (job design, performance appraisal, rewards, and training and development) in companies pursuing three distinct business strategies (dynamic growth, extract profit, and turnaround). They concluded that there are predictable relationships between business strategy and personnel policy choice but found no proof that these choices were systematically selected to fit particular strategies. They also found no conclusive evidence that a good fit contributes to greater organisational effectiveness. They suggest that fitting personnel policy choice is an important variable but that other factors, such as leadership and culture, must also be taken into consideration.

Schuler and Jackson further contend that as companies strive to achieve a greater fit between business and personnel strategies this will lead to continuous change in personnel management, with employees being exposed to a range of different practices in the course of employment. Employees may therefore be expected to exhibit different characteristics and to work under various sets of employment conditions at different stages in their working lives.

The Irish situation

There is little doubt that 'traditional' approaches to personnel management in Ireland have come under increasing challenge in recent years. There is also general agreement that such challenges mainly originate outside the sphere of personnel management (Beaumont 1995). Roche and Gunnigle (1995, 3) identify developments in the wider business context as the key catalyst in stimulating changes in industrial relations and personnel management:

> Never before has the analysis of industrial relations practices and policies been so closely tied to an appreciation of commercial and national and international political pressures. In the past the worlds of industrial relations practitioners and academics alike tended to be much more introverted and preoccupied with the internal dynamics of industrial relations systems, agreements and procedures ... Currently, these concerns, though not altogether displaced, often take second place to such issues as company performance, the union's role in contributing to business success, mission statements and quality standards, business units, employment flexibility and so on.

The most widely accepted explanation of changes in traditional approaches to personnel management is the increasingly competitive nature of product markets. In attempting to disaggregate the sources of increased competitiveness there is an amalgam of factors, most particularly the liberalisation of European and world trade, deregulation in product and service markets, improved communications and transport infrastructures, and greater market penetration by the emerging economies of southeast Asia (see Roche and Gunnigle 1995). These developments have particularly significant implications for Ireland as a result of its status as a small open economy that is heavily reliant on export performance. Such reliance on international trade exposes Irish businesses to volatility in the international economy.

The impact of increased competitive pressures on trading companies has been to focus attention on both cost *and* product innovation and quality as factors influencing competitive positioning and to create a 'flexibility imperative' whereby companies increasingly have to be responsive to consumer demand in areas such as customisation, delivery, and support services. The overall implication of these developments seems to have all but diluted the concept of companies competing on either a price (low cost) or product differentiation (premium price) basis. Increasingly it appears that all companies, not just the low-cost producers, must tightly control their cost structures. While the need to control labour and pay costs may be more intense in labour-intensive sectors, it is also important in other sectors as product and service market competition increases and profit margins tighten.

This conclusion finds support in a recent analysis of payment practices in Irish multinational companies. Roche and Geary (1994) noted that a significant trend during the nineteen-seventies and early eighties was for foreign-owned companies to concede above-the-norm pay increases. However, the authors note the abandonment of this approach since the mid-eighties, with most such companies settling within the norm. By and large, foreign-owned companies are more capital-intensive and have lower relative labour costs than their indigenous counterparts (Foley 1990). Extrapolating the logic of Roche and Geary's analysis, it appears that foreign-owned companies could absorb above-the-norm pay increases in previous years because of a combination of less intense competitive pressures and lower relative labour costs. In the face of significantly increased competition, however, labour costs have now become a focus of management control in foreign-owned companies to a degree only previously experienced in high-labour-cost companies, primarily of indigenous ownership.

Roche and Gunnigle (1995) further note that these competitive trends are increasingly penetrating the state-owned sector. A significant reason for this development is the erosion of state monopolies as a result of developments at European Union level (O'Connor 1995). An early example of a state company having to deal with increased competitiveness was that of Aer Lingus. Deregulation in the airline industry meant that the company was faced with increased competition on important routes. The resultant restructuring led to significant changes in employee numbers, employment patterns, and reward systems. The ESB and Telecom Éireann are now faced with EU-sponsored initiatives aimed at deregulating the electricity and telecommunications markets. Such changes are likely to have profound effects on personnel management strategies, policies and practices in these organisations. The conditions imposed by the Maastricht Treaty for entry to the third phase of economic and monetary union on issues such as interest rate convergence and the debt-GDP ratio pose considerable challenges for the Government, not least the issue of public sector expenditure. The completion of the internal market and removal of trade barriers also serve to expose many companies to increased international competition, with implications for personnel management at the level of the enterprise.

Reviewing the impact of the European Union on Irish industrial relations, Hourihan (1994) argues that EU membership has significantly affected the nature of national-level collective bargaining in recent years. He suggests that 'we may be seeing a new facet to the decision making process affecting industrial relations, with the European

Commission being afforded a validation role which directly affects the conduct of national level bargaining'(Hourihan 1994, 417). Hourihan argues that access to EU funds is being firmly tied to the acceptance or validation of policy decisions achieved at national-level bargaining by the European Commission and also that the use of EU funds may be linked to the adoption of labour market reforms put forward by Brussels. He suggests that such approaches imply a 'new dimension' that 'affords the European Commission an unheralded place in the formation of labour market policies within member states' (Hourihan 1994, 418).

THE GROWTH OF HUMAN RESOURCE MANAGEMENT

The preceding discussion has noted the marked increase in interest in more closely aligning business strategy with personnel management strategy and policy. Indeed it appears that this trend is set to continue, since the whole personnel and human resource sphere is seen as a neglected area of strategic management and because of its central role in implementing cultural and political changes in organisations (Beer et al. 1984; Fombrun, Tichy, and Devanna 1984).

The preceding chapter noted that the nineteen-eighties was a period of reappraisal for personnel management. Competitive pressures forced many companies to investigate different approaches to work-force management in areas such as job design, reward systems, and employee relations. However, by far the most widely debated development during this period was the emergence of human resource management (HRM). This was seen by many as a new development that contrasted with 'traditional' personnel management. Its apparently proactive stance was viewed as a significant departure from the traditionally reactive 'industrial relations' focus associated with established approaches to personnel management.

> The new approaches to industrial relations which adopted a managerialist rather than a pluralist stance, the restructuring possibilities, and the reduction in trade union power and influence were the back drop to what is now perceived as a new paradigm on which to base employment relationships. In the eyes of some commentators, Human Resource Management (HRM) came to represent the new paradigm, and the critical distinction drawn was the notion that HRM placed initiatives on people management at the strategic heart of the business ... The new flexibility agreements, new working practices, reorganisations, delayering activities, the flatter organisations, direct communications with the workforce, and stronger corporate cultures ... could be understood as a new, more coherent approach ... If this was propaganda, it was propaganda that managers themselves started to believe as the 1980s came to a close ... The real challenge is to try to discover what real attempts at strategic integration there are (Tyson, Witcher and Doherty 1994).

HRM involves the development of a strategic approach to work-force management (Beer et al. 1984; Guest 1987). It has its academic roots in two primarily distinct branches of the literature, both originating in the United States. The first of these is encompassed in the Harvard Business School model (Beer et al. 1984). This focuses on the individual employee as the key organisational resource, which the management must nurture and develop to maximise its contribution to the company. This model suggests that management adopt a coherent range of pro-employee or 'soft' personnel policies to ensure the attraction, retention and development of committed, high-performing employees.

The second source advocating increased strategic consideration of personnel management is the broader business strategy literature, specifically the work of Fombrun (see for example Fombrun, Tichy and Devanna 1984). This approach suggests that organisational performance can be substantially improved by integrating personnel management considerations into strategic decision-making to ensure that personnel policies complement business strategy. In contrast to the Harvard Business School model, this approach does not prescribe either a 'hard' or 'soft' approach to work-force management: rather, it suggests that the top management adopt the policies that best suit its particular circumstances and complement strategic purpose.

The nature of HRM[1]

In spite of a growing consensus on the nature of HRM, there remains considerable confusion about its distinctive characteristics, its applicability to organisations, and its contrasts with more 'traditional' approaches to work-force management. The most influential early work on HRM was conducted by Michael Beer and his colleagues at the Harvard Business School (Beer et al. 1984). Their model presents a broad causal map of the determinants and consequences of HRM policy choices, as outlined in fig. 2.7. Beer et al. describe HRM in generic terms as 'involving all management decisions and actions that affect the nature of the relationship between the organisation and its employees— its human resources.' Those in the top management, therefore, and particularly the chief executive, are seen as having the primary responsibility for aligning business strategy and personnel policy choice.

Fig. 2.7: Harvard Business School model of human resource management

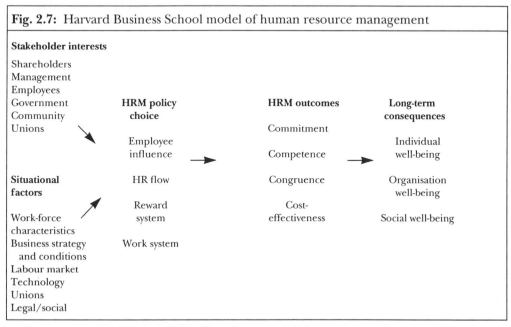

Source: Beer et al. (1984).

Four key components comprise the Harvard Business School model:
(1) stakeholder interests
(2) HRM policy choice
(3) HRM outcomes
(4) long-term consequences.

A central contention of the model is that personnel or HR outcomes are affected by policy choices made in four key areas:
(1) reward systems
(2) human resource flows
(3) work systems
(4) employee influence.

Each of these policy areas is seen as a key element of strategic choice that profoundly affects employees' behaviour and attitude towards the company. Strategic choice in these areas is influenced by broader contextual factors:
(1) situational constraints (including work-force characteristics, business strategy, management policy, labour market, etc.)
(2) stakeholder interests (shareholders, management, employees, government, etc.).

Decisions made in these policy areas are seen as affecting personnel or HR outcomes in the areas of employee commitment, congruence of employees' and management interests, employee competence, and cost-effectiveness. These outcomes are also seen as having broader long-term consequences for individual employees' well-being, organisational effectiveness, and social well-being.

Fig. 2.8: Definitions of human resource management

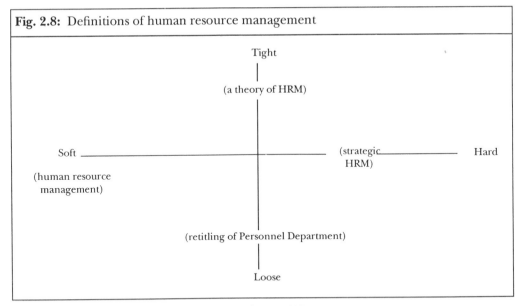

Source: Guest (1987)

On this side of the Atlantic, Guest's (1987) 'hard-soft, tight-loose' framework of HRM is possibly the most widely referenced (see fig. 2.8). The 'hard-soft' dimension refers to a spectrum ranging from a resource-based ('soft') managerial perspective, characterised by benign pro-employee policies, to a more calculated ('hard') management perspective where policy choice is driven by the need to complement business strategy and meet 'bottom line' financial criteria. The 'tight-loose' dimension refers to a spectrum ranging from HRM merely involving a retitling of traditional personnel management ('loose') with no real change in personnel practice to HRM becoming a clearly defined and articulated approach to work-force management, with an explicit and strong ('tight') theoretical underpinning (Flood 1989).

Guest proceeds to develop a theory of HRM in which he argues that companies will be more successful if they pursue four key HRM goals, namely

(1) strategic integration
(2) employee commitment
(3) flexibility
(4) quality.

He suggests that these HRM goals can be optimally achieved through coherent HRM policy choices in the areas of organisation and job design, management of change, recruitment, selection and socialisation, appraisal, training and development, rewards, and communication.

Guest identifies five necessary conditions for the effective operation of HRM:

(1) **Corporate leadership:** To ensure that the values inherent in HRM are championed and implemented.
(2) **Strategic vision:** To ensure the integration of HRM as a key component of the corporate strategy.
(3) **Technological/production feasibility:** Guest suggests that heavy investment in short-cycle, repetitive production assembly-line equipment mitigates against the job design principles and autonomous team-working necessary for HRM.
(4) **Employee relations feasibility:** Guest suggests that multi-union status, low-trust management-employee relations and an adversarial employee relations orientation mitigate against the implementation of HRM.
(5) **Management capacity:** To implement appropriate policies.

HRM v. traditional personnel management

When HRM is contrasted with more traditional personnel management, as in table 2.2, a number of key differences emerge. Firstly, it is argued that personnel management considerations are fully integrated with strategic decision-making in the HRM model, whereas in the traditional model the personnel contribution is less pronounced and issue-specific. A second contrast is that HRM is seen as essentially proactive and long-term, while the traditional personnel management approach is more reactive and adopts a shorter-term perspective. As to the desired mode of psychological contract, HRM is seen as facilitating employee commitment, while the traditional personnel management model is seen as a mode of managerial control over employees (Walton 1985).

A specific contrast in the employee relations sphere is that HRM is seen as essentially unitarist in perspective, involving no apparent conflict of interest between employers and employees. In contrast, 'traditional' personnel management is seen as grounded in the pluralist tradition and essentially concerned with managing the adversarial relationship between employers and workers. A related factor is that HRM is seen as focusing on relations between the (line) management and the individual worker, while the traditional model is seen as operating primarily through collectivist relations between the management and employee representatives. Another area of contrast is that

HRM is seen as operating most effectively in organic, fluid organisation structures, while 'personnel management' is felt to characterise more bureaucratic and rigid structures. As we have seen, HRM is seen to operate primarily through the line management, while the primary responsibility in the traditional personnel management model is vested in the specialist personnel function. The final perceived difference relates to the criteria used to evaluate effectiveness. HRM is seen as essentially focused on maximising the contribution of human resources to organisational effectiveness; in contrast, traditional 'personnel management' is seen as having more pragmatic objectives: the maximisation of cost-effectiveness.

Despite these argued contrasts between HRM and traditional personnel management, Guest cautions that this does not necessarily imply that HRM is better than 'traditional' personnel management. Rather, he suggests that traditional personnel management approaches may be more appropriate in certain organisational contexts, such as large bureaucratic companies or heavily unionised companies with adversarial collective bargaining traditions, while HRM may be appropriate in companies with more organic structures and characterised by more individualist, high-trust management-employee relations.

Table 2.2: Personnel management and human resource management compared

	Traditional personnel management	**HRM**
Contribution to corporate planning	Issue-specific	Integrated
Time and planning perspective	Short-term; reactive; marginal	Long-term; active; strategic
Psychological contract	Compliance	Commitment
Employee relations	Pluralist; collective; low-trust; adversarial	Unitarist, individual; high-trust
Organisation structures and systems	Bureaucratic, mechanistic; centralised; formal defined roles	Organic, fluid; devolved; flexible roles
Principal delivery mechanism	Specialist personnel management function	Line management
Aims	Maximise cost-effectiveness	Maximise HR use

Source: Adapted from Guest (1987).

Contradictions and inconsistencies in HRM

Several authors have identified a number of inherent contradictions and inconsistencies in HRM, particularly the 'soft' variant advocated by the Harvard Business School model (Legge 1989; Keenoy 1990; Blyton and Turnbull 1992; Cradden 1992). For example, Legge (1989) highlights the apparent paradox between the traditional commodity status of labour within the capitalist framework and the essentially unitarist perspective of HRM, which sees no conflict of interest between the management and workers. It has generally been accepted that in the capitalist framework there is an inherent conflict of interest between management and workers over the price of labour. Indeed this is the very basis for the existence of employee relations as a key concern of workers and management. However, the HRM perspective appears to ignore the 'inherence' of a conflict of interest but rather focuses on the achievement of congruence between management and employee interests and on achieving high levels of employee commitment. For example, Flood (1989) suggests that HRM emphasises the need for companies to focus on the extrinsic and intrinsic needs of employees and to develop employment practices that increase employee commitment. In a similar vein, Walton (1985) advocates that companies adopt policies that emphasise the mutuality of employer and employee interests to ensure employees' commitment to the achieving of organisational goals.

This focus on employee commitment not only seems incongruent with the pluralist perspective of the company (discussed above) but also appears to conflict with another basic tenet of HRM, namely that personnel considerations should be integrated with and complement business strategy. Clearly, many decisions that complement business strategy may not develop employee commitment. If, for example, a company's business strategy is to maximise short-term returns to the owners or shareholders, this may well involve decisions that do not develop employee commitment; for example, replacing labour with technology, contracting out certain tasks, or making employees redundant. A related issue is the suggestion that HRM involves the simultaneous achievement of higher levels of individualism and teamwork. These twin goals clearly have tremendous potential for conflict. For example, performance-related pay based on individual employees' performance may indeed conflict with teamwork, as can individual communications and negotiations.

High levels of flexibility are seen as a core objective of HRM. Guest (1987) suggests that increased flexibility involves the creation of structural mechanisms in companies to ensure responsiveness to changing environmental conditions. He suggests that such flexibility should encompass both functional and numerical flexibility. However, several authors have noted the difficulty of achieving congruence in different flexibility forms, namely numerical, functional and financial flexibility. It is clearly difficult to achieve high levels of functional flexibility (e.g. multi-skilling) where employees have a tenuous relationship with the company, as may result for example from attempts to improve numerical flexibility (Blyton and Morris 1992; Gunnigle 1992b).

Another contradiction in the HRM argument that personnel policies must be internally consistent arises in relation to job security. A prominent theme in the current literature is that for HRM to be effective, the management must provide implicit job tenure guarantees for employees (Beer et al. 1984; Guest 1987, 1989a; Walton 1985). For example, Guest (1989a) argues that job tenure commitments are a 'necessary' precondition to achieving a 'mutuality of management and employee interests,' which he suggests is a key policy goal of HRM. However, it is patently evident that high levels of competition and volatility in product markets have made job security increasingly difficult to achieve. Indeed, job security may itself be incompatible with broader business goals attributed to HRM, such as increased flexibility in responding to rapid changes in demand. In practice it would appear that some companies seek to achieve such flexibility by policies that actually reduce the likelihood of job tenure commitments—for example, using atypical forms of employment. On the issue of the practicability of achieving a 'fit' between business strategy and HRM policies (e.g. job tenure commitments) Blyton and Turnbull (1992, 10) comment:

> This is particularly problematic in highly competitive or recessionary conditions where the 'needs of the business' are likely to undermine any internal 'fit' with ('soft') HRM values: shedding labour for example will severely challenge, if not destroy, an organisation's HRM image of caring for the needs and security of its employees.

Another apparent inconsistency in HRM is the focus on achieving greater individualism in management-employee relations. As we have seen, employee relations in Ireland have been characterised by extensive reliance on collectivism, as manifested in, for example, relatively high levels of trade union density and low-trust management-employee relations (Whelan 1982). The 'soft' HRM approach, as outlined by the Harvard Business School model and by Guest, places the managerial emphasis on achieving high-trust relations between the management and employees and appears to have a preference for pursuing this goal in a non-union environment. Within the 'soft' HRM model, high-trust relations are pursued through managerial initiatives to increase individual employees' involvement and motivation and the adoption of techniques such as performance appraisal and performance-related pay. Such companies, therefore, attempt to create close management-employee ties and break down the traditional management-worker dichotomy, of which collective bargaining is seen as the principal manifestation.

Such initiatives are indicative of a unitarist management perspective, albeit a sophisticated variant, and have a potential for significant conflict with the pluralist perspective, characteristic of employee relations in Ireland. This unitarist perspective is described by Guest (1989a, 43) thus:

> HRM values are unitarist to the extent that they assume no underlying and inevitable differences of interest between management and workers ... HRM values are essentially individualistic in that they emphasise the individual-organization linkage in preference to operating through group and representative mechanisms ... These values ... leave little scope for collective arrangements and assume little need for collective bargaining. HRM therefore poses a considerable threat to traditional industrial relations and more particularly trade unionism.

HRM in practice

While the theoretical literature places much emphasis on the strategic nature of HRM, there is limited empirical evidence on the extent to which strategic approaches to HRM are adopted in practice. Indeed recent Irish research questions the extent of strategic HRM (Roche and Turner 1994).

Research on high-performing British companies by Tyson, Witcher and Doherty (1994) sought to examine whether companies attempt to achieve a fit between the business and HRM strategy, and if so, how. The research discovered three distinct approaches to corporate and business strategy formation and found common elements in the HR strategies adopted by the sample companies in the fields of management and employee development, employee relations, and organisation development. However, the integration of HR and business strategies occurs more naturally where there are core values and an explicit mission, thus suggesting, according to the authors, that integration is 'easier in more simple businesses.' At the strategic level the study failed to find any distinctive approach to human resource management, but it did find that these financially successful companies, in different ways, took human resource issues seriously. Thus, according to Guest and Hoque (1994, 44),

> while the link between practices and outcomes is tenuous, the key is strategic integration. What this means is that personnel strategy must fit the business strategy, the personnel policies must be fully integrated with each other and the values of the line managers must be sufficiently integrated or aligned with the personnel philosophy to ensure that they will implement the personnel policy and practice ... Where this can be achieved, there is growing evidence that a distinctive set of human resource practices results in superior performance.

As indicated in chapter 1, personnel management practice in Ireland has traditionally been associated with a strong 'industrial relations' emphasis. In this model relations between management and employees are grounded in the pluralist tradition, with a primary reliance on adversarial collective bargaining (Gunnigle and Morley 1993). Personnel management practice is seen as essentially reactive, dealing with various problematic aspects of work-force management (Shivanath 1987). Personnel policies and activities therefore tend to focus on short-term issues, with little conscious attempt to develop links with business policy. A key manifestation of the pluralist tradition at establishment level was a primary emphasis on 'industrial relations', with collective bargaining and related activities being the key role of the specialist personnel management function (Gunnigle, McMahon and Fitzgerald 1995). However, we have also seen that the nineteen-eighties were a decade of reappraisal for personnel management, both in Ireland and abroad. In Ireland the onset of recession lessened the need for many core personnel activities, such as recruitment and, particularly, industrial relations (Gunnigle 1992a). At the same time increased market competition forced many companies to seek ways of establishing a competitive advantage, including improved approaches to the work-force management of human resources.

Looking at contemporary developments, it appears that recession and subsequent recovery have led to a change in traditional approaches to work-force management, a greater devolution of personnel management activities to the line management, and the emergence of a greater strategic role for personnel management issues in a number of Irish companies (Turner and Morley 1995). In particular it is suggested that competitive pressures, reduced trade union power and new models of management practice have encouraged companies to adopt HRM-based approaches, which are seen as more strategic than 'traditional' personnel management (Flood 1989).

However, a problem with many analyses of change in organisational approaches to personnel management is that there is little consensus on the precise nature and extent of such change or how new developments contrast with more traditional approaches to work-force management. Much of this confusion seems to stem from the tendency to view HRM as an essentially distinct and homogeneous approach, incorporating a specific policy and combination of personnel policies (Gunnigle 1991, 1992a, 1992b). However, practice seems to indicate that there are numerous variants of HRM, incorporating different approaches to work-force management (Keenoy 1990). In Ireland it is suggested that there are four particular variants of HRM (Gunnigle, Morley and Foley 1995):

(1) **Traditional industrial relations:** In this model, HR considerations rarely concern strategic decision-makers; relations between the management and employees are grounded in the pluralist tradition, with a primary reliance on adversarial collective bargaining.

(2) **'Soft' HRM:** This approach emphasises the *human resource* aspect of the term 'human resource management'. This is the most visible form of HRM in Ireland, as practised by companies such as IBM, Digital, and Amdahl. It is characterised by a resource perspective on employees, incorporating the view that there is an organisational pay-off in performance from a combination of HRM policies that emphasise consensualism and mutuality of management and employee interests.

(3) **Neo-pluralism:** This second type of HRM involves moves towards greater consensualism and commitment in unionised companies. It is characterised by what might be termed a 'dualist' approach, involving the use of HRM techniques such as direct communication with employees and performance-related pay systems *alongside* established collective bargaining procedures. It is indicative of management approaches in a number of organisations, such as the ESB, Aer Rianta, and Analog Devices. While possibly less visible, and certainly less analysed, than 'soft HRM', this seems the most common form of HRM in Ireland.

(4) **'Hard' HRM:** This variant is characterised by the integration of human resource considerations into strategic decision-making to ensure maximum contribution to business performance. The emphasis here is on the *management* aspect of the term 'human resource management'. In this approach the company's human resources (incorporating not only employees but also subcontracted labour) are seen as similar to any other resource. Human resources therefore should be procured and managed in as cheap and effective a fashion as possible to ensure the achievement of the company's 'bottom line' objectives. Examples of this approach are most obvious in the adoption of 'atypical' employment forms, particularly the extensive use of sub-contracting and of temporary and part-time employees, to improve cost-effectiveness while meeting required performance standards.

CONCLUSIONS

This chapter has attempted to explore the links between business strategy, product market conditions and personnel management. It has focused particular attention on the issue of business and competitive strategies and the increased emphasis on more closely aligning business strategies and personnel policy choice. It also considered the development of human resource management. The idea of integrating personnel management considerations into strategic decision-making seems to stem from two contrasting sources in the literature. The first source is the 'personnel' literature and is based on the 'human capital approach' of the Harvard Business School model (Beer et al. 1984). This model is the basis for the 'soft' or benign approach to work-force management, whereby the senior management acknowledge that people are the company's most valuable resource and consequently seek to implement strategic decisions to make optimum use of this resource by adopting a range of personnel management policies designed to increase employees' commitment and involvement (Guest 1989a, 1989b; Storey 1989; Blyton and Turnbull 1992). The second source is the business strategy literature (specifically Fombrun, Tichy, and Devanna 1984) and is equated with what has been termed the 'business' or 'hard' approach to personnel management (Storey 1989, 1992; Keenoy 1990). This approach rationalises the strategic importance of personnel management considerations against colder economic criteria by suggesting that economic returns from human resources can be substantially improved by integrating personnel management considerations into business strategy. Blyton and Turnbull (1992) suggest that this approach is 'avowedly unitarist in outlook: a form of "utilitarian-instrumentalism" which provides a singular endorsement of managerialist views.' This view would seem to be confirmed by the proliferation of somewhat prescriptive configurations of product market, strategy and personnel policy choice, briefly discussed in this chapter. These seem to imply that there is a 'best policy' menu to suit an organisation's particular business strategy and product market conditions and that it is up to the senior management to find and implement this personnel policy menu (see Gunnigle, McMahon and Fitzgerald 1995).

The current literature indicates that decisions on personnel management policy choice represent an important strategic issue for organisations that significantly affect competitive strategies (Porter 1987), organisation structure (Chandler 1962), and organisation culture and climate (Chandler 1962; Porter 1985, 1987; Peters and Waterman 1982; Dastmalachian, Blyton, and Adamson 1991). Despite suggestions in the prescriptive management literature that companies should adopt specific 'best practice' modes in key areas of personnel management, it is increasingly acknowledged that the choice of optimal personnel policy is linked to the unique characteristics of the individual company. Consequently it is suggested that companies need to achieve a 'fit' between personnel policy choice and broader strategic considerations, particularly business strategy and product market conditions (Schuler 1987; Schuler and Jackson 1987a, 1987b).

In the Irish situation there has been little investigation of the links between business strategy, product market conditions, and developments in personnel management. In evaluating current developments in personnel management in Ireland there is a danger of confusing prominent examples of 'soft' HRM with the widespread pervasiveness of such approaches (Gunnigle and Moore 1994; Gunnigle et al. 1995). Indeed much of the evidence and support for HRM approaches emanates from the United States. However, the context of such developments in the United States is considerably different from that in Ireland, and it seems inappropriate to simply extrapolate from the American experience and infer similar trends here. Differences in industrial and employment structure and trade union density are some of the unique factors influencing approaches to personnel management in Ireland. This chapter has noted the different variants of HRM and reviewed some empirical evidence on its development in Irish companies.

3

Personnel Management and the Labour Market

M uch of the theory and debate surrounding the operation of personnel
management has focused on the development of policies and practices that
allow for the most effective use of an organisation's human capital—its
employees. Successive studies have sought to identify key indicators of strategic practice
in an effort to prescribe a set of core managerial principles on which effective human
resource management might be based (Guest 1989; Beer et al. 1984; Storey 1995).
However, one critical component of the equation appears absent all too often: the
workings of the labour market within which such practices are located.

Elliott (1991, 3) defines the labour market as the context within which the buyers and
sellers of labour come together to determine the pricing and allocation of labour
services. He further suggests that, of the many markets that exist in a modern economy,
the market for labour is the most important one. It is from selling their services in this
market that most families derive their income; it is also in this market that they spend
the largest part of their waking hours. When not working, many people devote a large
part of their time to acquiring the skills necessary for effective performance in this
market. The education and training people undertake during their lives is chiefly
designed to equip them with skills that enhance their performance in the labour market.
The link between personnel management and the labour market, therefore, is clearly
demonstrated, particularly where personnel management is concerned with managing
this labour in the most effective way possible.

This chapter examines the operation of personnel management in the context of the
labour market. Various theories of the labour market are examined, and the reality of
how labour markets operate is set down. The link between labour market theories and
personnel management is discussed; and finally a profile of the Irish labour market, in
terms of employment, education and demography, is presented.

THEORIES OF THE LABOUR MARKET
The labour market comprises all the buyers and sellers of labour, the buyers being the
employers and the sellers being the workers. It has long been recognised, however, that
labour markets differ from other markets in the economic system. Marshall (1920) held
that labour differed from other commodities because workers are inseparable from the

services they provide, i.e. they carry their history, their culture and their social norms into their place of work. Similarly Keynes (1936) recognised that the employment relationship differs from other contractual relationships because of its frequently long and indeterminable duration, which provides time for customs and norms, particularly those concerned with fairness, to build up around it. Marsden (1986) notes that several economists have attempted to develop economic theory in such a way as to take account of such influences, so that, while accepting that pressures of supply and demand, of competition and substitution are active in the labour market, so too are customs, social norms, group pressures and institutional rules active in shaping wage structures, labour mobility patterns, and other aspects of labour market behaviour.

In a broad sense, the behaviour of labour markets can perhaps be best understood by reflecting on the overlap between the three social sciences of labour economics, industrial relations, and industrial sociology. Each of these disciplines makes, to some extent, different predictions about human behaviour under similar circumstances and stresses different causes for observed patterns of behaviour. Thus, while labour economics examines the behaviour of employers and employees in response to the general incentives of wages, prices, profits, and non-pecuniary aspects of the employment relationship, such as working conditions, the greater part of industrial relations and industrial sociology deals with group activities, the internal dynamics of companies, social norms, and the processes of rule-making both within and outside the organisation. It is for this reason that there is no single theory of the labour market but rather a number of differentiated and often competing approaches. Three of the most prevalent perspectives will be examined here: the competitive approach (relating to a market approach to demand and supply), the institutional approach (referring to the critical role of institutions as the determinants of labour market operation), and the normative or radical approach (focusing on the traditional class struggle between owners of production and the workers).

The competitive model of the labour market

In the standard competitive model of the labour market, derived from neo-classical economics, it is presumed that people are rational economic maximisers, i.e. that they make rational choices to maximise the economic benefit to themselves. It is assumed that they have a set of preferences and will organise their time and effort so that they will achieve the highest rate of return possible to themselves. In the context of employment, a person will weigh up the marginal benefits of working as opposed to not working and so will take into account factors such as wages, time, leisure and so forth when making the decision to work. In this manner the equilibrium wage and the associated level of employment are determined by the intersection of labour supply and labour demand. This intersection produces a market-clearing wage, with the result that, at that wage, the quantity of labour willingly supplied exactly equals the quantity of labour willingly demanded.

Both Marsden (1986) and Beardwell and Holden (1994) identify a number of key presumptions that underpin this model of the labour market:

- The labour market comprises a large number of employers and employees, each with their own set of preferences based on utility or wealth maximisation.
- All other forms of labour market organisation develop out of competitive conditions.
- There are no constraints on entry to the labour market, i.e. new companies and new workers can enter the labour market at any time.

- Jobs in most companies can be done by a fairly large number of workers, provided they have the appropriate skills; in its most extreme form (homogeneous labour), all jobs can be done by all workers.
- The company can be treated as a transmission mechanism between markets, i.e. in-house training and work experience are of equal benefit to all firms and are therefore transferable.
- The only cost to the company of hiring labour is the wage; therefore there is no marginal gain in retaining existing workers rather than hiring new ones.
- There is perfect information: all workers and all companies know the state of the market and are instantly aware of any changes in the market.
- Technology is the chief link in the derived demand for labour, since it determines the skills that will be required from the labour market and the elasticities of substitution between different factors of production.

In the competitive model, adjustments to changes in product markets or production methods are made through the price mechanism: i.e. as costs increase, the price of labour decreases. In this way both employers and employees are price takers; companies will only employ as many people as it is economically viable to do so, bearing in mind the law of diminishing marginal returns, and workers will only choose to work where the cost of not working (or leisure) outweighs the benefits of being employed. In such a situation, unemployment does not exist, since wages are flexibly adjusted in line with labour supply.

The institutional model of the labour market

The debate on the validity of economic theories of the labour market has raged over the last few years, with many sceptics arguing that organisational and institutional factors and social norms have a greater influence on the behaviour of labour markets than pure labour market economics. Specifically, the tendency of employees to collectively represent themselves through the operation of trade unions has led in many organisations to a situation where the managerial prerogative to manage has been much diluted.

Perhaps the key fact that serves to differentiate the institutional model from the neo-classical model is that institutionalists do not agree that individuals behave independently of others: rather, they perceive that people formulate choices and preferences with regard to perceived choices and preferences made by others. In this way the notion of perceived equity and fairness enters into the equation. In a similar vein, organisations are to some degree constrained by the choices made by other companies operating in a given product or service market. Beardwell and Holden (1994) suggest that goals other than profit maximisation may be pursued, for example market share, organisational growth, or a target rate of return on capital present within the company. Institutionalists place a considerable emphasis on the role of group norms, customs and collective power in shaping labour market conditions such as wage rigidities, structured internal labour markets, and efficiency wages.

The radical model of the labour market

The radical approach is based on the traditional class struggle between workers and capital as presented by, among others, theorists such as Marx and Engels. As a theory of social change, Marxism has been concerned with the conditions under which the working class could develop sufficient unity and consciousness to challenge and then replace capitalism. Thompson (1983), in discussing the nature of work, indicates that the capitalist labour process is subject to a number of identifiable tendencies, whose critical features are deskilling, fragmentation of tasks, hierarchical organisation, the division between mental and manual work, and the struggle to establish the most effective means to control labour. Similarly, Braverman (1974) argues that deskilling is an inherent tendency of the capitalist labour process and that Taylorism or scientific management was an effort to relieve workers of their job autonomy and craft knowledge. The radical perspective, therefore, envisages an inevitable conflict between workers and managers as the owners of production where the division of labour is perceived as a means of constraining workers' power while greater specialisation of tasks serves to subordinate the worker.

Within this perspective the workers' capacity to resist exploitation and alienation lies in the development of collective representation through trade union organisation. It has been argued that resistance to specialisation and standardisation is not limited to the jobs workers do but rather extends to forms of work organisation and work structuring that are seen to segment the work-force and work-force solidarity; the adoption of elements of work-force flexibility that result in the creation of core and periphery labour markets is seen therefore as a covert managerial technique to further exploit labour.

THE OPERATION OF LABOUR MARKETS IN PRACTICE
Unemployment
A notable feature of most labour markets is the persistently high level of unemployment: contrary to the presumptions of the competitive model, not all those who are seeking employment can find it. Indeed it is a remarkable peculiarity of labour markets that unemployment can exist alongside wage inflation and job vacancies.

Wage rigidities
One of the key presumptions underpinning the competitive model of labour markets is that wages can be flexibly adjusted in line with demand for labour, i.e. that organisations can reduce wages as their demand for labour falls. In fact wages are likely to move upwards more readily than they move downwards, and often this downward wage rigidity is offered as a critical explanation for the nature and extent of current high levels of unemployment. More often, companies resort to recruitment freezes (see for example the cutback in recruitment in the public sector over the last few of years), reductions in overtime, and ultimately dismissals or redundancy as short-term reactions to demand for labour. Wage levels are also externally influenced by neo-corporatist agreements (PNR, PESP, PCW, etc.), Joint Industrial Councils, Government intervention, and so on.

Occupational segregation
Mainstream neo-classical theory usually starts from the presumption of an otherwise homogeneous market divided up only by the technical limitations on the substitutability of different skills and abilities and possibly by the constraints imposed by the need to certify the quality of skills. The labour market is structured into sub-markets by the restrictions on the substitutability between different kinds of labour. While competition between workers in different sub-markets may be very limited, each sub-market itself

remains a zone of competition, in which normal market relationships apply. Institutional writers have argued that institutional rules such as demarcation and apprenticeship arising out of collective bargaining, and company recruitment practices, can also play a large role in defining the limits of sub-markets.

In its most realistic form the labour market is divided into a number of occupational labour markets. Two discrete types of labour market may be said to exist: labour markets for unskilled or casual labour and occupational labour markets involving transferable skills. In other words, in the context of rational choice, individual workers seeking to maximise their net advantage will focus on searching for information about advantages in other firms and on obtaining access to different occupational labour markets through investment in training.

Internal labour markets

Doeringer and Piore (1971) define internal labour markets (ILMs) as internal administrative units within which the pricing and allocation of labour are governed by a set of administrative rules and procedures. A distinction is drawn between what are termed specific or non-transferable skills, for which there is no market outside the employing firm, and general skills, which can be applied in any organisational context. Individual employers have little incentive to invest in general skills unless other employers do likewise, because of the potential loss of their investment through labour turnover. It is argued that it is the policies that employers and workers develop in order to manage investments in such specific training that give rise to the development of structured internal labour markets. They argue that internal labour markets are a form of surrogate market that come about through technological and skill specificity. Organisation-specific training reduces employee mobility between companies; and companies realise further economies through on-the-job training and a system of job hierarchies that provides mobility chains or career progression up through the hierarchy. Formal patterns of progression between jobs are regulated through rules and customs and provide a sense of stability within organisations.

Doeringer and Piore further argue that mechanisms working within internal labour markets are governed by administrative rules rather than open market competition, and adjustments within these markets are mainly management-driven techniques, such as job evaluation, job design, wage and salary administration, and so forth. The use of personnel policies has the cumulative effect of building barriers to labour mobility, since accumulated rights are inextricably linked with tenure. Firms build ILMs to minimise the costs of investment in enterprise-specific human capital. ILMs are seen to determine wage and employment structures different from, but within, the constraints set by competitive market forces.

Wiliamson (1975) argues that ILMs are developed not so much to reduce the costs of investing in training but rather because the offer of more stable employment and of internal labour market conditions creates a situation in which it is in the workers' self-interest to promote the longer-term prosperity of the firm and hence to adopt a co-operative attitude.

FLEXIBILITY: DUAL AND SEGMENTED LABOUR MARKET THEORY

A notable feature of much of the recent HRM literature is the issue of flexibility within organisations. Boyer (1988) suggests that companies are both seeking structural changes to the design of companies and working to overcome 'institutional rigidities', while Sparrow and Hiltrop (1994) suggest that strategic pressures driving flexibility, such as competitive markets, low productivity, and a perceptible shift towards service sector employment, are forcing companies to review different ways of engaging and using labour. They suggest that companies are pursuing two opposing strategies, either relying heavily on the external labour market and low levels of employee involvement or favouring internal mobility and the development of multiple skills among existing employees.

So far the flexibility debate has focused on the contribution various employment strategies might make both to organisational adaptability and performance and increased opportunities for employees (Brewster et al. 1993; Marginson 1991; Berg 1988; Gunnigle and Daly 1992). These adaptability and performance improvements and increased employee opportunities are seen to be brought about through the development of numerical, pay or cost and functional flexibility (Atkinson 1984; Curson 1986; Pollert 1988, 1991; Green, Krahan and Sung 1993).

Fig. 3.1: The flexible firm

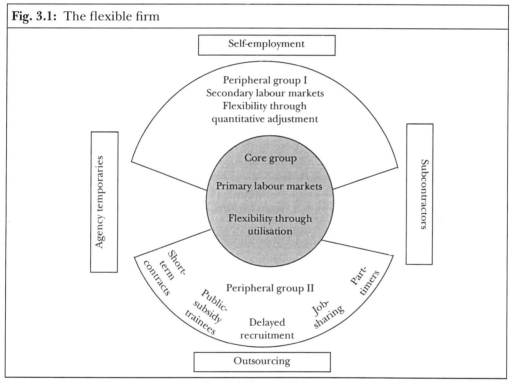

Source: Atkinson (1984).

The flexible firm model, as advanced by Atkinson (fig. 3.1), involves a reorganisation of firms' internal labour markets and their division into separate components, in which the workers' experience and the employer's expectations of them are increasingly differentiated (Atkinson and Gregory 1986). This hierarchical restructuring allows radically different employment policies to be pursued for different groups of workers. Within this framework the 'core' is composed of full-time staff, enjoying relatively secure, challenging jobs with good pay and employment conditions. Two sets of 'periphery' workers can be created. The first set are highly skilled, often technical or professional employees who are contracted into the company on fixed-term contracts and who enjoy relatively good conditions of employment. The second 'periphery' is composed of an amalgam of temporary, part-time and contract groups with less favourable pay and employment conditions and less job security or fewer training and promotion opportunities.

The flexible firm scenario suggests an attempt by organisations to increase flexibility in three key areas:

(1) **numerical flexibility**, incorporating the use of non-standard employment forms, which allows the organisation to hire and/or shed labour flexibly in line with business demands;

(2) **financial or pay flexibility**, whereby pay rates are linked to labour and product market conditions and pay increases for individual employees are variable and contingent on performance;

(3) **functional flexibility**, incorporating multi-skilling, which is defined as the expansion of skills within a work-force or the ability of companies to reorganise the competences associated with jobs so that the job holder is willing and able to deploy such competences throughout a broader range of skills.

The current literature reveals several strands within the flexibility debate. It is argued that competitive pressures are increasingly forcing organisations to increase their capacity to employ or shed labour more rapidly to achieve a better fit between work-force size and fluctuations in the demand for goods and services (Marginson 1991; Berg 1989; Boyer 1988; Dineen 1988). Consequently, non-standard employment in the form of temporary or casual workers, fixed-term contracts, home working and sub-contracting is seen to follow (Brewster et al. 1993; Hegewisch and Bruegel 1992; McGregor and Sproull 1992; Blackwell 1990; Meulders and Tytgat 1989; Lane 1988). Functional flexibility—concerned with the relaxing of demarcation lines and the adoption of broader job descriptions (Hunter and McInnes 1992; Blyton and Morris 1991)—is also seen as a mechanism for achieving greater organisational adaptability. Finally, while research does suggest that flexibilisation is on the increase, this may simply be occurring in reaction to depressed labour and product market conditions, rather than as a systematically planned emergence of the totally flexible firm. However, such apparently expedient responses to environmental conditions may well be sustained when the environment changes and as companies become more anxious to retain the advantages of certain flexibility forms (Hakim 1991).

Pollert (1991) indicates that prophesies of a 'radical break' in the climate of industrial relations, the nature and the 'future' of work have driven the whole flexibility debate into a 'post-industrial futurology', in which new types of work and new employment relations are being hailed as the novel and indeed path-finding developments of the new era. Similarly, Green et al. (1993) note that, despite some evidence of growing reliance on non-standard workers, it is not at all clear that employers are deliberately moving into flexible employment practices for the long-term strategic reasons that Atkinson identified.

PERSONNEL MANAGEMENT AND LABOUR MARKET THEORIES

The first two chapters examined the nature and scope of personnel or HRM, where, regardless of definition, both concepts can be viewed as attempts by employers to manage the employment relationship in line with the various external market conditions that affect their operations. This discussion on labour market functioning provides for varying perspectives on the role that personnel or HRM policies might play in determining the nature of this employment relationship. However, rather than describing an ideal version of personnel or HRM, labour market theories serve to explain why individual companies may vary the nature of their personnel policies in line with the prevailing economic climate they find themselves operating in. It is within this context that we now discuss how each of the various labour market hypotheses might view the role played by personnel or HR policies in their effect on established internal labour market structures.

Personnel/HRM and the competitive perspective

The competitive model assumes that as organisations face increased competition in their product markets they will continually seek new and better ways of reducing costs. From this viewpoint one can argue that the primary goal of personnel or HRM is cost minimisation and particularly the reduction of labour costs. Given the existence of wage rigidities implicit in the model, one would expect that companies will seek to reduce such rigidities by implementing structures and systems that allow for the more flexible deployment of labour.

Two particular labour pools are associated with the competitive model: the unskilled labour market and the skilled labour market. Taking the unskilled labour market first, the model assumes that labour turnover is high and that wage rates tend towards the market rate. Since a ready supply of unskilled labour is available in the external labour market, it is relatively easy and cost-efficient to hire such employees. Furthermore, as these employees do not have specific job knowledge or training, it is assumed that they will leave the company only when higher wages are offered elsewhere. For this reason, companies will accept high levels of turnover, since it is relatively easy to replace such workers and the costs of replacement are lower than the costs of providing incentives to retain them. Within such a scenario it is unlikely that organisations would adopt a 'soft' HRM approach. The competitive model also envisages a labour pool of skilled workers. In this instance structured internal labour markets are likely to exist, since, as companies contribute to the costs of training employees, they will have a vested interest in retaining them. In this situation it may be more cost-effective to develop structured internal labour markets that typically provide employment security, progressive wage increases based on tenure and opportunities for internal promotion than the costly alternative of recruiting and training.

The competitive model therefore suggests two possible scenarios that personnel or HRM might enact. The first is a 'no-frills' employment strategy that offers low-skilled work with little if any training and pays the market rate for labour. The second suggests the development of structured internal labour markets for skilled employment that may be linked to functional and financial flexibility. In both cases the primary driver of personnel or HRM policies is cost minimisation.

Personnel/HRM and the institutional perspective

The institutional perspective focuses on the process by which the employment relationship is regulated and in particular highlights the role played by various interest groups in the development of employment strategies and policies. While the competitive model focuses particularly on cost reduction, the institutional model is more concerned with reducing inefficiencies in the employment of labour. Specifically, it suggests that the actors in the labour process play a significant role in determining labour efficiency and advocates the use of various personnel or HRM policies that seek to alter the nature of power within companies. In practice, therefore, the institutional approach would perceive the central role of personnel or HRM as developing a unitarist perspective of the firm, whereby policies are introduced that seek to co-opt employees into the managerial vision of the company. One might therefore expect some elements of 'soft' HRM to be in evidence, such as employee involvement, TQM, and single-union agreements in exchange for greater flexibility and productivity agreements. Two scenarios are possible within the institutional framework: the first might involve the co-opting of unions in order to secure agreement through participative decision-making, while the second might result in greater individualising of the employment relationship as a means of marginalising trade union power and influence. In any event, the dominant HRM ethos espoused by the institutional model is the modification of existing power structures, through changing existing norms and behaviour patterns, in order to reduce inefficiencies.

Personnel/HRM and the radical perspective

The radical approach also focuses on organisational processes of regulating the employment relationship, but it differs from the institutional approach in that it presumes that all managerial activities are geared towards the creation of greater profits at the expense of the workers. In particular, personnel or HRM policies are viewed as deliberate means of exploiting labour and weakening the collective power of employees. Within this framework the adoption of, for example, the core/periphery employment model is seen to be a particular example of a 'divide and conquer' policy, where the management co-opt a selected number of core workers (who receive all the attendant benefits of security, training, promotion, and incentives) at the expense of the majority, for whom flexibility results in increased work intensification, greater direct control, diminished employment security, and possibly lower pay.

The radical perspective views all policies and strategies that seek to individualise the employment relationship as further evidence of the management's covert objective of reducing collective resistance. Within such a company the purpose of personnel or HRM, from the radical perspective, is not the reduction of costs or inefficiencies but the exploitation of labour through the extension of managerial control over the employment relationship (Beardwell and Holden 1994).

Having explored the various labour market theories and their perspectives on the role of personnel or HRM, the later section of this chapter provides details of the current nature of the Irish labour market as a prerequisite for later chapters on personnel and HRM at the operational level.

PROFILE OF THE IRISH LABOUR MARKET

Demography

The Republic's population of 3.6 million is the second-lowest in the EU. Irish society is likely to undergo a radical change over the next few years as the full effects of demographic changes work their way through the population. The ESRI Report (1994) estimated that the most striking features of demographic changes will be a drastic decrease in the number of children, a rapid fall in net entry into the labour force (from the year 2000 onwards), and a substantial reduction in the dependence ratio. The birth rate has been falling steadily since 1980, and, with increasing prosperity and employment opportunities, it is estimated that this trend is set to continue. However, the work-force will continue to expand in the medium term despite a falling birth rate. The proportion of people in the 15–64 and over-65 age categories increased by 3 and 2 per cent, respectively, between 1988 and 1991, while in the same period there was a decrease of 16 per cent in the 0–15 age group. An emerging tendency affecting participation in the labour force is for young people to remain in the education system for longer: in 1991 it was estimated that more than 50 per cent of those aged 15–24 were in full-time education.

Ireland has had a traditionally high level of emigration. While the nineteen-seventies witnessed a periodical reversal of this trend, net emigration resumed after 1979. This has increased over the eighties, rising from 9,000 in 1984 to 46,000 in 1989. Recession in the world economy, particularly in the United States and Britain, has stemmed the outflow in recent years, but emigration is expected to continue at substantial levels. A particular phenomenon within this trend is the growth in graduate emigration (from 5 per cent in 1982 to 20 per cent in 1988). The most popular destinations are, in order of priority, Britain, the United States, and continental Europe.

Employment and unemployment

As with its EU counterparts, Ireland continues to battle with persistently high levels of unemployment. The transformation from a relatively underdeveloped economy in the late nineteen-fifties to one capable of supporting industrial expansion and economic growth involved major changes in employment structure and a substantial relocation of the labour force. Taking the period since the fifties, the most significant change has been the decline in the agricultural work-force, from 451,000 in 1953 to 382,000 in 1960 (a decrease of 15.3 per cent). Trends in the sectoral distribution of employment indicate a progressive decline in agricultural and industrial employment and a dramatic rise in the service sector, particularly private services. Current data indicates that 57 per cent of the work-force is employed in services, with 28 per cent employed in industry and 15 per cent in agriculture. Much of the decline in industrial employment has been in traditionally labour-intensive sectors catering for the domestic market, such as construction and textiles.

The decline in manufacturing employment has been paralleled by substantial increases in productivity. Dineen (1993) argues that the expanded output of the foreign-owned manufacturing sector has not translated into corresponding employment gains, partly because of the effective use of new technologies, weak links with the rest of the economy, and repatriation of the gains to the parent company.

The growth of non-standard work forms has been observed in several OECD countries, including Ireland, since the middle to late seventies. However, while part-time employment as a share of total employment varies considerably between EU member-states, Ireland continues to record a below-average figure of part-time employment (tables 3.1 and 3.2).

Table 3.1: Part-time working in selected EU member-states

	As share of total employment		Average annual increase*
	1985 (%)	1994 (%)	1985–94 (%)
Denmark	24.3	21.2	–1.6
Greece	5.3	4.8	–0.5
United Kingdom	20.9	23.8	1.8
Spain	5.8	6.9	3.5
Ireland	6.4	10.8	9.3
Netherlands	22.4	36.4	12.5
EU†	12.5	15.3	3.7

* Countries ranked according to average annual increase.

† 1985 data excludes new German länder; 1994 data includes new länder. Figures for 1994 include 1993 data for Austria and Sweden.

Source: European Commission, *Employment in Europe*, 1995.

The sectoral changes in the structure of employment and the concomitant increase in female participation rates (at present around 33 per cent) are inextricably linked with changes in atypical employment. The sectoral shifts in employment are favourably biased towards greater female employment, with women proportionately over-represented in the expanding sectors. However, overall female participation rates are low by European standards.

Table 3.2: Employment changes, 1986–94

	1986 (000)	1994 (000)	Change, 1986–94
Full-time employment	1,029	1,077	+48 (+4.7%)
Part-time employment	66	137	+71 (+108%)
Total employment	1,096	1,214	+119 (+11%)

Source: CSO, Labour Force Surveys.

Of those 137,000 part-time workers in 1994, some 98,000, or over seven in ten, were women. In absolute figures, this indicates that over one in every five women in employment were working part-time: the comparable figure for men was just over one in twenty.

The greatest problem facing the economy is the high level of unemployment, at present amounting to some 13 per cent of the work-force. The dramatic growth in unemployment (by over 250 per cent since 1975) is largely attributed to weak international demand up to the middle nineteen-eighties and a prolonged period of fiscal rectitude since the early eighties. Economic recession in the early eighties, combined with the rapid growth in numbers joining the labour force, caused serious problems for employment creation and education and training. Employment contraction in the public sector further exacerbated the unemployment problem. Private services and foreign manufacturing firms have been the main source of employment growth, but this has not been enough to absorb the fall-out from agriculture and manufacturing.

Dineen (1993) suggests that the volatility of the labour supply will continue to influence the scale and nature of the unemployment problem in the decade ahead, while uncertainty on the demand side, particularly the output-employment relationship, the impact of new technologies and the increasing competition of the newly industrialising countries, will continue to threaten any fragile employment gains that are realised. He further indicates that appropriate domestic macro-economic, sectoral and fiscal (including tax) policies and institutional reform measures will need to be designed to ensure both that economic growth will be as employment-intensive as possible and that the labour market will function as efficiently as possible.

Education

High levels of education and training together with high unemployment make the Irish labour market one of the most attractive in the EU. Over the past decade the work-force has become increasingly better-educated, and a smaller proportion of young people is remaining in further education or training. A notable development has been the marked increase in numbers gaining technology-related qualifications.

Employers have, however, noted some areas of skills shortage. Particular areas of concern include craft categories (particularly in construction) and higher professional and managerial grades; specific areas include marketing and information technology. Greater levels of participation in higher education may also result in shortages of school leavers, particularly for lower entry-level positions.

Flexibility

Recent data for the Price Waterhouse Cranfield project (1992, 1995) indicates that there is some evidence to suggest that companies are making more use of some forms of flexible labour and that they are seeking changes in working practices that allow for easier deployment of employees among tasks.[1] However, non-standard employment forms or increases in functional flexibility do not necessarily signify the emergence of a flexible firm scenario but rather a segmented labour market at industry sector level (Flood 1988). While the evidence on both non-standard employment and functional flexibility indicates a trend towards greater flexibilisation, the emergence of the flexible firm is clearly not supported. Indeed, given the loose nature of the Irish labour market, one of the most surprising findings must surely be the large number of companies that have chosen not to adopt these strategies. And where they do occur the organisation-level data suggests that a relatively small proportion of the work-force is covered by them.

The contention that companies are consciously restructuring their work-force on a core-periphery basis is largely unsupported by recent research evidence (table 3.3).

Table 3.3: Proportion of work-force on non-standard contracts

	<1%	1–10%	11–20%	>20%
Part-time	39%	29%	5%	6%
Temp./casual	26%	43%	9%	5%
Fixed-term	37%	20%	5%	13%
Home work	44%	1%	—	—
n = 269.				

Source: University of Limerick (1992).

61

With respect to changes that have occurred in the last three years, there have been some increases in the use of part-time work, temporary or casual work, and fixed-term contracts. However, there is nothing inherently new about hiring part-time and temporary workers, and it is possible to rationalise the relative increases in these forms of employment through a link with the increase in service sector employment, a sector that has traditionally used these forms of employment. What is interesting, however, is that non-standard contracts in the form of part-time work, temporary or casual and fixed-term contracts and home work appear more common in the public sector than in the private sector. This sector, traditionally associated with relatively secure employment, has undergone severe contraction in recent times; this increased use of non-standard employment forms, therefore, might well be a reaction to the difficult economic environment such organisations find themselves in.

Interestingly, union presence does not appear to have a significant impact on the use of part-time work, temporary or casual contracts, or home work, while fixed-term contracts are more likely to be found in unionised companies. However, nationality of ownership does appear to influence the extent to which particular strategies are used. While part-time work is common among all ownership categories, employees in British-owned companies are more likely to be employed on this basis. However, temporary or casual work is more common in Irish and American-owned companies, and fixed-term contracts are more evident in Irish and British-owned companies. One might have expected greater evidence of the flexible firm emerging in non-Irish, and particularly American-owned, companies, since the breaking up of the work-force into core and periphery structures is considered an integral component of the HRM model (Guest 1987; Beer 1984; Gunnigle 1991).

The extent to which functional flexibility has been developed in Ireland is also subject to some doubt. There is some evidence that companies have sought changes in working practices to reduce demarcation levels between jobs (table 3.4).

Table 3.4: Change in specification of jobs over preceding three years

	Management	Prof./tech.	Clerical	Manual
More specific	25%	15%	12%	9%
No major change	38%	44%	50%	45%
More flexible	35%	29%	32%	24%
Don't know	0.4%	0.4%	1.1%	1.1%

$n = 269$.

Source: University of Limerick (1992).

Cross-tabulations with company ownership revealed that American-owned companies have made jobs most flexible among all employee grades. Similarly, some increases in flexibility are evident between sectors and in both unionised and non-unionised establishments. However, the flexible, multi-skilled craft worker with the potential to move freely between previously discrete, specialised areas of work has not emerged. As mentioned previously, functional flexibility is all too often limited to carrying out additional tasks that are secondary to a person's specialist skill and thus is more closely aligned to 'add-skilling' than multi-skilling per se.

In essence, then, while there is some movement by companies to generate some levels of flexibility, it would appear that the data collected by the Price Waterhouse Cranfield project does not support the emergence of the flexible firm model in Ireland. Despite the appeal of the flexible firm scenario in some quarters, the research evidence so far suggests that change in this area would appear to be much more closely aligned with 'gradual incrementalism' than with a 'radical post-industrial futurology' (Pollert 1991; Morley and Gunnigle 1993). Several criticisms have focused on the inherent weaknesses in the model, most notably its conceptually weak base (Pollert 1988, 1991) and the practical difficulties associated with its introduction (Keenan and Thom 1988; McInnes 1988). Indeed Elger (1991) suggests that the most striking feature of Atkinson's (1984) findings on functional flexibility is the modesty rather than the radicalism of the changes involved.

In consideration of the initial high level of general enthusiasm for the flexible firm model, it is somewhat surprising that it is left to the original authors to dispel some of the enthusiasm for their research. Atkinson and Meager (1986) emphasise that although the observed changes were widespread, they did not cut very deeply in most firms, and therefore the outcome was more likely to be marginal, ad-hoc and tentative rather than a purposeful thrust to achieve flexibility.

The creation of the flexible firm is neither unproblematic nor, in some cases, desirable. Hunter and McInnes (1991) note that temporary workers are seen to be less committed and reliable than permanent workers, while Geary (1992) found that conflict often arises between temporary and permanent workers and that the operation of core-periphery work-force scenarios can be seen as at odds with the whole policy of enlightened HRM.

This chapter has explored a number of pertinent labour market models that provide a framework for understanding the relationship between personnel or HR and labour market operation. Both these and the Irish labour market profile set the context within which personnel management operates. The following chapters explore in detail the key personnel management activities that take place at the organisational level.

4

Human Resource Planning, Recruitment, and Selection

Previous chapters have explored the nature of personnel management from both a conceptual and a strategic point of view and have outlined the key role played by the labour market in an understanding of personnel policy. In the following chapters the nature of personnel management at the operational level is discussed, and key personnel procedures and practices are outlined.

The operation of personnel management can best be viewed as a cycle of events. In the first instance the organisation determines the nature and calibre of the employees required for effective functioning (human resource planning). Next it establishes the employment relationship (recruitment and selection). Once this has been established the company develops a range of procedures and practices that facilitate the retention of those recruited. This stage will involve such practices as monitoring performance (performance appraisal), facilitating continuous improvement (employee development), determining the scope of the effort-reward bargain (reward practices), designing an effective system of work (job design), and, finally, managing the employment relationship (employee relations). However, while the practice of personnel management can be perceived as a cycle of events, this does not mean that each stage in the process is independent of the others. As will be seen in this and subsequent chapters, there is considerable interplay between all stages in the creation and development of an effective work-force. For the moment, however, we will concentrate on the first two stages of the employment cycle and focus specifically on human resource planning and on recruitment and selection.

THE PURPOSE OF HUMAN RESOURCE PLANNING

At a very general level, human resource planning can be said to be the basis of effective personnel management, since it involves forecasting human resource needs for the company and planning the steps necessary to achieve them. Boerlijst and Meijboom (1989) argue that European companies now appreciate that their survival depends on the quality of their staff and that their human resource management therefore requires a conscious and specific direction of effort in both the short and the long term. At its most basic level, human resource planning is concerned with ensuring that the

64

organisation employs the right quantity of staff with the necessary skills and knowledge for effective functioning. For many companies this constitutes a difficult process, since planning, by its nature, is fraught with tensions and unpredictability. The process is further complicated since, as Beardwell and Holden (1994) state,

> human resources are considered the most valuable, yet the most volatile and potentially unpredictable resource, which an organisation utilises. If the organisation fails to place and direct human resources in the right areas of the business, at the right time, and at the right cost, serious inefficiencies are likely to arise creating considerable operational difficulties and likely business failure.

The value of human resource planning may well have been overlooked in recent years, particularly in view of the current nature of the labour market, which is characterised by large numbers of relatively well-educated and trained people who are actively seeking employment. In many ways it can be argued that the pressure to plan human resource requirements has been offset by this 'loose' labour market, which allows employers to 'dip' into the market at will and be relatively assured of finding the calibre of worker required. However, labour markets by their nature are uncertain, and there is no guarantee that this situation will continue in the long term. Lundy and Cowling (1996) suggest that in today's environment, since fewer companies continue as bureaucratic and hierarchical structures, the perception might exist that frequent restructuring makes irrelevant any need to forecast and plan internal staff movements several years ahead. However, they suggest that, rather than nullifying the requirement for careful human resource planning, such new developments have attached increased importance to the process of facilitating the emergence of more flexible planning scenarios.

A further argument in favour of human resource planning is put forward by Walker (1988), who outlines a number of benefits that are perceived to be attached to the process of human resource planning:

- the reduction of personnel costs through the anticipation of shortages or surpluses of human resources, which can be corrected before they become unmanageable and expensive;
- the provision of a basis for planning employee development to make optimum use of workers' aptitudes;
- the overall improvement of the business planning process;
- the provision of equal opportunities for all categories of employees;
- the promotion of greater awareness of the importance of sound personnel management at all levels of the company;
- the provision of a tool for evaluating the effect of alternative personnel policies.

Ross (1982) suggests that, since human resource planning is future-oriented, there must be an explicit link between human resource planning and other organisational functions, such as strategic planning, economic and market forecasting, and investment planning. Human resource planning is a corporate-level activity that is dependent on effective business planning. It relies on the future plans and direction of the company and involves major policy decisions, which can only be taken by the top management. At the operational level, human resource planning involves catering for the human resource implications of operational business decisions, such as the termination of a particular product line. Operational plans may then form the basis of short-term action plans in a range of personnel areas from recruitment to dismissal. These may encompass the design of training programmes to upgrade operators' skills, recruitment schedules for graduate trainees, and forecasts of salary budgets for the next quarter.

Human resource planning therefore facilitates organisational functioning by evaluating current human resources, human resource use, and the human resource implications of change. Effective human resource planning helps in avoiding major discontinuities in human resource availability. It helps to determine future personnel strategies, to anticipate human resource-related problems, and to take positive action to ensure adequate human resources. It is a central component of an active personnel role whereby personnel practitioners can make a valuable contribution to strategic decision-making.

Fig. 4.1: Human resource planning process

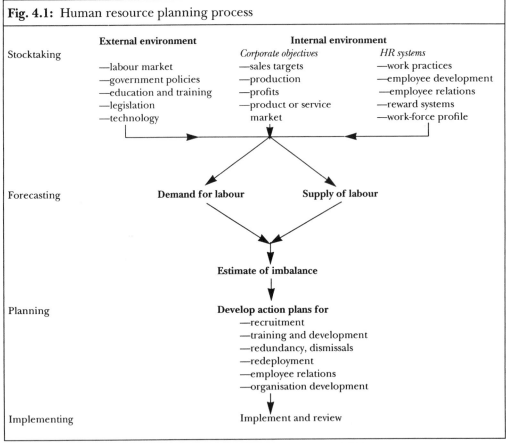

Source: Adapted from Beardwell and Holden (1994).

THE HUMAN RESOURCE PLANNING PROCESS

Human resource planning has traditionally started from the premise that a balance needs to be achieved between the supply of and demand for human resources. The central assumption underlying models of human resource planning is that the demand for labour is derived from corporate plans, while labour supply is derived either internally (from existing stocks of employees) or externally (potential employees in the external labour market). The reconciliation of the imbalance between the demand for and the supply of human resources leads therefore to the development of plans related to the functional activities of personnel management. A model of the human resource planning process is depicted in fig. 4.1.

The planning process outlined in fig. 4.1 identifies four key stages in the human resource planning process: stocktaking, forecasting, planning, and implementing. As mentioned at the beginning of this chapter, all these stages are linked and therefore form a cycle in which human resource planning affects and is affected by the range of personnel policy choices the company has available to it. (See chapters 1 and 2 for a detailed discussion of the dimensions of personnel policy choice.)

Stocktaking

The first stage in the development of human resource plans is the identification of a range of variables that influence organisational operations. The model depicts two particular categories of influencers: the external environment within which the company operates, and the internal organisational environment itself. (In chapters 1 and 2 much of the discussion focused on external factors that affect organisational functioning—such as Government policies, economic considerations, and product market conditions—while internally the link between business planning and personnel management was examined. In addition, chapter 3 outlined particular labour market considerations that have relevance for the operation of personnel management, while chapter 13 details aspects of the legislative environment that directly affect the employment relationship. Rather than duplicate the discussions of these chapters, it is proposed that the reader review their contents for a holistic understanding of their relevance to human resource planning.)

Sisson and Timperley (1994), in reviewing approaches to human resource planning, suggest that stocktaking involves analysing existing human resources, i.e. developing an accurate human resource profile where the work-force is evaluated and classified according to factors such as age, experience, and skills and abilities. It is suggested that stocktaking provides information on human resource capabilities and potential that helps in both succession planning and scheduling training and development programmes. Furthermore, Mayo (1991) advocates the use of job analysis to determine the knowledge and skills required for each job type; a skills audit to identify core abilities required and to develop a skills inventory of current employees; and a performance review to identify potential as well as future training needs. Bramham (1988) similarly suggests that human resource planning can aid in the assessment of the strengths and weaknesses of the present work-force, which might be analysed according to criteria such as age, sex, experience, skills or qualifications, and potential; while Beardwell and Holden (1994) further suggest that the analysis of present human resources leads to the development of

- recruitment plans—to avoid unexpected shortages;
- the identification of training needs—to avoid skill shortages;
- management development plans—to avoid managerial shortages or to avoid bottlenecks in the system;
- industrial relations plans—to avoid industrial unrest resulting from changes in the quantity or quality of employees.

A particular requirement of the stocktaking stage is the accurate profiling of the existing work-force. Specifically, the company needs to gather details on the present skills mix of its work-force in terms of education level, training level, job knowledge, and ability. Information of this kind should be readily available from existing personnel records, which will include CVs, performance reviews, job descriptions, and any job analyses that have been conducted. A skills profile should be read in tandem with existing work practices, technological processes employed, and corporate business strategy, which will therefore provide an accurate depiction of the current competence mix within the company.

Forecasting

The forecasting stage of the human resource planning model involves forecasting both the supply of and the demand for labour. This is probably the most difficult aspect of human resource planning, since it involves the company in making predictions of how many employees will be required for the future (demand analysis based on past trends and likely future business functioning) and determining where future employees are likely to be obtained (supply analysis). Planning is, by nature, a speculative process that relies heavily on past experience and the development of certain hypotheses concerning the future.

FORECASTING DEMAND FOR LABOUR

As indicated earlier, a preliminary step in developing human resource plans is the identification of clearly defined organisational objectives that indicate strategic purpose and direction. These may then be supplemented by more detailed operational plans, which outline the role of each function in facilitating the achievement of strategic goals. Cowling (1990) argues that the demand for labour can only be forecast with any degree of accuracy in the very short term and that while most managers will be aware of what their current requirements are, the issue of predicting requirements for the future is far more problematic. Bennison (1983) comments that

> the notion that it is possible to estimate future manpower needs, with the precision necessary to match policies of supply, is quite fallacious. Demand is particularly susceptible to changes in the outside world: wars, commodity prices ... foreign exchange difficulties too can cause problems in managing economies which, in turn, can affect the growth rate of organisations.

However difficult the process and however imprecise the results, some forecasting is required so that the company can make more informed decisions. Sisson and Timperley (1994) suggest that demand forecasting involves determining the general pattern of trading and production, product demand, technology and administrative changes, capital investment plans, market strategies, acquisitions, divestments, mergers, product diversification, and centralisation or decentralisation. As well as these demand factors one can also argue that a company's demand for labour will be affected by current legislative provisions, the prevailing economic climate, and the range of flexible choices available to companies (see the discussion of the flexible firm in chapter 3). Mayo (1991) further suggests that a knowledge of the following aspects of organisational functioning will facilitate improved demand forecasting:

- changes in requirements for management, geographically or in 'new business areas';
- new subsets of the company that may be required as the plan progresses and those that will no longer be required;
- changes in the number of particular types of job;
- the knowledge, skills, attitudes and experience that will be required of particular types of job;
- requirements for joint ventures and collaborative management;
- changes needed in career structures.

FORECASTING THE SUPPLY OF LABOUR

The forecasting of the internal labour supply constituted the central preoccupation of human resource planning throughout the nineteen-sixties and seventies and resulted in the development of a number of mathematical models for predicting labour attrition in a given period (Armstrong 1991). Sisson and Timperley (1994) provide a summary of the various types of models developed:

- 'renewal' or 'pull' models, where people are assumed to be 'pulled through' as a vacancy occurs through wastage or promotion and where vacancies in any grade are defined by outflows (wastage or promotion);
- 'linear programming' models for recruitment and deployment;
- 'camel' models, based on assessing promotion chances in a hierarchy, using age distribution and estimates about the future size of the human resource system;
- 'Markov' or 'push' models, based on predictable wastage patterns that are determined by length of service and a person's career.

Lundy and Cowling (1996) suggest that such quantitative approaches to the internal supply of human resources have focused on three key supply indices: wastage, absenteeism, and the age profile of the work-force.

Wastage (or labour turnover) refers to the proportion of a company's employees that leave within a specified period (usually calculated over twelve months) and therefore need replacing in order to maintain a constant number of employees in the company (Beardwell and Holden 1994). Employees may leave for many reasons, such as better opportunities elsewhere, dissatisfaction with the job, unrealistic job expectations, retirement, redundancy, and dismissal. An ability, therefore, to predict labour turnover is an important aspect of human resource planning and can facilitate the creation of personnel policies that improve retention rates, particularly for those employees the organisation has a vested interest in retaining (e.g. those who are highly skilled or those in whom the company has invested considerable training).

Measuring labour turnover is therefore a necessary prelude to planning and remedial action. One of the simplest methods of calculating wastage is through a turnover analysis:

$$\frac{\text{number of employees who leave in one year}}{\text{average number employed in the past year}} \times 100 = \%$$

Beardwell and Holden (1994) suggest that a turnover rate of 25 per cent is perfectly respectable in modern large-scale companies but that anything approaching 30–35 per cent should be cause for concern.

While the turnover index has the advantage of being easy to calculate and gives some indication whether losses are high or low, it is a relatively crude measure, since it does not provide details of the types of employees who are leaving or in which departments most losses are occurring. A calculation of the labour stability index can provide additional information about labour turnover; this is calculated as

$$\frac{\text{number of employees with more than one year's service}}{\text{total number employed one year ago}} \times 100 = \%$$

The stability index provides details on whether the organisation is retaining experienced employees, since it calculates and emphasises those who stay with the company. However, indices alone will not provide specific details on why the company is experiencing particular levels of wastage, and many companies therefore are adopting the 'exit interview' to help explain turnover. While companies vary in their design of exit interviews, the purpose is to provide information on why an employee has chosen to leave the company, and the employee may be asked to rate the company against a list of predetermined criteria, such as the attractiveness of the reward package, satisfaction with the job, supervisory arrangements, and so forth. Combined with turnover and stability indices, the information received from the exit interview can provide some useful indicators of potential problems with regard to various personnel procedures and practices.

Hill and Trist (1955), in conjunction with the Tavistock Institute, conducted a number of studies of labour turnover and developed what became known as the 'survival curve' (see fig. 4.2). The evidence from their studies suggested that the propensity to quit employment is highest during the early stages of employment but tapers away as employees settle down in the company.

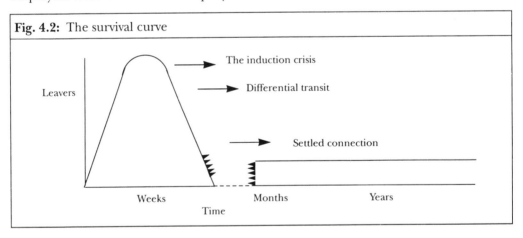

Fig. 4.2: The survival curve

Hill and Trist explained the survival curve as a social process that has three distinct phases. The first phase they labelled the 'induction crisis', at which time wastage or turnover is very high. Many reasons have been cited for the existence of the induction crisis; generally it is thought to arise because new employees find that the job is not what they imagined it would be, or find they are unhappy with the work environment, or perhaps find alternative work elsewhere that is perceived to be more attractive. The period covered by the induction crisis can vary considerably between companies and between job categories and in some cases can last up to two years. However, it is generally assumed to reach its peak after the first six weeks of employment. The second period is termed the 'differential transit', where, as the employee begins to feel more comfortable in his or her position and settles in to organisational life, wastage begins to decrease. The final stage is called the 'settled connection', and Hill and Trist suggest that employees who remain with the company for this length of time tend to be viewed as 'quasi-permanent'. At this stage there is a greater incentive to stay with the company than there is to leave and go elsewhere.

The survival curve is, in many ways, indicative rather than definitive, and while it does not take into account personal motivation or career expectations (career development is discussed in chapter 9), it suggests that there are inherent predictabilities in the process that allow companies to forecast wastage with some reliability.

Fig. 4.3: A model of employee absenteeism

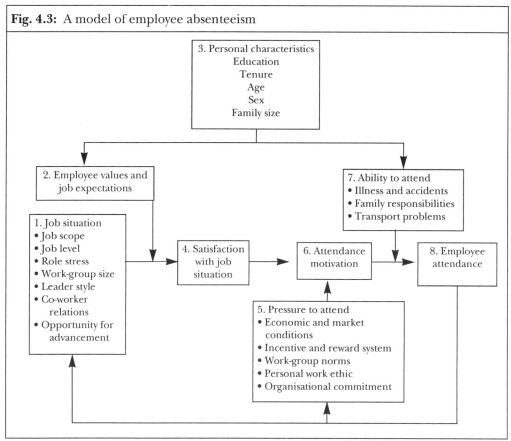

Source: Steers and Rhodes (1978).

ABSENTEEISM

Forecasting the stock of human resources requires an organisation to gather information on current levels of absenteeism and likely future trends. The Federation of Irish Employers (1980) has defined absenteeism as 'all absence from work other than paid holidays'. Steers and Rhodes (1978) developed a model of employee attendance that suggests, among other things, that an employee's attendance at work is a function of two particular variables: ability to attend, and motivation to attend. Ability to attend is chiefly concerned with illness or some incapacity that prevents an employee from attending work; in most cases this is involuntary absenteeism. Motivation to attend, on the other hand, is explicitly linked with the employee's feelings about the company and the job itself and whether he or she feels a pressure to attend work (see fig. 4.3).

Steers and Rhodes found a clear correlation between absenteeism trends and labour turnover trends. Interestingly, where employees are unhappy with their work situation (for whatever reason) and would like to leave but are unable to find alternative work, absenteeism rates tend to increase. However, where alternative work is more readily available, absenteeism rates are less likely to increase, but labour turnover becomes more frequent.

At the organisational level, information on absenteeism is typically gathered from attendance sheets, time cards, medical records, and other personnel files. The most common formula used to calculate absenteeism is as follows:

$$\frac{\text{Total absence (days/hours) in a particular period}}{\text{Total possible time (days/hours)}} \times 100 = \%$$

This index calculates the percentage of the total time available in a specified period that has been lost because of absence. Cowling (1990) suggests that there is a significant correlation between the nature of the job and absenteeism, pointing to job satisfaction as an important component of motivation to attend.

It is important therefore that organisations maintain accurate records of absenteeism and plot it regularly to discover any upward trends. High levels of absenteeism might point to inconsistencies between many of the personnel activities and therefore might require a company to rethink its strategy in respect of, for example, selection, supervision, job design, performance appraisal, discipline, or rewards.

AGE ANALYSIS

The third supply index that an organisation requires is an examination of the age distribution of each category of employee, for example to determine imminent retirement patterns, to plan recruitment policies, and to identify career and succession paths for those with future potential within the company. Lundy and Cowling (1996) suggest that plotting the age structure of a work-force throws into sharp relief whether, for example, a large proportion of employees are reaching retirement age, or whether the cadre of key executives is young and likely to be jostling each other for promotion in the near future. A predominantly mature age profile would suggest the need for a strong recruitment drive to fill the vacancies left by those about to retire. A predominantly middle-aged work-force might indicate potential (or existing) bottlenecks in the promotion system that, if unresolved, could create dissatisfaction and possible absenteeism or turnover problems (this can also be a feature of a young age profile). An age distribution that is heavily weighted at the young end and at the 'mature' end might lead to complications in engendering cultural norms and cohesive group dynamics. A balanced mix of ages is of course the ideal situation, where the company can develop and structure its internal labour market around progressive succession planning.

EXTERNAL SUPPLY

Chapter 3 drew attention to the importance of external labour market trends and the changing demography of the labour force. From the point of view of human resource planning the company will be particularly interested in, for example, current levels of unemployment (most especially in the local area), the changing structure of the work-force and its effects on recruitment and supply (for example, the increasing tendency to complete third-level education leads to fewer young people entering the labour force), the trend towards flexible employment choices with the concomitant increase in participation by women, and the current levels of education and training provision that determine the skills mix of the external labour market. All these factors serve to determine the outcome of the essential 'make or buy' question: is it more effective to seek prospective employees outside the company or should the company develop its own internal labour market? These decisions are made in view of the forecasted labour demand, strategic corporate plans, and external environmental considerations.

Planning

Once the organisation has forecast the likely demand for and supply of labour it can then estimate whether there are any imbalances between the two, i.e. whether it is faced with a labour shortage or a labour surplus. Where a shortage exists or is predicted, the company can decide to plan for recruitment or retraining, as appropriate. A labour surplus requires that a company makes plans for either redundancy, redeployment, retraining, or perhaps dismissals or short-time working. Regardless of the particular options open to it, the company's eventual decision will have consequences for the general nature of employee relations, the structuring of work, the reward package offered, and the structure of its internal labour market. For this reason the company needs to carefully weigh the attendant costs and benefits of whichever strategy it decides to employ.

Implementation

On completion of the human resource plans, the company implements its decision, and the cycle is once again set in motion. Since both internal and external environments are subject to considerable change over time, it is advisable that human resource plans be monitored and reviewed regularly and amended or redirected as required.

The human resource planning process identifies a range of personnel management options that are available to a company, depending on whether it forecasts a shortage or a surplus of labour in the future. The remainder of this chapter explores the process of recruitment and selection as a response to a perceived shortfall in required human resources.

RECRUITMENT AND SELECTION

The recruitment and selection process is essentially concerned with finding, assessing and engaging new employees. Its focus therefore is on matching the capabilities and inclinations of candidates against the demands and rewards inherent in a given job (Plumbley 1985; Herriot 1989). Much of the recent literature on personnel management has emphasised the necessity for the recruitment and selection of employees who are committed to the goals of the company. Plumbley (1985) suggests that the profitability and even the survival of an enterprise usually depend on the calibre of the work-force, while Pettigrew (1988) proposes that human resources represent a critical means of achieving competitiveness. It has been argued that recruitment and selection decisions are the most important of all decisions that managers have to make, since they are a prerequisite for the development of an effective work-force, while the costs of ineffectual commercial viability can often be attributed to decades of ineffective recruitment and selection methods (McMahon 1988; Plumbley 1985; Smith and Robertson 1986; Lewis 1984).

There are two distinct phases in this matching process: recruitment, which is concerned with attracting a group of candidates to apply for a given vacancy, followed by selection, the process of choosing the most suitable candidate from a pool of candidates identified through recruitment. The recruitment and selection process is outlined in fig. 4.4.

Fig. 4.4: The recruitment and selection process

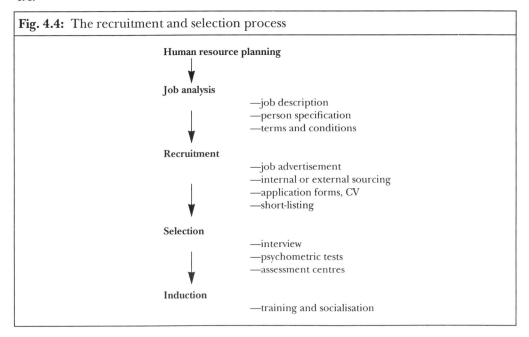

Job analysis

When an organisation makes the decision to fill an existing vacancy through recruitment, the first stage in the process involves conducting a comprehensive job analysis. This may already have been conducted through the human resource planning process, particularly where recruitment is a relatively frequent occurrence. Schneider and Schmitt (1986) define job analysis as a means of identifying the human behaviour necessary for adequate job performance. Based on the identification of such behaviour, theories about the kinds of people the job requires, in terms of knowledge, skills, and abilities, can be formulated, and procedures for the identification of such people can be developed. A number of different methods of job analysis have been developed over the years, many of which involve considerable statistical modelling; fig. 4.5 outlines nine of the most common job analysis techniques used in companies today.

Once a job analysis has been conducted the company has a clear indication of the particular requirements of the job and of where that job fits into the overall organisation structure. The job analysis then forms the basis for developing three critical recruitment and selection tools: the job description, the person specification, and the terms and conditions of employment.

Fig. 4.5: Advantages and disadvantages of nine methods of job analysis

1. Questionnaire method

Advantages	Good for producing quantitative information and can produce objective and generalisable results; cheap.
Disadvantages	Substantial sample needed; substantial foreknowledge needed to be able to construct questionnaire; respondents must be able and willing to give accurate replies

2. Check-list method

Similar to questionnaire method, but, since responses are either 'yes' or 'no', the results may be cruder or require larger sample; they tend to require fewer subjective judgments.

3. Individual interviews

Advantages	Very flexible; can provide detailed information; easy to organise and prepare.
Disadvantages	Time-consuming; expensive; difficult to analyse.

4. Observation interviews

Similar to individual interviews but give additional information, for example visual or auditory information; these contextual clues make it more difficult for the analyst to be misled; the methods may expose both the analyst and the worker to increased safety hazards.

5. Group interviews

Similar to the individual interview but less time-consuming for the analyst, and some claim that richer information is obtained, since interviewees stimulate each other's thought. They are more difficult to organise, and there is the danger that a group is over-influenced by one person.

6. Expert analysis

Advantages	Quick, cheap, and can be used for jobs that do not yet exist. Can avoid restrictive practices.
Disadvantages	The experts may not be true experts, and an unrealistic analysis may result.

7. Diary method

Advantages	Cheap, flexible, and requires little advance preparation. Useful for non-manual tasks, where observation is of limited value. Can also be used in jobs requiring a wide variety of tasks.
Disadvantages	Needs co-operation from respondents; tendency to keep incomplete logs, so frequent but minor items are often omitted.

8. Work participation method

Advantages	Can produce very realistic analyses.
Disadvantages	Expensive, time-consuming, and can only be used for jobs requiring short training and no safety hazards.

9. Critical incident method

Advantages	Focuses on the aspects of a job that are crucial to success.
Disadvantages	Often produces incomplete data that is difficult to analyse.

Source: Smith and Robertson (1993)

Job description

For many years job descriptions were often couched in vague terms to allow for any changes that might occur in the main job purpose over time. Furthermore, in many companies job descriptions were discussed in general terms at the selection interview and were not formally recorded or written down. This practice has been largely abandoned in recent years, particularly in view of the Terms of Employment Act, 1994, which requires all employers to furnish employees with written details of the terms and conditions pertaining to their employment or to refer them to where their job specification is to be found (company handbook, notice board, etc.). For this reason companies are paying careful attention to the development of job descriptions that are up to date, complete, and inclusive of all job requirements.

While job descriptions vary according to job classification or type, they typically conform to a set framework (fig. 4.6).

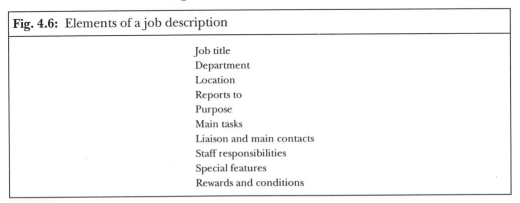

Fig. 4.6: Elements of a job description

Job title
Department
Location
Reports to
Purpose
Main tasks
Liaison and main contacts
Staff responsibilities
Special features
Rewards and conditions

The job description is essentially a broad statement of the purpose, scope, duties and responsibilities attached to the job and therefore the basis of the contract of employment. Furthermore, since job advertisements normally detail the job description, it is critically important that companies have a precise understanding of the nature of the job vacancy and that this realistic preview of the job be used to attract the most suitable candidates.

Person specification

Once the job description has been drawn up, the company can develop a person specification. This is essentially a description of the ideal person who will fit the job and should include details of the qualifications, knowledge, specific skills and aptitudes, experience and personal attributes that are required to do the job effectively. The person specification has a number of very important functions within the recruitment and selection process, since it not only describes the person required for the job but also determines where the company should concentrate its search and advertising efforts; it can facilitate systematic short-listing and will form the basis on which the selection criteria are determined. It is therefore of critical importance that the person specification exactly matches the job description, so that the most suitable job candidates can be attracted for selection.

Since, by their nature, personnel specifications describe the ideal candidate or job holder, it is often advisable to further discriminate between *essential* characteristics required for the job and *desirable* ones. This process further facilitates the assessment of suitability when the eventual selection is made. Rodger (1952) and Munro Fraser (1978) have developed somewhat similar categorisations that are considered useful for specifying the personal characteristics that can aid effective recruitment and selection; both these schemes are detailed in table 4.1.

Table 4.1: Person specification categories

Rodger (1952)
- Physical make-up: physique; health; appearance; speech.
- Attainments: education; training; experience.
- General intelligence: fundamental intellectual capacity.
- Special aptitudes: dexterity, numeracy, verbal, other.
- Interests: leisure, intellectual, practical, physical, social, artistic.
- Disposition: acceptability, interaction, impact on fellow-workers and management, dependability, stability.
- Circumstances: domestic, family; mobility; flexibility.

Munro Fraser (1978)
- Impact on others: first impressions; verbal ability.
- Qualifications: education, training, experience.
- Innate abilities: comprehension and capacity, conceptual ability, aptitude, intelligence.
- Motivation: objectives commitment, ambition, initiative.
- Emotional adjustment: coping with stress; working with others.

Both of the frameworks outlined in table 4.1 are useful, in that they establish general guidelines around which the person specification can be built. However, the company needs to take into account current equality legislation to ensure that the person specification is not discriminatory in any way (this question is discussed fully in chapter 13). Using the frameworks outlined above, fig. 4.7 illustrates a sample person specification that might be used for a graduate position as a personnel officer in a unionised multinational company.

The characteristics specified in fig. 4.7 can be weighted if required, so that in the case of a graduate position greater importance might be attached to educational attainments and skills than to work experience, which a graduate might not yet have gained. By attaching weights to the various criteria outlined, the process of eventual selection is facilitated, particularly where two or more candidates appear to be equally suitable.

In summary, then, one can suggest that a person specification must meet four particular requirements:

1. It must relate to a particular job and therefore closely match the job description.

2. It must be specific and detail exactly what is required to complete the job effectively: for example, 'extensive management experience' gives no indication of the quantity or quality of experience considered necessary for the job.

3. It must allow the company to differentiate between individual applicants, and ideally therefore the specification should be weighted or scaled to facilitate an accurate measurement of individual characteristics.

4. It must allow the company to assess whether a candidate meets it: i.e. all the characteristics specified must be capable of being measured and assessed. As an example, many person specifications require people who are 'highly motivated', yet motivation is inherently difficult to assess, particularly in an interview. (We will return to this later in the chapter.)

Fig. 4.7: Sample person specification: personnel officer

	Essential requirements	**Desirable requirements**
Education	Degree or diploma in business studies or related discipline	Specialisation in personnel management or training; membership of IPD
Experience	One year's experience in computerised personnel department with knowledge of selection, reward systems, and training	Two or more years' experience at personnel or training officer level in a manufacturing environment
Skills	Experience in use of appropriate computer programs; interviewing skills; negotiation skills	Knowledge of dedicated personnel programs; fluency in French
Motivation	Ambitious to succeed in personnel; willingness to expand personal competence base and manage self-development	Ability to motivate and influence others
Disposition, circumstances	Outgoing personality; ability to work as team member; adaptable	Flexibility in working patterns; ability to travel abroad as required

Terms and conditions

While in practice often included in the job description, the terms and conditions of employment refer specifically to the effort-reward relationship and so include details of the hours to be worked, methods of payment, job entitlements (holidays, bonuses, allowances, etc.), and other benefits. Since terms and conditions are often the most visible attributes of the job, they play an important role in the attraction of suitable candidates. Furthermore, as with person specifications, care must be taken to ensure that the terms and conditions of employment meet the requirements of employment legislation (see chapter 13).

RECRUITMENT

Once the job analysis stage has been completed, the company begins the process of recruitment to attract suitable candidates. Anderson and Shackleton (1986) indicate that the quality of new recruits depends on a company's recruitment practices and that the relative effectiveness of the selection phase is inherently dependent on the calibre of candidates attracted. Indeed Smith, Gregg and Andrews (1989) argue that the more effectively the recruitment stage is carried out the less important the actual selection process becomes.

Recruitment can be seen to have three important functions:
(1) to attract a pool of suitable applicants for the vacancy;
(2) to deter unsuitable candidates from applying;
(3) to create a positive image of the company.

The decision to recruit will normally involve the development of a job advertisement. This should include the job description, person specification, and details of the terms and conditions of employment, and is probably the most effective tool available, if completed correctly, for meeting the three key objectives outlined above. The advertisement itself should be striking, so that it will be noticed, and the key information relating to the job should dominate, so that it will attract those who might be suitable for the position.

Perhaps the most immediate decision facing recruiters is whether to recruit internally from those already employed by the company or to search the external labour market. The decision to access the internal labour market brings with it a number of distinct advantages. It is cost-effective, both in eliminating the need for external advertising and recruiting and also in reducing the induction or settling-in period. It is also considered to be good personnel practice, for not only can it be viewed as a positive motivator by current employees but the quality of the internal labour market is continually upgraded and maintained through high-quality recruitment, selection, promotion, career development, and multi-skilling. However, the company limits its potential range of candidates by limiting its search to the internal labour market, and often the introduction of 'new blood' can provide a rewarding stimulus and facilitate organisational dynamics.

A number of alternative recruitment methods are available to a company, the more salient of which are described briefly in table 4.2.

Table 4.2: Recruitment methods

Method	Comments	Advantages	Disadvantages
1. Internal: existing employees	Internal advertising may be requirement for some companies under union-negotiated agreements.		
1.1 Self-applicants		Inexpensive, quick. Motivation factor.	Can be indirectly discriminatory. No new talent into company.
1.2 Supervisor/manager recommendations		Know applicant's strengths, weaknesses and behaviour well.	Records of existing and acquired skills and experience need constant updating.
1.3 Succession planning		Training and development already in place, therefore succession smoother.	Information may be subject to bias.
2. Using existing contacts			
2.1 Unsolicited enquiries	Write-ins, personal enquiries on spec. NB: Should be handled courteously or may affect success-of other external methods	Less expensive. Know applicants are already interested.	Needs system implementation to cope. Need to review 'hold' file after certain period (six months?). May be indirectly discriminatory

2.2 Previous applicants	Maintain forms of unsuccessful applicants for given period and assess against new vacancies as they arise.	Can enhance company image if handled well. May speed process considerably.	As 2.1.
2.3 Previous employees	Particularly retired, or others leaving to unpaid job (e.g. new mothers or carers for elderly or ill dependants) in the 'would re-employ' category.	By changing terms of employment (especially by increasing flexibility or reducing hours). Could re-attract to part-time, flexible or temporary working to meet peak organisational demands. Known work behaviour.	Inbuilt flexibility requirement for employee not always feasible in given situations. Requirements for peaks of job may be outside remit of person.
2.4 Existing employee contacts	Existing employees encourage family, friends or contacts to apply for vacancies.	Employee may well know others with similar skills, knowledge, and attitudes. May have passed on knowledge of culture and job requirements.	May well be indirectly discriminatory if not combined with other methods. May be 'weaker' employees who recommend, whose attitudes etc. company does not wish to have reinforced through peer recruitment.
3. External contacts 3.1 Union referrals	Register kept by union of members seeking employment. Usual in some sectors (e.g. printing) where closed shop and/or custom-and-practice arrangements are traditional.	Confidence in skills. Cost.	Indirectly discriminatory. Overlooks those in work.
3.2 Professional referrals	Registers as above, particularly for professions, e.g. lawyers, doctors, accountants, engineers, linguists.	As 3.1.	As 3.1.
3.3 Employment exchange	Government provision. Network covering most towns and cities, acting as agents for potential employers and employees.	Variety of free services, which can be provided at national level. Speed. Perceived as socially responsible service within a	Unemployed rather than employed are registered, reinforcing labour exchange stereotype. As with all agencies, results reflect

	Particularly concerned with manual and junior positions.	secure, non-profit-making framework. Extremely valuable if effort made to cultivate contact.	quality of job description supplied.
3.4 Out-placement consultants	Providing practical help to redundant employees, enforced early retirees, etc.	Actively seeking to place, and may provide training required.	Available when recruitment needs reduce, and vice versa, reflecting economic situation.
3.5 Private selection consultants—local	Deal mainly with clerical, junior administration, shop staff, etc.	Reduce administration for employer. 'Normal' method in many places.	Employer pays for recruits. No guarantee against recruit leaving quickly. Some poor practice has led to employer distrust on occasions.
3.6 Management selection	Usually recruitment plus initial stages of selection of managerial, professional and specialist staff.	Specialist knowledge, objectivity, selection skills (especially when unusual recruitment need for company).	Payment by employer. May lack cultural awareness of company. Exclusion of internal applicants.
3.7 Search consultants ('headhunters')	Informal network of contacts keeping track of those likely to be in constant demand, especially senior management Promising candidates sought out and approached directly.	Possibility of joining can be discussed without commitment. Concentrates on those in employment.	Potential candidates outside head-hunters network excluded. Recruit may be headhunted again by same consultant! Cost (because labour intensive).
3.8 Schools and career service	Guidance and some testing of young people under 18. In-depth knowledge of potential applicants.	Useful source of 'raw' recruits to be developed by the company. Can assist in image enhancement. Cost.	Some 'guidance' of higher quality than other methods. Possibility of indirect discrimination if recruitment concentrated on one or two institutions.
3.9 Colleges	Recruitment of college leavers after conclusion of variety of courses. Tendency to recruit in local colleges in catchment area.	Work experience placements offer opportunity to preview. Increased employer impact on training provided, which can be very work-specific.	Tends to be once-yearly process. Recruits lack experience. Possible indirect discrimination.
3.10 Universities	Traditional 'milk round' by large national and international employers.	Can build strong relationship with those offering specialisms, pres-	Travel and accommodation costs can be high. Takes recruiters away

	Ad hoc enquiries by leavers. Frequently appointment boards provide full-time careers advisory service.	tige, etc. Sandwich and other work placements offer opportunity to preview potential.	from company for long periods.
3.11 Government training schemes	Government-funded initiatives aimed at specific skill shortages and/or disadvantaged groups.	Many skills provided at Government cost can be integrated with on-the-job experience. Opportunity to preview before offering permanent employment. Financial incentives.	Perception of 'cheap labour' can reduce company image unless well managed. Administration heavy. Training commitment required.
3.12 Temporary agencies	Provision of short or longer-term cover (an alternative to recruiting permanent employees).	Provide cover for coping with unexpected absence (e.g. illness), peaks in work loads, one-off or temporary requirement for skills (installation of new, specialist machinery), or transitional developments in work organisation.	Time scale often makes integration into company culture difficult. Quality can vary. Cost.
4. Advertising, media	An overlap between advertising and previous methods discussed frequently exists. Recruitment agencies can provide external expertise.		Essential for monitoring cost-effectiveness.
4.1 Press	Local and national papers, trade and professional journals.	Expensive, especially television and national press. Must be aimed at identified groups.	Only reach those using that medium.
4.2 Television	Includes teletext (Aertel) and view-data (Minitel).	Can provide non-recruitment advantages through increased customer awareness. Sound and vision used.	
4.3 Radio	Local, occasional national broadcasts.	Cheaper than television.	
4.4 Cinema		May be useful for 17 to 25-year-old groups, where several recruits	

needed; targets
likely to have some
prior knowledge.

Source: Beardwell and Holden (1994).

The choice of recruitment method is often determined by the nature of the position being advertised and whether the skills required for the job are in short supply or otherwise. For entry-level jobs, for example, it might be sufficient to advertise in local papers or to allow news of the position to be spread by word of mouth. However, where the position requires considerable experience or qualifications of a particular type, the company might have to consider advertising at national level in newspapers or trade or professional journals or employing the services of recruitment agencies or consultants.

Concomitant with decisions on the choice of recruitment method, the company must take account of the application process for vacancies. The most common methods involve the application form or the curriculum vitae (CV). The CV is probably the most common form of job application, and it generally tends to conform to a set standard: name, address, telephone number, date of birth, marital status (less frequent today), education and achievements, employment history, professional activities, and references. Most CVs are accompanied by a covering letter that seeks to 'sell' the applicant's suitability for the position; increasingly, however, companies are developing their own application forms, which seek to elicit job-specific information in a uniform way and which can enable comparisons to be made between applicants. Application forms elicit much the same information as is generally presented in a CV but also require the applicant to supply additional information in support of their application. In practical terms this requires applicants to again 'sell' their skills and to highlight the positive contribution they could make to the company.

Screening and short-listing

Once applications have been received, companies must devise means of analysing their contents and suitability for selection. In this respect the person specification becomes an invaluable tool for identifying suitable and unsuitable applicants. Dale (1995) suggests that there is an inherent tendency to compare applicants against each other rather than against the job requirements, and the biases and heuristics of the short-lister provide the underlying rationale that determines suitability. Using the example of a vacancy for an office manager, she identifies a short-listing matrix based on the person specification that can facilitate more informed decisions (see table 4.3).

Table 4.3: Short-listing matrix for position of office manager

Criteria	Candidate			
	1	2	3	4
Attainment				
Successful completion of further education course	Yes	Yes	Yes	Yes
Some job-related management training	Yes	No evidence	No evidence	Yes

Experience				
IT office applications	No evidence	Yes	No evidence	Yes
Customer service	Yes	Yes	Yes	Yes
Staff training and supervision	Yes	No evidence	No evidence	Yes
Record maintenance	No evidence	Yes	Yes	Yes
Abilities				
Communication skills	Untidy application	Yes	Application badly produced	Yes
Leadership skills	Trainer with no supervisory responsibilities	No evidence	No evidence	Yes
Planning and organisation	Poor organisation of information on form	No evidence	Application badly produced	?
Training and instructional skills	Yes	No evidence	No evidence	Yes
Aptitudes				
Customer-focused	No evidence	Yes	No evidence	Yes
Accuracy	No evidence	?	Application badly produced	Yes
Concern for quality	Untidy application	Yes	Application badly produced	Yes
Interests				
Involved with people	Yes	Solitary interests	No evidence	Yes
Learning and self-development	No evidence	Yes	No evidence	Yes

Source: Dale (1995).

The matrix is used essentially to eliminate those applicants who fail to achieve the minimum criteria and to further process those who are deemed suitable for interview or testing.

Selection

While the calibre of candidate is determined by the value of the recruitment process, the selection decision remains a difficult one. Dale (1995) proposes that

> most mistakes are caused by the fact that managers generally give little thought to the critical nature of the decisions. Employers are surprised and disappointed when an appointment fails, and often the person appointed is blamed rather than

recognising weaknesses in the process and methodology … Even the soundest of techniques and best practice (in selection) contain scope for error. Some of this is due to the methods themselves, but the main source is the frailty of the human decision makers.

A number of alternative selection techniques can be used to determine the suitability of an applicant. Before these are discussed, however, it is important to understand such terms as 'suitability', 'validity' and 'reliability' as they apply to the selection decision.

Suitability is largely determined by the nature of the job and the responsibilities that are attached to it. While the job description and person specification will largely determine specific job criteria, one can distinguish four generic criteria that can help to evaluate the relative suitability of an applicant:

1. The company requires a person who has the capacity to perform the tasks associated with a position to an acceptable standard. Previous work experience, educational attainments and the skill profile of the applicant will all provide a reasonable indication of work ability.

2. The company requires a person who has the ability to develop new knowledge and skills and to 'grow' with the job. Increasingly, as the nature of work changes and becomes more demanding, there is a strong orientation towards continuous development and competence upgrading. A person's previous history of skill development and his or her educational and training record can provide some useful indicators in this respect.

3. The company requires a person who will fit in to the company culture and has the capacity to work effectively within its structures and systems. The extent to which a person will fit in to the company is largely indeterminable, but some inference may be drawn from experiences in previous work environments and a determination of their ambitions and expectations.

4. The company requires a person who will work productively, is intrinsically motivated, and can establish co-operative relationships with other workers. While past behaviour is not the most reliable predictor of future intention, companies typically conduct reference checks to establish some idea of previous work behaviour.

Validity in the context of the selection decision concerns the extent to which the selection method used measures what it is supposed to measure: that is to say, can the company be assured (as far as this is possible) that there are no intervening factors or biases that are distorting the result that has been achieved? *Reliability*, on the other hand, refers to whether the same selection decision would again be reached if the decision were made by other people, i.e. that it is consistent.

To illustrate the relevance of both validity and reliability it is useful to use the example of the selection interview. If the interview is a valid selection technique then it should predict, with a high degree of accuracy, the expected work behaviour of a job applicant (validity). Were it a reliable selection technique, then, regardless of who makes the selection decision, the final result will be the same, i.e. if five managers were independently asked to interview a number of candidates and make a selection they would all choose the same candidate.

As indicated earlier, a number of alternative techniques are available that can aid the selection decision. The interview continues to enjoy considerable popularity among all organisations, and for many jobs companies may employ a series of interviews, ranging from the initial meeting to a second and often third interview. While interviews can be conducted either on a one-to-one basis or be panel-based, the principles of effective interviewing apply to both (these are discussed in the following pages).

Anderson and Shackleton (1993) provide an interesting comparison of some of the more commonly used selection techniques (see tables 4.4 and 4.5). However, they describe the selection interview separately, since the interview forms the basis of almost all selection decisions, and they suggest that the techniques outlined in table 4.5 should in fact be used to augment the interview decision.

Table 4.4: Different functions of the interview

Interview function	Appropriate stage in selection procedure	Interview functioning	Interviewer's objectives	Interviewee's objectives
1. Mutual preview	Phase I/II. Early stages of selection procedure probably following initial screening of written applications but preceding administration of main assessment techniques.	Informal, open-ended discussion to explain selection procedures and to offer career guidance counselling to interviewee by providing detailed and realistic job preview (RJP).	• To meet and 'set the scene' for applicant. • To inform applicants of company's selection procedure.	• To establish what will be involved at each stage in selection procedure. • To visit company 'on site'. • To obtain preview of job to allow self-assessment and self-selection.
2. Assessment	Phase II, one of a battery of candidate assessment techniques.	Formal, structured interaction guided by detailed job analysis and pre-formulated questioning strategy.	• To record answers to critical incident-type questions. • To probe and feed back results of other selection methods (particularly testing).	• To survive! • To obtain feedback and ensure accuracy of results of other methods.
3. Negotiation	Phase III. Final stage of selection procedure, immediately before, or after, offer of employment has been made.	Negotiation of outstanding points of difference, both interviewer and interviewee-directed and led.	• To ensure acceptance of job offer. • To facilitate job role transition. • To identify follow-up personnel procedures.	• To discuss contractual and non-contractual terms and conditions. • To facilitate job role transition. • To initiate the job change process.

Table 4.5: Main techniques of candidate assessment

Technique	Description	'Fit' with interview	Contribution to selection system
Psychometric testing	Standardised test of performance attitudes or personality. Major types:	Can precede or follow interview stage. Results can form basis of further inter-	*Ability tests* • High predictive accuracy for aspects of cognitive ability.

	• cognitive ability • personality • attitudes and values • career choice and guidance	view questions, or interview can be used to feed back test results. Personality tests are particularly useful in this respect and can facilitate probing questions at interview.	• 'Normed' results allow candidate to be compared with many similar people. Longer-term relevance, i.e. job role may change over time; ability remains relatively constant. *Personality tests* • Indications of inter-personal or managerial style that can be fol-lowed up at interview and/or compared with exercises in an AC. • 'Faking' scales built in to tests may detect high level of impression management and bias-ing of self-presentation.
Work examples	Pre-designed and con-structed samples of work performance designed to tap aspects of critical job perform-ance usually monitored and observed by trained experts, who rate can-didates on job-relevant dimensions.	Usually following initial interview and often conducted as part of an AC. Can therefore provide dynamic and highly job-relevant data for discussion at follow-up interview stage.	• High predictive accuracy. Directly relevant job tasks as samples of future behaviour. • Rated by observers on critical dimensions of job performance, some-times identical to those used for staff appraisal. • If constructed properly can add a sample of directly rele-vant candidate behaviour on segments of the job itself.
Assessment centres (ACs)	Multiple-method design, usually incor-porating testing, inter-views, and work sample exercises, where candidates are tested by observers on job-relevant dimen-sions. Can last from one to five days.	Usually the final stage of assess-ment to reach outcome decisions. because of cost of running ACs. Interviews usually conducted as integral part of an AC.	• All the above, as well as: • Opportunity to observe candidates over longer period in formal and informal situ-ations. • Multiple assessments by several assessors over several exercises can eliminate some individual biases associated with one-to-one interviews (see chapter 3).
Reference letter	Varies from very brief factual check (e.g. 'Did candidate hold this position between these	Commonly used as final check on candi-date after conditional offer of employment	• Best used as factual check only. • Most appropriate as final check: references

dates, as claimed?') to extensive rating of abilities, personality, and attitude to work.	has been made. Interview can throw up specific issues to be checked with previous employers by reference letter.	taken up with existing employer before offer of employment will not be popular with candidates!

Source: Anderson and Shackleton (1993).

Efficiency of the selection interview

Over the years, considerable research concerning both the validity and the reliability of the selection interview has been undertaken, often with conflicting results (Anderson 1992; Hunter and Hunter 1984; Wiesner and Cronshaw 1988). In reviewing this body of research, Anderson and Shackleton (1993) suggest that, from the point of view of validity and reliability, the overall efficiency of selection interview decisions has been much maligned in recent years, and they highlight a number of points that merit attention:

- Interviews can be much more accurate than many recruiters may believe.
- Structured interviews that are built around a pre-planned format are more valid and reliable than unstructured, non-directed conversations (Wiesner and Cronshaw 1988).
- Interviews are significantly more accurate if based on detailed job analysis techniques, where the decision reached is based on the application of both the job description and the person specification.
- The interview is an appropriate and fairly reliable method of assessing job-relevant social skills (Wagner 1949; Avery et al. 1987).
- Interviewers' accuracy varies, and recruitment decisions should always be validated, i.e. interviewers should check their decisions against subsequent job performance.

Errors and biases in selection

While the central question of whether interviewers are 'born, not made' remains unanswered, there is considerable evidence to suggest that the process of interviewing is all too often subject to a number of underlying biases and errors that adversely affect the selection decision (Anderson and Shackleton 1993; Waering and Stockdale 1987; Macon and Dipboye 1988; Anderson 1992; Dale 1995). While it would be untrue to suggest that all interviews are biased or error-prone, based on existing research Anderson and Shackleton (1993) have classified some of the more common errors and biases that can occur:

- The expectancy effect: Interviewers can form either a positive or a negative impression of a candidate based on the biographical information from the application form or CV, and this tends to have a bearing on all subsequent decisions (often termed 'gut instinct' or 'snap decision').
- The information-seeking bias: Based on their initial expectations, interviewers can actively seek information that will confirm their initial expectation.
- The primacy effect: Interviewers may form impressions about a candidate's personality within the first five minutes of meeting him or her and tend to be influenced most by what is said early in the interview.
- Stereotyping: Stereotypes can often be ascribed to particular groups of people based on sex, nationality, or family circumstances, although decisions based on them are in violation of equality legislation.

- Horns/halo effect: Based on information received, an interviewer may rate a candidate either universally favourably or universally unfavourably. Furthermore, negative information tends to influence more than positive information, and therefore even where there is a balance between positive and negative information, the overall impression will tend to be negative.
- Contrast and quota effects: Interviewers' decisions can be inherently affected by decisions made on earlier candidates and by pre-set selection quotas. Where a number of candidates have been selected for interview, those who are interviewed later are invariably compared with those who went before them, rather then being assessed specifically against predetermined criteria.

However rigorous the process, interviewing remains essentially a subjective process, and therefore the interviewer needs to ensure that, as far is possible, these errors or biases are eliminated from the process. The operation of panel interviews or successive interviews can obviate many of the inherent problems associated with interviewing and can ensure greater validity and reliability in the final decision. Furthermore, attention to effective interpersonal interaction, such as active listening and attendant non-verbal behaviour, competent questioning and a facilitative interview environment (free from noise and other distractions) can further ensure that the interview is as productive as possible.

Evenden and Anderson (1992) suggest that the choice of questions and the appropriate use of them can ensure greater balance and flow to the interview itself (see table 4.6).

Table 4.6: Types of interview questions

---

1 **Direct or closed**
These have the effect of yielding short answers such as 'yes,' 'no,' or 'sometimes': 'How did you travel?'

2 **Leading**
These lead the interviewee to give the answer the interviewer expects or wants to hear: 'We are always in flux. You do like change, don't you?'

3 **Topic-changing**
Moving the interview on to a new topic: 'Thanks for the information on your qualifications. Would you tell me how you chose your career route?'

4 **Probing and developing**
These enquire more fully into an area, or encourage building on an answer already given: 'Why did you say you prefer jobs that involve travel?'

5 **Open-ended**
These encourage full answers: 'Would you tell me about how you spend your leisure time?' 'Why did you apply for this particular job?'

6 **Reflecting back**
Reflecting back to the person what they have said by restating their reply: 'Promotion is very important to you, then?' 'Are you saying you're frightened by computers?'

① They are useful for the purpose of getting facts, but too much use leads to a staccato interview, and a short one if the applicant is nervous.

② There is no value in this type of question, unless the interviewers have self-deception in mind. Most interviewees would follow the lead.

③ Necessary to control the move through your plan and your timing. Helpful in creating a smooth flow in the interview.

④ Very important in seeking evidence and testing the interviewee's knowledge, experience, feelings, and attitudes.

⑤ The interviewee is given the opportunity to answer at length and to choose what to select to talk about. Very useful in getting the person talking and involved in the interview. Good for shy people if allied to gentle persistence.

⑥ These are important in making sure that your understanding is clear and accurate. It also shows that you are listening and interested in what the interviewee is saying.

Source: Evenden and Anderson (1992).

Placement, induction, and follow-up

When the selection decision is made, a job offer is made to the chosen candidate, and the unsuccessful applicants are notified. Where the selection process involved a number of internal applicants, due care should be taken in communicating the selection decision to them, particularly where they have been unsuccessful. A letter of offer can constitute a legally binding document, since it usually forms part of a legal contract of employment.

When the offer has been accepted, it is customary to have a period of induction for the successful candidate, which is designed to facilitate the smooth transition to work in the company. Induction periods vary from company to company and can last as long as three months. It is similarly common to find that the new recruit is 'on probation' for the first three months of employment, to determine whether events work out as expected (this largely depends on the job position). As discussed earlier in this chapter, labour turnover tends to be highest during the induction period, and therefore companies can reduce the induction crisis through a carefully managed socialisation process. This can involve furnishing the new employee with a company manual, explaining the nature of the business in greater detail, outlining the structure and hierarchy of the company, and providing a liaison to 'show them the ropes.' (Coaching, mentoring, facilitation and training and development as socialisation techniques are further discussed in chapter 9.) Positive reinforcement and feedback are critical considerations throughout the induction period, which can be facilitated by some form of interim performance appraisal; this can aid in the establishment of behaviour norms desired by the company.

RECRUITMENT AND SELECTION IN IRELAND

Having identified the processes of human resource planning and recruitment and selection, it becomes pertinent to explore current developments in these areas in Ireland. An examination of the Price Waterhouse Cranfield project data relating to recruitment practices indicates that a broad spectrum of recruitment methods is being employed (see table 4.7).

Table 4.7: Recruitment methods used in Ireland

	Managerial	Prof./ tech.	Clerical	Manual
From among current employees	53%	35%	46%	29%
Advertising internally	42%	39%	57%	41%
Advertising externally	65%	69%	46%	36%
Word of mouth	9%	12%	22%	37%
Recruitment agencies	41%	42%	28%	6%
Search or selection consultants	35%	24%	1%	.5%
Job centres	0.4%	1%	15%	26%
Apprentices	—	9%	4%	15%

Source: University of Limerick (1992).

Perhaps the most commonly recognised recruitment method is the advertisement, at local or national level. Plumbley (1985) suggests that where advertising judgments are based on reliable and relevant factors and where they are effectively communicated, external advertising serves as a powerful recruitment tool.

The data suggests that the external labour market is preferred when recruiting managerial and professional or technical staff, whereas the internal labour market is used more in the recruitment of clerical and manual grades. When filling managerial and professional or technical vacancies, companies favour external advertising above all other methods (64 per cent of respondents advertise managerial posts externally, while the equivalent figure for professional and technical posts is 68 per cent), while internal advertising is preferred for recruitment at clerical and manual levels. This may be evidence of a structured internal labour market, particularly for clerical positions, since traditionally career ladders and internal mobility are a particular feature of clerical work. Furthermore, at these levels it is often cheaper and quicker to avail of this recruitment method, as the necessary expertise may already be present in the company.

Using the internal labour market for recruitment purposes is not limited to internal advertising and may occur on a much more informal basis. Strauss and Sayle (1972) estimate that two-thirds of newly hired employees learn about their job through word of mouth from existing employees. Results from the PWCP survey suggest that this method of recruitment is more popular with clerical and manual positions than with higher-level vacancies (only 9 per cent of managerial positions are filled through word of mouth, while the corresponding figure for manual grades is 37 per cent), suggesting that the recruitment process for managerial and professional grades may be more formalised. Indeed when examining the use made of search or selection consultants one finds that it is mainly confined to the recruitment of managerial and professional or technical staff (35 and 24 per cent, respectively, compared with 1 and 0.5 per cent for clerical and manual grades). A similar trend is evident in the use of recruitment agencies. An important factor may be the costs of engaging such agencies, and, as a consequence, their use is often restricted to posts where the requisite skills are in short supply.

Company size appears to influence the recruitment methods used, particularly in relation to the recruitment of managerial staff and, to a lesser extent, professional and technical employees. No such correlation is evident, however, for the recruitment of clerical and manual staff. Similarly, larger companies make more use of the internal labour market for senior positions, where 60 per cent of companies employing more than 200 employees recruit managerial staff from present employees; the equivalent figure for those companies employing fewer than 200 employees is 46 per cent. This focus on the internal labour market may be linked to the practice of HRM, particularly aspects of career development and career counselling, much of which is evident in multinational subsidiaries and may thus provide a reasonable explanation for the relationship with company size.

A positive correlation was found between the frequency with which particular recruitment methods were used and the country of origin of the responding companies. The most significant difference occurs between Irish-owned companies and their American and EU counterparts, where, among employee categories, Irish-owned companies are seen to use their internal labour market to a lesser degree than the foreign-owned companies (see table 4.8).

Table 4.8: Recruitment methods and country of origin

	Managerial			Prof./tech			Clerical			Manual		
	Irish	US	EU	Irish	US	EU	Irish	US	EU	Irish	EU	US
Current employees	47%	59%	77%	31%	47%	38%	37%	61%	74%	23%	45%	40%
Advertise internally	38%	49%	49%	32%	55%	46%	49%	71%	77%	34%	55%	57%
Total	164	54	38	164	54	38	164	54	38	164	54	38

Source: University of Limerick (1992).

These results again are consistent with the contention that multinational companies promote the use of HRM policies, which is particularly evident in the development of their internal labour market through such techniques as progressive career planning and extensive communication and information sharing (see Gunnigle 1992; Murray 1984). Maintaining a robust company culture, shared by all employees, is a central aim of these companies; their greater reliance on the internal labour market, therefore, may well be a positive reinforcer of their cultural ethos.

The Price Waterhouse Cranfield project did not reveal any particular difference between the public and private sector with respect to their use of internal or external labour markets. However, in relation to specific recruitment methods it emerged that the use of recruitment agencies and search or selection consultants was more widespread in the private sector, among all categories of employees. A partial explanation for this may be that all the public sector organisations surveyed recognise trade unions, and many such unions insist that all vacancies be first advertised internally.

As identified earlier, selection tools available to companies range from the more traditional methods of interviews, application forms and references to more sophisticated techniques such as biographical data (biodata), aptitude tests, and psychological testing. Storey (1992) suggests that developments in the realm of selection lend some support to those who propound the HRM thesis, where a key feature has been the increase in testing designed explicitly to assess behavioural and attitudinal characteristics. He further indicates that the extent to which these more sophisticated and systematic approaches can be and are deployed depends largely on the sector circumstances and on the wider employment-management policies being pursued.

The data generated by the Price Waterhouse Cranfield Project indicates that relatively little use is being made by Irish companies of what are considered the more 'sophisticated' selection techniques. The picture emerging from the data suggests that the application form, the interview panel and reference checks are the most commonly used selection methods, while more sophisticated and reliable techniques such as biodata, testing, assessment centres and group selection are used in only a small proportion of instances. Table 4.9 presents the findings in descending order of frequency.

Table 4.9: Selection methods

	n	*%*
References	234	88
Application form	229	86
Interview panel	227	85
Aptitude tests	82	31
Psychometric testing	49	19
Group selection methods	19	7
Assessment centres	13	5
Biodata	13	5
Graphology	3	1

n = 267.

Source: University of Limerick (1992).

The interview is widely believed to be the most commonly used selection technique. For example, McMahon (1988) found that over 90 per cent of job categories were filled with the assistance of an interview; this high level of usage is confirmed in the PWCP sample (85 per cent). References also feature as a key tool in the selection process and are used primarily in conjunction with the selection interview. Furthermore, application forms as a key selection technique are much in evidence (86 per cent); but Guest (1983) cautions that, in this age of increasing numbers of applicants per vacancy, pre-selection devices are becoming more and more of a necessity, hence the importance of designing application forms in an analytical manner.

Biodata, assessment centres and testing are increasingly viewed as consistently valid predictors that are ideal as pre-selection devices, particularly where there are large numbers of applicants for relatively homogeneous positions (Muchinsky 1986; Hunter and Hunter 1984; Smith, Gregg and Andrews 1989). The use of these more sophisticated techniques is reported to be low in both Ireland (McMahon 1988) and Britain (Robertson and Makin 1986). However, there is evidence to suggest that testing in particular is becoming more widespread in the United States (Anderson and Shackleton 1986) and therefore linked perhaps to the HRM thesis, which is widely held to have originated in the United States. Again the figures presented in table 4.9 suggest that these techniques are not used to any great extent in Ireland at present.

Interestingly, the Price Waterhouse Cranfield project found that, while no substantial difference is evident in the use of the more traditional selection methods, large companies demonstrated a greater propensity to use more sophisticated techniques. Thus, while only 8 per cent of companies employing fewer than 200 employees use psychometric testing as a selection tool, 29 per cent of companies employing more than 200 use this technique. A similar picture emerges with respect to aptitude tests, where 41 per cent of those employing more than 200 employees use such tests; the corresponding figure for those employing fewer than 200 is 22 per cent.

A further interesting result is that American and EU-owned companies are more likely to use the more sophisticated selection techniques than their Irish-owned counterparts. For example, 37 per cent of American-owned companies and 29 per cent of EU-owned companies use psychometric or aptitude testing; the corresponding figure for Irish-owned companies is just 11 per cent. This confirms McMahon's (1988) finding that testing was largely confined to multinationals and may in some way be supported by Guest's (1988) contention that American industry is, on the whole, more receptive to experimenting with ideas derived from organisation behaviour and therefore more likely to use testing as a selection tool.

In summary, the picture emerging of the way in which companies approach the recruitment and selection process is relatively unsurprising, particularly given the loose nature of the Irish labour market. An oversupply characterises the labour market at present, resulting in a readily accessible pool of qualified young people available to fill vacant positions. Companies therefore have little difficulty in attracting candidates. However, with increasing importance being placed on having a well-developed, flexible work-force, greater demands may be placed on companies to develop mobile internal labour markets, and some of the more sophisticated selection techniques may see increased use in the future.

5

Employee Motivation and the Design of Work in Perspective

In 1971 Thomas Fitzgerald, writing in the *Harvard Business Review*, argued that motivation theory does not work and that we should discard the dismal vocabulary of motives, motivators and motivation and think about becoming a society of persons. His argument was based on the premise that the remedies advanced by prominent motivation theorists were inadequate because the seriousness of the motivation problem had been underestimated and in some respects misunderstood, as the problem of employee motivation is rooted in certain fundamental conditions of industrial society and its solution requires costly and extensive changes in our interdependent, closely linked systems. Truth, he argued, is sometimes damaged in the process of analysis and reconstruction, and concepts can easily become more real than the reality from which they were cut.

> When transplanted from the laboratory, the language of motivation may become subtly elitist by suggesting that the employee resembles a captive rodent in a training box equipped with levers, trick doors, food pellets, and electric grids ... When a man gets up in the morning, we can say that this act is a conditioned response to the stimulus of an alarm, but that doesn't tell us anything important (Fitzgerald 1971, 12).

Twenty-five years later this vocabulary prevails, promulgating such concepts as needs, wants and desires as central aspects of the human condition. However, it is recognised that effective management depends on a knowledge and understanding of human motivation that goes beyond any 'common sense conventional wisdom' (Litwin and Stringer 1968). While motivation as a concept is a complex phenomenon, any management practices that wish to make inroads in this area must be based on systematic knowledge about motivational processes that have relevance to the individual and relevance in the work-place. Managers confronted with organisational ills such as persistent absenteeism and turnover, low morale, expressed job dissatisfaction, poor job and organisational commitment or unacceptable quality, productivity or performance want, as Herzberg (1968) put it, 'the surest and least circumlocuted way of getting someone to do something.'

In this chapter we explore the concept of motivation and examine the relationship between motivational processes and that other important organisational factor, job design. Linking motivation and job design helps us to avoid the mistake of thinking that motivation is the only important determinant of work performance.

MOTIVATION: ROLE AND DEFINITION

Motivation at work has been the object of sustained attention since the emergence of industrial society. Steers and Porter (1987) advance a number of explanations for the prominence of motivation as a focal point. Firstly, they suggest that managers and organisational researchers cannot avoid a concern for the behavioural requirements of the company. The necessity of attracting the right calibre of employees and engaging them in such a way as to ensure high performance remains a central concern of the productive process. Secondly, they argue that the pervasive nature of the concept itself has resulted in its remaining as a central area of enquiry. As a complex phenomenon it affects a multitude of factors, and any worthwhile understanding of companies requires a deal of attention to be focused on this array of factors and how they interact to create certain outcomes. Thirdly, competitive trends of the business environment coupled with increased business regulation have forced companies to seek out any mechanisms that might improve organisational effectiveness and efficiency. The ability to direct employees' efforts towards these twin goals of effectiveness and efficiency are seen as crucial. A fourth reason for the sustained interest in motivation is the issue of technological advancement. A company must continually ensure that its work-force is capable and willing to use advanced manufacturing technologies to achieve organisational goals. A final reason, according to Steers and Porter, is the issue of planning horizons. Taking a longer-term view of the human resource in an attempt to build up a reservoir of skilled, enthusiastic employees has brought the concept of motivation to centre stage.

While there are several reasons why it remains a central area of enquiry, therefore, the study of motivation at work has been and continues to be based largely on analysing employees' behaviour at work, and so motivation theory is essentially concerned with explaining why people behave as they do, or why people choose different forms of behaviour to achieve different ends.

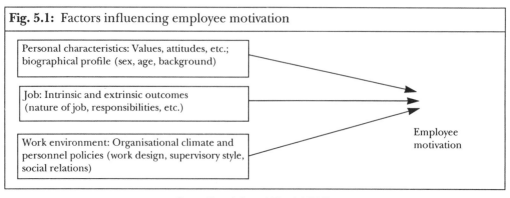

Fig. 5.1: Factors influencing employee motivation

Personal characteristics: Values, attitudes, etc.; biographical profile (sex, age, background)

Job: Intrinsic and extrinsic outcomes (nature of job, responsibilities, etc.)

Work environment: Organisational climate and personnel policies (work design, supervisory style, social relations)

Employee motivation

Source: Gunnigle and Flood (1990).

Traditional approaches to employee motivation have relied heavily on extrinsic factors, particularly pay. However, individual employee motivation and perceived job satisfaction will be influenced by a myriad of factors. Some will be related to individual employees and their personal characteristics. Others, such as supervisory relations or discretion, will stem from either the working environment or the job itself.

In relation to individual factors, it is important that companies select employees whose motives and work values 'fit' the organisational environment, management approach, and reward package. On the other hand the organisational climate, management style and design of work should facilitate good performance by providing adequate opportunity for employees to satisfy their varying needs. The management must be keenly aware of the need to motivate employees through both extrinsic and intrinsic outcomes. Extrinsic outcomes are tangible and visible and include such things as a pay increase or a company car. Intrinsic outcomes on the other hand relate to the satisfaction of personal wants and desires and include such things as increased autonomy and responsibility and feedback.

However, there is no simple answer to the crucial question: How do you motivate people? Herzberg (1968) perhaps best demonstrates the complexity attached to this question:

What is the simplest, surest, and most direct way of getting someone to do something? Ask him? But if he responds that he does not want to do it, then that calls for a psychological consultation to determine the reason for his obstinacy. Tell him? His response shows that he does not understand you, and now an expert in communication methods has to be brought in to show you how to get through to him. Give him a monetary incentive? I do not need to remind the reader of the complexity and difficulty involved in setting up and administering an incentive system. Show him? This means a costly training programme.

This remains a vital area of enquiry in the attempt to achieve and maintain high levels of motivation, especially in competitive industry, primarily because, according to Pettinger (1994),

there is a correlation between organisations that go to a lot of trouble to motivate their staff, and profitable business performance ... The ability to gain the commitment and motivation of staff in organisations has been recognised as important in certain sectors of the business sphere. It is now more universally accepted as a critical business and organisational activity, and one that has highly profitable returns and implications for the extent of the returns on investment that is made in the human resource.

The word 'motivate' was originally derived from the Latin *movere*, meaning 'to move'; modern interpretations are more all-encompassing, expressing various understandings of how we view people and organisations. Thus while Vroom (1964) conceptualises motivation as a process governing choices made by people or lower organisms among alternative forms of voluntary activity, Du Brin (1978) suggests that motivation centres on the expenditure of effort towards achieving an objective the company wants accomplished. Arnold, Cooper and Robertson (1995), using a mechanical analogy, suggest that the motive force gets a machine started and keeps it going and argue that motivation concerns the factors that push or pull us to behave in certain ways. Bennet (1991) suggests that an employee's motivation to work consists of all the drives, forces and influences—conscious or unconscious—that cause them to want to achieve certain aims.

Most of the early work on motivation was centred around getting more out of the employee, although many of the theorists were also concerned with finding an answer to the problem that was consistent with the essential dignity and independence of the person. Motivation theory bases its analysis of employees' performance on how work and its rewards satisfy individual employee needs. Numerous theories have been developed over the years to aid managements in identifying employees' motives and needs, the most influential of which will be discussed here.

The study of motivation at work has been based on analysing employees' behaviour at work. People react in different ways to different stimuli, and various theories of employee motivation seek to identify factors that induce good or bad performance and suggest how the management might apply these effectively at company level. Here we briefly examine some of the more influential theories on employee motivation and work design and evaluate their application in practice.

Motivation theory bases its analysis of workers' performance on how work and its rewards satisfy the individual employee's needs, the general conclusion being that if these needs are satisfied employees will be motivated to work at high performance levels, but if not, their performance will be less than satisfactory. Of course motivation is only one factor affecting performance; other factors, particularly technology, training, and individual ability, will have a significant influence on performance levels.

A central concern of the management is how to get employees to perform at the limit of their abilities. If this can be achieved, the management will have gone a long way towards creating a successful company. The understanding of human needs at work and the creation of a working environment that satisfies those needs is a key task of the senior management.

When discussing motivation theory it is useful to distinguish between content and process models of motivation. Content models focus on the wants and needs that people are trying to satisfy or to achieve within the situation, or *what* motivates human behaviour. They are dedicated to an exploration of individual needs, wants, desires, and aspirations. The content approaches discussed here are the *hierarchy of needs theory, the ERG theory*, the *acquired needs theory*, and the *dual-factor theory*. Process models attempt to show how the external context drives people to behave in a particular fashion and how managers can change the situation to better link the satisfaction of needs with performance, or *how* the content of motivation influences behaviour. The process approaches discussed here are *theory X theory Y, expectancy theory*, and *equity theory*.

Maslow's hierarchy of needs

Most managers today will be familiar with the hierarchical classification of human needs first proposed by Maslow (1943). Maslow, who was a clinical psychologist, suggested that human motivation is dependent on the desire to satisfy various levels of needs, and Maslow's hierarchy of needs is perhaps the most publicised theory of motivation. Based on the existence of a series of needs that range from basic instinctive needs for sustenance and security to higher-order needs such as self-esteem and the need for self-actualisation, it seeks to explain different types and levels of motivation that are important to people at different times.

In all, Maslow suggests that there are five levels of needs, ranked in the order shown, as this is the order in which the individual will seek to satisfy them. The ascending order of needs is important. Firstly, it implies that it is the next unachieved level that acts as the prime motivator; therefore people without the basic necessities of life will be motivated by basic physiological and, later, security needs. Only when these have been satisfied will higher-order needs become important. Only when all the lower-order needs are satisfied do higher-level needs act as a motivator: first esteem needs and ultimately self-actualisation.

Fig. 5.2: Maslow's Hierarchy of Needs

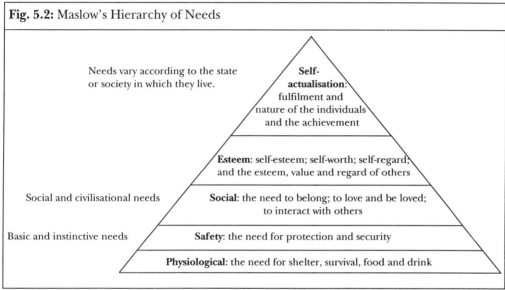

Needs vary according to the state or society in which they live.

Self-actualisation: fulfilment and nature of the individuals and the achievement

Esteem: self-esteem; self-worth; self-regard; and the esteem, value and regard of others

Social and civilisational needs

Social: the need to belong; to love and be loved; to interact with others

Basic and instinctive needs

Safety: the need for protection and security

Physiological: the need for shelter, survival, food and drink

Source: Maslow (1943)

The second implication of the ascending order of needs is that once a particular needs category is satisfied it ceases to have a significant impact on motivation. Any needs level therefore only motivates while it remains unachieved; once achieved it is the next level in the hierarchy that dominates.

Physiological needs include such things as food, shelter, clothing, and heat. These basic needs must be satisfied for the person to survive. In modern society it is employment and the income this generates that allows the individual to satisfy such needs.

Safety needs refer to such things as security at home, tenure at work, and protection against reduced living standards. Only when physiological needs have been satisfied will the individual concentrate on safety needs.

Social or love needs refer to people's desire for affection and the need to feel wanted. Our need for association, for acceptance by others and for friendship, companionship and love would also be included here.

Esteem needs cover one's desire for self-esteem and self-confidence and also one's need for recognition, authority, and influence over others.

Self-actualisation refers to the need for self-fulfilment, self-realisation, personal development, and fulfilment of the creative faculties (see fig. 5.3).

The hierarchy of needs theory states that a need that is unsatisfied activates seeking or searching behaviour. Therefore the person who is hungry will search for food, and the one who is unloved will seek to be loved. Once this seeking behaviour is fulfilled or satisfied it no longer acts as a primary motivator: needs that are satisfied no longer motivate. This clearly illustrates the rationale for arranging these needs in a hierarchy. However, people will seek growth when it is feasible to do so and have an innate desire to ascend the hierarchy. Such higher-order needs will act as a motivator when lower-order ones have been satisfied.

Self-actualisation is the climax of personal growth. Maslow describes it as the desire for self-fulfilment: the desire to become more and more what one is, to become everything that one is capable of becoming.

Fig. 5.3: The self-actualising person

1. Perceives people and events accurately, without undue interference from their own preconceptions.
2. Accepts self and others, including imperfections, but seeks improvement where possible.
3. Is spontaneous, especially in their thoughts and feelings.
4. Focuses on problems outside self, rather than being insecure and introspective.
5. Is detached, so that they are not unduly thrown off course by awkward events.
6. Is autonomous, and remains true to self despite pressure to conform.
7. Appreciates good and beautiful things, even if they are familiar.
8. Has peak experiences of intense positive emotions of a sometimes mystical quality.
9. Has close relationships, but only with a few carefully chosen people.
10. Respects others, avoids making fun of people, and evaluates them according to their inner qualities rather than race or class.
11. Has firm moral standards and sense of right and wrong, though these may be different from many other people.
12. Is creative; this is perhaps the most fundamental aspect of self-actualisation and is seen as the result of the other aspects listed above. By being open-minded and open to their experience the self-actualising person sees things in novel ways and can draw novel conclusions from established information.

Source: Sugarman (1986).

Maslow's theory has been the subject of much commentary and criticism over the years. Firstly, his work was based on general studies of human behaviour and motivation and therefore was not directly associated with matters central to the work-place. Arising from this the theory is extremely difficult to apply, because of the illusive nature of the needs identified, particularly in the context of the work-place. Researchers have also found little support for the concept of exclusive pre-potency. A more realistic view is that people have several active needs at the same time, which implies that lower-order needs are not always satisfied before one concentrates on higher-order needs. Another criticism of this approach is that career advancement may be the true factor underlying changes in need deficiencies. Research demonstrates that as managers advance in companies their lower-order needs diminish; simultaneously they experience an increased desire to satisfy higher-order needs. Finally, it has also been suggested that the theory attempts to demonstrate an imputed rationality in human actions that may not necessarily exist. The conceptualisation of our needs in such a logical sequential fashion, while useful as a frame of reference with which we can all compare ourselves, has not resulted in convincing evidence among the research community.

Other inconsistencies that research has thrown up include the fact that needs do not often group together in the ways predicted; the restricting of the concept of need to a purely biological phenomenon remains problematic; and needs, while often realistically described, are done so with insufficient precision.

Overall, Maslow's needs hierarchy appears to be a convenient way of classifying needs but has limited utility in explaining work behaviour. Its primary value has been that it highlights the importance of human needs in a work setting.

Existence-relatedness-growth (ERG) theory

ERG theory, as developed by Alderfer (1972), reduces Maslow's fivefold needs category to a threefold taxonomy. A second difference, stemming from criticisms of Maslow's approach, is that less emphasis is placed on a hierarchical order of lower and higher-order needs, inferring that all needs levels may be influential at the same time.

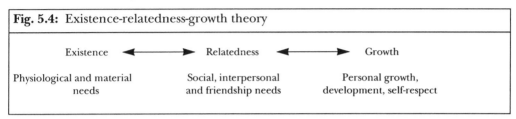

Fig. 5.4: Existence-relatedness-growth theory

Existence ◄───►	Relatedness ◄───►	Growth
Physiological and material needs	Social, interpersonal and friendship needs	Personal growth, development, self-respect

Source: Alderfer (1972).

Another important variation is the proposition that an already satisfied lower-order need may be reactivated as a motivator when a higher-order need cannot be satisfied. An employee who has satisfied basic material and social needs may be concerned with their personal growth and development (e.g. promotion). If there is no scope for such development they may revert back to a preoccupation with previously satisfied needs (e.g. social or financial). The other implication, referred to above, is that more than one needs category may be important at any one time.

Acquired needs theory

An alternative approach, developed by McClelland (1961), concentrated on identifying motivational differences between people as a means of establishing which patterns of motivation led to effective performance and success at work. McClelland distinguishes three basic needs in addition to physical drives:

Need for achievement: the desire to consistently want challenging tasks demanding responsibility and application.

Need for power: the need for control over people.

Need for affiliation: the need for good social and personal relations with people.

McClelland suggested that these needs are acquired and developed over one's life. Depending on which needs are dominant, these will exert varying influences on work performance. People with a high need for achievement tend to have a strong motivation to take on challenging tasks and to do them better. This, combined with a moderate to high need for power and a lower need for affiliation, has been suggested as a good indicator of success in senior management (McClelland and Boyatzis 1982). An important implication of this approach is that if such needs are acquired, they may be developed through appropriate environmental conditions that facilitate the emergence of the desired needs profile.

McGregor's theory X, theory Y

Unlike previous approaches that concentrated on analysing the motivations of people at work, McGregor (1960) examined managerial assumptions about employees and the implications of such assumptions for managerial approaches to issues such as control, job design, and remuneration systems. He identified two very different sets of assumptions about employees' behaviour and motivation, termed theory X and theory Y.

Organisational approaches to work-force management differ considerably, and these contrasting frameworks are useful in helping to analyse and explain management styles. Both classifications represent extreme styles or approaches to people management. In practice, companies may adopt elements of both approaches but often with a particular leaning that indicates a preference for one or other approach.

Fig. 5.5: Theory X, Theory Y

THEORY X	THEORY Y
Employees are inherently lazy, dislike work will do as little as possible. Consequently, workers need to be corrected, controlled and directed to exert adequate effort.	Employees like work and want to undertake challenging tasks. If the work itself and the organisational environment is appropriate, employees will work willingly without need for coercion or control.
Most employees dislike responsibility and prefer direction.	People are motivated by needs for respect, esteem, recognition and self-fulfilment.
Employees want only security and material rewards.	People at work want responsibility. The majority of workers are imaginative and creative and can exercise ingenuity at work.

Source: Gunnigle and Flood (1990)

Traditional autocratic management approaches were clearly based on theory X assumptions. Despite considerable academic and practical support, it would seem that theory Y has not got the whole-hearted backing of many senior managers. Consequently its application has often been restricted to once-off initiatives designed to deal with particular problems or issues rather than reflecting a change in corporate approaches to the way employees are managed.

Dual-factor theory

Herzberg (1968) was equally concerned about the impact of work and job design on motivation. He saw the key to improving employees' motivation as job satisfaction. Herzberg felt that by identifying the factors at work that produced the greatest levels of satisfaction (or dissatisfaction) it would be possible to design jobs that provided job satisfaction, thereby encouraging higher levels of performance. His approach concentrated on identifying the factors that contributed most to employees' satisfaction at work (called 'motivator' factors). He also sought to identify those factors that influenced levels of employee dissatisfaction ('maintenance' v. 'hygiene' factors). Herzberg concluded that these two sets of factors were inherently different in their impact on motivation and performance. A central aspect of Herzberg's dual-factor theory is that only by varying motivator factors can the management improve performance and motivation. Varying maintenance factors will reduce levels of dissatisfaction but will never act as a motivator.

The implication here is that management can only stimulate employees' motivation by designing jobs to incorporate the motivator factors (i.e. jobs that encourage and facilitate responsibility, advancement, and recognition). Herzberg believed that high levels of job satisfaction could be achieved by altering the job content to allow for personal growth and development while also ensuring that the job context (pay, working conditions, etc.) was appropriate. This process became known as *job enrichment*.

Herzberg's approach has gained considerable recognition, particularly for differentiating between the impact of intrinsic and extrinsic factors on employees' motivation. Criticisms have focused on the reliability of its application to all types of jobs (not just professional or white-collar) and the view of job satisfaction as being almost synonymous with motivation.

Fig. 5.6: Herzberg's dual-factor theory of work motivation

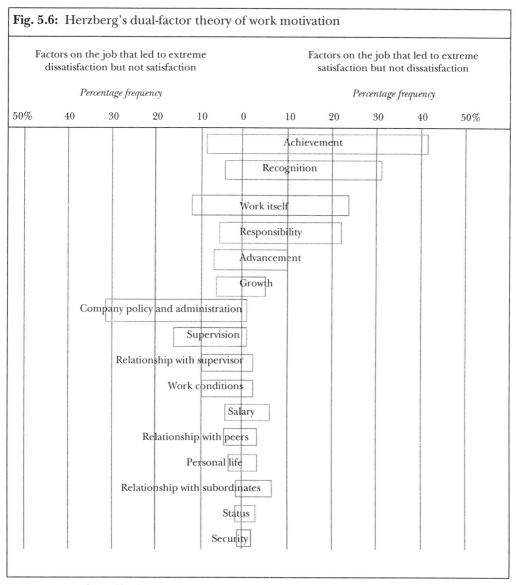

Source: Herzberg, F., *Work and the Nature of Man*, Staples Press, New York 1966.

Expectancy theory

Most of the approaches discussed above represent attempts to identify a general set of employee needs that cause workers to behave in a certain way. The belief is that by identifying such needs management can provide for their ease of achievement, so facilitating improved performance. Many of these approaches rank such motives or goals in a hierarchical order, with self-actualisation as the ultimate motivator.

Most managers, however, will probably point out that employees differ markedly in their motivation. It is possible to find two employees, similar in age, sex, background, etc., one of whom will strive to achieve high performance levels, undertake additional tasks, etc., while the other is content to get by doing the minimum acceptable to the company. How does one explain such variations? One approach that avoids attempts to find a definitive set of employee motives but seeks to explain individual differences in goals, motives and behaviour is expectancy theory.

Associated with Vroom (1964), expectancy theory focuses on the relationship between the effort put in to the completion of particular activities by the individual and the expectations concerning the reward that will accrue as a result of expending the effort. Expectancy theory attempts to combine individual and organisational factors that influence this causal effort-reward relationship. Broadly speaking, this theory argues that people base decisions about their behaviour on the expectation that one or another alternative behaviour is more likely to lead to needed or desired outcomes. The relationship between one's behaviour and particular outcomes is affected by individual factors such as personality, perception, motives, skills and abilities and by organisational factors such as culture, structure, and managerial style (the context in which one is operating). Expectancy theory therefore avoids attempts to isolate a definitive set of employee motives but rather seeks to explain individual differences in terms of goals, motives, and behaviour. It postulates that employee motivation is dependent on how the employer perceives the relationship between effort, performance, and outcomes.

'Expectancy' is the probability (assigned by the individual) that work effort will be followed by a given level of achieved task performance. It refers to the perceived probability that a particular level of effort will lead to desired performance levels. If the desired outcome (e.g. bonus pay) demands a given level of performance (e.g. production goals), the individual employee must believe that that level is achievable or they will not expend the necessary effort. (If I tried, would I be able to perform the action I am considering?) 'Instrumentality' is the probability (assigned by the individual) that a given level of achieved task performance will lead to various work outcomes or rewards.

Expectancy theory therefore suggests that employees' decisions on how they perform are based on their perception of desired outcomes, whether performance targets are achievable, and an evaluation of the likelihood that by achieving these targets they will realise their desired outcomes. (Would performing the action lead to identifiable outcomes?)

'Valence' is the value attached by the individual to various work outcomes or rewards. It is thus a measure of the strength of attraction that a particular outcome or reward has for the individual employee. (How much do I value these outcomes?)

The model suggests that the person's level of effort (motivation) is not simply a function of rewards: they must feel that they have the ability to perform the task (expectancy), that this performance will influence the reward, and that this reward is actually valued. Only if all conditions are satisfied will employees be motivated to exert greater effort. It is critical therefore that people can see a connection between effort and reward and that the reward offered by the company will satisfy employees' needs. However, there is no simple formula, since people possess different preferences for outcomes and have different understandings of the relationship between effort and reward. They may well be motivated in very different ways. Among the criticisms levelled at the theory are the difficulty associated with testing the theory empirically and the fact that it assumes a type of rationality with respect to how the individual thinks and behaves that may not exist.

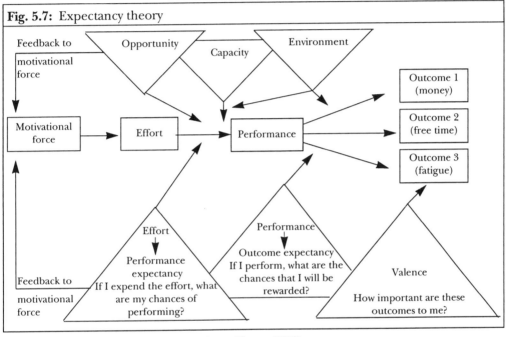

Fig. 5.7: Expectancy theory

Source: Umstot (1988).

This approach suggests that employees will expend a high level of effort if they believe it will result in performance levels that will be rewarded by valued outcomes. These valued outcomes may vary among different people: one may value money, another promotion, yet another recognition. However, it is not only the outcome that is important but also the belief that valued outcomes can be achieved through improved effort and performance.

In relation to the implications of expectancy theory for management, Vroom (1964) suggests that managers must seek to understand individual employees' goals and motives and ensure that these are clearly and positively linked to desired performance levels that in turn are achievable from the employee's view. Nadler and Lawler (1979) go a little further and highlight specific areas for management action:

- the need to establish what are valued outcomes;
- the need to specify desired and achievable performance levels;
- the need to ensure that there is a clear link between effort, performance, and desired outcomes;

- the need to ensure adequate variation of the outcomes available;
- the need to ensure equity and fairness for the individual employee.

Expectancy theory does not attempt to identify a universal set of motivational factors: rather it highlights the importance of a range of potential motivating factors. These may be either intrinsic or extrinsic. Intrinsic outcomes are those originating from doing the job (sense of achievement, satisfaction) while extrinsic outcomes are those provided by other people, particularly the management, and include pay, promotion, etc.

Equity theory

The concept of 'a fair day's work for a fair day's pay' is often used to express how the parties to the labour process wish to perceive the employment relationship. Equity theory—sometimes referred to as justice theory—resembles expectancy theory in that it sets out the individual's cognitive process that determines whether or not they will engage in the effort-reward bargain within the framework of the social exchange process.

Developed by Adams (1965), the equity theory of motivation is based on the comparison between two variables: inputs and outcomes. Inputs refer to what the individual brings to their employment and include such things as effort, experience, and skills. Outcomes describe the range of factors the employee receives in return for their inputs, for example pay, recognition, fringe benefits, and status symbols. Adams suggests that individual expectations about equity correlations between inputs and outcomes are learned during the process of socialisation in the home or at work and through comparison with the inputs and outcomes of others. He suggests that people can
—change inputs, e.g. can reduce effort if underpaid;
—try to change their outcomes, e.g. ask for a pay rise or promotion;
—psychologically distort their own ratios by rationalising differences in inputs and outcomes;
—change the reference group with which they compare themselves in order to restore equity.

Huseman, Hatfield and Miles (1987) enumerate the core propositions of equity theory as follows:

1. People evaluate their relationships with others by assessing the ratio of their outcomes from and inputs to the relationship against the outcome-input ratio of a comparable person.
2. If the outcome-input ratios of the person and the comparable other are deemed to be unequal, then inequity exists.
3. The greater the inequity the person perceives (in the form of either over-reward or under-reward), the more distress the person experiences.
4. The greater the distress a person experiences the harder they will work to restore equity. Among the possible equity restoration techniques are distorting inputs or outcomes, disregarding the comparable other and referring to a new one, or terminating the relationship.

Employees will therefore formulate a ratio between their inputs and outcomes and compare it with the perceived ratios of inputs and outcomes of other people in the same or a similar situation. If these two ratios are not equal, the person will take action in an attempt to restore a sense of equity.

A good deal of research has been devoted to testing the relationships advanced by

Adams, particularly those that focus on employees' reactions to pay. Overall, this research provides support for Adams's theory of employees' reactions to wage inequities. Mowday concludes that the research support for the theory appears to be strongest for predictions about underpayment inequity. Furthermore, equity theory appears to offer a useful approach to understanding a wide variety of social relationships in the work-place.

Table 5.1: Equity theory research on employees' reactions to pay

Study	Equity condition	Method of induction	Task	Dependent variables	Results
Adams (1963)	Overpayment; hourly and piece rate	Qualifications	Interviewing	Productivity, work quality	Hourly overpaid subjects produced greater quantity; piece-rate overpaid subjects produced higher quality and lower quantity than equitably paid subjects
Adams and Jacobsen (1964)	Overpayment; piece rate	Qualifications	Proof-reading	Productivity, work quality	Overpaid subjects produced less quantity of higher quality
Adams and Rosenbaum (1962)	Overpayment; hourly and piece rate	Qualifications	Interviewing	Productivity	Hourly overpaid subjects produced more quantity, while piece-rate overpaid subjects produced less quantity
Anderson and Shelly (1967)	Overpayment; hourly	Qualifications, importance of task	Proof-reading	Productivity, work quality	No differences were found between groups
Andrews (1967)	Overpayment and under- payment; piece rate	Circumstances, previous wage experiences	Interviewing, data checking	Productivity, work quality	Overpaid subjects produced higher quality and under- paid subjects produced greater quantity and lower quality
Arrowood (1961)	Overpayment; hourly	Qualifications, work returned	Interviewing	Productivity	Overpaid subjects had higher productivity
Evans and Simmons (1969)	Overpayment and under- payment; hourly	Competence, authority	Proof-reading	Productivity, work quality	Underpaid subjects produced more of poorer quality in competence condition; no difference found in other conditions
Friedman and Good- man (1967)	Overpayment; hourly	Qualifications	Interviewing	Productivity	Qualifications induction did. not affect productivity; when subjects were classified by perceived qualifications, un- qualified subjects produced less than qualified subjects
Goodman and Fried- man (1968)	Overpayment and under- payment; hourly	Qualifications, quantity v. quality emphasis	Questionnaire coding	Productivity, work quality	Overpaid subjects produced more than equitably paid subjects; emphasis on quantity v. quality affected performance

Goodman and Friedman (1969)	Overpayment; piece rate	Qualifications, quantity v. quality emphasis	Questionnaire scoring	Productivity, work quality	Overpaid subjects increased productivity or work quality, depending on induction
Lawler (1968b)	Overpayment; hourly	Qualifications, circumstances	Interviewing	Productivity, work quality	Overpaid (unqualified) subjects produced more of lower quality; subjects overpaid by circumstances did not
Lawler, Koplin, Young and Fadem (1968)	Overpayment; piece rate	Qualifications	Interviewing	Productivity, work quality	Overpaid subjects produced less of higher quality in initial work session; in later sessions subject's perceived qualifications and productivity increased; the need for money was related to productivity for both groups
Lawler and O'Gara (1967)	Underpayment; piece rate	Circumstances	Interviewing	Productivity, work quality	Underpaid subjects produced more of lower quality and perceived their job as more interesting but less important and more complex
Pritchard, Dunnette and Jorgenson (1972)	Overpayment and underpayment; hourly and piece rate	Circumstances, actual change in payment	Clerical task	Performance satisfaction	Circumstances induction did not result in performance differences for piece rate, but some support was found for hourly overpay and under-pay
					Changes in pay rate supported hourly predictions; some support found for piece rate overpayment prediction but not for underpayment
Valenzi and Andrews (1971)	Overpayment and underpayment; hourly	Circumstances	Clerical task	Productivity, work quality	No significant differences found between conditions; 27% of underpaid subjects quit; no subjects in other conditions quit
Wiener (1970)	Overpayment; hourly	Qualifications, inputs v. outcomes, ego-oriented v. task-oriented	Word manipulation		Outcome-overpayment subjects produced more; input-overpaid subjects produced more only on ego-oriented task
Wood and Lawler (1970)	Overpayment; piece rate	Qualifications	Reading	Amount of time reading, quality	Overpaid subjects produced less, but this could not be attributed to striving for higher quality

Source: Mowday (1987).

108

WORK DESIGN

The nature of work organisation and design will significantly influence the degree to which work is intrinsically satisfying for employees and to which it promotes high levels of motivation. Companies should carefully consider their approach to work organisation and choose the approach that best suits their particular needs.

The study of individual tasks in companies has long been of interest, and theory and research in the area have attempted to describe strategies for changing or refining jobs so as to enhance variables such as performance, motivation, satisfaction, commitment, and absenteeism. There is a body of opinion that sees at least some of the roots of the industrial and indeed social problems of modern societies in the nature of poorly structured work. The central view of the various schools of thought, according to Kelly (1980), is that the organisation of work on the basis of task fragmentation is counterproductive. It is suggested that the situation can be remedied by reversing the division of labour and meeting the social needs of people at work as well as the economic needs of employers. The central issue therefore in Lupton's (1976) words is 'how to design for best fit.'

Over the years the field of job design has been characterised by shifts from one theoretical view to another. The primary shifts have been from task specialisation (e.g. Taylor 1911) to job enlargement (e.g. Walker and Guest 1952), to job enrichment (e.g. Herzberg 1968), to socio-technical systems theory and the quality of working life (QWL) movement (e.g. Cherns and Davis 1975), to high-performance work design (e.g. Buchanan and McCalman 1989).

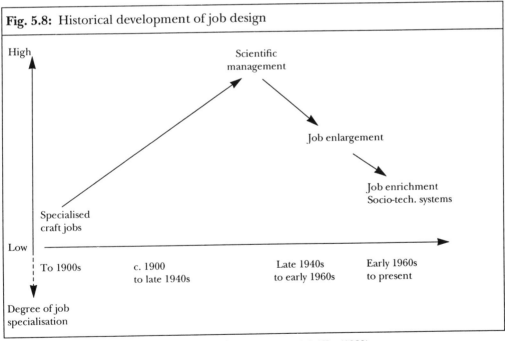

Fig. 5.8: Historical development of job design

Source: Adapted from Moorhead and Griffin (1989).

Broadly conceived, work organisation refers to the way the various tasks in the company are structured and carried out. It reflects the interaction of management style, the technical system, human resources, and the company's products or services. Davis (1966) defines the process of job design as that which is concerned with the 'specification of the contents, methods, and relationships of jobs in order to satisfy technological and organisational requirements, as well as the social and personal requirements of the job holder.' In line with this definition, table 5.9 demonstrates that the reason employers restructure jobs is a mix of improving productivity, reducing or eliminating organisational problems, and providing satisfying work for employees.

Table 5.9: Reasons for introducing job changes

| | Birchall and Wild | | Reif and Schonerbek | | Total |
	Blue-collar	*White-collar*	*Blue-collar*	*White-collar*	
System output					
Productivity	12	9			21
Costs	5	3	21		29
Quality	7	5	13		25
Down time	1				1
Inventories	1				1
Skills	2	2			4
Flexibility	3	3			6
Specialisation			14		14
System changes					
Introduction of					
automated equipment	2	1			3
Introduction of					
new plant	3	2			5
Personal problems					
Labour turnover	6	5		6	17
Absenteeism	4	1			5
Attract labour	1				1
Improve labour					
relations	2	2			4
Concern for employee					
Worker morale	10	7	15		32
To give meaning					
to work	4	4			8
Monotony			11		11
Eliminate social					
problems	3				3
Others	8	3	4	6	21
Total	74	47	78	12	211

Source: Birchall (1975).

Cherns and Davis (1975) identify three parties with an explicit interest in job restructuring, employee motivation, and satisfaction and work performance. The first, they claim, is labour, primarily represented by trade unions and other organised bodies. Unions are seen to be interested in 'the conditions of work, learning and adaptability, reward and satisfaction, and future structures of formal relationships with management.' The second party to the process is the management; they are interested in the efficient use of their human resources through the development of appropriate work methods. Finally there is the state. The government is seen to be concerned with matters related to labour and management because of the integral part they play in the successful running of the economy. Human resource planning, training and education, income policy, unemployment and the enhancement of industrial democracy projects are, Cherns and Davis argue, typically regulated by institutions of the state.

The design of individual jobs is seen to particularly affect employees since it influences job content, employees' discretion, the degree of task fragmentation, and the role of supervision. We suggest that decisions on the organisation of work are primarily a management responsibility and that the particular approach chosen will be a good indicator of corporate beliefs about how employees should be managed and jobs structured and about the role of supervision. It will also reflect the company's approach to many aspects of personnel management as manifested in attitudes to recruitment, employee development, motivation, rewards, and management-employee relations.

Task specialisation

Variously referred to as task specialisation, scientific management, and Taylorism, the traditional approach to the organisation of work was dominated by a desire to maximise the productive efficiency of the company's technical resources. Choices on the organisation of work and the design of jobs were seen as being determined by the technical system. The management's role was to ensure that other organisational resources, including employees, were organised in such a way as to facilitate the optimal use of the technical system. This efficiency approach is based on scientific management principles and has been a characteristic of employers' approaches to job design since the turn of the century. Jobs were broken down into simple, repetitive, measurable tasks whose skills could be easily acquired through systematic job training.

Fig. 5.10: Traditional approach to job design

Characteristics	Outcomes
Bureaucratic organisation structure	Tight supervisory control
Top-down supervisory control	Minimal need for employee discretion
Work planning separated from execution	Work measurement
Task fragmentation	Reliance on rules and procedures
Fixed job definitions	Job specialisation
Individual payment by results	Reduced job flexibility
	Short training time
	Little employee influence on job or work organisation

Source: Gunnigle and Flood (1990)

The rationale for this approach to work and job design was based on 'technological determinism', whereby the company's technical resources were seen as a given constraint and the other inputs, including employees, had to accommodate the technical system. It also reflected managerial assumptions about people at work. Close supervision, work measurement and other types of controls indicate a belief about employees akin to McGregor's theory X: they suggest that employees need to be coerced to work productively and that this is best achieved by routine, standardised tasks.

This traditional model of job design has undoubtedly had positive benefits for many companies. It helped improve efficiency and promoted a systematic approach to selection, training, work measurement, and payment systems. However, it has also led to numerous problems, such as high levels of labour turnover, absenteeism, and low motivation. Short-term efficiency benefits therefore were often superseded by long-term reductions in organisational effectiveness. Many behavioural scientists argued that organisational effectiveness could be increased by recognising employees' ability and giving them challenging, meaningful jobs within a co-operative working environment.

More recently the increased emphasis on improving quality, service and overall competitiveness has led to the emergence of other schools of thought aimed at restructuring work systems to increase employees' motivation, commitment, and performance. Much of the focus of the work of the successors to task specialisation has been on the restructuring of jobs to incorporate greater scope for intrinsic motivation. Subsequent schools questioned traditional management assumptions about why employees worked. The traditional approach saw employees as essentially instrumental in their attitudes to work; jobs were seen as a means to an end, and it was these extrinsic rewards that motivated employees. Consequently employers created work systems that closely circumscribed jobs, supervised work, and rewarded quantifiable performance.

Job enlargement

The job enlargement and job enrichment schools differ in their relative emphasis: the former makes one's job 'bigger', while the latter adds some element to the job that is dedicated to increasing the employee's psychological growth. Job enlargement grew from the arguments of humanitarians in the nineteen-fifties that production methods prevalent at the time created poor working conditions, which led to high levels of job dissatisfaction. The proposed solution was job enlargement, which, when introduced, would lead to more variety and less routinised work.

This assumption was drawn on by Walker and Guest (1952) in their study of car assembly lines. They studied 180 workers and identified six main characteristics of mass-production technology: (1) repetitiveness, (2) low skill requirement, (3) mechanically paced work, (4) little alteration of tools or methods, (5) low requirement for mental attention, and (6) minute sub-division of the product. Their conclusion was that the solution to the ills of mass-production technology lay in job enlargement, but their proposals have generated some debate. The disputed issues centre around meaning and methodology. Walker and Guest viewed job enlargement as 'the combination of more than two tasks into one.' However, this did not in any way distinguish it from 'job extension', which could possibly be nothing more than the addition of more meaningless tasks (Wall 1982). It has been argued that there is no explicit theory on which the concept of job enlargement can become a model of job restructuring. There is no motivation theory, according to Buchanan (1979), on which job enlargement stands. Aldag and Brief (1979) note that job enlargement experiments failed to use a conceptual framework of how the structuring of jobs should actually be executed.

Furthermore, Buchanan (1979) argues that job enlargement studies have largely ignored external variables and people's differing attitudes to work.

Job enrichment

Largely attributed to Herzberg (1968), job enrichment was developed for the advancement of the dual-factor theory of work motivation. The job enrichment approach suggested that employees gain most satisfaction from the work itself and that it was intrinsic outcomes arising from work that motivated them to perform well in their jobs. In his celebrated article 'One more time: how do you motivate employees?' Herzberg (1968) established the concept of vertical loading as a means of moving away from the addition of 'one meaningless task to the existing (meaningless) one.' Vertical loading, dedicated to the addition of more challenging dimensions to the job, remains the mainstay of job enrichment.

Fig. 5.11: Principles of vertical job loading

Principle	Motivators involved
A. Removing some controls while retaining accountability	Responsibility and personal achievement
B. Increasing the accountability of people for their own work	Responsibility and recognition
C. Giving a person a complete natural unit of work (module, division, area, etc.)	Responsibility, achievement, and recognition
D. Granting additional authority to an employee in their activity; job freedom	Responsibility, achievement, and recognition
E. Making periodic reports directly available to the worker rather than to the supervisor	Internal recognition
F. Introducing new and more difficult tasks not previously handled	Growth and learning
G. Assigning people specific or specialised tasks, enabling them to become experts	Responsibility, growth, and advancement

Source: Herzberg (1968).

In a similar treatise on intrinsic outcomes and job satisfaction, Hackman and Oldham (1980) enumerate three basic conditions for promoting job satisfaction and the motivation of employees:
• Work should be meaningful for the doer.
• Doers should have responsibility for the results.
• Doers should get feedback on the results.
This approach suggests that it is the design of work and not the characteristics of the employee that have the greatest impact on employees' motivation. Hackman and Oldham identified five 'core job characteristics' that needed to be incorporated into job design to increase meaningfulness, responsibility, and feedback:
(1) Skill variety: the extent to which jobs draw on a range of different skills and abilities.
(2) Task identity: the extent to which a job requires the completion of a whole, identifiable piece of work.
(3) Task significance: the extent to which a job substantially affects the work or lives of others, either within or outside the company.

(4) Autonomy: the freedom, independence and discretion afforded to the job holder.

(5) Feedback: the degree to which the job holder receives information on their level of performance, effectiveness, etc.

Having identified the factors necessary for promoting satisfaction and intrinsic motivation, the next stage is to incorporate these characteristics in jobs through various job redesign strategies. Hackman and Oldham suggest five implementation strategies for increasing task variety, significance and identity and creating opportunities for greater autonomy and feedback:

1. **Form natural work groups**: Arrange tasks together to form an identifiable, meaningful cycle of work for employees, i.e. responsibility for a single product rather than small components.

2. **Combine tasks**: Group tasks together to form complete jobs.

3. **Establish client relationships**: Establish personal contact between employees and the customer or final user.

4. **Vertically load jobs** (see fig. 5.11): Many traditional approaches to job design separate planning and controlling (management functions) from executing (employee's function). Vertically loading jobs means integrating the planning, controlling and executing functions and giving the responsibility to employees (e.g. responsibility for materials, quality, deadlines, budgetary control).

5. **Open feedback channels**: Ensure maximum communication of job results (e.g. service standards, faults, wastage, market performance, costs).

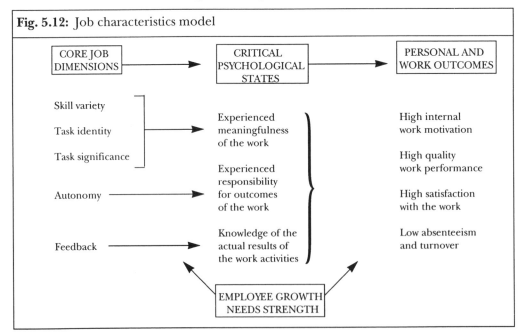

Fig. 5.12: Job characteristics model

Source: Hackman and Oldham (1980)

These changes would then have positive long-term benefits both for the company and the individual employee. Not all employees are expected to respond favourably to such redesign initiatives; only those with a strong desire for achievement, responsibility and autonomy will be motivated by increased intrinsic satisfaction and hence motivated to perform better. For others such change might be a source of anxiety and lead to resentment and opposition to changes in the work system.

The 'quality of work life' movement

Concern with the nature of work organisation and its potentially adverse effects on employees' motivation have caused many companies to take steps to ensure that job design incorporates the intrinsic needs of employees. This has been manifested in the emergence of the 'quality of work life' movement, aimed at eliminating many of the problems associated with traditional work systems, making work more meaningful for employees, and ensuring positive benefits for employers.

Apart from the job enrichment initiatives mentioned above, the QWL movement has also been characterised by steps to increase employees' influence and involvement in work organisation and job design. Again this challenges some traditional management assumptions about employees: it involves recognising that employees can make and want to make a positive contribution to organisational decision-making; it assumes that such involvement is valued by employees and that it results in increased commitment, responsibility, and performance.

Increased employee influence in work system design also addresses the issue of employee supervision as an aspect of the management role. If employees are to be involved in making decisions about the organisation of work and to be responsible for the subsequent execution of such decisions, much of the 'control' aspect is removed from the supervisory role. It necessitates a change in attitude to work-force management. Supervisors become less concerned with monitoring and controlling employees' performance and more involved in advising and facilitating employees in carrying out their jobs.

This approach requires high levels of commitment and trust from both management and employees. Management must feel confident that employees have the required competence and will use their greater levels of influence positively and to the benefit of the company. Employees must be happy that their increased commitment and sense of responsibility will not be abused or exploited by employers.

Various mechanisms are available for increasing the level of employees' participation in the design and operation of work systems. Possibly the best-known approach is quality circles. These are small groups of employees and managers who meet together regularly to consider means of improving quality, productivity, or other aspects of work organisation. They are seen as having played an important role in the success of Japanese companies and have been successfully applied in western economies, including Ireland.

There are numerous other participative and consultative mechanisms that may be established and can work effectively in the appropriate organisational environment. Creating such an environment has become an important concern for companies. Past experience in applying various techniques for improving employees' motivation and involvement have demonstrated that these operate best where there is a change in the overall corporate approach. The issue for senior management is how to create a corporate culture whose values, beliefs and practices establish an organisational environment within which employees are highly committed to and work towards the achievement of business goals.

High-performance work design

Recent commentators, such as Buchanan and McCalman (1989), suggest that the previously limited impact of job design theories is a weakness that needs to be remedied. Job design 'has tended to be regarded as an isolated management technique aimed at local organisational problems and at individual jobs rather than realising that it must form part of the whole company philosophy, through all levels, if it is to be really successful.' The motive behind high-performance job restructuring is the desire and the need to improve the overall competitive position of the company. 'The new strategic imperatives require new work organisation strategies' (Buchanan and McCalman 1989). This is clearly reflected in what is termed the high-performance literature (Vaill 1982; Perry 1984; Lawler 1986; Buchanan and McCalman 1989) and indeed the excellence literature (Peters and Waterman 1982; Moss Kanter 1983; Quinn Mills 1991). All contributors emphasise the need to empower employees in an attempt to make the company more effective. This is achieved through a group or team-based work structuring approach in an attempt to develop a highly skilled, flexible, co-ordinated, motivated work-force and a leaner, flatter, more responsive organisation. Mooney (1988) argues that this body of literature represents a basic reassessment of the value of a person's worth to the company, resulting in many of the core assumptions of the traditional model of organisation being jettisoned.

The high-performance concept, advocating an integrative approach to the structuring of work and the management of the human factor, has its roots in the individualistic and group approaches to job restructuring of the previous decades. There is a shift in language and emphasis away from job enlargement, job enrichment and quality circles towards a more all-inclusive approach, linking individual contributions, group performance and competitive advantage, which, according to Buchanan and McCalman (1989), afford to these traditional strategies a new acceptability. They argue, therefore, that the label 'high-performance' reflects a strategic shift in our approach to the management of human assets and may serve to encourage a wider understanding of the application of traditional job restructuring techniques, variations of which have enjoyed a renaissance in recent times in the light of the strategic imperative of the nineteen-nineties.

As a means of distinguishing high-performance work design from previous movements, Mooney (1988) draws on the differences between system and value changes within companies. As the concept implies, a system change simply means changes in methodology or ritual, he argues. Many of the previous job design schools were built on principle. On the other hand value changes, according to Mooney, run deeper, involving a refocus on fundamental business tenets. Thus, while the high-performance school involves system changes to accompany the new emphasis, they are driven and sustained by value changes dedicated to the creation of a revised understanding of and a new order in work-place relations.

THE CHOICE FOR COMPANIES

The issues of employee motivation, organisation and work design are related to broader corporate choices about the nature and role of the company. Employee performance will be influenced by a variety of factors relating to both the individual and the work context. The work environment is seen as particularly important. As information technology becomes more flexible in its application, employers have possibly greater scope for introducing changes in work organisation. Apart from the necessity for management commitment and positive beliefs about people at work, these changes have broader implications for other personnel management policy choices. In particular it is important that any changes in work organisation complement decisions taken in other personnel areas, especially in human resource planning, selection, employee development, employee relations, and remuneration.

Employee selection and development are particularly significant, since corporate choices on work and job design need to dovetail with work-force needs and motives. The degree of congruence between the work system, job design and employees' needs will be a major influence on overall employee relations.

6

Reward
Management

Reward management is a critical component of work-force management strategies, particularly in helping to attract and retain employees and also in influencing performance and behaviour at work. 'In the 1990s there is a recognition that compensation practices must be relevant to a world where there is unrelenting competition at every level and more awareness that labour productivity is a key dimension of making a profit' (Sanfilippo and Weigman 1991). Pay, incentives and benefits are of central importance to employees and companies alike, and subsumed under the label 'reward management' are a myriad of objectives relating to human resource plans and business strategies, high performance and continuous improvement, the satisfaction of individual needs and wants, cultural maintenance, and the promotion of teamwork. High or low pay, the nature of incentives and the range of fringe benefits in existence provide a valuable insight into the corporate approach to human resources. How the reward package is structured and applied will have a significant impact on employees' performance.

Rewards, therefore, are more than just direct wages and salaries paid. Additional direct payments in the form of bonuses and other incentives are used extensively. A growing cost for many employers is that of employee benefits, which represent indirect reward, because employees receive the value of the benefits without getting direct cash payments (Mathis and Jackson 1994). The reward package is often one of the largest costs faced by employers, many having labour costs as high as 50 per cent of all operating costs. Although the calculation of the total cost of a reward system is reasonably straightforward, the value derived by employers and employees is much more difficult to identify.

This chapter explores employee rewards. Pay, incentives and benefits as possible components of the reward package are defined, and the objectives and scope of reward management are examined. Issues in the design of an effective reward system are considered, and the meaning, purpose and methods of job evaluation are set out. The choice of pay, incentive and fringe benefits available to a company is presented and examined. Finally, the debate on pay as a motivator is briefly discussed.

THE SCOPE OF REWARD MANAGEMENT

As with the design of the work system, a company's reward system is a powerful indicator of its philosophy and approach to work-force management. Three aspects of the reward package are worth distinguishing at the outset: pay, incentives, and benefits. *Pay* refers to the basic wage or salary an employee receives. *Incentives* refer to the rewarding of an employee for effort that results in performance beyond normal expectations. *Benefits* refer to indirect rewards, such as VHI cover and pension entitlements.

In relation to incentive schemes that emphasise differential rewards based on performance as a means of increasing motivation, it is not axiomatic that higher motivation will follow. Such schemes have numerous drawbacks, in their design, operation, and negative side-effects. For this and other reasons many companies use standard pay rates that do not vary according to performance. In establishing a remuneration system a company must weigh the motivational aspects of a performance-related scheme against its drawbacks in the form of operational and other difficulties. It must be established in the context of the company's strategic needs and human resource profile and be part of the overall human resource approach, encompassing other motivational factors appropriate to the company and relevant to the work-force.

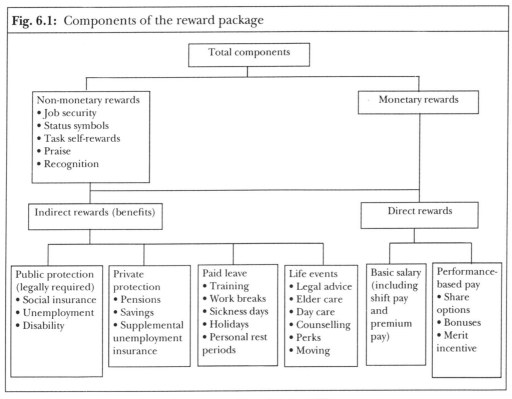

Fig. 6.1: Components of the reward package

Source: Adapted from Schuler (1995).

Schuler (1995) enumerates a number of core objectives underlying a company's reward package:

- **It serves to attract potential employees.** In conjunction with the company's human resource plan and its recruitment and selection efforts, the reward package and its mix of pay, incentives and benefits serve to attract suitable employees.

- **It assists in retaining good employees**. Unless the reward package is perceived as internally equitable and externally competitive, good employees may leave.
- **It should serve to motivate employees**. The reward package can assist in the quest for high performance by linking rewards to performance, for example by having an incentive element.
- **It contributes to human resource and strategic business plans**. A company may want to create a rewarding and supportive climate, or it may want to be an attractive place to work so that it can attract the best applicants. The reward package can assist with these plans and also further other organisational objectives, such as rapid growth, survival, or innovation.

The reward package therefore is important to the company because it helps to attract and retain employees and to influence performance and behaviour at work. Concomitantly it is important to employees because it provides the means of satisfying basic needs and may also allow them to satisfy less tangible desires for personal growth and satisfaction.

TOWARDS AN EFFECTIVE REWARD SYSTEM

Important considerations in the design of a company's reward system will be the relative emphasis on extrinsic versus intrinsic rewards, and the role of pay and whether it is contingent on individual performance and its compatibility with the company's business goals and other personnel policies. This latter issue is particularly significant, since the company's reward system must complement overall business objectives and other personnel policy choices.

Decisions on the company's cost structure and market strategy will influence the reward strategy. A high-volume low-cost strategy may constrain the company in its ability to provide expansive rewards. On the other hand a product innovation strategy may require a comprehensive reward system that attracts and retains high-calibre staff. The reward system must also 'fit' other personnel decisions. Recruitment and selection will provide a particular work-force profile, and the reward system must cater for their various needs. The reward system must also complement personnel practices in areas such as employee development and promotion.

The design and implementation of an effective reward system has proved a difficult task for many companies. Beer et al. (1985) suggest that many employees' grievances and criticisms of reward systems can mask more fundamental employee relations problems. Because extrinsic rewards are a tangible outcome of an employee's relationship with a company, they are an obvious target for discontent with the employment relationship. Dissatisfaction with elements of this relationship, such as the supervisory style or opportunities for personal development, may manifest themselves in dissatisfaction with aspects of the reward system. Consequently, companies experiencing problems with their reward system should examine decisions taken on other personnel policy issues, such as selection, employee relations, or work design, rather than making piecemeal changes to the rewards package.

Another potential problem concerns suggestions that pay should be contingent on individual performance. Support for contingent payment systems is based on the concept that it is fair and logical to reward individual employees differentially, based on some measure of performance. While this principle is rarely a source of contention, problems may arise in attempting to develop reliable and acceptable mechanisms for evaluating employees' performance. These include the limited criteria used (e.g. work study), inconsistency of application (e.g. performance appraisal), or bias or inequity in employee evaluations. A more fundamental issue may be resentment towards the exercise of managerial control by means of performance measurement and reward distribution, which is inherent in many 'reward-for-performance' approaches.

In attempting to develop an effective reward system, Lawler (1977) highlights the following essential characteristics:

(1) **Reward level:** The reward package must satisfy basic needs for survival, security, and self-development.

(2) **Individuality:** Apart form satisfying basic needs, the reward system must be flexible enough to meet the varying individual needs of the company's employees.

(3) **Internal equity:** Rewards must be seen as fair when compared with others in the company. Criteria for the allocation of rewards should be equitable and clear; these should be communicated and accepted by all parties and applied consistently throughout the company.

(4) **External equity:** Rewards must be seen as fair when compared with those offered for comparable work outside the company.

(5) **Trust:** Management and employees must believe in the reward system, employees accepting that certain rewards will be forthcoming when the relevant criteria are met, management trusting that employees will perform at an appropriate level in return for such rewards.

The objectives of an effective reward system therefore encapsulate the identification of prevailing market trends, balancing individual and group needs with organisational needs or constraints, ensuring fairness and equity, inducing and rewarding higher levels of performance, and working within the law.

In her study of motivation and personnel practices in the civil service, Blennerhassett (1983) found that the reward system satisfied basic needs for a reasonable standard of living (through adequate salaries) and security (through employment tenure guarantees and a good pension plan). On the issue of individuality the system fared less well. The range of rewards was considered inadequate to meet staff needs. It was also felt that the criteria for distributing rewards were relatively inflexible and did not adequately reflect individual performance. Incremental salary scales and other procedures militated against the use of financial or other extrinsic rewards for motivating employees. Criteria for the distribution of other rewards, such as promotion or 'nicer' jobs, were unclear, and there was little evidence that good performers were rewarded better than poor performers. On internal equity the evaluation depended on whether seniority is accepted as an equitable basis for distributing rewards. Decisions on the distribution of key rewards such as pay and promotion were based on seniority, with little attempt made to relate such decisions to any measure of individual performance. The system rated highly on external equity, as measured by the ability of the civil service to attract and retain staff.

In the private sector one might expect greater variations in the design of reward systems and increased flexibility in the criteria applied in the distribution of rewards. Since pay is a key factor influencing both where and how people work, any discussion of extrinsic rewards must give due consideration to its important role in work-force management.

121

DETERMINING THE RELATIVE VALUE OF JOBS

Of primary importance is the establishment of basic pay levels for various jobs. Here again the company must be aware of the need to establish pay equity. This initially applies to external comparisons with pay levels in other companies: comparable pay rates influence a company's ability to attract and retain employees. Suitable comparable companies should be chosen to maintain pay competitiveness while keeping wage costs at reasonable levels. Pay levels will be influenced by factors in the broader business environment, such as:

(1) **Economic climate:** Here factors such as levels of inflation, disposable income and industrial activity will exert both direct and indirect influences on payment levels by affecting employment levels, demand, consumer price indices, etc.

(2) **Labour market:** The state of the labour market will be influenced by general economic factors. It will also depend on labour supply and demand for certain skills and on local factors such as the level of company closures, emigration, etc. Information on local and national pay rates can be obtained through wage surveys of comparable companies.

(3) **Government policy:** The Government will exert considerable influence on pay levels, both indirectly (fiscal policy) and directly through what it pays its own employees (state and state-sponsored sector), national pay guidelines, minimum pay levels (Joint Labour Committees), and legislation (e.g. equal pay).

(4) **Trade unions:** Through collective bargaining, trade unions will seek to improve or at least maintain their members' earning levels. Such claims will generally be based on comparability, differentials, and cost-of-living increases. They will also depend on factors relating to the company itself. Managerial policy and style in managing employees will affect approaches to the supervision, development and payment of employees. The company's competitive position will influence its ability to reward employees. These factors help determine the company's position as a low, high or average payer, which in turn will influence the choice of comparable companies for pay purposes, trade union approaches, and employees' expectations.

Companies must also strive to maintain internal equity in determining differential pay rates for various jobs. The establishment of an internal pay structure involves deciding the relative value of jobs within a company and results in the creation of a hierarchy of job grades. The perceived equity of internal job grades will influence employees' performance and commitment. Grading can equally be a source of grievance and conflict.

Establishing fair and consistent pay rates and differentials between jobs is an important step in developing an effective reward system. Management will want to ensure that jobs that contribute most to the company are rewarded appropriately. They will also be keen to ensure that conflict over pay and job grading is kept to a minimum by establishing an equitable and consistent system for grading jobs and determining differentials. Aspirations for pay equity can be partially satisfied by ensuring that pay rates are competitive in comparison with other companies. Before this, however, the company should establish an acceptable mechanism for internally grading and evaluating jobs.

The initial stage in establishing the relative worth of jobs is an analysis of job content. This will often be achieved through systematic job analysis, which should provide detailed information on the duties, demands, responsibilities and skills of the various jobs in the company. Such information may then be used to establish the company's grading structure and to decide related pay levels through some method of job evaluation.

APPROACHES TO JOB EVALUATION

Job evaluation is often described as being concerned solely with the techniques used to establish the comparative worth of jobs within a company, but it is also, according to Armstrong and Baron (1995), about making decisions on what people should be paid for the work they do. We suggest that it is a technique for determining the relative worth of jobs within a company so that differential rewards may be given to jobs of different worth. It operates by examining job content and placing jobs in a hierarchy according to their contribution to the attainment of corporate objectives. Fowler (1996) notes that

> selecting the right job evaluation system is crucial if the resulting pay frameworks are to be consistent with an organisation's structure, style and values. There is no one best scheme. Each organisation needs to assess its own requirements and set these against the range of available methods.

Armstrong and Baron (1995) cite the following key purposes of job evaluation:

- to provide a rational basis for the design and maintenance of an equitable and defensible pay structure;
- to help in the management of the relativities existing between jobs within the company;
- to enable consistent decisions to be made on grading and rates of pay;
- to establish the extent to which there is comparable worth between jobs so that equal pay can be provided for work of equal value.

Job evaluation schemes are commonly grouped into non-analytical schemes and analytical schemes. *Non-analytical* schemes involve the making of comparisons between whole jobs, without analysing their constituent parts or elements. Among the main schemes here are job ranking, job classification, and paired comparison. *Analytical* schemes involve jobs being broken down into a number of critical factors, which are then analysed and compared, using a quantitative measure. Among the main analytical methods are points rating, the Hay method, and more recently competence-based job evaluation.

We now turn to a description of the non-analytical and analytical schemes mentioned.

Job ranking

Ranking is the simplest method of job evaluation and, according to Armstrong and Baron (1995), 'is almost intuitive.' It aims to judge each job as a whole and determine its place in a job hierarchy by comparing one job with another and arranging them in perceived order of importance, their difficulty, or their value to the company. No attempt is made to quantify judgments. A ranking table is then drawn up, and the jobs thus ranked are arranged into grades. Pay levels are then agreed for each grade. Sometimes a single factor, such as skill, is used; alternatively a list of factors is used, such as skill, responsibility, complexity, physical demands, etc.

Armstrong and Baron (1995) list the following advantages and disadvantages of job ranking:

Advantages:

- It is in accord with how people instinctively value jobs.
- It is simple and easily understood.
- It is quick and cheap to implement, as long as agreement can be reached on the rank order of the jobs without too much argument.
- It is a way of checking the results of more sophisticated methods to indicate the extent to which the hierarchies produced are felt to be fair—but this may simply reproduce the existing hierarchy and fail to eliminate the sex bias.

Disadvantages:

- There are no defined standards for judging relative worth—and therefore no rationale for defending the rank order: it is simply a matter of opinion.
- Ranking is not acceptable as a method of determining comparable worth in equal-value cases.
- Evaluators need an overall knowledge of every job to be evaluated, and ranking may be more difficult when a large number of jobs are under consideration.
- It may be difficult, if not impossible, to produce a fair ranking for jobs in widely different functions where the demands made on them vary significantly.
- The division of the rank order into grades is likely to be somewhat arbitrary.

Overall, job ranking as a method of job evaluation is most useful for small companies with a limited range of jobs to evaluate.

Job classification

This method is more complex than job ranking, in that classes or grades are established and the jobs are then placed into the grades. It begins, therefore, not by ranking jobs but by agreeing a grading structure. At the beginning the number of grades and the particular criteria for these grades are agreed, so that for each grade there is a broad description of its key characteristics. The number of grades is usually limited to between four and eight, between each of which there are clear differences in the demands made by any job within its appropriate grade. In establishing the grades, 'benchmark' jobs, considered to be particularly characteristic of each grade, are chosen, and, using detailed job descriptions, all other jobs are evaluated by comparison with both the benchmark job and the criteria for each grade. Evaluated jobs are then placed in their appropriate grades.

The advantages of job classification include

- its simplicity and the ease with which it can be understood;
- greater objectivity than job ranking;
- the fact that standards for making grading decisions are provided in the form of the grade definitions.

There are also significant disadvantages:

- The basis of the job evaluation is either one factor or an intuitive summary of many factors.
- It is difficult to apply with more complex jobs, where duties and skills do not fit neatly into cne grade but overlap with other grades.
- It may not be able to cater for a wide range of jobs or for senior jobs, where grade descriptions have to be very general.
- Because it is not an analytical system it is not effective as a means of establishing comparable worth and is unacceptable in equal-value cases.

Paired comparison

More sophisticated than the previous two methods, the paired-comparison approach is based on the premise that it is more reasonable to compare one job with another than to consider a larger number of jobs together. The method requires the comparison of each job individually with every other job, until one builds up a rank order of jobs. When a job is deemed to be of higher worth than the one it is being compared with it is awarded two points; if it is deemed to be of equal worth it receives one point; and if it is found to be of less worth it receives no points. The points are then totalled for each job and a rank order is produced.

The main advantage of this approach is that it is easier to compare one job with another at a time, which results in greater consistency. The main disadvantages are that it relies on whole-job ranking, which is difficult, and there is a limit to the number of jobs that can be ranked.

Points rating

Points rating is a widely used method of job evaluation. It involves breaking down each job into a number of component job factors and then analysing these separately defined factors, which are assumed to be common to all jobs. It is based on the assumption that the degree to which differences in the job factors arise will accurately reflect the actual difference between total jobs. The selection of the job factors is critical. Benge (1944), who first promoted the method, suggested that it should be limited to the following five factors, which he believed were the universal factors found in all jobs: skill requirements; mental requirements; physical requirements; responsibility; and working conditions. Each of these job factors can then be broken down into a number of sub-factors. The sub-factors of responsibility, for example, might well include financial, quality, equipment and materials, training, and other. Once the factors and sub-factors have been agreed, point values are then allocated (see Table 6.1).

Table 6.1: Points rating job evaluation

			LEVEL		
	1	2	3	4	Total
Factor	Minimum	Low	Moderate	High	points
Responsibility					
(a) Financial	10	20	30	40	
(b) Quality	10	20	30	40	
(c) Equipment	10	20	30	40	
(d) Training	10	20	30	40	
(e) Other	10	20	30	40	200
Working conditions					
(a) Hazardous	15	30	45	60	
(b) Unpleasant	10	20	30	40	100

Source: Gunnigle and Flood (1990)

In the example shown here, responsibility is twice as important as working conditions, while in relation to working conditions, hazardous conditions get more points than those that are simply rated as unpleasant. The various jobs can then be evaluated and placed in their appropriate grades. We suggest that this can be done by either taking one factor and evaluating its significance in all jobs under consideration or taking each job and evaluating it in terms of all job factors. The former approach is recommended, as it concentrates on the comparable worth of jobs in terms of a specific factor, and this information can be brought together at the end to give a total picture of relative job worth.

Among the advantages of this system are:

- It is systematic and analytical, in the sense that it compares jobs on a factor-by-factor basis.
- The standards of comparison are clearly defined.

Frequently cited disadvantages include the following:

- It is complex and difficult to understand.
- It can be time-consuming and expensive.
- Although analytical, it still relies on a good deal of subjective judgment.
- It may be impossible to put numerical values on different aspects of jobs, since skills are not always quantifiable in this way, particularly when comparing the skills required in jobs of often disparate demands and responsibilities.

Fig. 6.2: Primary factors in the Hay method

PROBLEM-SOLVING (MENTAL ACTIVITY)	KNOW-HOW	ACCOUNTABILITY

The amount of original, self-starting thought required by the job for analysis, evaluation, creation, reasoning, and arriving at conclusions.
    Problem-solving has two dimensions:
• The degree of freedom with which the thinking process is used to achieve job objectives without the guidance of standards, precedents, or direction from others.
• The type of mental activity involved; the complexity, abstractness or originality of thought required.
    Problem-solving is expressed as a percentage of know-how, for the obvious reason that people think with what they know. The percentage judged to be correct for a job is applied to the know-how point value; the result is the point value given to problem-solving.
	The total of all knowledge and skills, however acquired, needed for satisfactory job performance (evaluates the job, not the person).
	Know-how has three dimensions:
	• The amount of practical, specialised or technical knowledge required.
	• Breadth of management, or the ability to make many activities and functions work well together; the job of company president, for example, has greater breadth than that of a department supervisor.
	• Requirement for skill in motivating people.
	    Using a chart, a number can be assigned to the level of know-how needed in a job. This number—or point value—indicates the relative importance of know-how in the job being evaluated.
		The measured effect of the job on company goals.
		    Accountability has three dimensions:
		• Freedom to act, or the relative presence of personal or procedural control and guidance, determined by answering the question, 'How much freedom has the job holder to act independently?'—for example, a plant manager has more freedom than a supervisor under his or her control.
		• Dollar magnitude, a measure of the sales, budget, value of purchases, value added or any other significant annual money figure related to the job.
		• Impact of the job on dollar magnitude, a determination of whether the job has a primary effect on final results or has instead a sharing, contributory or remote effect.
		    Accountability is given a point value independent of the other two factors.

Note: The total evaluation of any job is arrived at by adding the points for problem-solving, know-how, and accountability. The points are not shown here.

Source: Shuler (1995).

126

Hay method

The Hay method (or Hay plan) is one of the most widely used job evaluation methods in the world and is generally classified as a points-factor rating. Traditionally associated with managerial and professional jobs, it is becoming more widely used for technical, clerical and other positions. The method relies on three primary factors, namely know-how, problem-solving, and accountability (see fig. 6.2). It combines aspects of points rating and factor comparison. Point values are established for each job, using the factors set out in the table, and jobs are compared with one another on each factor.

Points-factor schemes of this kind are popular because people generally feel that they work. Among the frequently quoted advantages are:

- the wide acceptance of the approach;
- the fact that evaluators are forced to consider a range of factors and therefore avoid oversimplification;
- a higher level of objectivity than other approaches;
- the fact that many external comparisons are available, because of the widespread adoption of the method.

Disadvantages include

- the degree of complexity;
- the fact that because of its standardised nature it may not reflect a company's real needs;
- the fact that despite the impression of objectivity, human judgment is required in the process.

Fig. 6.3: Comparison of conventional job evaluation and competence-based job evaluation

COMPONENT	SKILL-BASED EVALUATION	JOB-BASED EVALUATION
1. Determination of job worth	Tied to evaluation of skill blocks	Tied to evaluation of total job
2. Pricing	Difficult because overall pay system is tied to market	Easier, because wages are tied to labour market
3. Pay ranges	Extremely broad: one pay range for entire cluster of skills	Variable, depending on type of job and pay grade width
4. Evaluation of performance	Competence tests	Performance appraisal ratings
5. Salary increases	Tied to skill acquisition as measured by competence testing	Tied to seniority, performance appraisal ratings, or actual output
6. Role of training	Essential to attain job flexibility and pay increases for all employees	Necessitated by need rather than desire
7. Advancement opportunities	Greater opportunities: anyone who passes competence test advances	Fewer opportunities: no advancement unless there is a job opening
8. Effect of job change	Pay remains constant unless skill proficiency increases	Pay changed immediately to level associated with new job
9. Pay administration	Difficult, because many aspects of pay plan (training, certification) demand attention	Contingent on complexity of job evaluation and pay allocation plan

Source: Adapted from Shuler (1995, 398).

Competence-based job evaluation

Variously referred to as competence-based, skill-based, or knowledge-based, this is a system whose emphasis is on an evaluation of the person who performs the job and their competence and performance abilities rather than on the job title or grade. For example, if the previously described job evaluation methods had at their core the principle of 'paying for the job,' competence-based evaluation has as its central tenet 'paying for the person.' Armstrong and Baron (1995) argue that competence-based job evaluation is growing in importance because much greater significance is now attached to knowledge work, and more emphasis is being placed on flexibility, multi-skilling individual and team autonomy, and empowerment.

Armstrong and Baron (1995) highlight three approaches to developing competence-based job evaluation:

1. Take an existing analytical scheme and modify the factor plan to make it more competence-related by reference to an existing competence framework.
2. Take existing competence frameworks and adapt them to develop a competence-based scheme.
3. Conduct a special analysis of generic and job-specific abilities to produce a competence framework and develop a scheme from this analysis.

Among some of the abilities likely to be examined or considered in any of these approaches are interpersonal skills, communication skills, reasoning and critical thinking ability, technical knowledge, business knowledge, decision-making ability, team working and leadership skills, resource management capabilities, and planning, organising and problem-solving abilities.

The advantages of competence-based job evaluation include the following:

- It provides a framework for relevant, continuing employee development.
- It can assist in making the company more flexible through an ever-expanding focused skill base.
- There is a clear focus on the person.

The following are among the disadvantages often cited:

- The competence movement has been accused of being vague in its terminology.
- It can be as complex and difficult as any other form of job evaluation.
- It can lead to too much emphasis being placed on the skills and knowledge the person brings to the job and not enough on the output from that job.

CRITICISMS OF JOB EVALUATION

Fowler (1996) suggests that

> job evaluation, once a highly regarded management tool, has come under fire in recent times. Its critics say that because it assesses the job rather than the job holder, it fails to recognise the contribution of the individual. It has also been argued that the detailed job descriptions involved in some schemes serve to inhibit flexibility.

Edwards, Ewen and O'Neal (1995) enumerate a number of weaknesses associated with traditional job evaluation. They suggest that it leads to an inappropriate focus on promotion, where people are led to believe that a job is more important than the person in the job. Secondly, they emphasise its inability to reward knowledge workers, on the basis that traditional job-based pay systems, which reward position in the hierarchy, do not work well for those whose performance is based on specialised applied learning rather than on general skills. Thirdly, they point to its inability to keep pace with high-speed organisational changes and emergent employee roles.

The potential for error in human judgments that forms a central part of the process is perhaps one of its greatest drawbacks. Despite some of the obvious benefits of job evaluation, it is not infallible. It attempts to create a consistent and equitable system for grading jobs; however, it depends on the judgment of people with experience and training, requiring them to make decisions in a planned and systematic way, and the results do not guarantee total accuracy.

Choosing and introducing the job evaluation scheme

The introduction of job evaluation will have a tremendous impact on company pay structures and employee relations generally. Therefore, any decisions should only be taken after careful deliberation. Fowler (1996) suggests that a job evaluation scheme needs to be determined primarily by setting the characteristics of different methods against the company's circumstances and objectives. In this respect he suggests that the following questions are useful:

1. Is the principal aim to meet the requirements of equal pay legislation?
2. How many different jobs are there to be evaluated?
3. How complex is the pay structure?
4. What are the factors or characteristics to which the company wishes to allocate monetary value within the pay structure?
5. Is the scheme intended for making market comparisons?
6. Is there an advantage in using a computerised system?

The introduction of job evaluation can be a complex process, and it is often useful to seek expert advice and guidance in the early stages. Such an expert would usually be responsible for advising on the technical aspects of the scheme and assisting with decisions on the type of scheme to use, the establishment and composition of overseeing committees, the training of job analysts, and communicating the details of the scheme to all concerned.

In relation to participation they suggest that at all stages in the process the staff should be kept adequately informed. It is vital that those who will be most directly affected by the scheme should know its objectives, its content, and how it will operate. Middle management and supervisors are critical here: they will play a vital role in implementing the scheme, and it is imperative that they understand it and appreciate their role in its operation.

The reward package: pay, incentives, fringe benefits

Determining the worth of a job and the setting down of basic pay levels are critical aspects of the process of establishing a pay system. Choosing the actual payment system is the other critical aspect.

The choice of reward system is an important consideration for companies. It will partially reflect the corporate approach to human resource management and will affect such areas as employee relations, supervisory style, and employee motivation. The particular package offered will be determined by a variety of factors related to the company, the general business environment, and the work-force.

In relation to choices of payment schemes, Mooney (1980) feels that these are related to characteristics of the company and the product. In particular he identifies the significance of the following elements:

(1) **Company ownership:** A continuing influx of foreign companies will increase the use of performance-related bonus schemes.

(2) **Size:** Performance-related schemes are more common in larger companies, while small firms tend to rely on flat rates only.

(3) **Technical system:** Companies operating large batch production techniques—which are common in Ireland—are more likely to use performance-related payment systems.

(4) **Labour costs:** Mooney feels this is the most important factor influencing the choice of payment system. Flat-rate-only or company-wide schemes dominate in capital-intensive companies, while individual or group incentive schemes are popular in companies with high labour costs.

Overall, as with other aspects of personnel management, the corporate approach to rewards should complement the company's strategic business goals, personnel policy, and other personnel activities.

There are numerous options in the type of pay and incentive and benefits package a company might adopt. The more common types of payment systems are discussed below. Benefits available in Ireland are then considered.

Flat rate systems

FLAT RATE ONLY

A traditional approach to reward, flat rate pay schemes pay a person for time on the job, and no incentive is provided for actual performance. They are popular because of their simplicity and ease of administration. They are particularly useful for managerial and administrative jobs, where specific performance criteria are difficult to establish. They help attract employees to the company, but their motivational potential in encouraging good performance is thought to be limited.

In Mooney's (1980) study of wage payment systems in Ireland he found the flat rate system by far the most popular, particularly for indirect employees. However, he also found that the use of approaches that combine the flat rate with incentive payments based on some measure of performance was on the increase.

ANNUAL HOURS CONTRACT

As with the flat-rate-only system, this is based on the premise that one is paid for the time spent on the job. However, in this instance working time is organised on an annual rather than a weekly basis; the annual hours contract will therefore specify the number of hours to be worked in the year rather than the week. Originally developed in Scandinavia, this system, according to O'Sullivan (1996), is increasingly being regarded in Ireland as an important alternative to the standard 39-hour week plus overtime.

O'Sullivan cites a number of advantages to be gained from this approach. From the company's perspective there will often be an improvement in unit costs and productivity, the elimination of large-scale overtime, a closer match between output and demand, and a reduction in absenteeism. From the employee's perspective the benefits include improved basic pay, stability of earnings, and increased leisure time. The disadvantages cited by O'Sullivan include the necessity to recoup money owing to the company if an employee leaves during the year and the reorganisation and cultural and value changes that are necessary with this approach.

Fig. 6.4: Methods of calculating annual hours contract

There are two ways of calculating the contract, which produce the same result:

(1) Standard working week formula

Calendar year:	52.18 weeks (inc. leap year)
Annual leave:	4 weeks
Public holidays:	1.8 weeks
Average working week:	46.38 weeks × 39 hours
Annual hours:	1,808.82 (net basic working hours)

(2) Annual working formula

In a complete calendar year there are an average of 365.25 days, which comprise 8,766 hours.

Example:

Employee works 39 hours a week.

$$\frac{39 \times 365.25}{7} = 2,035 \text{ hours a year}$$

Less annual and public holidays:	2,035
20 days' annual leave:	7.8 × (20)
9 public holidays:	7.8 × (9)
	– 226.2
Employee available to work:	1,808.8 hours per year

Source: O'Sullivan (1996).

INCENTIVE SYSTEMS

The use of incentives is not a new phenomenon, performance-related pay (PRP) schemes having formed a significant part of the traditional remuneration package in many companies; indeed Roots (1988) traces their use to Biblical times. McBeath and Rands (1989) define performance-related pay as 'an intention to pay distinctly more to reward highly effective job performance than you are willing to pay for good solid performance,' the objective being to develop a productive, efficient, effective company (Hoevemeyer 1989).

Performance-based incentive schemes fulfil a number of functions, among the principal ones being:

- to ensure an adequate supply of skilled and trained employees in response to fluctuating labour demands; while choice is more repressed in turbulent economic circumstances, people making an employment decision will look not only at the terms of employment but also at the total remuneration package, including variable and incentive pay;
- to elicit from employees, both individually and collectively, performance that reinforces the strategic direction of the company; one of the main underlying assumptions therefore is that pay has the potential to motivate.

FLAT RATE PLUS INDIVIDUAL PRP

Many commentators suggest that the individual rewarding of performance has a strong motivational impact. Payment is related to the individual employee's contribution; the required performance levels and related financial rewards are specified, and these are achievable immediately after these performance criteria have been met.

Despite the popularity that individual PRP schemes have achieved in the recent past, according to Appelbaum and Shapiro (1991) they have a number of potential flaws. Firstly, they result in a preoccupation with the task at hand and do not relate individual performance to the larger company objectives. Secondly, they work against creating a climate of openness, trust, joint problem-solving, and commitment to organisational problem-solving. Thirdly, they can divide the work-force into those supporting the plan and those not in favour, which can create adversarial relationships.

FLAT RATE PLUS GROUP OR TEAM-BASED PRP

The greatest problem associated with individual PRP schemes is therefore not that they will not work but rather that they will focus the attention and effort in a direction that does not necessarily aid in the achievement of the strategic goals of the company. In recognition of these and related problems, many companies have turned to group or team bonus schemes.

Payment systems that pay a flat rate plus an incentive based on group, team or sectional performance are used where it is difficult to measure individual performance or to avoid some of the harmful side-effects of individual-based schemes while providing some incentive that is related to a measure of performance. Daley (1991) defines group bonus schemes as 'the application of payment by results schemes to a group or team where the bonus payments are divided among team members on a pre-agreed basis.' As with individual schemes, there is a wide range of schemes from which a company can choose, but Ost (1990) feels that all incentives based on group or team work are subject to a number of guiding premises:

1. They always have one or more explicitly stated unit or firm-level performance goals that can only be achieved through teamwork.
2. A team-based incentive system always contains a reward component that is contingent on the successful achievement of those goals.
3. The reward must be perceived by the employee as resulting from contributions he or she has made.
4. The reward must be perceived as a fair reward.
5. The behaviour and the rewards offered must clearly signal what is meant by good performance.

PIECEWORK

This involves payment solely by performance. While it remains popular in specific areas (e.g. for seasonal work in agriculture and for outworkers), it is unacceptable to many employees, since it provides no guarantee of a minimum income to satisfy basic requirements for both individual and social well-being.

GAIN-SHARING SCHEMES

These systems incorporate arrangements that reward employees for improvements in corporate performance through profit sharing, share ownership, or some other reward mechanism. Gain-sharing schemes differ from more traditional profit-sharing arrangements in that they link rewards based on corporate performance to changes in managerial policy and style that incorporate greater employee influence, involvement, and participation.

The direct effects of such schemes on employee motivation are believed to be poor, because of the weak relationship with individual performance and the lack of immediacy. However, they are seen as having important long-term benefits in increasing employees' participation, awareness, and commitment.

Most gain-sharing schemes involve either profit sharing or employee share ownership. Profit sharing is a scheme under which employees, in addition to their normal remuneration, receive a proportion of the profits of the business. Profit sharing may take a number of forms, and it is largely at the discretion of the employer to decide to what measure of profit the incentive should be tied, what percentage should be allocated, and how it should be administered.

Employee share ownership schemes involve the allocation of company shares to employees according to an agreed formula. Interest in Ireland in employee share ownership schemes has traditionally been relatively low (Long 1988). The growth, small though it has been, is rooted in the Finance Acts, 1982–84, which were driven by Government commitment to 'ensuring the success and efficiency of Irish industry and the prosperity and security of Irish workers for the future.' More recent changes, however, have served to further undermine the already narrow base of share ownership in Ireland when the then Minister for Finance, Bertie Ahern, removed tax incentives for employee share schemes. While resultant action was a dilution rather than removal, employees and employers may be more reluctant to adopt such schemes in what could be described as an atmosphere of uncertainty.

Gain-sharing arrangements incorporating either profit or equity sharing are generally linked to organisational attempts to increase employee involvement and commitment. Armstrong and Murlis (1988) enumerate a number of objectives underlying such schemes:

* to encourage employees to identify themselves more closely with the company by developing a common concern for its progress;
* to stimulate a greater interest among employees in the affairs of the company as a whole;
* to encourage better co-operation between the management and employees;
* to recognise that employees have a moral right to share in the profits they helped to produce;
* to demonstrate in practical terms the good will of the company to its employees;
* to reward success in businesses where profitability is cyclical.

Such schemes have become particularly popular in Britain and the United States and have been linked to corporate success on such criteria as market share, profitability, and quality.

MERIT RATING

In recent years there has been an increasing trend towards relating pay more closely to performance. Fowler (1988) suggests that a number of companies are moving towards the evaluation of employees' performance against specified objectives and using this as a basis for deciding on merit awards. He also notes the extension of performance-related pay systems into the public sector, the use of performance appraisal for all grades of employees, and attempts to move away from regular increments to increases based on some evaluation of individual performance.

Bowey and Thorpe (1986) suggest that there is a positive correlation between variable individual incentive payments and improvements in costs and quality. However, they also point to potentially adverse effects on attitudes to work and employee relations. A continuing problem with merit-based pay is finding an acceptable mechanism for equitably and consistently assessing performance; otherwise merit-based payments can lead to problems as a result of resentment at managerial control or inequity or inconsistency in performance evaluation. An important factor seems to be the extent of employee involvement, with schemes that require extensive consultation having a greater chances of success. Murlis (1985) identifies six factors that underpin successful merit-based reward systems:

- an equitable mechanism for performance measurement incorporating performance appraisal;
- consistency of rewards among individual employees;
- managerial flexibility in linking reward decisions to organisational needs to attract and retain employees;
- simplicity in understanding and application;
- good basic reward package;
- clearly defined employee development policy.

It is important that management clearly outline the main performance criteria and reward employees accordingly. Employees' acceptance of merit-based pay will depend on perceived equity in performance evaluation. It demands a climate of trust and fairness—the main responsibility for whose development lies with management.

Trade unions are often opposed to payments based on individual performance, preferring collective increases achieved through management-union negotiations. Grafton (1988) feels that schemes that operate merit increases in addition to general salary awards are less likely to cause opposition by employees, as they operate as a discretionary element that does not cut across the collective bargaining role of the trade union. In an appropriate organisational climate, merit-based pay can be effectively used to augment negotiated pay and benefit increases and stimulate improved employee and organisational performance.

COMPETENCE OR SKILL-BASED PAY

The concept of skill-based pay is not particularly new. According to O'Neill and Lander (1994), while relatively limited in application it has been used for years under names such as pay for knowledge, competence pay, pay for skills, and multi-skilled pay. While there may be slight technical differences in these terms, they are generally used interchangeably.

Skill-based pay is a payment system in which pay progression is linked to the number, kind and depth of skill that people develop and use. Armstrong (1995) emphasises the fact that it involves paying for the horizontal acquisition of the skills required to undertake a wider range of tasks, or for the vertical development of the skills needed to operate it at a higher level, or the further development of existing skills. In this way competence or skill-based pay is directly linked to competence or skilled-based job evaluation, described earlier. In its operation there will usually be a basic job rate for the minimum level of skill. Above this level, people will be paid for new skills acquired that assist them in performing their jobs as individuals or members of a team.

O'Neill and Lander (1994) cite four principal reasons for the increasing adoption of skill-based pay:

- the need to develop and maintain productive efficiency through increased output,

often combined with a smaller work-force and fewer levels of supervision;
- the need to make more flexible use of the existing work-force to cover absenteeism, turnover, and production bottlenecks;
- the need to support new technologies, such as computer-aided manufacturing, and new value systems, such as total quality management;
- the need to build higher levels of involvement and commitment and increased teamwork and to provide more enriched jobs that provide greater reward opportunities for employees.

In relation to the spread of incentive schemes, Ireland has in recent years seen a number of shifts in the application of such schemes as a cure for low productivity. This change has been from a preoccupation with the productivity bargaining of the nineteen-sixties, measured day work in the seventies (exorbitant levels of tax in the seventies, according to Clarke (1989), rendered bonuses and merit rewards ineffectual as a cure for low productivity), to PRP in the eighties (Grafton 1988). As the operating environment became ever more complex during the eighties, companies turned increasingly to performance appraisal and merit pay (Randell 1989). Table 6.2 provides some evidence of the increased popularity of incentive schemes in many Irish companies.

Table 6.2: Use of incentive schemes in Ireland

	Managerial	Prof./tech.	Clerical	Manual
Employee share options	20.4	11.9	8.2	7.8
Profit sharing	15.2	11.5	10	89
Group bonus scheme	13	11.5	9.7	12.6
Individual bonus/commission	30.1	22.2	13.8	11.5
Merit/performance-related pay	46.1	39	28.6	13.4

Source: University of Limerick (1992).

The growth of incentive schemes has been linked to the inexorable trend towards relating pay more closely to performance. However, the take-up of incentive schemes in Ireland is correlated with company ownership: American-owned companies on the whole appear far more likely to employ incentives than others, particularly Irish indigenous companies, which demonstrate a low take-up among the range of incentives (Gunnigle et al. 1994).

It is evident that incentive schemes can take a number of forms, and the question facing most companies is not which type of incentive scheme to pick but rather which package or combination of methods will be most successful in fulfilling the company's strategic goals. In the implementing of incentive schemes, Balkin and Gomez-Mejia (1987) emphasise a number of issues that must be addressed:

(*a*) the number of different forms to offer;
(*b*) the relative importance of each form;
(*c*) the proportion of the work-force to which each form may be applicable.

The responses to these questions will be determined by the objectives of the incentive system itself and whether the company sees enhanced performance, cost containment or employee retention as the overriding objective of the incentive system. It must be realised, however, that while incentive schemes represent a potentially effective tool,

135

they are not a panacea for all organisational ills. Incentive schemes will only fulfil their true potential if existing barriers to individual, group or organisational effectiveness have been removed. Such schemes do not represent a mechanism for compensating for wage differentials, nor for overcoming inadequacies in the production system.

Fringe benefits

In general, fringe benefits (both statutory and voluntary) are estimated to constitute an additional 25 to 30 per cent of the value of basic weekly pay for manual grades; for clerical, administrative and managerial categories a figure of 15 to 35 per cent should be added. However, the relative addition is primarily related to the level of fringe benefits voluntarily agreed at company level, particularly items such as company cars, pensions, health and insurance cover, and sickness benefit, and can therefore vary considerably between companies.

Fringe benefits are normally the result of voluntary agreements between employees (or their representatives) and the management. Significant differences also exist between blue and white-collar workers. Some general guidelines on the nature of fringe benefits in Irish companies are outlined below.

MATERNITY LEAVE

Female employees are entitled to a minimum of fourteen weeks' unpaid maternity leave in accordance with the Maternity (Protection of Employees) Act, 1981, and the Worker Protection (Regular Part-Time Employees) Act, 1991. Such employees are also entitled to unpaid time off for ante-natal and post-natal care. Employees on maternity leave are paid an allowance under the terms of the social welfare legislation. (For a more detailed discussion see chapter 13 on labour legislation.)

CHILD CARE FACILITIES

A small number of Irish companies provide child care facilities for staff. At present there are about fifty state-financed nurseries sponsored by health boards, mostly for families with special needs. There are nurseries in four state-sponsored companies in Dublin and approximately ten in third-level educational institutions.

CAREER BREAKS

Provision for career breaks is rare in Irish private-sector companies; such schemes are, however, becoming increasingly widespread in the public sector. These provide for unpaid leave up to a maximum of three years. Where schemes exist in the private sector they are normally shorter, generally one to two years.

HOLIDAYS

The great majority of companies provide annual leave entitlements greater than the statutory minimum of fifteen days a year. This can vary from eighteen to twenty-three days, the average being twenty days. Legislation provides for eight public holidays a year; some companies also grant Good Friday, which is not a public holiday, as a day off.

ADDITIONAL HOLIDAY PAY AND BONUSES

Practice varies enormously on this issue. However, many larger private-sector companies make such payments. These are typically in the form of either additional holiday pay (from one to several weeks' pay), end-of-year or Christmas bonus (one to several weeks' pay), and discretionary payment or gifts for special occasions (such as long service or marriage).

MANAGERIAL INCENTIVE SCHEMES

A large number of companies operate incentive bonus schemes for managerial grades. However, there are considerable variations in the level of payment and the grades involved. Typical criteria for incentive payments include company performance (particularly profitability), sales, and output.

SICKNESS PAY

There is no legal obligation on companies to provide sickness pay to employees. However, a large number of companies provide some kind of sickness pay during defined periods of absence from work because of illness or injury. A survey carried out by the Federation of Irish Employers in 1990 found that of the 515 companies questioned, 351 (68 per cent) had sickness pay schemes for full-time manual workers and 424 (82 per cent) had schemes for white-collar grades. Of the 168 companies that employed part-time workers, 62 (37 per cent) extended their sickness pay schemes to cover these employees.

Sickness pay schemes normally provide that once a particular service requirement is fulfilled, employees receive full pay (inclusive of social welfare payments) for a finite period (which may vary from a few weeks to a year). It is normal practice for employers to take into account the benefit payable to employees by the Department of Social Welfare, as well as income tax rebates, in calculating how much the company should pay to make up the total benefit. This can be achieved by either paying the total benefit through the payroll and recovering social welfare cheques from employees or by paying a 'topping-up' element, with the employee retaining social welfare benefits.

HEALTH INSURANCE

The state provides free health care to those on very low incomes through the medical card system. There is no legislative requirement on employers to provide employees with the coverage of a private medical insurance scheme. However, health insurance is available to individuals through the Voluntary Health Insurance (VHI) Board. This is a state-sponsored body that is wholly financed by members' contributions and provides a range of insurance cover, depending on the level of contribution. The VHI has over a million members and is the monopoly provider of private health insurance. VHI contributions are fully deductible for income tax purposes. The Federation of Irish Employers estimates that over 75 per cent of private-sector companies have VHI schemes for employees. Over half of the white-collar schemes and one-third of the manual grade schemes incorporate a contribution by the employer to the cost of such schemes.

CANTEEN FACILITIES

There are no statutory requirements for the provision of canteen facilities. However, the Safety in Industry Act, 1980, requires that 'where more than five people are employed, there must be adequate provision for boiling water and taking meals.' In practice the majority of larger employers provide some form of canteen facilities. These may be subsidised by up to half the economic cost of meals. Tea and coffee facilities may also be provided at a subsidised rate.

SPORTS AND RECREATION FACILITIES

These are typically restricted to larger companies, which may contribute some of the costs of their operation.

COMPANY CARS

The majority of larger companies provide company cars for senior managers and in some instances for sales staff. The price of such cars varies considerably according to range but is normally between £11,000 and £26,000. Where cars are supplied, the company normally also pays for insurance, tax, petrol, and service. Where employees use their own cars on company business, firms normally pay a mileage allowance, typically from 25p to 60p a mile, depending on engine size. Company cars are taxed as benefits in kind at a cash equivalent of 20 per cent of the original market price. This is reduced where the employee pays the cost of fuel (3 per cent), insurance (2 per cent), service (2 per cent), and tax (0.5 per cent).

PENSION SCHEMES

There is no legislative requirement for employers to provide employees with a pension scheme. However, most larger companies have pension schemes, particularly for managerial grades. The majority of these schemes are contributory. Most schemes are based on a normal retirement age of sixty-five, although some are based on retirement at sixty. A survey of 579 companies conducted by the Federation of Irish Employers in 1988 found that 79 per cent had a pension scheme for all or some employees. The normal contribution by employees was 5 per cent of annual earnings. Company pension schemes are governed by the Pensions Act, 1990.

The state provides a basic pension at the age of sixty-five. This is related to means but is independent of income and is non-contributory; there is no income-related state pension scheme. Private occupational schemes provide earnings-related pensions to supplement state entitlements, and the state actively encourages the introduction of such schemes through various tax concessions. The Pensions Act, 1990, is designed to protect the rights of members of private occupational pension schemes. It provides for the control of schemes through a regulatory body, the Pensions Board, and deals with funding, benefits, and information disclosure.

OTHER BENEFITS

Some companies give employees a discount on the company's products or services or occasionally provide them free of charge. Other popular benefits are death-in-service benefits in conjunction with the pension scheme, free or subsidised health insurance, and share option schemes. Few companies provide employees with low-interest or interest-free loans.

In relation to the evidence on the provision of benefits, the Price Waterhouse Cranfield project indicates an increase in the use of non-money benefits. Such an increase, however, has not been universal. Companies of American and British origin were far more likely to have such schemes in operation than public or indigenous companies. Recognition of a trade union was also found to have an influence, with those companies not recognising unions reporting a much greater tendency to include non-money benefits in the reward package than those in which there was a union presence.

Fig. 6.5: Change in use of non-money benefits by company origin

	Ireland	Britain	United States
	%	%	%
Increase	15.6	35.7	31.3
Decrease	0.7	—	2.1
No change	79.4	64.3	62.5
Don't know	4.3	—	4.2
	n = 141	n = 14	n = 48

Source: University of Limerick (1992).

Pay as a motivator

The utility of pay in motivating and promoting performance has been a subject of debate for many years, with empirical and theoretical support for both sides of the argument (Bevan and Thompson 1992). Most managers instinctively believe that money is a motivator, even though empirical evidence to support this is far from conclusive (Fowler 1991; Goffee and Scase 1986). Indeed the failure of such schemes in some instances to fulfil their potential has been attributed to a flawed theoretical base (Pearse 1987), which in many instances serves to undermine effectiveness by demotivating employees (Sargeant 1990; Deci 1982).

Perhaps the key conclusion that can be drawn from the available evidence, both academic and empirical, is that pay is a complex, multi-faceted factor that serves as both a tangible and an intangible motivator, offering intrinsic and extrinsic rewards. The applicability of pay-related incentive schemes within a wide range of organisational contexts is therefore difficult to generalise on and is largely dependent on organisational circumstances and prevailing conditions.

Notwithstanding the reservations expressed, however, pay and benefits are increasingly becoming areas of extreme importance in determining the effectiveness of a company. In his treatise on how to motivate employees, Herzberg (1968) suggested that a 'kick in the pants' produces movement but not motivation. Kohn (1993) argues that the same is true of rewards.

> Punishment and rewards are two sides of the same coin. Rewards have a punishment effect because they, like outright punishment, are manipulative. 'Do this and you'll get that' is not very different from 'Do this or here's what will happen to you'. In the case of incentives, the reward itself may be highly desired, but by making that bonus contingent on certain behaviours, mangers manipulate their subordinates, and that experience of being controlled is likely to assume a punitive quality over time.

Herzberg has further argued that the fact that too little money can irritate and demotivate does not mean that more and more money will bring about increased satisfaction, much less increased motivation.

Pay is important to employees. It provides the means of living, eating, and achieving other personal or family goals. It is a central reason why people hold down jobs and move between jobs. However, the important question is not how important financial incentives are as such but whether they motivate employees to perform well in their jobs.

Once an employee has been attracted to a company and the job, the role of money as a motivator is debatable. Clearly money—or the lack of it—can be a source of dissatisfaction and grievance. However, if the employee is reasonably happy with their income, does that income induce them to perform at high levels of performance? Many of the theoretical prescriptions suggest that money is important in satisfying essential lower-order needs; once these are out of the way it is factors intrinsic to the job that are the prime motivators, especially self-actualisation. Others suggest that money is important at all levels and, as expectancy theory indicates, may be a prime motivator where it is a valued outcome and where there is a strong link between effort and performance and the achievement of greater financial reward.

During the nineteen-sixties and seventies many organisational behaviourists emphasised the importance of job enrichment and organisation development, and it became quite popular to discount the importance of money as a motivator (Biddle and Evenden 1989). The current emphasis on performance, productivity and cost reduction has tended to focus on primary job values, such as employment security, benefits, and—particularly—the pay package. Most managers will agree that remuneration, especially the money element, has an important role in motivating employees. However, it is only one factor in the total motivation process. Clearly many people are not primarily motivated by money but by other factors, such as promotion prospects, recognition, or the job challenge itself. All employees do not have a generalised set of motives: rather, a company's work-force will comprise people with varying sets of priorities relating to different situations and work contexts, resulting in differing motives and goals. These motives and goals will vary both between employees and with individual employees over time. For example, a young single person may give priority to basic income and free time, and the job itself may not hold any great interest; later that person, now married and with a mortgage, may be more concerned with job security and fringe benefits such as health insurance and pension.

From the motivational point of view, effective payment systems should—

(1) be objectively established;

(2) clarify the performance level required and the rewards available;

(3) reward the achievement of required performance levels adequately and quickly;

(4) ensure that employees have the ability, training resources and opportunity to achieve the required performance level;

(5) recognise that financial incentives are only one source of motivation and design the job to ensure that employees can satisfy other needs through their work (e.g. achievement, challenge);

(6) take regular steps to identify employees' needs and ensure that these can be satisfied within the organisational environment.

Clearly, employees must value financial rewards. If employees are paid at a very high level or are simply not concerned with financial rewards, higher pay will have little incentive value. At this stage other factors related to the job and work environment must have the potential to motivate employees.

Secondly, if money is a valued reward, employees must believe that good performance will allow them to realise that reward. This suggests that pay should be linked to performance and that differences in pay should be large enough to adequately reward high levels of performance. This approach obviously rejects remuneration systems that equally reward good, average and poor performance, such as regular pay increments based on seniority.

Equity is an important consideration. Employees must be fairly treated in their work situation, especially as regards the perceived equity of pay levels and comparisons with fellow-employees. They will be keen that rewards (pay, incentives, and benefits) adequately reflect their contribution (effort, skills, etc.). Should employees feel that they are not being treated fairly on these criteria, performance levels may fall.

Finally, employees must believe that the performance level necessary for the achievement of desired financial rewards is achievable. The required performance criteria and levels should be clearly outlined and communicated to employees. Companies must also ensure that employees have the necessary ability, training, resources and opportunity to achieve such performance levels; otherwise employees will either not be able to or will not try to expend the necessary effort.

Even where these factors are present, success is not guaranteed. For example, an incentive scheme based on production figures may be established to encourage employees to achieve high performance levels; however, unofficial norms established by the work-group may dictate 'acceptable' performance levels and ensure that they are not exceeded, through various social pressures. Equally such an approach may signal to employees that management are clearly in charge and may either lessen employees' feelings of control and competence or encourage conflict over the standards set.

It should always be appreciated that while pay is an important source of motivation it is not the only one. To motivate effectively, financial incentives should be structured in such a way as to highlight the link between effort and performance and the reward, to adequately reward good performance, and to be equitable in the eyes of employees. The remuneration system should be viewed as part of a total motivational process that allows for individual differences and provides motivational opportunities through additional extrinsic and intrinsic factors, particularly self-fulfilment.

7

Managing and
Appraising Performance

The management of performance is a key variable in the effectiveness and growth of an organisation. In view of the strategic pressures driving companies, it is becoming increasingly evident that they will need to carefully monitor performance if they are to realise improvements in productivity and growth.

Sparrow and Hiltrop (1994) emphasise a number of important organisational and social variables that influence performance priorities. Among these are the tendency towards organisational de-layering, with its concomitant widening of spans of control; devolution of accountability and responsibility; changing career and job expectations; the increased use of more flexible working arrangements; and the greater individualising of the employment relationship. All these factors are having an effect on the nature of the employment relationship and are placing increasing importance on the ability of companies to manage the performance of their staff. However, effective performance management does not operate in a vacuum and must take account of the related personnel policy choices of job design (see chapter 5), reward management (chapter 6), and the principles of effective employee development (chapter 9).

The emphasis in this chapter is on exploring the dimensions of performance management and on outlining a range of considerations relating to the development and operation of effective performance appraisal systems. The chapter concludes with an examination of recent developments in the area of performance management and current performance appraisal practices in Ireland.

THE NATURE OF PERFORMANCE MANAGEMENT

The current literature on managing job performance reveals several terms that are often used interchangeably, such as 'performance appraisal', 'performance assessment', 'performance evaluation', and 'job appraisal'. However, in general they are all concerned with measuring a person's performance in a given job against predetermined work standards and involve designing a formal system to facilitate observation, monitoring, analysis, feedback, and target-setting. Armstrong (1995) indicates that performance management as a concept emerged in the late nineteen-eighties as a result of a growing recognition that a more continuous and integrated approach was needed to the managing and rewarding of performance. He further notes that many of the more recent developments in performance appraisal have been absorbed into the concept of performance management, which is 'a much wider, more comprehensive and more natural process of management' (Armstrong 1995, 431).

Sparrow and Hiltrop (1994) suggest that performance management is essentially a strategic management technique that links business objectives and strategies to individual goals, actions, performance appraisal and rewards through a defined process. They stress that the most important feature of an effective performance management system is its ability to be seen as a method of continuously securing improvements in the performance of teams and individuals against predefined business strategies and objectives. Lockett (1992) indicates that the core objectives of performance management are (a) the continuous improvement of business performance in the areas of customer service, product quality, and market leadership, and (b) the continuous development of organisational capability through the design of effective production systems, the development of organic structures, the enhancement of employees' performance in line with business demands, and the expansion of product or service lines.

Table 7.1: Characteristics of good and bad performance management systems

Good	Bad
• Tailor-made to fit the particular needs and circumstance of the organisation	• Lack of strategic direction, with no clear objectives
• Congruent with the existing culture insofar as they support the achievement of high performance standards but will help to change or reshape that culture if necessary	• Rivalry and territorialism between departments
	• Persistent failure to meet objectives and deadlines
• Support the achievement of the organisation's mission and the realisation of its values	• Lack of clear accountabilities and decision-making
• Define the critical success factors which determine organisational and individual performance	• Confusion over roles in organisation
	• Middle managers feel unable to influence events
• Clarify the principal accountabilities of managers and staff so that they are fully aware of their objectives, the standards of performance expected of them, and the quantitative key performance indicators which will be used to measure their achievements	• Absenteeism, sickness and/or overtime out of control
	• Work-force and middle managers resistant to change
	• High turnover amongst key posts
• Enable systematic review of performance against agreed criteria in order to establish and act on strengths and weaknesses, identify potential, plan and implement career development and training programmes and provide a basis for motivation through intrinsic and extrinsic rewards	• Staff appraisal lacks credibility
	• PRP scheme regarded as ineffective
	• Lack of detailed information on costs and contributions
	• Poor budgetary control and plan
• Develop PRP systems which provide incentives and rewards as motivators for improved performance	• Outdated or inadequate management information systems
• Provide an integrated approach to increasing motivation and commitment, which combines the impact of results-orientated performance appraisal and PRP systems with the actions that management and individual managers can take, such as career development and succession planning programmes to develop attitudes and behaviours which lead to better performance	• Lack of structural career and succession planning process

Source: Philpott and Sheppard (1993). Copyright © L. Philpott and L. Sheppard, 1993. Reprinted with permission.

Philpott and Sheppard (1993), from their analysis of performance management in operation, outline a number of characteristics of effective and ineffective performance management systems (see table 7.1). In a similar vein the research of Fletcher and Williams (1992) suggests not only that most of the companies studied were a long way from operating sophisticated personnel management but that for most of them performance management was synonymous with performance appraisal, or performance-related pay, or both. They comment (Fletcher and Williams 1992, 47):

> There is, of course, much more to it than that. The real concept of performance management is associated with an approach to creating a shared vision of the purpose and aims of the organisation, helping each individual employee understand and recognise their part in contributing to them, and in so doing manage and enhance the performance of both individuals and the organisation.

The various definitions of performance management suggest that it is essentially a management process of linking individual, group and organisational performance with the main strategic objective and values. It is therefore a company-wide activity that is concerned with the continuous assessment and review of performance against predetermined strategic objectives.

There are a number of marked similarities between the performance management system and management by objectives (MBO), since both systems set objectives, require the identification of performance measures, and involve continuous appraisal and feedback. However, Fowler (1990) suggests that performance management goes further than MBO, in that it is applied to all staff (not just managers, as was traditionally the case with MBO), includes greater qualitative performance indicators, and focuses more on corporate goals and values than on individual objectives. In a similar vein, Armstrong (1995) differentiates performance management from traditional performance appraisal, indicating that it does not represent an activity that is imposed on managers and that it is primarily owned and driven not by the personnel department but by line managers.

THE PROCESS OF PERFORMANCE MANAGEMENT

A central tenet of effective performance management is that a participative approach is taken to the system design. This implies involving all organisational actors in jointly determining the nature and scope of the system. The system should have the full commitment of the top management yet not be viewed as a top-down affair (Wright and Brading 1992).

Armstrong (1995) suggests that performance management be regarded as a flexible process and presents a conceptual framework of the performance management cycle (see fig. 7.1). This model is based on the premise that all work performance is driven by the range of corporate strategies and objectives, which are broken down and translated into essential functional or departmental objectives. A performance contract is developed that outlines the tasks, knowledge, skills and abilities that are required to achieve these objectives. Built in to the model is the requirement for continuous feedback on performance, with the possibility of interim reviews. The system further prescribes the operation of one formal review a year, where employees and managers constructively evaluate performance and identify a new performance contract. This review typically takes the form of an annual performance appraisal, which will be described in the next section. Continuous employee development is an inherent aspect of the process, where specific training requirements are identified at the review stage and informal training and learning through coaching, mentoring and self-development are encouraged throughout the year.

Fig. 7.1: A conceptual framework for performance management

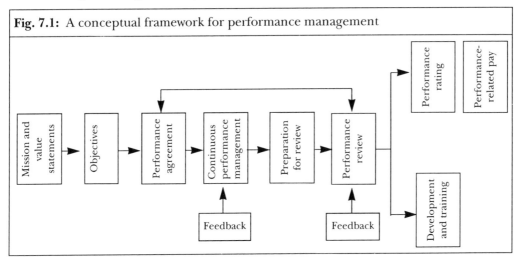

Source: Armstrong (1995).

The model identifies two further components: performance rating and performance-related-pay. Armstrong suggests that these are not inevitably associated with performance management *per se,* while Wright and Brading (1992) argue that formal ratings of performance should be avoided if possible and the focus brought closer to qualitative outcomes. However, while there is an increasing tendency to link rewards with performance (see chapter 6), it is recommended that decisions on pay be separated from the performance review, to facilitate the developmental nature of performance management (Armstrong 1992; Evenden and Anderson 1992).

Performance appraisal

Performance appraisal can be described as a systematic approach to evaluating employees' performance, characteristics or potential with a view to assisting with decisions in a wide range of areas such as pay, promotion, employee development, and motivation. We suggest that the performance management loop provides the framework within which systematic appraisal can take place (see fig. 7.2).

The appraisal of performance is likely to take place daily, often on a very informal basis, for example through casual meetings, informal discussions between supervisor and staff, team briefing, and so forth. However, the establishment of a formal appraisal system is a necessary prerequisite of effective performance management, since it provides a dedicated period for managers or supervisors to meet their staff and discuss a range of factors pertaining to work performance. Evenden and Anderson (1992) identify a range of perceived benefits associated with effective performance appraisals, some of which are presented in table 7.2.

145

Fig. 7.2: The performance management loop

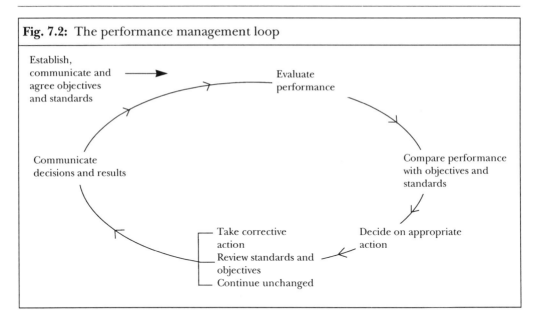

Table 7.2: Benefits of performance appraisal

Benefits to managers
- Opportunity to learn about employees' hopes, fears, anxieties and concerns relating to both their present job and their future
- Chance to clarify and reinforce important goals and priorities
- Mechanism for measuring changes in employees' work performance
- Opportunity to motivate staff by recognising achievements
- Clarification of overlap or ambiguities that may exist in the work structure

Benefits to employees
- Opportunity to receive feedback on how performance is viewed in the company
- Opportunity to communicate views about the job
- Opportunity to discuss career options
- Recognition of tasks carried out well and objectives achieved
- Basis for identifying training and development needs

Benefits to the company
- Assistance with succession planning and the identification of future potential
- Facilitation of human resource planning through competence analysis
- Method of ensuring harmony between business objectives and employee performance
- Generally improved communications throughout the company
- Opportunity to improve performance

Source: Evenden and Anderson (1992).

The performance appraisal system can be seen to have many interrelated functions, including performance evaluation and target setting, the establishment of work standards, the identification of skills gaps, and the facilitation of communications and motivation. In some instances the process of evaluation can become the overriding consideration of the appraisal process, and often the motivational and developmental aspects receive little consideration. Given that the annual appraisal may represent the only formal one-to-one meeting the manager or supervisor has with his or her staff, the onus is on the manager or supervisor to ensure that adequate attention is paid to all aspects of the appraisal process. However, in spite of their perceived benefits, performance appraisal schemes are not a panacea for poor management or fundamental weaknesses in organisation structure or design, and therefore, as mentioned earlier, the company must take cognisance of the range of policies, systems and procedures that affect work performance.

Randell (1994) suggests that an examination of a company's appraisal scheme can show a great deal about how the company views its staff and how they should be managed and developed. Adopting the approach that beliefs about human behaviour at work can be broadly classified, he suggests that appraisal systems are developed according to what those who design them view as the *causes* of work performance:

- Where the past is seen as a reasonable determinant of present and future work behaviour, the performance appraisal scheme will focus on a comprehensive assessment of past strengths and weaknesses. This view is largely connected with reinforcement theories of motivation, whereby good performance is rewarded in the hope that it will be repeated, while poor performance is discouraged or punished to decrease the likelihood of its occurring in the future.
- Where the 'here and now' is seen as the critical determinant of work behaviour, the appraisal system will focus on factors such as employees' understanding and learning. This approach draws heavily on cognitive psychology and equity theories of motivation, where employees' perception of the work situation is seen to determine subsequent behaviour.
- Where the 'pull' of future events desired by employees is seen as the prevailing influence on work behaviour, appraisal systems will emphasise rewards and opportunities. This approach draws on expectancy theories of motivation and focuses on self-fulfilment to encourage desired work behaviour.

There are two underlying principles associated with all three perspectives: a desire to add to the individual's capacity for doing an existing job, and a need to maintain or improve motivation.

Methods of performance appraisal

There is considerable variety in the range of performance appraisal techniques that can be used by companies. A summarised description of the most commonly used techniques is presented in table 7.3, and a number of these will be examined in closer detail.

Table 7.3: Performance appraisal techniques

Method	Characteristics	Strengths	Weaknesses
Rating	Appraiser specifies on a scale to what degree relevant characteristics (normally related to job-related behaviour or personality) are possessed by appraisee	Ease of comparison; range in complexity from very simple to very involved, using descriptions of behaviour or performance	Subjective; personality or behavioural traits difficult to measure

Ranking	Appraiser ranks workers from best to worst, based on specific characteristics or overall job performance	Simple; facilitates comparisons	Little basis for decisions; degrees of difference not specified; subjective
Paired comparison	Two workers compared at a time and decision made on which is superior, resulting in a final ranking order for full group	Ease of decision-making; simple	Difficult with large numbers together with weakness attributed to ranking
Critical incident	Appraiser or supervisor observes incidence of good and bad performance. These are used as a basis for judging and assessing or discussing performance	Job-related; more objective	Needs good observational skills; time-consuming
Free-form	General free-written appraisal by appraiser	Flexible	Subjective; difficulty of comparison
Performance or objectives-oriented systems	Appraiser evaluates degree to which specific job targets or standards have been achieved	Job-related; objective; participative	Needs measurable targets; danger of collusion
Assessment centre	Appraisees undergo a series of assessments (interviews, tests, simulations, etc.) undertaken by trained assessors	Range of dimensions examined; objective	Expensive; not necessarily job-specific
Self-assessment	Appraisees evaluate themselves using a particular format or structure	Participative; facilitates discussion; promotes self-analysis	Danger of lenient tendency; potential source of conflict between appraiser and appraisee

Rating usually involves the appraiser rating the employee's performance and behaviour against a predetermined scale. These ratings, based on a sequential scale, can be made against a series of relatively standard headings, which tend to include generalised performance characteristics or particular personality traits. Rating scales are often used in conjunction with results-oriented schemes, which measure performance against a set of objectives. In such cases rating scales are used to indicate the extent to which an employee was successful in achieving the objective. Two examples of the use of rating scales in results-oriented schemes are illustrated in tables 7.4 and 7.5, which contain extracts from performance plans used in a large manufacturing company in Ireland.

Table 7.4: Extract from performance appraisal form for managers, manufacturing firm

Employee's name:
Job title:
Appraiser:
Appraisal period:
Date of appraisal:

Section 1: This section outlines the key roles and abilities that managers must demonstrate to perform their jobs effectively. Using the rating scale below, evaluate the extent to which the manager named above demonstrates effectiveness in each of the areas identified. Enter n.a. for those areas that are not relevant to the manager's current position.

	Rating
1. Planning	
—manages systems and processes	—
—sets measurable goals and targets	—
—assigns tasks responsibly	—
2. Production	
—motivates others positively	—
—demonstrates personal commitment	—
—facilitates co-operative environment	—
3. Team building	
—manages conflict	—
—facilitates participation	—
—develops interaction	—
4. Coaching	
—develops others	—
—communicates effectively	—
—understands interaction	—
5. Innovation	
—divergent thinking	—
—challenges processes	—
—stimulates change	—

Rating scale:
1. Negative results: did not achieve objectives
2. Mixed results: achieved some objectives
3 Good results: achieved most objectives
4. Very good results: achieved all objectives
5. Strong results: achieved all and exceeded some objectives
6. Excellent results: exceed most objectives
7. Outstanding results: exceeded all objectives

Table 7.5: Extract from performance appraisal form for employees, manufacturing firm

Employee's name:
Job title:
Appraiser:
Appraisal period:
Date of appraisal:

Section 1: This section outlines the key roles and abilities that employees must demonstrate to perform their jobs effectively. Using the rating scale below, evaluate the extent to which the employee named above demonstrates effectiveness in each of the areas identified. Enter n.a. for those areas that are not relevant to the employee's current position.

1. Quality of work: the extent to which the quality of work is accurate and thorough
2. Dependability: the extent to which the employee can be relied on to do a good job
3. Judgment: the extent to which the employee makes rational choices
4. Organisation: the extent to which the employee can plan and structure work
5. Communication: the extent to which the employee can transmit and receive information in a comprehensive manner
6. Adaptability: the extent to which the employee can cope with change and uncertainty

Rating scale:
1. Negative results: did not meet expectations
2. Mixed results: met some expectations
3. Good results: met most expectations
4. Very good results: met all expectations
5. Strong results: met all and exceeded some expectations
6. Excellent results: exceed most expectations
7. Outstanding results: exceeded all expectations

Armstrong (1995) argues that while rating scales are a convenient means of comparing employees and arriving at an evaluation, they tend to ignore the complex set of variables that determine work performance and are a highly subjective method of assessment. Furthermore, it is particularly difficult to achieve any great level of consistency with rating scales, since, as we have seen, they are highly subjective, and some appraisers will be more generous than others. A further problem associated with both rating and ranking methods is the error of central tendency, that is, a tendency to veer towards the middle point on such scales and so to ascribe average values to performance.

One means of improving consistency might be to require appraisers to make a forced distribution of assessment that involves plotting overall evaluation against the normal distribution curve. An example of this might be where, if there are twenty employees in a particular department or section, the overall distribution of performance should appear as follows:

Excellent	5%	=	1 employee
Good	15%	=	3 employees
Average	60%	=	12 employees
Poor	15%	=	3 employees
Unsatisfactory	5%	=	1 employee
Total	100%	=	20 employees

A problem with this technique is that there is no rule that suggests that performance or ability should be normally distributed, and to assume so is to ignore the myriad of variables such as culture, production norms, supervisory arrangements and personal motivation that can have an effect on work performance.

An alternative to forced distribution might be the forced choice technique, which seeks to avoid the error of central tendency. Again appraisers are asked to rate performance against a predetermined scale, but this technique does not have a middle or average value. We use the example of measuring initiative to demonstrate the forced choice technique (see table 7.6).

Table 7.6: Example of forced choice appraisal technique

Criterion	Evaluation choices (tick as appropriate)			
Initiative	Takes responsibility and uses it well	Keen to take on new tasks	Needs direction	No initiative

Behaviourally anchored rating scales (BARS) were developed to reduce rating errors, and they include a number of performance dimensions, such as teamwork. Armstrong (1995) provides an example of BARS in operation (see table 7.7).

Table 7.7: Example of BARS

A. Continually contributes new ideas and suggestions. Takes a leading role in group meetings but is tolerant and supportive of colleagues and respects other people's points of view. Keeps everyone informed about own activities and is well aware of what other team members are doing in support of team objectives.
B. Takes a full part in group meetings and contributes useful ideas frequently. Listens to colleagues and keeps them reasonably well informed about own activities while keeping abreast of what they are doing.
C. Delivers opinions and suggestions at group meetings from time to time but is not a major contributor to new thinking or planning activities. Generally receptive to other people's ideas and willing to change own plans to fit in. Does not always keep others properly informed or take sufficient pains to know what they are doing.
D. Tendency to comply passively with other people's suggestions. May withdraw at group meetings, but sometimes shows personal antagonism to others. Not very interested in what others are doing or in keeping them informed.
E. Tendency to go own way without taking much account of the need to make a contribution to team activities. Sometimes uncooperative and unwilling to share information.
F. Generally uncooperative. Goes own way, completely ignoring the wishes of other team members and taking no interest in the achievement of team objectives.

Source: Armstrong (1995).

Results-oriented schemes are based on the underlying principles of 'management by objectives' (MBO), which include the specification of objectives, participation in agreeing objectives, the measurement of performance against objectives, and finally feedback and monitoring. In the results-oriented system, performance is measured against previously agreed targets or key result areas. As with MBO, there is a particular requirement for targets to be jointly set between manager and employee to ensure commitment to the process and allow for renegotiation as required. This type of appraisal scheme requires managers to have a comprehensive understanding of the nature and scope of the employee's job and demands high levels of vigilance in observation, target-setting, feedback, and future planning. While it is a useful technique, it can pose difficulties where the job is subject to considerable variation or where it is largely dependent on the performance of other jobs. Furthermore, there is a strong emphasis on measurable and quantifiable criteria, which might overshadow more qualitative criteria such as work behaviour and interaction.

Where jobs are difficult to quantify, the ***critical incident technique*** might prove useful. This requires the appraiser to identify three or four critical components of the job and assess performance according to how well these tasks were completed. It can be costly to perform, particularly as it may involve considerable observation, which can generate negative feelings from employees, who may feel threatened by the process; and where the appraisal takes place annually it can be difficult to constructively discuss key incidents that took place more than six months earlier.

The *free-form appraisal technique* is completely unstructured and essentially involves the appraiser writing a narrative discussion of the employee's performance. While it allows considerable discretion to the appraiser, who is not constrained by set criteria, this discretion can result in considerable inconsistencies and does not allow for effective comparisons.

360-degree feedback is a relatively new appraisal technique, also known as 'multi-rater assessment' and 'multi-sourced assessment', that has gained popularity in recent years. Ward (1995) and Garavan and Morley (1997) suggest that it is designed to provide a complete multi-dimensional overview of an employee's performance. The appraisal takes into account skills, abilities, and work behaviour, and information is obtained from records, reports, the person being appraised, and colleagues. Structured questionnaires are designed and are administered to relevant assessors, completed anonymously, and then returned to the employee. This technique is particularly comprehensive and provides a multi-faceted assessment of work performance, taking into account a range of variables that might not be considered where the appraisal is conducted by one manager. However, as this technique provides such a broad range of information, there may be a need to train employees in its interpretation and provide counselling where required.

Most appraisal techniques require some element of target setting for their effective operation. Objectives and target setting can help to provide clarity, realism and precision and allow both parties to focus on the same criteria during discussion. Evenden and Anderson (1992) suggest that to improve the motivational aspects of appraisal each job should be broken down into its key areas and then objectives for each area developed. They describe key areas as the main tasks that need to be done so that effective contributions can be made to departmental and, through them, company objectives. In identifying targets and objectives, Evenden and Anderson (1992, 267) suggest the use of a few essential rules to facilitate the target-setting process, whereby targets—

• should not be too numerous;
• should be set jointly by manager and employee;
• should be related to agreed personal objectives (of the employee);
• should be revisable and not too rigid;
• should be clear, concrete, and challenging;
• should identify constraints that may affect achievement;
• should identify time scales, review dates, and milestones on the way;
• should link target-setting into the action plans.

The appraisal interview

A number of the principles of effective interviewing were outlined in chapter 4, and many of these have application here. Of particular importance is the preparation for the interview itself. Most formal appraisal interviews take place once a year, even though there may be continuous review throughout the year. For this reason both managers and employees need to set aside time to carefully think about the appraisal process, the targets that were previously identified, work performance over the period, particular variables that may be affecting successful completion of work tasks, and the range of developmental opportunities that might have application in developing action plans for the future.

Adequate notice of the appraisal interview is an essential element in facilitating thorough preparation. Employees need to determine not only how they have performed over the past year but what their key expectations might be in relation to their career and skills development. Equally, managers need to be assured that they are familiar with all aspects of employees' performance so that constructive, motivational feedback can be provided. A rule of thumb for appraisal interviewing is to focus on *behaviour,* which the employee can change if required, rather than *personality,* which is rather more constant and very difficult to modify. It is in this respect that predetermined objectives and associated standards and targets come into play.

The appraisal interview is perhaps the most difficult interview a manager has to conduct, since the twin goals of performance evaluation and motivation facilitation are not necessarily compatible. Evaluation requires a manager to act as judge, and yet the developmental aspect of appraisal demands a more facilitative, supportive approach. When these are combined with the inherent pitfalls of the interviewing process (see chapter 4), the result can often lead to interaction that is stressful and demanding for both the manager and the employee.

There are three particular interviewing styles often associated with the appraisal interview: the 'tell-and-sell' approach, the 'tell-and-listen' approach, and the 'problem-solving' approach.

The *tell-and-sell* approach is directive and authoritative in nature and involves the manager telling the employee how he or she has evaluated performance and then attempting to convince the employee of the fairness of the assessment. This approach is invariably one-directional, from the manager to the employee, and provides very little opportunity for the employee to participate in the evaluation process. The likely response from the employee is a defensive one, and where he or she has no input into setting action plans for the future there is likely to be little commitment to any follow-up action. Bearing in mind the key perceived benefits of appraisal, outlined in table 7.2, it is unlikely that this approach would facilitate their attainment, and it is not therefore recommended as good practice.

The *tell-and-listen* approach is similar in some respects to the one just outlined, but some attempt is made to involve the employee in the process. In this approach the manager again communicates his or her evaluation of performance to the employee and then actively encourages the employee to respond to the evaluation given. However, human nature being what it is, particularly in respect to being told rather than being asked, it is unlikely that this approach is any more effective over time than the first one.

The *problem-solving* approach is based on the premise that the appraisal process is one that is jointly conducted by the manager and the employee. Here the manager first asks the employee to discuss performance against agreed targets and to express any problems that might be affecting work behaviour. Rather than being given an evaluation, the employee is free to comment and to concentrate on particular aspects of performance, and the manager provides feedback on performance. This approach advocates conducting an evaluation after the interview, taking account of the contribution made by the employee towards their own evaluation.

Evenden and Anderson (1992) put forward a set of guidelines that can facilitate effective appraisal interviewing:

- Begin the interview with a clear statement of the purpose of the meeting, which will ensure that both parties are aware of the rationale for the interview.

- Attempt to establish rapport and put the employee at ease. While this is a difficult process and is heavily dependent on the nature of the relationship between the parties, it can be facilitated by ensuring that adequate notice of the interview has been given to the employee and he or she has had time to prepare for it.
- Discuss the main tasks and responsibilities undertaken by the employee and invite comments. This stage should take account of any self-appraisal that has been conducted and should focus on the objectives and key tasks of the job.
- Ensure that a balanced discussion takes place. The manager is required to praise the employee for good performance but also to be frank in discussing any perceived weaknesses. The focus should be on the attainment of work targets and standards.
- Encourage the employee to talk frankly about any frustration in the job and any problem areas. Questioning style is particularly pertinent here, especially if the employee is unsure about or unwilling to admit to problems or difficulties.
- Encourage the employee to develop self-analysis and self-discovery, particularly in relation to developing action plans for the future. Greater commitment to new objectives and plans is likely where the employee can make a contribution towards determining them.
- Bring the interview to a close with a summary that clarifies what action is expected for the coming appraisal period.

Once the interview has been conducted and feedback given to the employee, it is important to ensure that the focus on performance is not neglected until the next appraisal interview. The performance management cycle requires a continuous alignment of work targets with key business objectives, and therefore performance should be reviewed throughout the year. Expectations created at the appraisal interview, for example promotion prospects or training initiatives, should be acted on to ensure that the motivational aspects of performance appraisal are not disregarded. Above all, however, a genuine commitment to the process of performance management is required of all managers and employees if the process is to be effective.

Performance appraisal in Ireland

Available empirical data on performance management in Irish companies is limited. However, Shivanath (1987), in her study of personnel management practices, found a high incidence of performance appraisal among Irish companies (80 per cent). The Price Waterhouse Cranfield project data (University of Limerick 1992) suggests that performance appraisal is a well-established practice, with 65 per cent of respondent companies indicating that they regularly undertake performance appraisal.

A recent study of performance appraisal by McMahon and Gunnigle (1994) suggests that while performance appraisal is seen to be a regular feature in most companies, there appears to be a relative absence of appraisal in the public sector and small indigenous private-sector companies (see table 7.8). These results are disturbing, particularly as the public sector is such a large employer. However, it is not altogether unsurprising to find that large multinationals report a high usage of formal performance appraisal. It has been seen throughout this book that the multinational employers have a greater disposition towards what are termed HRM practices, and performance management is seen as an important variable in stimulating and maintaining a culture that promotes high performance.

Table 7.8: Performance appraisal use by size, sector, and nationality

	Public		Private Irish		Foreign	
Size:						
<100	1	(25%)*	8	(27%)	11	(73%)
100–499	2	(40%)	9	(60%)	18	(100%)
>499	8	(36%)	11	(92%)	6	(100%)

n = 126
*Percentage of total surveyed in these categories.

Source: McMahon and Gunnigle (1994).

The research further identified a range of key objectives associated with performance appraisal in Ireland; overwhelmingly the priority for companies appears to be the improvement of future work performance (see table 7.9).

Table 7.9: Objectives of performance appraisal in Ireland

Objective	%
Improve future performance	98
Provide feedback on performance	96
Agree key objectives	95
Identify training needs	95
Strengthen employee's commitment and motivation	89
Improve communications	84
Assess promotion potential	82
Career counselling	77
Assist personnel decisions	70
Aid salary review	64
Secure feedback on supervisory or managerial effectiveness	63

Source: McMahon and Gunnigle (1994).

McMahon and Gunnigle further compared the objectives of performance appraisal in Ireland with those in Britain and the United States (see tables 7.10 and 7.11).

Table 7.10: Objectives of performance appraisal in Britain

Objective	%
To review past performance	98
To assess training and development needs	97
To help improve current performance	97
To set performance objectives	81
To assist career planning decisions	75
To assess future potential or promotion	71
To assess increases or new levels in salary	40
Other (e.g. updating personnel records)	4

Source: McMahon and Gunnigle (1994).

Table 7.11: Objectives of performance appraisal in United States

Objective	%
Reward	85.6
Counselling	65.1
Training and development	64.3
Promotion	45.3
Manpower planning	43.1
Retention v. discharge	30.3
Validation of selection technique	17.2

Source: McMahon and Gunnigle (1994).

What is particularly interesting is the variability between objectives in different countries. The tables reveal broad similarities between objectives in Ireland and Britain, but the American objectives are markedly different. One possible explanation for this might be the greater propensity of American companies to individualise the employment relationship and to operate performance-related payment systems (see chapter 6 for a detailed discussion), and so the focus of performance appraisal is intrinsically linked with the reward system.

It is worth noting that 64 per cent of responding companies indicated that a key objective of performance appraisal is to aid salary review. In discussing the process of performance management earlier in this chapter we suggested that decisions about pay and rewards should be made separate from the performance appraisal decision, to avoid the developmental aspects of appraisal being subsumed by anxieties over monetary reward. Thus, while performance-based payment systems are not particularly widespread in Irish companies, decisions on rewards appear to be a dominant characteristic of many appraisal systems.

Table 7.12: Performance appraisal scheme types used in Ireland

	Number	%
Results-oriented	45	62
Trait rating scales	37	51
Descriptive essay	32	44
Critical incidents	16	22
Forced choice	11	15
BARS	11	15
Forced distribution	7	10
Ranking	7	10
Other (e.g. peer and group appraisal, assessment centre)	15	21

Source: McMahon and Gunnigle (1994)

With respect to the types of appraisal systems employed, McMahon and Gunnigle found considerable variation within and between companies (table 7.12). The results-oriented technique continues to have relatively wide application in Ireland, as has the use of rating scales. In describing the various appraisal techniques earlier, we suggested that rating scales are often attached to results-oriented schemes to facilitate the evaluation of performance against agreed targets. The research further suggests that companies employ different types of appraisal scheme for different categories of employees and may also combine appraisal schemes to facilitate improved evaluation. Comparisons with types of schemes used in Britain and the United States reveal that results-oriented schemes, trait ratings and descriptive essays are a particular feature of appraisal schemes in both countries.

In summary, it is suggested that organisations are paying careful attention to the process of performance management and are employing a range of performance appraisal schemes to facilitate work performance. Given the requirement for high-performance work organisation (as described in chapter 5), one might have expected a somewhat greater use of performance appraisal systems. However, as the pressures for competitive functioning intensify it is likely that companies will pay more rather than less attention to performance management in the future.

8

Training and Development: Policy and Context in Ireland

T he last few years have witnessed considerable efforts to improve the national system of training and development. Much of this renewed effort has been brought about by heightened international competition, technological advancements leading to the emergence of skill gaps in certain industries, and renewed pressure to provide increased incentives for organisation-level training. The combined effect has been the dilution of the essentially voluntarist nature of the state's role in training and development and a move towards a more interventionist approach.

The approach of this chapter is essentially policy-based. It examines training and development at the macro or national level, while company-level training and development, focusing on procedures and practices, is discussed in the following chapter.

HISTORICAL OVERVIEW OF TRAINING AND DEVELOPMENT

The development of a national training and development framework can be viewed as a series of distinct phases, originating with the guild system around the eleventh century and developing with considerable statutory reform in the last century. Table 8.1 provides a chronological overview of some of the stages in this development.

Table 8.1: Development of national training infrastructure

1898	Agricultural and Technical Instruction (Ireland) Act	First form of regulated apprenticeship
1930	Vocational Education Act	Established VECs to provide nationwide system of continuing education
1931	Apprenticeship Act	Set up apprenticeship committees to regulate apprenticeship training
1959	Apprenticeship Act	Established An Cheardchomhairle to co-ordinate and regulate apprenticeship system
1967	Industrial Training Act	Established AnCO to promote training and to assume responsibility for industrial and commercial training, including apprenticeship

1987	Labour Services Act	Established FÁS to provide, co-ordinate and promote training activities
1988	Galvin Report	Drew attention to inadequacies of existing management development initiatives and necessity for greater investment in such initiatives at company level
1990	Culliton Report	Recommended reorganisation of FÁS and re-directing resources to providing training for those at work and preparing for work
1992	Apprenticeship system revisited	Apprenticeship system reorganised along lines of competence-based standards
1996	Forthcoming White Paper on training and development	Will focus on state's role in assisting industry to create a learning environment

Source: Adapted from Heraty (1992).

To trace and fully understand the origins of the national training system it is necessary to consider the beginnings of vocational education, since it was from initiatives in this area that vocational education and training as we now know it gradually evolved.

The guild system

The history of training in Ireland can be traced back as far as the guild system. The Norman conquest of England in the eleventh century brought with it the guild system from continental Europe, with merchants settling in England using this system to control and regulate trades. This system was to follow the invaders into Ireland and to introduce the English influence on trade and training.

The guilds became self-contained and self-perpetuating through a process of controlled apprenticeships, which provided each craft with a ready supply of trained craftsmen but in numbers that left the power and control of each guild in the hands of a few. Training became an integral feature of these apprenticeships. The apprentice was viewed as his master's property, bound by contract to serve the master faithfully for seven years while simultaneously learning his trade. The origins of craft apprenticeships can be traced to this era.

Industrial development

The gradual decline of the guilds in continental Europe and England coincided with the rise of the factory system of production in the late eighteenth century. Over time this system was further developed through the application of scientific techniques for controlling and measuring work, which were aimed at eliminating inefficiency. A result of such application was the introduction of the concept of the division of labour, which organised work into particular skills, crafts, and tasks, combined with the mechanisation of the production process.

The rapid growth of industrialisation and its increased use of the division of labour gave rise to a form of work classification that still exists and is taken to be synonymous with the existing distribution and nature of occupational work categories. Groups within the labour force became broadly categorised as managerial, clerical, technical, skilled, semi-skilled, and unskilled. This categorisation also reflected the growing organisation of trade unions among particular groups of workers, for example the skilled in craft unions, semi-skilled and unskilled in general unions, and clerical and technical in white-collar unions. A recognisable training entity was mostly associated with craft apprenticeship, and this was to become the central element of the earliest initiatives in vocational education and training.

Statutory reform

In an attempt to formalise and regulate technical and scientific education, the City and Guilds of London Institute was established in 1878. Through an examination system it encouraged the development of courses and formulated standards of attainment. About this time also some significant developments took place in Irish centres, including Bolton Street College in Dublin and the Crawford Institute in Cork.

The British government responded to this change of emphasis by introducing the Technical Instruction Act, 1891. This made provision for the financing by local authorities of technical education in schools and was seen as a new departure in satisfying the training needs of industry, which had previously been largely privately financed. This legislation was soon followed by the *Agricultural and Technical Instruction (Ireland) Act, 1898*, which introduced the first form of regulated apprenticeship in Ireland and specified that all training and instruction for apprentices be given on the job.

Following the establishment of the Irish Free State in 1922 it became clear that the system of apprenticeship training could be classified as aspirational in nature and was proving to be of little value to apprentices. Independence set the development of the Irish economy in motion, and a government-appointed Commission on Technical Education in 1926 was highly critical of the educational system, particularly its inability to meet the development needs of trade, industry, and agriculture. In particular, statutory reform was recommended to alleviate the inconsistencies of the previous system.

The *Vocational Education Act, 1930*, introduced a new structure by establishing thirty-eight vocational education committees (VECs), which were responsible for the provision of a suitable system of continuing education and technical education in their counties or cities. An emphasis was placed on 'vocational training', which was defined as full-time second-level training in literacy and scientific subjects, augmented by some concentration on manual skills. Despite these new initiatives the overall picture of apprenticeship training remained much the same; there was no compulsion on employers to send apprentices on any of the courses organised by the VEC, and many continued their practices unchanged.

Arising from the recommendations of the 1926 commission, the *Apprenticeship Act, 1931*, attempted to achieve the reorganisation of the apprenticeship system. This was the first systematic effort at regulating the apprenticeship system. The main provision was the formation of apprenticeship committees, with responsibility for regulating apprenticeship training in the designated fields: construction, electrical, and so forth. These committees formulated rules governing the length of apprenticeship, age limits for entry, educational requirements, wage levels, the number of hours to be worked, and the regulation of training courses. Employers were obliged to release apprentices for these courses, provided such a course was available within three miles of the work-place and took place during normal working hours.

This Act is now perceived as having been largely ineffective, as it merely laid down basic rules for the co-ordination of the apprenticeship system. There was evidence of considerable variation in the standards of training programmes available to apprentices and, in some instances, abuses of the apprenticeship system. To compound these difficulties, certain trades were in demand by industry—for example engineering and construction—while others were in decline. The organisation of apprenticeship schemes was scattered among the thriving industries—such as transport, steel, textiles, and footwear—leaving other sections lagging behind.

In an effort to alleviate these problems a Commission on Youth Employment in 1943 recommended the establishment of a National Apprenticeship Committee to control and co-ordinate apprenticeship training. Such a committee would have overall responsibility for all trades and so replace the existing committee system. There was general recognition that the origination of apprenticeships on a committee basis was ineffective and led to quality problems and other inconsistencies.

Statutory reform continued in the form of the *Apprenticeship Act, 1959,* which attempted to address the problems caused by the multiple responsibilities allocated under the 1931 Act. A national apprenticeship board, An Cheardchomhairle, was set up to co-ordinate the apprenticeship system. This body, which was given the authority to examine the methods used by any trade for the recruitment and training of apprentices, had a number of specific objectives, including the setting down of appropriate educational qualifications, ensuring the release of apprentices to technical colleges, providing on-the-job training, and establishing a system of examination on the practice and theory of each trade.

While this board was successful in its aims to a large degree, outside of the apprenticeship system there was little recognition of the need for, or value of, training.

Economic stagnation

The Irish economy at this time was inwardly focused, with the policies adopted by Éamon de Valera and successive Fianna Fáil Governments concentrating on the imposition of trade barriers and the preservation of ownership of industry at national level. Manufacturing industry was still in its infancy compared with agriculture and commerce and merited little attention in national planning terms. Indeed foreign ownership of industry was barred, and there was inappreciable emphasis on export markets and foreign trade. With the exception of the statutory reform on the apprenticeship front, no coherent training policies were pursued at national level.

Ireland remained slow to recognise the need for training outside of the apprenticeship system. At national level the Government adopted an essentially voluntarist approach. Training was held to be the preserve of joint negotiation between both sides of industry, with the Government's role defined in purely advisory and facilitative terms. The industrial sector was largely left to its own devices to provide the skills necessary for its growth and development. De Valera's philosophy of keeping Ireland for the Irish, with little emphasis on export markets and foreign trade, left small opportunity for the expansion of indigenous industry and even less for the importing of new technologies and systems from abroad.

Ireland experienced a shortage of skilled labour in the early nineteen-fifties, especially in the engineering field (Garavan et al. 1995). However, there was little coherent response at a policy level. By the end of the fifties there was no shortage of criticism of the training system. Suggested reforms included direct financial aid from the Government to companies for apprenticeship training and the introduction of some system of statutory training levy whereby companies that did not themselves train might contribute to the training costs of others.

Significantly, perhaps, this lack of progress towards reform was marked by the fact that neither side of industry was motivated to press for serious change in the voluntarist structure of training provision. Employers, though pressed in some sectors by skill shortages, were prepared to pay the wages necessary to poach from their competitors the skilled labour they required. Trade unions concentrated on consolidating the apprenticeship system, following the logic that maintaining defensive control over conditions of entry led to skilled labour attracting a good price. The principle of voluntarism and the maintenance of the status quo, therefore, appeared to suit everybody.

Moves towards institutional reform

As the nineteen-sixties dawned it seemed increasingly clear that the voluntarist approach to training was failing to meet national needs. There were not enough skilled workers, and the lack of training outside the apprenticeship system, combined with the narrow content of apprenticeship training itself, resulted in Ireland lagging behind most of its Continental competitors in the average skill levels and educational qualifications of its work-force. However, if the diagnosis of Ireland's training ills was fairly clear, agreement on a possible cure was altogether more contentious. The Department of Labour and the educational establishment were somewhat more advanced than industry in recognising the need for reform. Employers and trade unions remained unconvinced and, to a large degree, unconcerned that there was a serious problem with a voluntarist system that allowed both sides to pursue their different interests in relative harmony, through the apprenticeship framework. Skilled labour could attract a good price. Employers were left to train or not to train according to their short-term cost criteria, while negotiation between the two sides of industry and the Government remained a purely facilitative one (Heraty 1992). Relative, if fragile, economic security allowed this complacency to flourish.

It was to take the perception of harsher economic conditions in the early nineteen-sixties and a new determination on the part of the Government led by Seán Lemass to inspire attempts at serious reform. There is considerable agreement that this Government was responsible for dragging the Irish economy into the twentieth century (Breen et al. 1990). Ireland had joined the International Monetary Fund (IMF) in 1957 and shortly afterwards the World Bank. The Economic Development Report of 1958 added its impetus to the liberalisation of trade and commerce, and a more outward-looking economic view began to emerge. Controls on foreign ownership of industry were removed in 1963, import tariffs were removed over the period 1962–64, and in 1965 the Anglo-Irish Free Trade Area Agreement and the General Agreement on Tariffs and Trades (GATT) were signed.

These initiatives reflected Government policy aimed at creating a more open economy, with the emphasis on attracting foreign investment. A cornerstone of this policy was the encouragement given to foreign companies to establish in Ireland, through tax incentives, capital investment grants, advance factories, and other facilities. With the arrival of these companies vocational and skills training took on a new impetus, although the skill base remained very weak. The influx of these multinational companies, many of which espouse the training and development of employees as a priority investment, represents a landmark influence on training in Ireland that has persisted to the present day. Tourism and agriculture were also selected for development, with a view to reaching foreign markets. The Farm Apprenticeship Board was set up in 1963 to provide training for young farmers, and the Council for Education, Recruitment and Training in the Catering Industry (CERT) was established to handle education and training in the tourism sector.

This change in economic policy led to a considerable reduction in emigration and in fact resulted in many emigrants returning to Ireland to work or to establish their own business.

In response to a report on vocational education by the International Labour Organisation in 1962, a Dáil committee was set up in 1963 to tackle the problem of retraining the unemployed. The bulk of those unemployed were unskilled and in dire need of training if the kind of work-force necessary for attracting foreign companies was to be readily available. The middle nineteen-sixties were a watershed in national training policy, when the recognition of a number of significant issues was instrumental in the subsequent change of direction (Garavan et al. 1995). The general conclusions reached were that

- the voluntarist system facilitated the perpetuation and enhancement of familiar problems and allowed them to continue untackled;
- there was no effective national body to keep apprenticeship and other training activities under review;
- there was an insufficient number of skilled workers to meet the growing demands of the developing economy;
- a small number of employers trained well—such as Guinness and Bewley's—and their skilled workers were often poached by those who invested little in training;
- the state itself provided a poor example, with inappreciable investment in training in the public sector;
- training methods were poor, with few formal qualifications, and the training situation was in considerable need of improvement.

In response, the White Paper of 1965 adopted many of the recommendations of the ILO report and set about establishing a national industrial training authority.

The period from 1967 to 1980 is characterised by upheaval and reform of the training system at national and corporate level. The *Industrial Training Act, 1967*, repealed the 1959 Act and established An Chomhairle Oiliúna (AnCO). This body was empowered to assume responsibility for all industrial training, including apprenticeship, and its functions included the provision of training at all levels of industry and the provision, facilitation, encouragement, assistance, co-ordination and development of training initiatives.

The activities of AnCO were grouped into three key areas:

Training advisory service: Through this service, trained advisers of development agencies (including the IDA, SFADCo, and Údarás na Gaeltachta) acted as consultants to industry. Their activities incorporated the assessment of company training needs, the drawing up of training plans, and the sanctioning of grants to industry.

Training for individuals: Training centres were established to provide a range of courses aimed at unemployed or redundant workers, those seeking retraining for new skills, and school leavers, and at assisting some community-based initiatives.

Apprenticeship training: AnCO was empowered to make detailed provisions for the training of apprentices; designated sectors in this regard included the construction, engineering, metals, electrical, motor, furniture, printing and dental craftwork areas.

Finance for AnCO was provided mainly by the Government, but the Act also allowed for the imposition of a levy and grant scheme to underwrite training costs and to heighten awareness of the economic benefits of investment in training. The scheme itself took several factors into consideration, including company size, gross payroll level, and the amount of training provided. The levy amounted to between 1 and 1¼ per cent of annual gross payroll. Varying portions of the levy could be recovered: for example, companies with fewer than fifty employees could claim back 90 per cent, while those employing between 51 and 500 could claim back between 50 and 90 per cent. An upper limit of £50,000 was payable to any one company, or £2,800 in respect of any one employee. The general purpose of the scheme was to tax prime industry into accepting its responsibility for its own training while simultaneously fostering a systematic approach to training and development.

The 1967 Act represented a significant change in policy, reflecting an interventionist strategy aimed at sweeping away the concept of voluntarism. It also heralded an institutional role for a national training agency.

The early nineteen-seventies saw a considerable upsurge in economic activity, with the influx of multinational companies creating valuable employment for skilled and semi-skilled employees. This buoyancy was short-lived, however. The economy drifted into crisis from the middle seventies onwards as a result of the recession brought about by the oil price shocks and the resultant increase in unemployment. High levels of Government borrowing for current expenditure led to a soaring foreign debt. Spending on education and training was severely curtailed during this period, and companies, faced with rising costs and shrinking markets, cut back on non-essential spending. As a consequence, training and development activities were severely curtailed.

The economic conditions of the late seventies focused considerable attention on AnCO. The multiplicity of agencies seeking resources, paralleled by the growing scarcity of funds, was now a serious problem (Heraty 1992). The perception of widespread duplication of functions precipitated severe criticisms of AnCO, the more salient of which were the following:

- Considerable doubt was expressed about the quality of the training and the competence of AnCO to provide such a wide range of training activities.
- There was considerable evidence to suggest an overdependence on AnCO as a supporter of training.
- AnCO's concept of training was felt by many employers to be too concerned with paperwork, which was seen to create a situation where training specialists were ultimately judged on their ability to recover the levy paid rather than the innovation or relevance of their training activities.
- Considerable resentment was building up over AnCO's access to European Social Fund money, with accusations being made concerning the duplication of courses that were already available in many of the technical colleges, the redirection of funding away from education and towards AnCO, and the lack of any coherent, integrative policy on management training.
- The lack of a strategic focus and the industry-based nature of training schemes militated against the development of an economy-wide strategy for training.

In 1985, in the midst of a sea of criticism, the Confederation of Irish Industry carried out a comprehensive analysis of the national training system and called for an extensive review of the levy scheme. The main arguments are worth recording and may be summarised as follows:

- In a period of rapid technological and market changes, education and training are crucial factors in the struggle to improve competitiveness and achieve further employment.

- The Government is responsible for ensuring the provision of basic education and transferable skills that are necessary for entering employment.
- Enterprises are responsible for the provision of relevant specialised training that is necessary for their economic development.
- Industry recognises the need to provide for retraining and the continuing education of its existing work-force, particularly in technical fields.
- Employers and employees have a mutual interest in availing of education and training.
- Employees should be willing, in their own interest, to invest in further education and training, outside working hours if necessary.
- Recognition was given to the historical position of apprenticeship in the sphere of education and training of craft workers, and it was pointed out that the decreasing role of craft workers in manufacturing industry must be recognised, together with an increasing demand for technicians and skilled operatives.

White Paper on Manpower Policy

A White Paper on Manpower Policy was published in September 1986, which examined the role of all those involved in training policy and put forward a number of proposals for action:

1. While the primary responsibility for providing training rested with employers, Government intervention was necessary to ensure that the quality and quantity of training available conformed to policy objectives.

2. The question of the multiplicity of agencies responsible for training could be addressed through the amalgamation of a number of agencies into one authority.

3. The levy-grant scheme should be reorganised and based on a more selective approach (i.e. linked to approved company development plans and concentrated on key skill areas).

4. The apprenticeship system should be revised and modernised with a view to developing a system based on standards achieved to ensure a satisfactory balance between supply and demand and a reduced cost to the state while still maintaining quality.

5. Deficiencies in management training should be identified under the auspices of an advisory committee.

While the White Paper caused considerable consternation among those involved in training at the time, it also provided the impetus to the Government to make significant institutional reform and to streamline the national training system.

Labour Services Act

The Government's response to the White Paper was the enactment of the Labour Services Act, 1987, which represented the first attempt in twenty years at state level to reform the training system and bring it into alignment with economic objectives pursued by the Government. This Act provided for the establishment of An Foras Áiseanna Saothair (FÁS) as an amalgamation of the National Manpower Service, AnCO, and the Youth Employment Agency. CERT was excluded, largely because of the tourism lobby, which argued that because of the skill shortages and the importance of tourism as an employment growth sector, CERT should remain independent and provide a specialised service.

The Act set out a number of key functions for FÁS, including the provision of training and retraining for industry and the management of particular employment schemes to assist in the reduction of unemployment. Specifically, the policy allocated to FÁS was that it should adopt a customer-centred approach, regionalise its operations, and give a high priority to meeting the needs of the long-term unemployed.

The Minister envisaged FÁS as a labour-intensive service, doing invaluable work for the economy and the community and offering job satisfaction to its own employees. He did not, however, visualise any real dismantling of the existing services of the NMS, YEA or AnCO but instead saw them being adapted over time to achieve a more regionally based and integrated service. His aspiration was for FÁS to move towards the provision of more effective services at local level. The period between 1987 and 1991 therefore represented a time of significant change for FÁS. In the immediate aftermath of the Act a meaningful shift in its activities was evidenced, away from company-based facilitation activities towards an increase in community and youth employment training programmes.

While a considerable amount of FÁS's activities are directed towards reducing unemployment and fostering community initiatives, it still provides services to industry. This service now operates on a regional basis, using a network of training advisers. There are also industry experts at national level who oversee the development of FÁS's activities in relation to the various industrial sectors, through liaison with the Industrial Training Committees, which supervise the identification and planning of training in their appropriate sectors.

Advisory Committee on Management Development

A review of statutory and institutional reform over the years shows a consistent focus on apprenticeship training, youth employment schemes, training for the unemployed, and the like. Little attention was given to management training and development, and it was not until 1986 and the White Paper on Manpower Policy that explicit reference was made to the importance of management development.

Under the direction of Paddy Galvin, the Advisory Committee on Management Development was set up to evaluate the quantity and quality of existing provision for the development of managers. The committee reported in 1988 that economic performance is significantly influenced by the quality of organisational management. A number of key strengths of the management training and development system were identified, including the quality of the main providers, the standard of general education, the wide choice of provision, and experimentation with different delivery systems. The report also drew attention to a number of specific weaknesses and made recommendations for action. The most salient findings concerning both the weaknesses identified and the recommendations made are summarised in table 8.2.

Table 8.2: Summary findings of the Advisory Committee on Management Development

Issue to be addressed	Recommendations
Insufficient level of commitment and expenditure on management development initiatives	Increased commitment an urgent national priority; establish action group on management development to promote management training

Lack of understanding of what is involved or what constitutes good practice in management training and development	Develop a set of national guidelines on management development to be used as a code of practice
Lack of a common core of relevant business knowledge and skills	Adjustment of business education to reflect business needs; broadly common curriculum to be offered by providers of business education
Difficulties experienced by small businesses in implementing management policies	Provision of incentives for small firms to draw up and implement management development programmes
Ambiguity and inconsistency of state's role in funding post-experience management training	State funding to be redirected away from providers of training and towards users of training; closer alignment of employment of funds with economic policy
Separate training for public and private-sector managers not in national interest	Merger of management training activities of IMI and IPA

In particular, the committee reported that half of the top companies spent less than £5,000 on management development activities, while over one-fifth of them spent nothing. In its recommendations it highlighted the strategic importance of management training and development and stressed the necessity for it to be closely integrated with the strategic business objectives of the company. While the report was criticised on the grounds that it was over-prescriptive and that its case analysis was highly selective, it is recognised that its proposals represented a progressive development in emphasising the need for investment in training and development at all levels of a company.

PROVISION OF TRAINING AND DEVELOPMENT SERVICES

As a result of many of these initiatives, the provision of training and development services has grown considerably in recent years. While FÁS has a recognised role to play at state level in the provision of training services, both to industry and to the unemployed, there are numerous other participants involved in the training arena. The more widely recognised of these are described briefly.

Irish Institute of Training and Development

The IITD, founded in 1969, is a professional body that caters for those concerned with training and development in business, industry, consultancy, and the community. The institute's aim is to provide for the growth of those involved in training and development and, by doing so, to become the Irish voice for the development of people at both organisational and individual level. Membership at present stands at about 1,300, organised through a National Council and ten chapters around the country. The institute provides a range of services, including local meetings, a bi-monthly journal, seminars and workshops, an annual conference, and a mechanism for the representation of members' views to the Government and other institutions. The IITD also grants its own certificate and diploma in training and development as well as continuing professional development programmes at centres throughout the country.

Irish Management Institute

The IMI is a leading provider of management training, with the declared aim of providing leadership in the development of Irish management competence. It has approximately 1,300 members and provides a range of advanced management and specialist programmes, both open and customised, that are dedicated to raising the level of corporate performance.

Institute of Personnel and Development

The IPD is a professional body for those concerned with personnel management. It operates a part-time education scheme to prepare people for a career in personnel management, specifically the Diploma in Personnel Management and the Certificate in Personnel Practice; these courses are administered by a number of universities and colleges. The institute also provides an information and advisory service to members, arranges a number of conferences, workshops and seminars throughout the year, and publishes journals, books and monographs in the personnel management field.

Institute of Public Administration

The IPA provides a range of educational, training and development services designed to meet the changing demands on public servants. In particular it offers a wide range of courses on general business services, sectoral programmes for specific public sectors, and professional education services, including courses accredited by the NCEA and programmes accredited by the institute itself.

Other institutions

A considerable range of undergraduate, postgraduate and post-experience programmes is provided by universities, colleges and privately funded educational establishments throughout the country, and a number of institutes have been established to cater for professional development in select disciplines. The large growth in private-sector employment in recent years has also seen a considerable increase in the numbers of consultants who provide expertise in a range of training and development activities.

NATIONAL TRAINING POLICY IN REVIEW

There is a growing recognition that training policy at the national level has resulted in a number of inconsistencies, and there is a perceived need for a reorienting of training policy to take greater cognisance of the needs of industry. A number of criticisms have been levelled at the existing national training system that are worth reporting.

The Culliton Report

In 1992 the Culliton Report made two specific recommendations about training and development at the national level.

- The provision for training at work is inadequate. New structures are needed to remedy the situation. An institutional reorganisation of FÁS should be adopted to reflect the sharp distinction between support activities for the unemployed and industry-relevant training. These two activities should as a minimum be separated into two distinct divisions; in the long term a more radical approach may be necessary.
- A greater proportion of FÁS resources and activities should be allocated to industry-relevant training directed towards those at work and those preparing for work.

While acknowledging the role of the Labour Services Act, 1987, in shifting emphasis away from in-company training to schemes such as the Social Employment Scheme and other youth employment initiatives, these recommendations clearly espouse an interventionist approach on the part of the state. The Culliton Report pointed out that about 90 per cent of the budget of FÁS was absorbed by activities that could not generally be described as training. Roche and Tansey (1992) argued that FÁS is a complex organisation with multiple objectives, both economic and social, coupled with a wide span of activities and programmes. They also suggested that FÁS is deserving of closer analysis because of its position and the national resources it has responsibility for managing.

IBEC analysis of industrial training

The Irish Business and Employers' Confederation carried out a comprehensive review of industrial training in 1994, which identified a number of perceived weaknesses in the national training system. The following is a summary of the issues identified:

- National policy on training is seen to be primarily driven by the state, with the result that employers have only a consultative role and are not directly represented on important bodies.
- The training support scheme is held to be inadequate, with insufficient state support for industrial training.
- The provision of training is fragmented among state agencies, education institutions, consultancies, private training organisations, and industrialists.
- Companies need to invest more in training, but the real problem in many small firms may have less to do with increasing their investment in training and more to do with the need to get a better return on any investment made.
- There is a serious imbalance of resources allocated between support for training for the unemployed and training for those in employment: the report cited an expenditure of £280 million for the unemployed and £1.8 million for those in employment.

The report, while acknowledging the passive role played so far by employers and the inadequate provision that resulted, concluded with a number of recommendations that would facilitate a greater contribution from employers. These are summarised in table 8.3.

Table 8.3: IBEC recommendations for industrial training

- The development of a national training policy for the employed and the co-ordination of Government services to support industry.
- The researching of industry's training needs to clearly articulate the training needed in important business growth areas to support business development; direct consultation and the development of pilot projects would be an essential part of this function.
- The promotion of truly effective and cost-efficient training that supports organisational objectives and improved performance.
- The development of a national framework of vocational qualifications, both for off-the-job and in-company training.
- The generation of greater awareness of the contribution that well-structured training can make to business competitiveness.
- The development of appropriate initiatives to satisfy the training and development needs of small businesses.
- The securing of direct financial support for training initiatives that meet criteria and standards laid down,

the actual training to be carried out by approved trainers, of which FÁS would be one option; in this way, company-relevant training would receive a greater level of support.
- The improvement of the quality and design of training programmes for those in employment.
- The promotion and establishment of a quality training mark, with the objective of developing company accreditation as a requirement for the future availability of grant-aided training.
- The development of initiatives to meet gaps in the provision of training, particularly in the service sector.
- The representation of the interests of industry on sectoral and educational bodies in the planning and organisation of education and training for industry.

Source: Garavan, Costine, and Heraty (1995).

Trade unions and training

There are indications that a broadening of the trade union view of training and development is occurring. The Irish Congress of Trade Unions has emphasised the fact that in the area of raising the skill levels of existing employees, Irish firms lag well behind their Continental counterparts (Duffy 1993). In outlining an argument for improving this situation, Duffy refers to several deficiencies in the Irish training scene, including:
- the need for companies to engage in greater consultation with trade unions in the area of training and development;
- the focus on very job-specific training, without any element of personal development;
- the tendency of firms to design their training with a view to maximising the recovery of grants, rather than focusing on the needs of people being trained;
- the absence of formal training agreements.

Duffy goes on to state that training requirements fall into two broad categories: the need to continue upgrading existing skills, and the need to meet the challenges of a total change in work practices brought about by changes in technology. These general themes are also embraced in a report commissioned in 1993 by the ICTU, *New Forms of Work Organisation: Options for Trade Unions,* in which the need to ensure adequate skills training as well as providing opportunities for personal development is associated with the introduction of new work organisation strategies. In addition, the joint general president of SIPTU, William Attley, has stated his belief that the success of the economy depends in large measure on high levels of skills and knowledge and that it is the intention of the unions to press for this vision of a highly skilled and flexible work-force (Attley 1994).

Garavan, Costine and Heraty (1995) suggest that, taking an overall view, a number of inconsistencies exist in the area of national training and development policy. The following is a summary:
- The state has handled its own training badly. It exhorts private enterprise to develop and implement corporate training plans and yet does not itself operate such a process.
- During the last ten years or so the Government has invested heavily in training, almost to the point where companies have become dependent on such funding, with very uneven results. The cumulative effect of all state intervention has been to represent training to employers as something that is essentially provided by external agencies. Studies carried out by FÁS have highlighted the prevalence of inadequate levels of training provision, a fact reinforced more recently by the report *Industrial Training in Ireland* prepared by Roche and Tansey (1992). Indeed it is their

contention that employers are reluctant to provide anything more than the basic minimum level of training for their employees.

• Since the middle nineteen-eighties there has been a preoccupation with training to reduce mass unemployment, particularly youth unemployment. This in turn has switched the emphasis of national training strategies away from the existing business enterprise and its needs and towards the creation of a network of non-business organisations. Because of this, the value of training for organisational improvement has been diminished in the eyes of many employers.

• With regard to providing the critically required impetus to the concept of continuing training, the Labour Services Act, 1987, seems less than effective legislation. It does not make a significantly positive statement about the role of training within companies and the need to allocate more resources and commitment in this vital area. Among the specific issues it fails to embrace are the following:

1. The stipulation that a minimum amount of total labour costs be allocated towards training. It is suggested that, to respond effectively to initiatives in other countries, an initial level of 2 per cent should be included, with tax relief applicable to any expenditure above this statutory minimum.

2. The necessity for companies to draw up an annual training plan, which would include details such as the use of training for technological and other major organisational changes; the types of general training activities to be undertaken and the resources being committed to them; and the qualifications of the training specialist charged with implementing the training plan. Such a planning process would encourage companies to treat training as a strategic activity rather than perceiving it as an operational activity with a limited contribution to make to business success.

3. The need to focus on the quality of training at national and company levels. Those responsible for the allocation of funds for training should satisfy themselves about the nature of the training requirements, the quality of the delivery mechanism, and, in particular, the qualifications and credibility of the trainers who provide it. This stipulation should be equally applicable to in-house specialists and external consultants. Furthermore, multiple-assessment criteria should be employed: evaluation in terms only of numbers trained should not be considered sufficient.

The recognition of a link between investment in education and training initiatives has caused many EU countries to be concerned with policy reform in the area of training and development. The Minister for Enterprise and Employment, Richard Bruton, in his address to the annual conference of the Irish Institute of Training and Development in 1996, referred to the forthcoming White Paper on Labour Markets and emphasised the necessity for industry to take ownership of the requirement for investment in training and development. He indicated that the policy objectives of the White Paper would take into account various means of increasing employment intensity and opening access to labour markets to those with disadvantages. He cautioned that the ability to offer attractive packages to multinational corporations is rapidly diminishing and that there is a growing need to 'put human resources into the balance sheet' and for the state to examine how it can assist industry in creating a learning environment. (At the time of writing, no further details exist of the content or direction of the forthcoming White Paper.)

Roche and Tansey (1992) highlight the continuing importance of economic training to encourage the delivery of high-quality training as a national priority. In particular, they emphasise a key set of benefits that are seen to be associated with strategic economic training:

- It promotes national economic development by ensuring that the potential for national economic growth is maximised. Insufficient training or a poor level of training can lead to skill shortages, which can inhibit the growth of the economy.
- Economic training improves individual productivity.
- Economic training has the potential to improve an industry's adaptability and its capacity to absorb changes in product and process technologies.
- Extensive economic training facilitates the introduction of more advanced physical capital.
- The existence of a pool of highly skilled labour at all levels is used as a mechanism for attracting foreign industry to Ireland.
- A skilled labour force becomes a significant differentiation factor within a single market.

In view of the recognition of the value and economic necessity of training and development and of all partners at the macro level, it remains to us to investigate training and development at the micro or company level. The following chapter discusses training and development at the level of the firm and examines the processes by which companies can seek to achieve efficiency returns on their training investment.

9

Managing Employee Development

An organisation's employees are increasingly seen as critical competitive resources that, if developed effectively, contribute significantly to the attainment of strategic business goals. Block (1990) argues that there is a growing realisation that strict controls, greater pressure, more clearly defined jobs and tighter supervision have in the last fifty years run their course in their ability to give companies the productivity gains required to compete effectively in the market. Iles (1994) points out that the importance of people to organisational success is often acknowledged in rhetoric, as in company reports and media statements, but not much manifested in practice. However, it is increasingly recognised that the future cannot be merely an extrapolation of the past, and attention therefore is focusing on various means of using human resources to create and sustain competitiveness.

This chapter examines the personnel policy dimension of employee development, focusing particularly on the process of employee development at the company level and the principles of learning that underpin effective training practice, and explores the nature of current employee development practices in Ireland.

ORGANISATIONAL REQUIREMENT FOR EMPLOYEE DEVELOPMENT

In recent times much has been written about the development of employees as a means of increasing the effectiveness of the company. Traditionally, competitiveness was gained either through financial efficiency, marketing capability, or technological innovation. However, increased international competition and rapid technological development are leading to the realisation that the primary source of competitive advantage in the future will be the creation of new knowledge that is disseminated through the company and in turn leads to continuous innovation (West 1994). This view is shared by both Senge (1990) and Stata (1989), who suggest that the ability of a company to learn faster than its competitors may yet become the only sustainable competitive advantage. Furthermore, the move towards organisational de-layering and employee empowerment and the adoption of some elements of the 'flexible firm' model require a culture of continuous development and competence upgrading. The more the learning capability is increased, therefore, the more adaptable and successful the company can become.

This burgeoning interest in training and development can perhaps be attributed both to the popularisation of Porter's (1980, 1990) notion of competitive advantage and to the idea of excellent companies that has emerged from, among others, Peters and Waterman (1982), Ouchi (1981), and Pettigrew, Hendry, and Sparrow (1988). Companies are continually being urged to strive for competitive advantage and to use a variety of tools to achieve this: total quality management, information technology, JIT, and so forth. However, these are merely means of assisting a company in designing a business strategy that tackles the question of achieving competitiveness. The execution of strategy lies in the hands of individuals, and therefore no matter how good the strategy is, if it fails to take account of the people element it is doomed to failure at worst or to partial success at best. The key to competitive advantage might therefore be said to be the company's work-force. People possess the abilities and skills that must be developed, channelled and exploited to attain a sustainable advantage over competitors. If the primary factor in obtaining this competitive advantage is perceived to be the work-force, then the company must adopt the view that employees are part of the global value chain of that company and need to be considered at every stage in the strategic planning process.

> If the people in the company are not mobilised to produce the right quality of product or service, on time and every time, then the enterprise will fail. Thus people must be considered a factor of equal importance to finance, marketing, production and so forth in the business planning equation, because they are the medium through which plans are turned into successful reality (McEwan et al. 1988).

The last two decades have witnessed considerable change, with many of these changes—demographic shifts, heightened competition, changing work patterns, complex technologies—having a significant impact on the nature and scope of employees' development. In particular, McLagan (1989) identified reduced cycle times, a focus on higher-quality output and team-based approaches to work design as significant factors that require greater flexibility and commitment from employees. Similarly, Barrow and Loughlin (1992) suggest that companies in the nineties require that employees

- have the ability to learn new skills and adapt to changing circumstances;
- can conceptualise the contribution of their role to organisational effectiveness;
- are capable of working in flatter structures and without supervision;
- have the ability to manage the interface between customers and the organisation;
- possess capabilities such as problem solving, creative thinking and innovativeness.

All these requirements place considerable responsibility on the personnel and training departments to ensure that employees are equipped to meet the demands required of them for competitive functioning.

Definition of terms

Within the field of corporate training a number of terms—training, development, learning, education—are often used interchangeably, while there is also a growing body of literature on the concepts of human resource development and the 'learning organisation'. Much of this variation in terms arises where different authors seek to focus on or emphasise different elements of the training process. For the purpose of clarification each of these terms is described in brief, while table 9.1 illustrates some important distinguishing features of the more commonly used terms.

Education: Educational objectives have traditionally been couched in general or abstract terms and are often perceived as person-oriented rather than job-oriented. In its true sense, education refers to the assimilation of knowledge and understanding, which can be far broader than the work context within which a person may operate.

Training: While no standard definition of training exists, it is generally expressed in behavioural terms and, in a narrow sense, refers to the acquisition of the knowledge, skills and abilities required to perform effectively in a given role. Each training intervention requires some change in performance, and, for the most part, new performance requires some form of learning to occur.

Learning: For the most part, learning is perceived as a process through which people assimilate new knowledge and skills that result in relatively permanent changes in behaviour. Learning can be conscious or unconscious, formal or informal, and requires some element of practice and experience.

Development: Development is a broad concept that is future-oriented and concerned with the growth and enhancement of the individual. In organisational terms it refers to the acquisition of skills and abilities that are required for future roles in the company.

Human resource development: This concept has largely developed alongside the strategy literature and generally refers to the development of a strategic organisational approach to managing employee development. It advocates the strategic linking of training and development activities to corporate objectives and a central role for line managers in developing employees.

Learning organisation: The literature on the learning organisation as a distinct concept is relatively new, and again, while there is no agreement on what exactly constitutes a learning organisation, it is generally described as a participative learning system that places an emphasis on information exchange and on being open to enquiry and self-criticism. It therefore describes a company that facilitates continuous development and consciously transforms itself.

Table 9.1: Distinctions between learning, training, development, and education

| | Learning | Training | Development | Education | |
				Informal	Formal
Focus of activity	On values, attitudes, innovation, and outcome accomplishment	On knowledge, skills, ability, and job performance	On individual potential and future role in work-place	On personal development and the experience of life	On structured development of individual to specified outcomes
Clarity of objectives	May be vague and difficult to identify	Can be specified clearly	Objectives stated in general terms	Objectives are unique to individual and may not be clearly articulated	Objectives stated in general terms
Time-scale	Continuous	Short-term	Long-term	Lifelong	Specified period: e.g. ten years

Values that underpin activity	Assumes continuous change; emphasises breakthrough	Assumes relative stability; emphasises improvement	Assumes continuous change; emphasises maximising potential	Assumes incremental change; emphasises improvements	Often assumes stability; emphasis on breakthrough
Nature of learning process	Instructional or organic	Structured or mechanistic	Instructional or organic	Instructional or organic	Structured or mechanistic
Content of activity	Learning how to learn, values, attitudes relevant to work	Knowledge, skills and attitudes relevant to specific job; basic abilities	Interpersonal, intrapersonal, and life skills	Life experience provides basis for education	Imposed and specified curriculums
Methods used	Informal learning methods, learner-initiated methods	Demonstration, practice, feedback	Coaching, counselling, guidance, mentoring, peer learning	Experience, observation, experimentation, and reflection	Lectures, guided reading, debate, self-managed learning
Outcomes of process	Individuals learn how to learn and create own solutions	Skilled performance of tasks that make up job	Improved problem-solving, decision-making, intrapersonal, interpersonal competence	Personal outcomes internal to individual	External specified outcomes
Learning strategy used	Inductive strategies	Didactic, tutor-centred	Skill-building and inductive strategies	Inductive strategies	Combination of didactic, skill-building and inductive strategies
Nature of process	Inside-out: seeks to do for self	Outside-in: done by others	Combination of outside-in and nside-out	Inside-out: seeks to do for self	Largely outside-in: done by others
Role of professional trainer	To facilitate and guide	To instruct, demonstrate, and guide	To guide, instruct, coach, counsel, and mentor	Minimal: largely individual-directed	To act as expert, instruct, facilitate, and guide to learning resources
Document trainer philosophy	Existentialism; self-managed process	Instrumentalism: transferring knowledge using formal methods and measuring results	Existentialism: one-to-one learning, self-managed learning	Existentialism: totally self-managed	Combination of instrumentalism and existentialism
Type of need emphasised	Individual and organisational needs	Organisational needs	Organisational and individual needs	Individual needs	Institutional and individual needs
Process of evaluation	Continuous evaluation	Evaluation against specific job performance standards	Evaluation of skills and effectiveness	Evaluation against life goals and personal development	Evaluation in terms of pass v. fail levels

Link with corporate aims and strategies	Directly aligned with company's vision and requirements for success	Not necessarily linked to company's aims and goals	Directly aligned with company's aims and requirements for future but depends on type of development	No link to company's aims and goals	Not necessarily linked to company's aims and goals
Pay-back to company	Immediate and continuing	Almost im- mediate in form of skilled per- formance	Medium to long- term pay-back	No direct pay-back	Long-term at most

Source: Garavan, Costine, and Heraty (1995, 4–5).

One further term merits a mention here. The term 'employee development' is becoming increasingly popular both with academics and students and with the Institute of Personnel and Development, which divides its professional studies syllabus into three essential areas, using the term 'employee development' to denote aspects of the course that relate to the management of organised learning interventions at work. In this book we use the terms 'training and development' and 'employee development' interchangeably and view them as deliberate organisational interventions that seek to enhance the knowledge and competence of employees.

Training policies

A training policy reflects the company's attitude towards employee development and governs the priorities, standards and scope of its training activities. In this way it provides the framework within which all planned interventions take place. A company's policy towards employee development can be placed on a spectrum where, at one end, training is viewed as an expense and only occurs as the need for it arises and, at the other end, employees are seen as a potential source of competitive advantage and therefore training and development is a central organisational concern. In this respect all companies have a training policy, whether explicit or implicit, positive or negative. The extent to which they develop positive training policies is contextually bound and is influenced by factors such as prevailing employment legislation (e.g. equality, health and safety), the state of the labour market (whether skilled labour is readily available or can be contracted in or out), available resources that can be allocated to training, prevailing views on the value of training (particularly at senior and strategic levels), the nature of the product or service market (see chapter 2 for further clarification), and, in some cases, the expectations of employees themselves. Furthermore, organisations can differentiate themselves as 'desirable' employers by providing a range of employee and career development opportunities designed to attract and retain the required calibre of employee. Such an approach requires a high level of co-ordination between employee development and the range of other personnel policy choices, such as recruitment and selection, performance appraisal, reward systems, and employee relations.

In the current training literature there are a myriad of training models that have developed over the years, ranging from the reactive, ad hoc varieties to those that seek to describe training and development in strategic terms. A selection of these models is presented in table 9.2, which illustrates the range of approaches companies can adopt towards employee development.

Table 9.2: Comparative summary of employee development models

Model	Characteristics	Focus	Limitations
Unsystematic model	Unplanned approach; lack of training policies; individuals largely responsible for own development	Operational	Ad hoc; reactive; training viewed as cost rather than investment
Problem-centred model	Identification and prioritisation of performance problems coupled with generation and evaluation of results	Operational	Highly reactive; high risk of inaccurate identification of priority problems
Systematic model	Grounded in systems theory; highly structured; rational means of directing resources; cyclical process from identification of needs to evaluation of outcomes	Operational	Very simplistic; low applicability in times of uncertainty; does not recognise individual differences; ignores context
Cycle-of-training model	Adopts a stake-holder approach; views training as total organisational process; considers wider organisational implications	Semi-strategic	HR considerations not linked with business planning; does not consider line management role in training and development
Effectiveness improvement model	Advocates close relationship between line and staff managers; uses performance audits as management tool	Semi-strategic	No incorporation of HR considerations in strategic business planning; organisational culture and role of top management not considered
Business-focused strategic model	Relates training needs to business requirements; identifies external triggers for change; highlights top and line management support	Strategic	Inadequate consideration of the training context; ignores nature of individual as learner

Source: Heraty (1992).

The employee development model adopted by a company gives a useful indication of the training policy it will employ. In a company that adopts the unsystematic framework, for example, one would expect little integration of employees' considerations into strategic decision-making or broader business issues. The opposite holds true for companies that adopt the more strategic models, where employee development considerations play a critical role in the formulation of strategic business plans.

Learning principles and conditions

Since all training involves some form of learning, and since effective training is dependent on the extent to which the knowledge gained results in improved performance, it becomes pertinent to explore some of the principles underlying effective employee development. From a training and development view, learning may be summarily described as a complex process of acquiring knowledge, understanding, skills and values in order to be able to adapt to the environment in which we live (Garavan, Costine and Heraty 1995). Such adaptation generally involves some recognisable change in behaviour, though this is not always so.

Revans (1982) identified four cardinal conditions for successful learning:

1. The subjects are motivated to learn of their own volition and not solely at the will of others.

2. They may identify themselves with others who may not only share their needs but may also satisfy some of these needs.

3. They can try out any new learning in actions of their own design.

4. Within a reasonable time they can attain first-hand knowledge of the results of their trials.

These factors have important implications for the design and delivery of training programmes and suggest that the choice of training approach and method must take cognisance of the following principles:

- *Motivation to learn*: The employee must want to learn and therefore, in order to be committed to the process, must perceive that the learning event will result in the achievement of certain desired goals.
- *Involvement of the learner*: The training or learning should be seen as an active rather than a passive process. Briscoe (1987) and Pont (1991) suggest that adults learn more effectively when they are actively involved in the learning process.
- *Reinforcement and feedback*: Employees should be given an opportunity to practise what they have learned and should be provided with continuous feedback on their performance. This facilitates continuous improvement, and employees can engage in goal-setting to heighten the learning process. In tandem with this the training event must allow employees sufficient time both to absorb the material and to practise or test new knowledge and skills.
- *Meaningfulness of the material*: The nature of the training or learning intervention must be seen to be relevant to the employee's work. Wexley and Latham (1991) suggest that to increase meaningfulness, trainees should be provided with an overview of the material to be learned; the material should be presented using examples, concepts and terms familiar to the learner; material should be sequenced in a logical manner; and complex intellectual skills should be composed of simpler, subordinated skills whose attainment is essential before the complex skills can be acquired.

It is critical to recognise that employees are not homogeneous but represent a diverse group of people who happen to be working in the same company. Each person brings a unique set of experiences and expectations to the learning event, which can shape the level of learning that takes place and the degree to which the learning becomes a significant aspect of subsequent behaviour. A number of pertinent factors determining individual differences have been identified by Buckley and Caple (1992), which include the employee's age (affects attitudes, motivation, and interests), level of intelligence and ability (affects preferences for structured or unstructured learning events), background and emotional disposition (can result in predetermined perceptions of the value of training), learning style and preference, and finally trainability or motivation to learn (affects aptitude for improved performance and expectations of training outcomes).

An understanding of learning styles is particularly important, since the training method chosen by an organisation must take cognisance of particular learning preferences that individual employees might express. For example, some people may learn more effectively in a structured training environment using concrete examples, whereas others might prefer a more informal conceptual framework. Mumford (1986) suggests that a failure to take account of different learning styles can have seriously negative implications for the training process, while Garavan, Costine and Heraty (1995), quoting Arment (1990), indicate that

(*a*) by the time we reach adulthood each of us has developed our own method of learning, reflected in a unique and well-established learning style;

(*b*) trainers also have well-established learning styles and preferences;

(*c*) the more compatible the style of learning with the approach to training adopted, the more likely it is that a positive learning experience will occur.

Transfer of learning

The term 'learning transfer' refers to the extent to which skills and abilities acquired during a training session are applied to the work situation or to the learning of a new but related skill. Reid et al. (1992) distinguish between two types of positive learning transfer: vertical and lateral.

Vertical transfer occurs where one subject area acts as a basis for another, for example where a foundation course in business forms the basis on which learners can progress to greater specialism or diversification, when they can apply the general principles learned at the foundation level. In the training context this involves the acquisition of additional knowledge or skills that build on existing skills and abilities.

Lateral transfer occurs where the same type of stimulus requires the same response. In this respect, training simulates a particular type of task and provides the learner with an opportunity to practise in a 'safe' environment. Reid et al. use the example of the simulations that are used to train pilots. Buckley and Caple (1992) suggest that positive transfer will have taken place if the trainee is able to apply on the job with relative ease what has been learned in training (lateral) or is able to learn a new task more quickly as a result of earlier training on another task (vertical).

In some circumstances 'negative transfer' occurs, possibly as a result of past learning experiences that contradict present practice or where the learning experience creates inhibitions that impede the acquisition of new skills. An illustration of the former might be where a person who learns to drive on one side of the road finds it difficult to drive on the other side while abroad; this is particularly so where the driver is distracted or stressed. The particular choice of training method, style of trainer or indeed the training situation might, individually or combined, serve to inhibit the learning process and so result in negative learning transfer.

As an addendum to the above, two further sets of factors may also play a part in determining the scope of learning transfer: organisational factors and social factors. Latham and Crandall (1991) identify pay and promotion policies as key organisational variables that influence the level of training transfer because they affect the expectations of the training outcome. Bandura (1986) suggests that trainees may believe they are capable of carrying out specific behaviour but may choose not to do so because they believe it will have little or no effect on their status in the company. This highlights the necessity for employee development practices to take cognisance of the key learning principles discussed earlier.

Two significant social variables that affect transfer are peer group influences and supervisory support. Garavan, Costine and Heraty (1995) indicate that peer interaction can provide support and reinforcement not only for the learning but also for the application of learning to the job. Failure to achieve this support can result in alienation during and after training. Supervisory support is also a critical factor: good supervisory support increases trainees' expectations that the learning skills will be valued by the organisation.

The process of employee development

Once the training policies have been developed, the organisation needs to translate the key training objectives into action. At this stage a training plan is drawn up that seeks to merge individual and organisational requirements into a clear course of action. A model of the training process is presented in fig. 9.1.

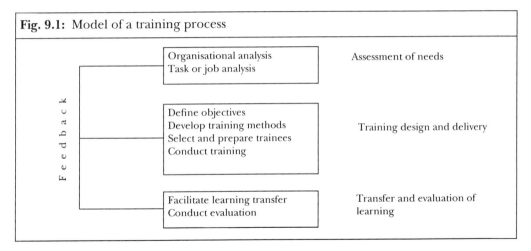

Fig. 9.1: Model of a training process

The first stage in the training process is the identification of training needs or training needs analysis (TNA). In a particular company a need is a discrepancy or gap between what is and what ought to be, for example desired performance against actual performance. 'Training needs' refers therefore to any shortfall between current knowledge, skills, attitudes etc. and the level required now or in the future. This training gap is illustrated in fig. 9.2.

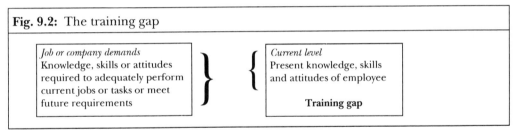

Fig. 9.2: The training gap

Source: Armstrong (1987).

Training needs can be current or future, or both. Current needs arise where inconsistencies emerge in the present training system and the company must act to remedy the situation. Garavan, Costine and Heraty (1995) view this as a reactive needs analysis, which usually provides a short-term solution. Future needs, on the other hand, arise from organisational changes and are usually diagnosed by active needs identification. They are prompted by internal and external factors such as strategy change, work restructuring, product or service diversification, the introduction of new technology, skills inventories matched against future requirements, or the like. Such needs are usually more developmental in nature, and there can be a temptation to dismiss them and deal only with immediate needs. In such circumstances it is difficult to imagine how employee development can make a strategic contribution to effective corporate functioning.

Identifying training needs

Needs analysis is a central component of the training process, as it ensures that training and development occurs only where there is a valid need for it. Many companies invest considerable resources in training but often fail to examine how effectively it can meet the business objectives. Needs analysis must therefore be viewed as a systematic process of determining and ordering training goals, measuring training needs, and deciding on priorities for training action.

Needs manifest themselves in a number of ways. Although there is much emphasis on identifying the needs of individual employees, needs can occur at three levels (see table 9.3). All these groups influence each other: organisational needs highlight needs for particular groups and so carry implications for individual needs.

Table 9.3: Level of training needs analysis

Level	Concern
Organisational	What does the company need to achieve its goals? Has it got the capability? Are there any strategic long-term objectives to consider?
Job or occupational	Special skills, knowledge or attitude training needs for particular jobs
Individual	Where individual skills fall short of those required

Source: Boydell (1983).

An organisational review is undertaken to systematically uncover and analyse long-term training and development needs throughout the company. Wexley and Latham (1991) suggest that organisational analysis involves an examination of how the company interfaces with the external environment. The environment in which the company operates can be a critical factor in determining whether training and development should be conducted; specifically,

- if the training and development function is to survive it must be supported financially by the company; the level of this support is determined by the overall profitability of the company;
- the environment in which a company operates can affect training and development needs; it can influence the way employees do their jobs, how decisions are made, and the types of skills and levels of flexibility required.

182

Sparrow and Bognanno (1993) refer to the development of a competence profile for the organisation as a whole and suggest that there are four different categories of competence that a company needs to recognise:

(1) **emerging competences**: those that will require greater emphasis as the company pursues its particular strategic path;

(2) **maturing competences**: those that are becoming less relevant, perhaps because of technology or work restructuring;

(3) **transitional competences**: those required of people during any change process, such as a high tolerance of uncertainty or an ability to manage stress and conflict;

(4) **core competences**: those that are central to a company's performance and so have continuing relevance.

By compiling a competence profile, the authors suggest that the company can attach a 'shelf life' to its existing range of skills, knowledge and abilities and can therefore estimate where training gaps exist.

A comprehensive job analysis provides information on the duties required of and the responsibilities attached to various jobs. Priority areas for individual training and development can then be identified to bridge the training gap. Performance standards in these areas may be specified in accordance with criterion behaviour: what the employee is expected to be able to do at the end of the training. A range of data sources is available to a company that can be used to compile a training needs analysis; this is presented in table 9.4.

Table 9.4: Data sources for identification of training needs

Level	Source	Training need implications
Organisational	Corporate objectives	Emphasise direction training must take
	Staffing plans	Current capability v. future needs
	Skills inventories	Areas needing development
	Organisational statistics	Identifies trends and problem areas (absenteeism etc.)
	System changes	New equipment or systems call for training
	Management requests	May apply in other areas too
	Exit interviews	May identify problems such as poor supervision etc.
Operational	Operational staffing plans	Profiles future requirements, indications, etc.
	Job analysis, job description	Indicates exact requirements of each job
	Task analysis	Very detailed job analysis
	Person specifications	Profiles skills and characteristics job holders need
	Training surveys	Up-to-date information on needs
	Performing the job	Shows trainer the needs of a new recruit
	Observe output	This may be delegated to line manager
	Review literature	Journals, guidelines, approaches of other companies
	Ask questions	Of the job holder, the supervisor, the manager
	Working groups	Combine several viewpoints
	Analyse operating problems	Differentiate environmental problems etc.
Individual job	Appraisal, career development etc.	Identifies weaknesses and development needs
	Interview	Self-analysis involves the worker, increasing motivation

Questionnaire	Gives employee time to consider their needs
Individual job analysis	Compared with job description
Tests	Of knowledge, skill, achievement
Attitude surveys	Determining morale and motivation
Training progress charts	Up-to-date records
Assessment centres	Intensive assessment
Manager's recommen-dation	The manager can identify individual needs

Source: Garavan, Costine, and Heraty (1995).

Design and implementation of training programme

Once a needs analysis has been completed, the organisation can set particular training objectives. Arising from the prioritising of training objectives, the company will then choose the categories of employees that require the particular training and then select the most appropriate method to be used. However, in many companies the training method is chosen before the participants are identified, and problems can arise where a method chosen is inconsistent with the learning styles and preferences of the trainees.

The range of training methods available is considerable, and companies, when deciding on the most appropriate method to use, must take cognisance of the principles of learning discussed earlier, the needs of the employees to be trained, and the logistics of training that affect every company. Table 9.5 provides a comparison of some of the more commonly recognised training interventions; while this table is not exhaustive, it highlights key characteristics of each approach that merit some consideration.

Table 9.5: Training and development methods

Method	Advantages	Disadvantages
On-the-job methods		
'Sitting by Nelly': learning job from co-worker	Inexpensive; natural learning; high transfer of learning	May pick up bad habits; often time-consuming; feedback may not be supportive or constructive
Coaching: supervisor guides and develops employee	Job-relevant; facilitates succession planning and employee relations	Adversely affected by time constraints and work pressures; individual attention may be limited
Mentoring: manager guides, counsels, and encourages development	Flexible; useful for socialisation, succession planning, and manage-ment development	Contact may be infrequent; manager may not have required mentoring skills or may not be committed to process
Job rotation: range of place-ments within the company	Relatively inexpensive; provides exposure to many situations; facili-tates interdepartmental relations	May be unsettling; may lack direction; may be inconsistent; difficult to monitor
In-house courses	Can be tailored to specific company needs; range of techniques—cases, projects, etc.—can be based on real problems	High opportunity costs because of absence of trainee from work; participation may be quota-based; can become an exercise in head-counting (quantity v. quality of courses)

184

Off-the-job methods

External courses: educational or skill-based	Exposure to broader range of knowledge and views; promotes net-working; useful for acquisition of specialised knowledge or skill	Learning transfer may be difficult; can be very expensive and time-consuming; may raise employees' expectations
Workshops: active discussion	Particularly suitable for managers; group approach facilitates problem-solving; high learning transfer	Requires advance notification and prepar-ation by participants; may be difficult to manage
Computer-based training	Individually focused; self-paced learning; performance is easily monitored; large numbers can be readily trained	Expensive to design; some employees may have a phobia about computers; learning situation is contrived
Open or distant learning	Facilitates career development; useful for self-motivated employees; participants direct pace of learning	Very expensive; high drop-out rate; time-consuming; can be difficult to balance work load and learning
External placements	Provides useful external perceptions; builds external networks; facilitates attitudinal change	Learning transfer may be limited; can be very costly; may be perceived as a junket; difficult to manage and control learning

Source: Adapted from Garavan, Costine, and Heraty (1995).

All training methods have their own particular strengths and can be modified to suit the company's requirements. The most important criterion in the choice of training method is the extent to which it meets the particular objectives that have been established. Once the training method and trainees have been identified, the company can conduct the actual training or learning event. When this stage of the training process is completed the next phase is evaluating the impact of the training itself.

Evaluation of training

The evaluation of training and development activities ensures that control is maintained over the training process and allows for assessment of the outcome, methods and overall impact of any training and development programme. Buckley and Caple (1992) describe evaluation as the process of attempting to assess the total value of training, that is, the cost-benefit and general outcomes that benefit the company as well as the value of the improved performance of those who have undertaken training. Easterby-Smith (1986) describes three general purposes of training evaluation:

- **summative**—testing to determine whether training and development was effective and achieved its objectives;
- **formative**—qualitative analysis of training as it is occurring to determine whether improvements or adjustments are required;

- **learning**—assessing the extent to which the trainee can transfer the learning acquired back to their job performance.

The systems approach to training evaluation as proposed by, among others, Hamblin (1974) and Kirkpatrick (1959), analyses the contributions that training makes at different levels within the company and requires that data be quantifiable and based on predetermined objectives. Such models propose a hierarchy of evaluation, where each level requires a different evaluation strategy and is seen as a measure of the progressive transfer and application of training content. This hierarchical approach to training evaluation is presented in table 9.6.

Table 9.6: Levels of training evaluation

Level	Description	Methods	Assessment
1. Reaction	Seeks opinions of trainees	Questionnaires at end of training	Easy to collect; subjective; does not evaluate learning or learning transfer
2. Learning	Seeks knowledge, principles and facts learned by trainees	Tests, exams, projects before training and after training is completed	Evaluates level of learning; does not measure impact of learning on job performance
3. Behaviour	Seeks to determine positive changes in behaviour	Observation; measurement before start and after return to job	Objective assessment of impact of training on job performance; can be difficult to assess in some jobs
4. Results	Seeks to determine contribution to organisational objectives	General indicators (profits, turnover, etc.); specific indicators (absenteeism, accidents)	Evaluates return on investment of training expenditure; difficult to quantify

Evaluation constitutes the final stage in the training and development process, and, while difficult to measure, it provides information that is critical to effective organisational functioning. A lack of training evaluation can result in inappropriate training, which is wasteful of both financial and human resources. The difficulty for most companies lies in identifying a set of measurable criteria that can facilitate the effective evaluation of employee development interventions. In particular, many of the perceived benefits of employee development, such as improved morale, increased job satisfaction, and improved employee relations, are by their nature difficult to demonstrate in quantitative terms, and many companies therefore limit their activities to a level 1 (reaction) evaluation.

Employee development is not limited to the provision of a number of formal training interventions. As the term itself implies, development is a continuing process, and learning can be viewed as an inherent process that spans the period of the person's employment with the organisation. For this reason many companies are developing a range of continuous development initiatives and establishing a number of planned structures that facilitate a person's lifelong learning experience. A number of these initiatives are now discussed.

Management development

Definitions of management development abound, but the difficulty with defining the concept lies in the debate on what exactly constitutes management and managerial work. Seminal work by both Stewart (1976, 1991) and Mintzberg (1973) reveals managerial work to be fragmented and disparate, with short time horizons and conducted within complex social networks. There are various views on the rationale for management development itself. Some theorists view management development as a means of engendering organisational change (Marsh 1986; Lippitt 1982), as a tool in facilitating quality and excellence (Alexander 1987; Nagler 1987), as a means of establishing core company values and strong corporate culture (Fulmer 1986), or as a determining factor of organisational success (Walsh 1996).

Mumford (1987) describes management development as an attempt to improve managerial effectiveness through a planned and deliberate learning process, while Molander (1986) views it as 'a conscious and systematic process to control the development of managerial resources in the organisation for the achievement of goals and strategies.' Armstrong (1991) adopts a broader view in suggesting that management development incorporates any attempt to develop the effectiveness of the management pool and to equip managers to deal with change and future job requirements.

Storey (1994) differentiates between two divergent models of management development. The first views management development as a highly structured, top-down event with a strong emphasis on structured training programmes that all managers must progress through in order to rise up the ranks. The opposite approach is far more decentralised and places the emphasis on self-development, where the individual manager devises his or her own development plans and in effect owns the process. Within these two models a variety of management development approaches may be adopted, ranging from educational programmes (the MBA route is most common in Ireland) to mentoring, coaching, action learning, and natural learning.

Gunnigle and Flood (1990) suggest that management development activities are based on the premise that a company can develop and improve its managerial talent over time, and therefore that a strong link with a performance appraisal system is essential to identify current levels of performance and assess performance over time. Garavan, Costine and Heraty (1995) propose that the development of essential managerial qualities involves three main areas of training:

(1) the acquisition of knowledge, including the professional, technical, organisational and business environment information required for all managerial tasks;

(2) the acquisition of skills in areas such as problem-solving, communication, motivation and negotiation that are necessary for effective managerial functioning;

(3) the development of aptitudes and attitudes such as judgment, creativity, flexibility, initiative, self-reliance and respect for ethical standards that are required for high performance.

Mabey and Salamon (1995) outline a number of organisational 'agendas' for investing in management development. These are presented in table 9.7.

187

Table 9.7: The many agendas of management development

Type	Characteristic	Assumptions	Questions and problems
Functional— performance: 'a garage'	Knowledge, skills or attitudes to improve performance, bring about change, and increase national stock of managers	• Training needs can be objectively identified and matched against training	• Overlooks other factors influencing the impact of MD on performance
Political— reinforcement: 'a cascade'	MD acts as extension of company's political order	• Top team's perception of how organisational performance is to be improved is correct	• MD dogmas are frequently dependent on one or two key figures; what happens when they go?
	Programmes (e.g. culture change) propagate skills and attitudes believed by top team to be necessary to turn company around	• 'Recipe for success' can be translated into an MD programme and cascaded down the company	• Approach leaves little opportunity to be questioned, and career costs of doing so may be high; such a climate defies genuine commitment
Compensation: 'a reward'	MD activities are offered as compensation for deprivations of employment: e.g. • as welfare substitute • as alternative focus to alienating work-place • to promote self-development	• Such activities encourage employees to acquire a habit of learning	• This approach deflects attention from causes of alienation, offering a palliative instead • It is deceptive—and morally dubious—to 'use' education in this manner
Psychic defence: 'a displacement'	MD provides a safe situation in which to discharge anxieties by giving access to or participation in more strategic matters	• Managers need a social system for defending their psyche against persecutory anxiety arising from their competitive career drives • Apparently fair appraisal systems, target-setting and ordered management succession help reduce fear of disorder and chaos if latent competition were to leak out	• Would greater self-development and self-determination in the work-place necessarily lead to unbridled and selfish anarchy? • Only a few MD activities would typically provide an opportunity for such displacement

Source: Mabey and Salamon (1995, 147–8).

Career development

While both organisations and individuals are paying increasing attention to the planning and management of careers, the concept of career is becoming much more difficult to define. Accelerated economic change, corporate de-layering and an increase in the use of outsourcing have combined to challenge the traditional perceptions not only of a 'job for life' but also of the existence of established, easily identifiable career paths and development initiatives. The concept of career is essentially perceptually based, and there is no complete agreement about what it is. Greenhaus and Callanan (1994) describe a career as the pattern of work-related experiences that span the course of a person's life. From an employee's point of view this will comprise the sequence of jobs that people pursue throughout their working life. In organisational terms career development is a systematic process in which the company attempts to assist employees in the analysis of their abilities and interests and to guide their placement, progression and development while with the company.

The process of career development requires an understanding both of the stages of career development and of the various careers that individual employees might pursue. Driver (1982) differentiates between four different types of career:

(1) **steady state:** a career choice represents a lifetime commitment to a particular occupation;

(2) **linear:** the employee moves 'up the ladder' in one particular occupation;

(3) **spiral:** the employee remains in a particular occupation for a lengthy period (seven to ten years) and then chooses another occupation that builds on acquired skills and abilities;

(4) **transitory:** the employee's choice of career changes frequently, with each move signifying a change in direction.

Career development can further be understood in terms of a person's life-cycle, where, as they progress through the various stages in their life, different needs, concerns and aspirations take priority. Table 9.8 summarises the relationship between a person's life stages and career cycle.

Table 9.8: Life and career stages

Stage		Characteristics
1	Childhood	Focus on ego-identification; development of self concept; search for values and roles; formulation of interests and capabilities
2	Early adulthood (growth, exploration)	Self-identification through role and occupational analysis; closer identification of needs, interests, and capabilities; potential conflict between need to establish identity and feeling of losing autonomy
3	Adulthood (establishment)	Focus on establishing self in work and life situations; clear career pattern; search for stability and personal security
4	Late adulthood (maintenance)	Emphasis on acceptance and consolidation of position; possible review and modification of life or work role; concern with providing for and guiding new generation
5	Maturity, decline	Conclusion of career role; acceptance of life and career pattern; preparation for post-work challenges

Source: Gunnigle and Flood (1990)

189

Nicholson and West (1988) propose a transition-cycle model of job change in companies and identify a set of strategies that companies might adopt to facilitate the smooth transition from one job to another. Such transitions can include both the transition from education to work and relocation within the company, including transfers, promotions, and moves to group-based work design.

Fig. 9.3: The transition cycle

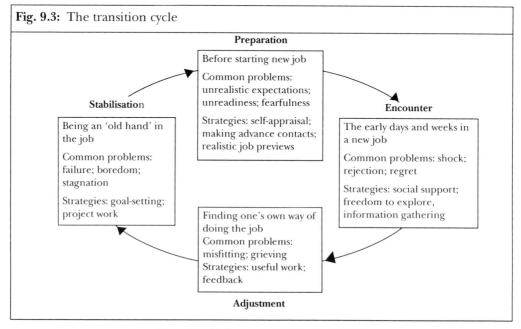

Source: Arnold, Cooper, and Robertson (1995).

One significant problem experienced by many companies is the mis-match of employees' expectations about the job and career prospects and the reality of the situation. This in part may explain the 'induction crisis' experienced by many companies, where several new employees leave the company within the first six weeks of starting employment. Companies can reduce the extent of this problem by developing a 'realistic job preview', which attempts to describe the job and the company as seen by those who work there. In this way job applicants can self-match their skills, abilities and aspirations against the realistic job description provided.

The socialisation of employees in new work roles is critical and can be facilitated through the establishment of informal support networks. Once employees become comfortable with their role and develop an understanding of the work environment, the company needs to concern itself with providing challenging work and feedback on performance. The danger exists that employees will become dissatisfied with the work or the development opportunities available; for this reason career management should be a central concern at every stage of the employment relationship.

Nicholson and Arnold (1989) identify four common shortcomings of organisational career development systems:

- **restricted**: where (while it is acknowledged that some are inevitable) the company creates unnecessary restrictions, such as non-promotional transfers between functions;

- **political**: where career opportunities can be blocked by managers who perhaps seek to advance their own interests at the expense of individual employees;
- **mechanistic**: where career moves are controlled by rules and procedures that do not allow for exceptions and fail to take account of changing circumstances;
- **neglected**: where possible career paths are simply not identified and no-one can see the way forward.

Russell (1991), Mayo (1991) and Iles and Mabey (1993) variously define career development or career management intervention as any efforts by companies to assist people in managing their careers. Several such interventions have been identified over the years, and the more salient of them are outlined in table 9.9.

Table 9.9: Career development techniques

Technique	Description
Succession planning	The company identifies or 'earmarks' employees considered suitable for key positions in the future and provides the necessary experience, training etc. to enable such employees to take up these positions.
Career counselling	The company appoints an external counsellor (in some cases an internal manager may adopt the role) to assist individual employees in clarifying their ideas about self and work. Psychometric tests are often used to identify career opportunities for individual employees.
Skills inventories	The company develops detailed records on the skills, experience, qualifications and expertise accumulated by each employee, coupled with information on people's career preferences and objectives.
Mentoring programmes	The company develops a system whereby an older, more experienced worker acts as a role model for a younger employee and supports, guides and counsels them through their time with the company.
Educational opportunities	The company actively promotes continuous development and provides information and financial support on both internal and external courses, training, and conferences.

The establishment of formal career management techniques is a useful managerial tool that can be used to build an effective internal labour market. Similarly, it is of benefit to employees where the system used takes cognisance of individual career aspirations and the creation of a range of opportunities that facilitate and encourage continuous development.

The learning organisation

Recent years have witnessed a burgeoning interest in continuous development as a corporate concern, and this increased interest has given rise to a body of literature on the notion of the 'learning organisation'. While there is no complete agreement on a definition of this concept, it has been described as an organisation that facilitates the learning of all its members and consciously transforms itself (Pedler, Boydell, and Burgoyne 1989). It is a place where

people continually expand their capacity to create the results they truly desire,

191

where new and expansive patterns of thinking are nurtured, where collective aspirations are set free, and where people are continually learning how to learn together (Senge 1990).

West (1994) suggests that the concept of the learning organisation is embedded in the notion that innovative companies should be designed as participative learning systems, which place an emphasis on information exchange and on being open to enquiry and self-criticism; while Pedler, Boydell and Burgoyne (1989) propose that a learning organisation is one that

- has a climate in which people are encouraged to learn and to develop to their full potential;
- extends its learning culture to include customers, suppliers, and other significant stakeholders;
- makes human resource development strategy central to its business policy so that the process of individual and organisational learning becomes a major business activity.

Calvert et al. (1994) maintain that learning organisations use learning as a means of attaining their goals and create structures and procedures that facilitate and support continuous learning and development. An attempt is made to link individual and organisational performance, which is often reflected in the reward choices made by the company. However, the process of becoming a learning organisation is not easily realised, since it requires fundamental changes in how people think and interact and involves a comprehensive evaluation of deeply held assumptions and values. As with any change process, the move towards adopting the learning model is often viewed with suspicion and distrust by those who are averse to changing all that has traditionally been stable and consistent and moving towards a situation where they are required to take responsibility for their continuous development and competence improvement.

The problem for most companies lies in what is described as 'transition management' (Perry 1983; Buchanan and McCalman 1989). While identifying the work and organisation design features that one wishes to implement is comparatively straightforward, it is much more difficult to determine how to take the company and its employees through the actual transition. Garavan, Costine and Heraty (1995) propose that the driving force for managing the movement towards a learning organisation must reside at the top of the company. However, by its nature a learning organisation cannot be constructed by a management directive: instead it must be pursued by effectively influencing, persuading and communicating at all organisational levels. It means

- attending to the requirements of all employees and groups and building a sense of cohesion and group purpose and support;
- identifying and satisfying individual motivational and developmental needs;
- harnessing the efforts of all employees to meet the desired goal.

It therefore requires the establishment of a clear vision of what needs to be achieved and the adoption of appropriate strategies to make this possible.

The premise of most of the available literature on the learning organisation is perhaps overprescriptive, and the concept itself may be difficult to comprehend, since, by its definition, companies never reach the stage at which they can be said to have fulfilled the criteria required to become a learning organisation. Notwithstanding this, the principles on which the concept is founded represent a set of ideals to which most companies would aspire, namely the creation of an organisational climate that facilitates continuous development, a system that rewards continuous improvement, and a structural design that promotes continuing learning.

EMPLOYEE DEVELOPMENT PRACTICES IN IRELAND

As we saw in chapter 8, Ireland has seen considerable debate on the uncompetitiveness of its indigenous firms in the traded area. Concomitantly, the low profitability of private industry during the prolonged recession of the nineteen-eighties has led to a skill gap in many industries and an overall lack of investment in human capital (Culliton 1992; OECD 1990). The challenge facing Irish companies, as with their counterparts in the European Union, is the mobilisation of human resources as a prerequisite for the tight, efficient and productive implementation of business strategies. The question is, to what extent are companies actively meeting this challenge?

Training expenditure

Unlike some of their Continental counterparts, Irish companies are not required to invest a minimum proportion of annual turnover or its equivalent in updating the skills and knowledge of their employees, nor are they obliged to make known the amount they spend annually on training and development (Heraty and Morley 1994). Fox (1987) argues that problems continually arise in drawing up statistics on training and development, since companies have differing perceptions of what constitutes training; and since many companies tend to rely on informal training strategies and mechanisms, the problem of quantifying training expenditure are further compounded. However, data from the Price Waterhouse Cranfield project (University of Limerick 1992) indicates that training expenditure has increased over the last few years among all companies surveyed (fig. 9.4). Larger companies reported higher-frequency increases, particularly in the managerial and professional categories; but increased spending on management development was a general feature of the research findings.

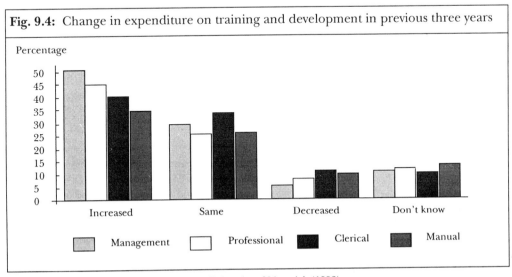

Fig. 9.4: Change in expenditure on training and development in previous three years

Source: University of Limerick (1992).

193

Responsibility for employee development

Employee development has traditionally been seen as the preserve of personnel and training departments. However, much of the recent training literature has suggested that the site of responsibility for many 'traditional' personnel activities has gradually been shifting towards the line management, particularly in the area of employee development (see Garavan, Costine, and Heraty 1995; Webster 1990; Harrison 1992; Ashton 1984). Heraty (1992) in a study of fifty-eight Irish companies found that while line managers were becoming increasingly involved in training and development, this involvement was largely limited to the delivery of training, whereas policy formulation was the preserve of personnel or training departments. The Price Waterhouse Cranfield project data presents some variations on this (table 9.10). The table reveals considerable evidence of strong line involvement in policy formulation, with almost 40 per cent of respondents reporting that training and development policy decisions are jointly taken by the HR department and line managers.

However, it is also apparent that line managers have considerable discretion in this area, with almost a quarter of those surveyed reporting that line managers are totally responsible for training and development policy decisions; compare this with sole HR department responsibility at 11.2 per cent. Interestingly, when asked whether line management responsibility had changed over the last three years, 34.9 per cent (94) reported that it had increased and 55.6 per cent (149) that it had remained the same, while 5.2 per cent reported that it had decreased. If change took place, therefore, it was far more likely to have been an increase rather than a decrease.

Table 9.10: Responsibility for employee development policy decisions

HR department and line management	39.4%	(106)
Line management	23.4%	(63)
Line management and HR department	18.2%	(49)
HR department	11.2%	(30)

(*n* = 248)

Source: University of Limerick (1992).

However, Ashton (1984) cautions that different training and development activities require varying degrees of line management involvement and that some form of role clarification is necessary as a basis for developing a strategically oriented training and development function; otherwise problems will arise concerning ownership of the function.

Analysis of training needs

The analysis of employees' training needs is a prerequisite of effective training and development practice (Donnelly 1987; Buckley and Caple 1992). However, just 63 per cent (170) of respondents to the Price Waterhouse Cranfield project survey indicated that they analyse the training needs of their employees. Specifically, over two-thirds (69.4 per cent) of the private-sector companies did so, while just over half (53.4 per cent) of the public-sector companies did. The general low level of analysis is surprising, particularly in the light of the overall reported increase in spending on training and development, and raises the question of how effective the result actually is. Furthermore, larger companies were found to be much more likely to analyse training needs than were smaller companies.

Table 9.11: Identification of training needs

Performance appraisal	59.5%	(160)
Annual career development interviews	38.7%	(104)
Succession plans	26.4%	(71)
Planned job rotation	23.0%	(62)
International experience schemes	17.0%	(46)
Formal career plans	15.2%	(41)
'Highflier' schemes for managers	9.7%	(26)
Assessment centres	4.5%	(12)
(Actual numbers in parentheses.)		

Source: University of Limerick (1992).

A variety of techniques was used for collecting information on training requirements (see table 9.11). Among companies of all sizes, performance appraisal emerged as the most commonly used method of identifying needs. Interestingly, private-sector companies appeared to rely on this mechanism to a far greater degree than the public sector (69.4 per cent, compared with 37.9 per cent), while non-union companies' use was higher than that of unionised companies (70.2 per cent, compared with 57.7 per cent). Of particular interest is the fact that while a large proportion of companies use performance appraisal to identify potential for future development, only 34.6 per cent of the companies reported that their managers had received training in performance appraisal.

Employee development activities undertaken

The evidence so far suggests that companies are taking their training responsibilities seriously and that considerable training and development is being undertaken at the company level. In particular, the Price Waterhouse Cranfield project noted that management development is a strong organisational concern and the level of activity in this area in increasing. Table 9.12 indicates a range of management development activities that were cited by responding companies.

Table 9.12: Management development

Staff communication	50.9%	(137)
Motivation	49.1%	(132)
Team building	41.6%	(112)
Delegation	39.0%	(105)
Performance appraisal	34.6%	(93)
Foreign language	15.0%	(41)
(Actual number of firms in parentheses.)		

Source: University of Limerick (1992).

Training in communications emerged as the most popular management development activity, particularly in unionised companies. This would appear to correspond to the trend towards more direct communication with employees that is increasingly prevalent in employee relations (Gunnigle and Morley 1993). Larger companies were found to have delivered a broader range of management development initiatives than smaller companies, particularly in the areas of team building, motivation, and delegation: the largest companies surveyed were twice as likely to provide training in these areas as the smallest ones. These results are not surprising, since the Galvin Report (1988) highlighted the particular problems faced by small firms in implementing a management development policy. Cross-tabulations with sector did not reveal significant differences, except in the area of training in performance appraisal, where managers in private-sector companies were more likely to have received training than their public-sector counterparts (38.8 per cent, compared with 24.1 per cent).

Heraty (1992) similarly found a strong tendency towards management development, with 79 per cent of respondents providing training in this area. Her study also revealed a strong focus on supervisory training (81 per cent), health and safety training (76 per cent), and technical training (67 per cent). One could argue that there is nothing surprising in these results, since technological change, legislative provisions and the move towards organisational restructuring are forcing companies to provide training in such areas. Furthermore, given the prevailing competitive environment and with it the organisational requirement for greater flexibility and quality and the demand for individual career development opportunities, one might have expected evidence of greater development in these areas (31, 29 and 12 per cent, respectively).

Walsh (1996), referring to a forthcoming national study of management development in Ireland, indicates that historically low levels of investment in management development have improved somewhat over the last number of years. However, he cautions that the issue of maximising the benefits from an experienced and competent managerial work-force remains a central concern for many organisations.

Evaluation of employee development initiatives

Heraty (1992) differentiated between 'hard' and 'soft' evaluation criteria. Hard criteria are concerned with measurable outcomes and would encompass numbers and categories of employees trained, the number of days' training undertaken, the contribution towards particular cost savings, and perhaps examination pass rates. Soft criteria are far more difficult to quantify and would involve evaluating the extent to which demands for trained staff are met, job performance after training, an improved ability to recruit internally, and also improved product or service quality. Her research indicated that while there is an increased focus on evaluation, the tendency is all too often to focus on the hard criteria, which indicate neither the quality nor the effectiveness of the training.

The Price Waterhouse Cranfield project reported that 63.7 per cent of responding companies consciously monitor the effectiveness of their training programmes. A combination of evaluation techniques was used, and these can be said to range from very informal mechanisms, such as feedback from line managers and trainees, to more quantifiable methods, such as tests and formal evaluation after training (see table 9.13). The findings indicate that respondent companies tended to place a large emphasis on informal mechanisms of evaluation and were much less likely to use more structured mechanisms, such as formal evaluation after training or tests. This is indicative of training and development in general, where a difficulty arises in ultimately determining the 'value added' of training.

Table 9.13: Evaluation of employee development

	Use		Do not use	
Informal feedback from line management	98.8%	(164)	1.2%	(2)
Informal feedback from trainees	97.5%	(155)	2.5%	(1)
Formal evaluation immediately after training	76.6%	(89)	23.3%	(27)
Formal evaluation some months after training	49.4%	(42)	50.6%	(43)
Tests	47.4%	(37)	52.6%	(41)
(Actual numbers in parentheses.)				

Source: University of Limerick (1992).

Overall, recent evidence would indicate that considerable training and development is taking place in Irish companies and that there is a conscious attempt not only to distribute responsibility for training decisions but also to monitor the effectiveness of training activities. In view of the prevailing economic climate, companies are increasingly under pressure to seek a maximum return on available resources, and employee development may yet be viewed as the most effective means of sustaining organisational effectiveness.

10

Employee Relations: Institutions and Actors

E mployee relations is probably the most significant aspect of the work of personnel practitioners. Indeed the traditional role of the personnel manager in most Irish companies might more appropriately be described as 'industrial relations manager', given their primary concern with collective bargaining and trade union interactions. While the last decade has undoubtedly witnessed some diminution of this *industrial* relations emphasis and a consequent broadening of the personnel role, employee relations remains a most critical area of personnel activity.

This chapter sketches the nature of employee relations, describes the Irish context, and considers the parties involved in employee relations interactions. Particular attention is paid to the role of trade unions and state institutions in employee relations. (The role of employers and employers' organisations is discussed in chapter 11.)

THE NATURE OF EMPLOYEE RELATIONS

As has often been noted, the very nature of employee relations is a source of some confusion (Tiernan, Morley, and Foley 1996). Traditional definitions have focused on the concept of *industrial* rather than *employee* relations; such an approach reflected an emphasis on the formal regulation of the employment relationship through collective bargaining between organised employees and employers. This perspective remains significant as employers, trade unions and governments seek to develop rules and norms to govern employment relations at enterprise, industrial, national and supranational levels. However, as the nature of employment has changed, the concept of 'employee relations' has achieved increased prominence and is seen as embracing more than just industrial relations. In this book the term 'employee relations' is adopted as a generic one that embraces all employer, employee and state interactions on employment matters. It focuses on the nature of the relationship between the parties to the labour process, embraces both collectivist and individualist approaches, and includes state, industrial and enterprise-level arrangements. It primarily involves the following issues: (*a*) collective bargaining; (*b*) communications policy and practice; (*c*) grievance handling; (*d*) discipline administration; (*e*) joint decision-making and problem-solving; (*f*) the management of change; and (*g*) aspects of social responsibility. In most of these issues trade unions may play an important role. However, they are not a prerequisite, and employee relations is a critical personnel management concern in non-union as well as in unionised companies.

Employee relations in Ireland

Employee relations practice in the great majority of medium and large companies in Ireland has traditionally been associated with a strong collectivist emphasis (Roche 1990). In this model, relations between the management and employees are grounded in the pluralist tradition, with a primary reliance on adversarial collective bargaining.

> Over a wide range of industries and services, employers and unions have conducted their relations on the basis of the premise that their interests were in significant respects different and in opposition ... These differences of interest were reconciled on an ongoing basis through what is sometimes known in the academic literature as 'collective bargaining pure and simple' (Roche 1990, 22).

This pluralist tradition is manifested in relatively high levels of union density, well-developed collective bargaining institutions at establishment level, and employee relations as the key role of the specialist personnel function (Gunnigle and Morley 1992).

As in many industrialised countries, Ireland in the nineteen-eighties witnessed considerable change in the environment and practice of employee relations. From an employer perspective the onset of recession lessened the emphasis on hitherto core work-force management activities, such as recruitment and, particularly, employee relations. Trade union membership fell significantly in the period 1980–87, and industrial unrest also declined significantly over the decade (Roche and Larragy 1989; Roche 1992a, 1994a; Brannick and Doyle 1994). At the same time many companies sought to establish a competitive advantage through improvements in quality, service, or performance. Consequently, it is argued that there has been greater innovation in employee relations practice, particularly in areas such as work systems, rewards, and management-employee communications (Hannaway 1988, 1992; Murray 1984; Flood 1989; Garavan 1991).

In relation to Government approaches to employee relations a number of significant issues emerge. At a general level, Governments have had a largely benign approach to organised labour. The traditional approach of the Government to employee relations has been grounded in the 'voluntarist' tradition. This meant that employers and employees or their representative bodies were largely free to regulate the substantive and procedural terms of their relationship with a minimum of intervention from the Government or its agencies (Hillery 1989, 1994; Breen et al. 1990; Roche 1994b). However, we have more recently witnessed a significant growth in state involvement in the employee relations sphere (see later discussion in this chapter).

An important aspect of public policy in employee relations is the constitutional support for the concept of freedom of association. Article 40.6.1 of the Constitution supports the right of people to form and join associations or unions; however, there is no statutory provision for trade union recognition, and there is no legal obligation on employers to recognise or bargain with unions. (The issue of union membership and recognition is addressed later in this chapter.).

Another important aspect of public policy relates to approaches to industrial development. Since the middle nineteen-sixties Government policy has actively encouraged direct foreign investment. There are now over a thousand foreign-owned companies operating in Ireland, with an emphasis on the engineering (including electronics) and chemicals sectors; these companies employ some 100,000 employees. The United States and Britain have been the principal sources of overseas investment.

On the employee relations front it certainly appears that multinational companies have been a source of innovation in management practices, particularly in the application of new approaches in personnel and employee relations and in expanding the role of the specialist personnel or employee relations function (McMahon et al. 1988; Gunnigle and Flood 1990). However, it would also seem that multinational companies pose unique challenges in the employee relations sphere, particularly in their ability to switch the place of production and also to adopt employee relations styles that challenge the traditional pluralist model (Kelly and Brannick 1988; McGovern 1988, 1989a, 1989b).

A critical first step in grappling with the study of employee relations in Ireland is appreciating the range and nature of the actors and institutions involved in our employee relations system. The key parties include individual workers, trade unions, worker representatives, employers and management, and Government agencies. The interaction of these parties in employee relations will also be heavily influenced by contextual factors such as economic conditions, historical and political factors, and developments in technology. Table 10.1 outlines the main parties involved in employee relations.

Table 10.1: Employee relations: the main parties

Individual employees		Managers
Trade union representatives	*Employer-employee relations*	Employers' associations
Government bodies		Courts and tribunals

Source: Gunnigle, Garavan, and Fitzgerald (1992).

The most critical actors in our employee relations system are trade unions, employers and employers' organisations, and the state. The roles of trade unions and the state are reviewed below, while employer approaches are considered in the next chapter.

TRADE UNIONS

As we have seen in chapter 1, the historical development of personnel management is inextricably linked with the growth of organised labour through the trade union movement. Modern trade unionism has its roots in the factory system and the dramatic changes brought about by the industrial revolution that began in England in the eighteenth century and later spread to the rest of Europe and to North America. The growth of the factory system heralded a change from a largely peasant society based on agriculture and craft production to an industry-based society characterised by new social divisions, where people worked together in larger numbers and relied on wages for their existence (Gunnigle, Morley, and Fitzgerald, 1995). In the face of authoritarian management styles and poor working conditions and lacking in economic or political power, these new factory workers were poorly positioned. It was not until the growth of organised labour through the trade union movement that employees' concerns could command the attention and action of factory owners and managements.

Despite Ireland's relatively recent history of industrialisation, trade unions were well established in Dublin, Belfast and Cork by the early years of the twentieth century (McNamara, Williams, and West 1988; Gunnigle, Morley, and Fitzgerald 1995). The development of trade unionism in England profoundly influenced events in Ireland. The passing of the Trade Disputes Act, 1906, often referred to as the 'Bill of Rights for workers', provided legal immunity for unions involved in strikes and authorised peaceful picketing. Increased conflict between employers and unions characterised this early period and came to a head in the Dublin lock-out of 1913. These events precipitated the increased organisation of workers into trade unions and employers into employers' associations. It also served to increase employers' emphasis on employee relations as a significant management activity. Over time, the fledgling union movement was reluctantly accepted, and employers began to take steps to accommodate it. Employee relations moved towards a more conciliatory approach based on collective bargaining, which in turn led to the increased use of employee relations specialists within companies (Gunnigle et al. 1992).

Trade union objectives and legal status

Essentially, trade unions are organisations that aim to unite workers with common interests. They seek to define those interests, express them, and collectively advance them. A trade union's basic strength lies in its ability to organise and unite workers. Through joining trade unions, it is argued, workers provide themselves with the collective means of redressing the imbalance in bargaining power that is otherwise perceived to exist between individual workers and their employers (Gunnigle, Morley, and Fitzgerald 1995). While workers may join trade unions for numerous reasons, the most common include the desire to influence pay claims, to have protection against management actions, and an ideological belief in the role trade unions play in a democratic society (Tiernan, Morley, and Foley, 1996). Sydney and Beatrice Webb, who wrote the first comprehensive history of trade unions and early collective bargaining, came up with what was long accepted as the most comprehensive definition of a trade union (Webb and Webb 1920): 'a continuous association of wage earners with the objective of improving or maintaining conditions of employment.' Although this definition accurately embraces the work-place role of trade unions, it does not capture their broader social role in advancing workers' interests in the political arena (Salamon 1992; also see Gunnigle, Morley, and Fitzgerald 1995).

For our purposes, trade unions may be viewed as permanent associations of organised employees whose primary objectives are
- to replace individual bargaining with collective bargaining, thereby redressing the balance of bargaining power in favour of employees and reducing the management's prerogative in employment-related matters;

- to facilitate the development of a political system where workers' interests have a greater degree of influence on political decisions, resulting in an economic and social framework that reflects the interests of wage earners;
- to achieve satisfactory levels of pay and conditions of employment and to provide members with a range of services.

The main legislation dealing with the formation and operation of trade unions is the Trade Union Acts, 1941 and 1971, and the Industrial Relations Act, 1990. The legal definition of trade unions provided for in the legislation is very broad and extends to employers' organisations (Kerr and Whyte 1985). This legislation stipulates that, apart from certain 'exempted' bodies, only 'authorised' trade unions holding negotiating licences are permitted to engage in collective bargaining on pay and working conditions.

Trade unions will only be granted a negotiating licence where they register with the Registrar of Friendly Societies and meet the notification criteria (eighteen months), membership criteria (at least 500 members) and financial criteria (minimum deposit of £5,000) set out in the legislation (Gunnigle, Morley, and Fitzgerald 1995). While unions with head offices outside the Republic are not necessarily required to adhere to these requirements, they must be legally recognised trade unions in their country of origin and meet some prescribed guidelines in relation to their controlling authority; otherwise they must meet the notification, membership and deposit requirements set out above.

The legislation also provides for the operation of a number of 'exempted bodies'. These bodies are not required to hold a negotiating licence to engage in collective bargaining and include work-place ('staff' or 'house') associations or unions, some civil service associations, and teachers' associations (Kerr and Whyte 1985).

The principal legislation governing the operation of trade unions is the Industrial Relations Act, 1990. This deals with trade disputes, immunity, picketing, secret ballots, injunctions, and trade union rationalisation. It provides for the protection from civil liability of those who organise or engage in trade disputes. It further provides for the protection of union funds against actions for damages and the legalisation of peaceful picketing in trade disputes. The Act requires unions to conduct a secret ballot of all members of the union who could be reasonably expected to take part in the strike before engaging in industrial action. It recognises 'secondary picketing' (picketing an employer other than the primary employer involved in the dispute) only where it is reasonable for workers to believe that the second employer was acting to frustrate the industrial action by directly assisting the primary employer.

Trade union types

Irish trade unions are normally organised on an occupational basis. This means that workers tend to join a particular union because of the job or trade in which they are employed. Trade unions in Ireland have traditionally been grouped into three broad categories, namely craft unions, general unions, and white-collar unions. However, it should be noted that it is extremely difficult to categorise unions as 'pure' craft, general or white-collar, since many deviate from a tight definition of their category on some dimension (Gunnigle, Morley, and Fitzgerald 1995). For example, general unions may have white-collar and craft workers among their membership, and not all 'craft' unions operate a recognised apprenticeship system. This occupational categorisation should therefore be viewed as indicative rather than definitive.

CRAFT UNIONS

Craft unions cater for workers who possess a particular skill in a trade where entry is restricted through apprenticeship or otherwise. Prominent examples of such occupational categories are electricians and fitters. Craft unions represent the earliest form of union organisation and have their origins in the early unions that emerged in England at the beginning of the nineteenth century. These 'model' unions, as they came to be called, confined their membership to skilled categories, such as printers and carpenters, who had served a recognised apprenticeship in their particular trade. The first English craft union to organise in Ireland was the Amalgamated Society of Engineers, which established branches in the early eighteen-fifties (Boyd 1972). While the early craft unions only represented a small proportion of the labour force, the organisation of workers into craft unions was critical in establishing trade unions as legitimate institutions representing workers' interests in relation to employers and the government.

Craft unions have traditionally protected their trades by ensuring that only those workers holding union cards carry out certain types of skilled work. It is suggested that such unions, by controlling entry to the craft, have traditionally held considerable negotiating power. This strategy is often criticised as being a source of restrictive work practices and demarcation disputes.

Increased mechanisation and consequent de-skilling have had a detrimental impact on the membership and power of craft unions, as reflected in the reduction in their share of union members from a high point of 17 per cent in 1940 to approximately 11 per cent in the late nineteen-eighties (Roche and Larragy 1989). Indeed some older craft unions have ceased to exist, as their traditional craft was rendered obsolete by developments in technology and work practices. However, craft unions remain an integral part of Ireland's employee relations landscape. Figures from the Irish Congress of Trade Unions suggest that the three main engineering craft unions—the Amalgamated Engineering and Electrical Union (AEEU), the Technical, Engineering and Electrical Union (TEEU), and the National Union of Sheet Metal Workers of Ireland (NUSMWI)—make up 6 per cent of the membership of the ICTU, while the main building unions—the Union of Construction, Allied Trades and Technicians (UCATT), the Building and Allied Trades Union (BATU), and the Operative Plasterers' and Allied Trades Society of Ireland (OPATSI)—account for just under 4 per cent (ICTU 1990; Gunnigle, Morley, and Fitzgerald 1995).

GENERAL UNIONS

Unlike the restrictive recruitment strategies of craft unions, general trade unions adopt an open approach, taking into membership all categories of workers, regardless of skill or industry. Despite this open recruitment approach, however, general unions have traditionally catered for semi-skilled and unskilled workers; in more recent years some general unions have attracted white-collar and some craft categories into membership.

The growth of general unions is rooted in the increased number of unskilled or general workers employed in the factories and other large companies that characterised late nineteenth and early twentieth-century Britain. Their initial recruitment drives focused on categories such as general labourers and dock workers. These 'new' unions were more militant than the traditional craft unions of the period, and in addition to their aggressive bargaining approaches they were noted for their political consciousness.

While general unions catering for unskilled workers such as labourers and dockers existed in Ireland from the eighteen-sixties, they came to play a more active role in industrial and political life in the early years of the twentieth century (Gunnigle, Morley, and Fitzgerald 1995). A significant development was the establishment of the Irish Transport and General Workers' Union (ITGWU) in 1909, led by Jim Larkin. The ITGWU and some other general unions organised such categories as dockers, carters and railway workers and became engaged in a series of disputes culminating in the Dublin lock-out of 1913. While this dispute at first dealt a severe blow to the general unions, they slowly recovered and reorganised. Union membership grew from 130,000 in 1914 to 300,000 in 1922, with the ITGWU accounting for 130,000 of these (Boyd 1972; McNamara, Williams, and West 1988).

General unions are typically the largest unions, and today they account for approximately half of all trade union members. General unions are common in all types of organisations and in all industrial sectors. The largest is the Services, Industrial, Professional and Technical Union (SIPTU), with a membership of 199,000 (Department of Enterprise and Employment 1993). It was created in 1990 by the merger of the two largest unions, the ITGWU and the Federated Workers' Union of Ireland (FWUI). Other large general unions are the Amalgamated Transport and General Workers' Union (ATGWU) and the Marine Port and General Workers' Union (MPGWU). Recent figures from the ICTU suggest that the three largest general unions represent some 45 per cent of all ICTU members.

WHITE-COLLAR UNIONS

White-collar unions primarily cater for professional, supervisory, technical, clerical and managerial categories. These unions have experienced a significant growth in membership, particularly from the late nineteen-sixties and into the eighties. The share of members in white-collar unions increased from 24 per cent in 1940 to over 35 per cent in the eighties. In the period 1966–76 white-collar unions increased their membership by 71 per cent, compared with a growth in union membership generally of 30 per cent (Roche and Larragy 1989). The dramatic growth in employment in the services sector, particularly the public sector, was a significant factor in the growth of white-collar unionisation. While traditionally white-collar workers were generally reluctant to join trade unions, changing attitudes, combined with the significant advances in pay and conditions secured by blue-collar unions, encouraged hitherto conservative white-collar workers to unionise.

Recent figures from the ICTU show that the five largest public-sector unions—the Irish Municipal, Public and Civil Trade Union (IMPACT), the Communications Workers' Union (CWU), the Irish Nurses' Organisation (INO), the Civil and Public Services Union (CPSU), and the Public Service Executive Union (PSEU)—account for almost 17 per cent of the ICTU membership, while the three principal teachers' unions—the Irish National Teachers' Organisation (INTO), the Association of Secondary Teachers, Ireland (ASTI), and the Teachers' Union of Ireland (TUI)—account for over 8 per cent (Gunnigle, Morley, and Foley 1995). We also find that in the financial services two unions—the Irish Bank Officials' Association (IBOA) and the Manufacturing, Science and Finance Union (MSF)—account for another 8 per cent of ICTU membership. Other important unions catering for white-collar employees are the Irish Distributive and Administrative Trades Union (IDATU) and the Irish National Union of Vintners', Grocers' and Allied Trades Assistants (INUVGATA). It should also be noted that many white-collar workers are members of general unions, particularly SIPTU.

Trade union structure

Turning to the actual operation of trade unions, three different levels may be identified, namely (*a*) work-place level, (*b*) branch level, and (*c*) national level. This structure is illustrated in fig. 10.1. Ultimate decision-making authority in a trade union is vested in the membership and executed through resolutions passed at the annual delegate conference. It is the responsibility of the union executive to carry out policy decisions reached at the annual conference. The primary role of the union official is to carry out the operational aspects of the union's role, servicing the membership through assistance and advice.

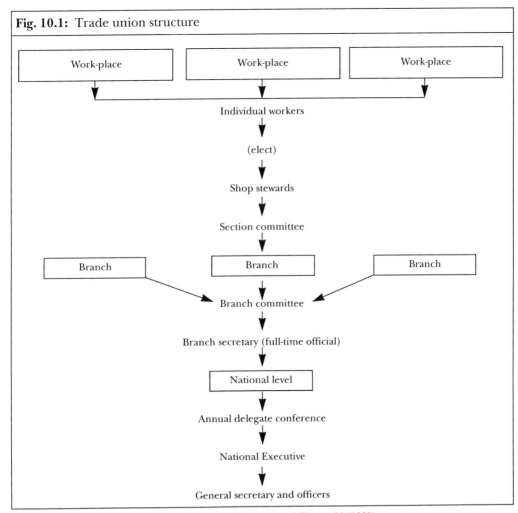

Fig. 10.1: Trade union structure

Source: Gunnigle, McMahon, and Fitzgerald (1995).

The **shop steward** is the principal trade union representative in the work-place. Shop stewards are elected by fellow-members at elections that normally take place once a year. A number of shop stewards may be elected to represent different sections within the work-place. The shop steward's role is to represent the interests of union members on work-place issues, to liaise with union officials, and to keep members informed of union affairs. Shop stewards may become involved in much work-place bargaining involving local grievances or disputes. On more important issues their role is to support the union official and give feedback to the membership. It should be noted that shop stewards are employees of their organisations and therefore must perform their normal work and duties. The Department of Enterprise and Employment's *Code of Practice on the Duties and Responsibilities of Employee Representatives*, issued under the terms of the Industrial Relations Act, 1990, provides that employee representatives should be afforded reasonable time off to perform their representative duties (Department of Enterprise and Employment 1993). They are also charged with representing their members in a fair and equitable manner. It has become the custom and practice in a number of companies for shop stewards to be given some time off to perform their union duties and to have access to certain necessary facilities, such as clerical and secretarial support. However, these are generally minimal, a fact that may be related to the small scale of most Irish organisations (Gunnigle, Morley, and Fitzgerald 1995).

The *section committee* consists of union members elected by fellow-members who work in a specific section of the establishment. Its main role is to help shop stewards to perform their tasks effectively. Shop stewards within an establishment frequently form themselves into a committee so that they can meet regularly, discuss common problems, and decide on policy and work-place employee relations issues. Such a committee is called a *shop stewards' committee*. All these shop stewards normally belong to the same union; a committee comprising shop stewards from different unions is normally called a *joint shop stewards' committee*.

The *branch* is the basic organisational unit in a trade union. In Ireland a trade union branch normally comprises a group of union members from different companies in the same geographical area; occasionally a branch may comprise union members from one large business enterprise. A branch manages the internal affairs of the union in its particular area and strives for improvements in the terms and working conditions of its members. The affairs of the branch are managed by the *branch committee*. This committee is elected at the annual general meeting of the branch, which is also the forum for electing delegates from the branch to attend the annual delegate conference of the union.

Both the branch committee and the branch members are served by a *branch secretary*. In larger unions this person is normally a full-time union official, whose role is to administer the affairs of the branch and to negotiate terms and conditions for all branch members with the management.

At national level the election of union officers takes place at the *annual delegate conference*. It is here that motions concerning trade union policy, usually emanating from branches, are discussed and voted on. If approved by the conference such a resolution becomes ultimately union policy. The annual conference comprises branch delegates together with the union's *national executive*. The national executive is responsible for carrying out the decisions of the annual conference and appointing branch officials and other union staff. The *general officers* of the union are usually full-time union employees and normally include the *general president*, *general secretary*, and *general treasurer*.

Irish Congress of Trade Unions

The Irish Congress of Trade Unions is the national co-ordinating body of the Irish trade union movement; it is estimated that some 97 per cent of Irish trade unionists are members of affiliated unions (ICTU 1993). Important unions not affiliated to the ICTU are the National Bus and Rail Union (NBRU), the Psychiatric Nurses' Association (PNA), and the Dairy Executives' Association (DEA).

While the ICTU acts as the representative of the collective interests of the trade union movement, individual unions retain a large degree of autonomy, and the ICTU relies on the co-operation of affiliated unions in promoting its overall goals (Gunnigle, Morley, and Foley 1995). The ICTU plays an extremely important role at national level, representing union views to the Government and other institutions. This role is particularly significant in centralised pay negotiations. Along with the other social partners—the Government, employers, and farming representatives—it is a party to national negotiations on pay and other aspects of social and economic policy. It is the vehicle through which trade unions decide on participation in centralised pay bargaining, approve any agreement thus concluded, and ensure that affiliated unions adhere to the terms of such agreements. The ICTU also represents trade unions on several national bodies and provides union nominees for the conciliation and arbitration services.

Ultimate decision-making power in the ICTU is vested in its annual delegate conference, where delegates from affiliated unions consider motions presented by the various unions and those adopted become ICTU policy. A number of important committees operate under the auspices of the ICTU executive. A Disputes Committee deals with inter-union disputes in relation to union membership. The Demarcation Tribunal deals with inter-union disputes in relation to work boundaries. The Industrial Relations Committee has the particularly important responsibility of granting authorisation for an 'all-out picket' in industrial disputes. (This requires all union members employed in the company where the dispute exists not to pass the picket, provided the picket is peaceful, is at the place of work of the employer, and is 'in contemplation or furtherance of a trade dispute.' For this purpose a secret ballot of all union members must be held and the aggregate majority must be in favour of such industrial action. Individual unions can only sanction a 'one-union picket', where only members of the union in dispute are obliged not to pass.)

Trade union density

The most widely used indicator of trade union penetration in a country is union density, which comprises two key measures: (*a*) the proportion of the work-force (which includes those employed and those seeking employment) who are trade union members ('work-force density') and (*b*) the proportion of employees who are union members ('employment density').

As noted in chapter 1, Ireland has traditionally been characterised by relatively high levels of trade union density. There is a total of approximately sixty-five trade unions, catering for a membership of about 460,000, which represents a work-force density of 43 per cent and an employment density of 56 per cent. As can be seen in table 10.2, work-force density has fallen from a high point of 55 per cent in 1980 to its present level of approximately 43 per cent. Indeed the nineteen-eighties witnessed the most serious decline in trade union density since the thirties (Roche 1989). This is principally attributed to macro-economic factors, particularly economic depression, increased unemployment, and changes in employment structure involving decline or stagnation of employment in traditionally highly unionised sectors (indigenous manufacturing and the public sector) and growth in sectors that have traditionally posed difficulties for union penetration (foreign-owned manufacturing and, particularly, private services) (see Roche and Larragy 1989, 1992; Roche 1992, 1994).

Table 10.2: Trade union membership, 1945–90

Year	Membership	Employment density	Work-force density
1945	172,300	27.7	25.4
1960	312,600	49.6	45.4
1975	448,800	59.3	52.3
1980	527,200	61.8	55.2
1981	524,400	61.5	53.5
1982	519,900	60.3	51.4
1983	513,300	61.1	49.7
1984	500,200	60.7	48.2
1985	483,300	59.9	46.6
1986	471,000	58.0	45
1987	457,300	56.2	43.1
1988[*]	470,644	57.1	44.2
1989[*]	458,690	55.6	43.4
1990[*]	462,451	54.6	43.2

[*]Figures for 1988–90 are estimates and are derived from the annual membership of unions affiliated to the ICTU.

Source: UCD DUES Project (1992).

With regard to more recent trends, provisional figures from the Department of Enterprise and Employment (formerly the Department of Labour) based on returns from unions affiliated to the ICTU suggest that trade union membership rose from approximately 470,000 in 1988 to approximately 477,000 in 1992, and the department suggests that this trend was sustained up to 1993 (ICTU 1993; Department of Enterprise and Employment 1993). This increase appears to reflect the fact that more people are now at work than ever before.

Looking at comparable figures in other countries, we find that levels of union density in Ireland are quite high, as illustrated in table 10.3.

Table 10.3: Trade union membership: employment density by country

Sweden	85%
Denmark	73%
Finland	71%
Norway	57%
Ireland	55%
Belgium	53%
Luxembourg	50%
Austria	46%

Australia	42%
New Zealand	42%
Italy	40%
Britain	40%
Canada	35%
Germany	34%
Japan	27%
Netherlands	25%
United States	16%
France	12%

Source: Visser (1991).

Turning to the distribution of trade union membership by size of union, we find considerable imbalance, as illustrated in table 10.4. At one extreme a relatively small number of large unions represents almost three-quarters of the total union membership, while at the other extreme we find some forty small unions catering for approximately 12 per cent of total membership (Gunnigle, Morley, and Fitzgerald 1995).

Table 10.4: Trade union membership by size of union, 1991

Members	Unions	Percentage of total union membership
Fewer than 1,000	17	1.3%
1,001–2,000	10	3.0%
2,001–5,000	11	6.7%
5,001–10,000	6	9.7%
10,001–15,000	3	8.0%
Over 15,000	8	71.3%

Note: This table refers only to trade unions holding negotiating licences under the Trade Union Acts and therefore excludes a number of representative bodies that operate as trade unions but do not hold such a licence.

Department of Enterprise and Employment (1993).

A related and important development in trade union structure since the nineteen-eighties has been the significant increase in the number of union mergers. The aggregate number of unions in Ireland has declined dramatically in recent years, falling from over ninety in the nineteen-sixties to some sixty-five in 1991 (Gunnigle, Morley, and Fitzgerald 1995; see table 10.5). The merger in 1990 of the two largest unions, the ITGWU and FWUI, to form SIPTU was probably the most significant union merger in Ireland. It is estimated that SIPTU, the largest union in the country, now caters for some 40 per cent of total trade union membership.

Table 10.5: Number of trade unions in Ireland, 1980–90

Year	Number of unions
1980	86
1981	86
1982	83
1983	80
1984	78
1985	77
1986	77
1987	76
1988	74
1989	68
1990	65

Source: Department of Enterprise and Employment (1993).

Union membership and recognition at company level

The extent of trade union membership and recognition and the nature of management-union interactions are key indicators of management approaches to and changes in employee relations. This aspect incorporates both the extent of union recognition and, where unions are recognised, the nature of management-union relations. A particular issue in the context of Irish employee relations is trade union recognition and the future role of collective bargaining.

A number of commentators have identified changes in the extent and nature of collective employee representation as a critical aspect of change in management approaches to employee relations (Purcell and Gray 1986; Purcell 1987; Salamon 1992). Collectivism in employee relations incorporates the extent to which the management acknowledges the right of employees to collective representation and the involvement of the collective in influencing management decision-making. A critical aspect of collectivism in employee relations is therefore the extent of trade union recognition and, where unions are recognised, the nature of management-union relations.

As we have seen, employee relations in Ireland has traditionally been associated with a strong pluralist orientation, characterised by comparatively high levels of union density and recognition and a reliance on adversarial collective bargaining (Hillery 1989; Roche 1990; Gunnigle and Morley 1992; Gunnigle et al. 1994). Despite some commentaries to the contrary, trade unions remain integral to the fabric of Irish employee relations. Data from the Price Waterhouse Cranfield study indicates that levels of union density in Irish organisations are quite high, with almost two-thirds of respondent firms reporting that more than 50 per cent of their staff were union members (Gunnigle and Morley 1992; Gunnigle, Morley, and Fitzgerald 1995). As expected, levels of unionisation were positively associated with company size, with large employers likely to have higher union density. Union penetration also tends to be strongest in the public service and 'traditional' manufacturing; for example, Hourihan (1995) estimates that union density is approximately 76 per cent in the public service but only 25.4 per cent in the private sector. The Price Waterhouse Cranfield study also found that union density was particularly high in the public sector.

Table 10.6: Trade union density at company level

Proportion of employees in trade unions	%
0	18.3
1–25%	6.4
26–50%	10.9
51–75%	18
76–100%	42.3
Don't know/missing	4.1
n = 269	

Source: University of Limerick (1992); also see Gunnigle, Morley and Turner (1993).

Trade union recognition is a critical barometer of 'collectivism' in company-level employee relations, since the granting of such recognition remains largely an issue of management prerogative. This is not to say that trade union action or the decision of the Labour Court may not convince employers to accede to union recognition but rather to acknowledge the reality that at present the decision to concede recognition is largely a matter of management discretion. Salamon (1992, 476) defines trade union recognition as

> the process by which management formally accepts one or more trade unions as the representative(s) of all, or a group, of its employees for the purpose of jointly determining terms and conditions of employment on a collective basis,

and goes on to suggest that union recognition is

> perhaps the most important stage in the development of an organisation's industrial relations system ... [conferring] legitimacy on the trade union's role of representing and protecting its members' interests in the workplace.

We have seen earlier that the constitutional guarantee of freedom of association, embodied in article 40.6.1.iii of the Constitution, confers on citizens the right to form and join associations or unions. The Constitution guarantees this right subject to 'public order and morality' and provides that laws may be enacted for the 'regulation and control in the public interest' of the exercise of this right. However, while the Constitution supports the freedom of workers to organise into associations and unions, there is no apparent obligation on employers to recognise or bargain with such unions (Commission of Inquiry on Industrial Relations 1981). Although the Labour Court may issue a recommendation in recognition disputes, such recommendations have no legal effect (see the later discussion on the Labour Court); indeed recent evidence suggests that Labour Court recommendations in favour of union recognition are often ignored by employers (Gunnigle 1995a).

It should be noted that constitutional support for the concept of freedom of association has also been interpreted as including an implied right not to join trade unions or associations where people do not wish to do so. This was demonstrated in a Supreme Court case in 1961 involving industrial action by a section of a company's work-force to enforce a 'closed shop'. The Supreme Court held that while the Constitution conferred on employees the right to join trade unions it also included an implied right not to join, and on this basis it found against the union and its actions (*Educational Company of Ireland v. Fitzpatrick and others,* IR 323, 1961).

Historically it is suggested that the lack of a statutory mechanism for facilitating union recognition in Ireland was not problematic, since most larger employers tended to recognise and conclude collective agreements with unions (Gunnigle, Morley, and Fitzgerald 1995). This phenomenon has been attributed to a tradition of trade union recognition and reliance on collective bargaining (Roche 1989; Roche and Turner 1994). However, it is equally clear that the decline in union membership in the nineteen-eighties and the increased incidence of union avoidance among some employers has made union recognition an increasingly significant issue in employee relations (McGovern 1989; Gunnigle and Brady 1984; Gunnigle 1995).

Table 10.7: Trade union recognition in longer-established companies

Union recognition	Number of firms	%
Yes	207	77
No	57	21
Missing/don't know	5	2

n = 269

Source: University of Limerick (1992); see also Gunnigle, Morley, and Turner (1993).

Looking at the empirical evidence, we see that levels of union recognition in Ireland remain quite high. Data provided by the Price Waterhouse Cranfield study indicates that the great majority of longer-established Irish companies recognise unions (see table 10.7). In general the research evidence seems to indicate that union membership remains quite robust, with high levels of union recognition and union density in most Irish companies. However, we have seen that union penetration tends to be strongest in the public service and 'traditional' manufacturing. It may therefore be useful to look outside these sectors for a more reliable indicator of the role of trade unions. Some of the most interesting evidence on trends in union recognition emerge from a recent study of newly established companies in Ireland (Gunnigle 1995a, 1995b; also see Sheehan 1996). This study found a high incidence of non-unionism, with 53 per cent of firms not recognising unions, as opposed to 21 per cent in the Price Waterhouse Cranfield study (see tables 10.8 and 10.9). The incidence of non-union status was mainly related to ownership and industrial sector and largely confined to American-owned firms in 'high-technology' sectors.

Table 10.8: Trade union recognition in newly established companies, by country of ownership

Union recognition		Ownership			Total	
	Irish	American	European	Other		
Yes	82%(9)	15%(4)	100%(8)	57%(4)	25	(47%)

No	18%(2)	85%(23)	0	43%(3)	28	(53%)

Source: Gunnigle (1995a).

Table 10.9: Trade union recognition: newly established v. longer-established companies

Union recognition	Longer-established Public & private sector (n = 269)	Private sector only (n = 182)	Newly established (n = 53)
Yes	77%	72%	47%
No	21%	28%	53%
Missing	2%	0	0

Source: Gunnigle (1995).

Alternatives to trade unions

Before we complete our discussion of trade unions it should be noted that while unions have been the most conspicuous means of representing employees' interests, there are other approaches that may be adopted. The most obvious of these is individual bargaining, whereby workers negotiate terms and conditions of employment directly with employers on a person-to-person basis. Such individual bargaining may be attractive to workers in a strong bargaining position by virtue of their valued skills or knowledge, especially where such skills or knowledge are in short supply. However, it is traditionally argued that individual bargaining does not suit the needs of most workers, since it places them at a bargaining disadvantage vis-à-vis employers. Indeed this has been a traditional selling-point of trade unions: that collective employee representation through trade unions serves to counterbalance employers' bargaining power and thus redresses the perceived bargaining disadvantage of the individual worker.

Another approach that workers may adopt is to use work-place or staff associations to represent their interests. Company-based staff associations usually represent employees' interests through consultation with the senior management on collective as well as individual issues. They have traditionally been associated with white-collar grades, particularly professional and managerial staffs (Gunnigle, Morley, and Fitzgerald 1995). The use of staff associations is often seen as an improvement on individual bargaining. By joining together, it is argued, workers can present a more united front to employers and redress the perceived bargaining imbalance associated with individual bargaining. An important consideration, particularly among some employers, is that staff associations provide for a modicum of collective employee representation without the introduction of a 'third party'—the trade union—into the employee relations process at the establishment level. Employees may also sometimes prefer to use staff associations. The traditional association of trade unions with the interests of 'blue-collar' workers may create a 'snob factor', which encourages employees to join or remain in staff associations (Gunnigle, Morley, and Fitzgerald 1995). Employers may also see staff associations as 'easier' bargaining partners, less likely to engage in confrontational or adversarial bargaining approaches (Gunnigle 1995b). However, this factor is also a source of the most far-reaching criticism of staff associations, namely that they suffer from a lack of independence from the employing company. A related disadvantage is the absence of an external organisation structure and of resources with which to provide bargaining expertise or legal advice.

Some indicative contrasts between trade unions and staff associations are shown in table 10.10. It is important to note that these generalisations may not characterise all trade unions or staff associations.

Table 10.10: Trade unions and staff associations: indicative contrasts

	Trade unions	*Staff associations*
Objectives	1. Replace individual bargaining with collective bargaining	Similar but less ideological commitment
	2. Pay and employment conditions	Yes
	3. Political	No
Controlling authority	Union head office; normally strong role for ICTU	No external authority
Rules, procedures	Detailed constitution, often with strong political dimension	None or brief constitution; oriented to firm
External resources	Access to external expertise and resources; influence on national issues (e.g. incomes policies)	None except by contracting in
Methods	Collective bargaining: adversarial orientation	Consultative
Use of sanctions	Prepared to use strike weapon	Most unlikely
Services to members	May have range of services	Limited

Source: Gunnigle, McMahon and Fitzgerald (1995).

THE ROLE OF THE STATE

This section considers the role of the state in employee relations. It focuses on the four main methods by which the state may intervene in employee relations: (*a*) as an employee relations policy-maker, (*b*) as a provider of machinery for the resolution of disputes, (*c*) as a legislator, and (*d*) as an employer.

Policy: state approaches to employee relations

We have seen in chapter 1 that the Irish employee relations system has historically been described as a voluntary one. This is generally taken to indicate an approach in which the role of the state in employee relations has been restricted to establishing essential legislative rules and providing mediation and arbitration machinery, leaving employers and employees relatively free to develop work rules and procedures to suit particular company contexts. This strategy has been termed 'auxiliary state control' and was the dominant approach of Governments towards employee relations up to the end of the nineteen-seventies (Roche 1989). In general, it is suggested that Governments have been supportive of trade unions and a consensus approach to employee relations. This approach was largely a historical legacy of the British voluntarist tradition. However, since the early eighties it would appear that the British and Irish governments have taken markedly contrasting approaches in the areas of pay and employee relations. In Britain, Conservative governments have taken steps, both legislative and otherwise, to reduce union power and ensure that wage levels and other employee relations outcomes are determined by market forces. In Ireland the voluntarist tradition has been considerably diluted in recent years; in contrast to Britain, however, this change has taken the form of greater centralisation and state intervention in employee relations (Roche 1989; 1994b). In the period 1970–82 Ireland had a series of national agreements on pay and related employment issues. These were hailed as important vehicles in delivering wage restraint, reduced industrial conflict, and low inflation; however, they failed to deliver, and the period was characterised by high levels of inflation, wage drift, and industrial conflict. Central agreements were abandoned by the somewhat disillusioned social partners—particularly employers—and there was a brief return to decentralised bargaining in the period 1982–86.

In a time of severe fiscal rectitude the Fianna Fáil Government revived central agreements through the Programme for National Recovery (1987–90). This period was characterised by very moderate wage increases and high growth in GDP. Much of the credit for such success has been attributed to centralised agreements, although it is possible to argue that this period would have been characterised by low pay increases and low levels of industrial conflict regardless of whether pay was negotiated centrally or locally.[1] Recent Governments have been strong advocates of centralised agreements on pay and other aspects of economic and social policy, involving negotiations with the main social partners. In the area of employee relations the achievement of a high level of national consensus through a model of 'bargained co-operation' has been the most significant development. (The impact of centralised agreements is discussed in further detail in chapter 12.)

Machinery for resolution of disputes
In the area of the resolution of disputes the state provides a number of specific agencies to deal with employee relations matters: the Labour Relations Commission, the Labour Court, rights commissioners, the Employment Appeals Tribunal, and equality officers. The adoption of the Industrial Relations Act, 1990, introduced a new framework under which some of these institutions must operate. (The provisions of this Act are outlined in chapter 13.) This section briefly considers the role of the various dispute resolution institutions; their operation is summarised in fig. 10.2.

LABOUR RELATIONS COMMISSION
The Labour Relations Commission was established under the Industrial Relations Act, 1990. It is a tripartite body with employer, trade union and independent representation and is charged with the general responsibility for promoting 'good industrial relations'. The commission provides a comprehensive range of services designed to help prevent and resolve disputes; the main functions are as follows:

- the conciliation service;
- the industrial relations advisory service;
- the preparation of codes of practice relevant to industrial relations after consultation with unions and employers' organisations and the provision of guidance on such codes of practice;
- the appointment of equality officers and the provision of an equality service;
- the selection and nomination of people for appointment as rights commissioners;
- the commissioning of research into matters relevant to industrial relations;
- the review and monitoring of developments in the area of industrial relations;
- assisting joint labour committees and joint industrial councils in the exercise of their functions.

Fig. 10.2: State institutions for resolution of disputes

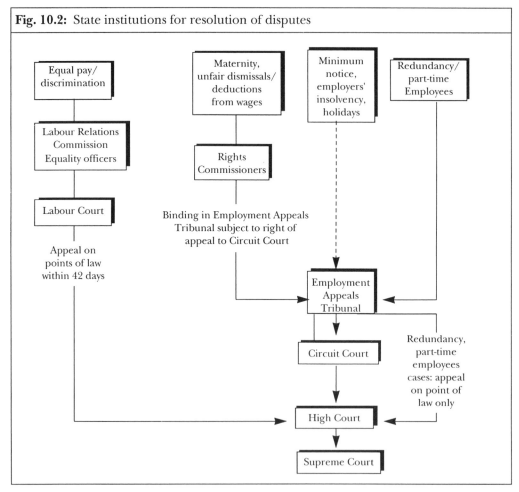

Source: Adapted from Wallace (1987).

A critical aspect of the work of the Labour Relations Commission is its *conciliation service*. Together with the Labour Court (see below), the role of conciliation is to assist in the resolution of cases referred by parties in dispute. These are normally issues where the parties have failed to reach agreement or compromise at local level. The conciliation service was formerly provided by the Labour Court; the relocation of the service is designed to give a new impetus to the role of conciliation and encourage the conflicting parties to take more responsibility for the resolution of disputes. It is hoped that this will encourage the resolution of disputes at the earliest possible stage of the dispute-settling machinery rather than having issues progress almost automatically to a full Labour Court investigation. The normal pattern for an issue being processed to conciliation, and possibly to full Labour Court investigation, is outlined in fig. 10.3.

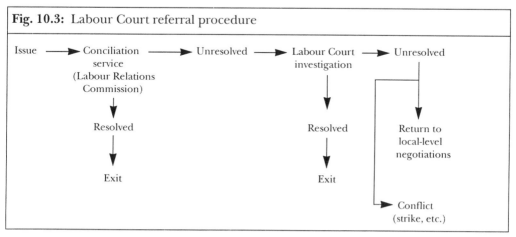

Fig. 10.3: Labour Court referral procedure

Source: Gunnigle, Morley, and Foley (1995).

The conciliation process involves an industrial relations officer (IRO) presiding over a meeting of the conflicting parties. Having listened to the parties in dispute, the IRO may hold separate meetings ('side conferences') with both to get a better idea of the basis of the dispute and what is required to resolve the issue. The IRO can then attempt to guide the parties towards an acceptable solution. Conciliation is essentially voluntary, with the IRO acting as a facilitator in the search for an acceptable solution.

The success rate in resolving issues at conciliation has fluctuated over the years, and there have been frequent criticisms of both employers and unions for abusing the system through unwillingness to settle at conciliation. However, conciliation generally has a good record in resolving disputes, as demonstrated in table 10.11.

Table 10.11: Conciliation service referrals, 1971–92

	Number of disputes in which conciliation conferences were held	Number of disputes settled at conciliation (% in parentheses)
1971	628	429 (68)
1972	713	443 (62)
1973	855	487 (56)
1974	951	646 (68)
1975	1,108	576 (52)

1976	1,071	581	(54)
1977	1,175	638	(54)
1978	1,288	651	(51)
1979	1,301	633	(49)
1980	1,375	693	(50)
1981	1,582	766	(48)
1982	1,855	927	(50)
1983	2,090	1,114	(53)
1984	1,750	1,037	(50)
1985	2,021	1,355	(67)
1986	1,892	1,268	(67)
1987	1,787	1,151	(64)
1988	1,571	1,064	(68)
1989	1,450	1,019	(70)
1990	1,552	1,143	(74)
1991	1,880	1,598	(85)
1992	1,935	1,451	(75)

Source: Labour Court and Labour Relations Commission, annual reports.

Table 10.12 provides greater detail on the work of the conciliation service in the period 1991–92. This data indicates that conditions of employment, special pay increases and basic pay claims constituted the main issues dealt with in that period.

Table 10.12: Conciliation service activities, 1991–92

	Disputes			Meetings	Settled
	Private sector	Public sector	Total		
1991	1,303	577	1,880	2,485	85%
1992	1,388	547	1,935	2,450	75%

Source: Labour Relations Commission, annual reports.

While the main focus of the conciliation service is on dealing with actual disputes, the role of the advisory service is to help identify problems that may give rise to employee relations difficulties and to provide direction and advice in resolving such problems. The advisory service represents something of a new departure in the role of dispute resolution agencies. It has as its central brief the task of preventing industrial disputes by encouraging 'good industrial relations policies, practices and procedures' in companies facing management-labour difficulties. The Labour Relations Commission is also responsible for undertaking or commissioning research, as well as monitoring developments in the general employee relations arena.

One of the principal new functions of the Labour Relations Commission is preparing codes of practice on a range of matters in industrial relations (unspecified). While codes of practice are set in a statutory framework, they are not directly enforceable, in that a breach of the code will not incur any civil or criminal sanction. The codes of practice are intended to give guidance to employers and trade unions on particular issues and to have strong moral authority. So far two codes of practice have been prepared, the *Code of Practice on Dispute Procedures Including Procedures in Essential Services* and the *Code of Practice on the Duties and Responsibilities of Employee Representatives and the Protection and Facilities to be Afforded Them by Their Employer.*

The Industrial Relations Act, 1990, also gave to the Labour Relations Commission the responsibility for assisting joint industrial councils (JICs) and joint labour committees (JLCs) in the discharge of their functions. The LRC's main role is to provide industrial relations officers to chair a number of JICs and JLCs. JICs are permanent voluntary negotiating bodies whose task is to facilitate collective bargaining at industry level in certain sectors. They comprise representatives of employers and trade unions from within the relevant industry or sector. JICs may be registered with the Labour Court; at present three are registered, for the footwear and construction industries and the Dublin wholesale fruit and vegetable trade (Gunnigle, Morley, and Fitzgerald 1995). There are a further eleven unregistered JICs, in the following industries: bacon curing; bakery and confectionery; banks; electrical contracting; flour milling; grocery, provision and allied trades; hosiery and knitted garments manufacture; printing and allied trades in Dublin; state industrial employees; woollen and worsted manufacture; and Telecom Éireann.

Joint labour committees are statutory bodies comprising employers' and trade union representatives and independent members that regulate wages and conditions of employment in areas where collective bargaining is poorly established. At present there are fifteen JLCs, covering approximately 88,000 workers (Labour Relations Commission 1992). JLCs exist in respect of the following industries: aerated waters; agriculture; brush and broom manufacture; catering (excluding Dublin); contract cleaning (Dublin); hairdressing (Cork); hairdressing (Dublin); handkerchief and household goods; hotels (excluding Dublin and Cork); law clerks; provender milling; shirtmaking; tailoring; women's clothing and millinery; and the catering industry in Dublin and Dún Laoghaire. JLCs are charged with determining legally binding minimum wages and conditions of employment for those workers represented by them. The JLC submits proposals to the Labour Court for minimum wage rates or for regulating conditions; if the Labour Court accepts the proposals then it makes an employment regulation order (ERO) giving statutory effect to the proposals. Employment regulation orders are enforced by inspectors appointed by the Minister for Enterprise and Employment.

THE LABOUR COURT

The Labour Court is the principal institution for facilitating the resolution of trade disputes (Gunnigle, Morley, and Fitzgerald 1995). It was established by the Industrial Relations Act, 1946, as amended by the Industrial Relations Acts, 1969 and 1976. The Industrial Relations Act, 1990, assigned many of the functions previously held by the Labour Court to the Labour Relations Commission (most notably the conciliation service).

The principal role of the Labour Court is to investigate and make recommendations on cases referred to it by parties in dispute. These are normally issues where the parties have failed to reach agreement or compromise at local level. At the first stage of a Labour Court investigation the parties are obliged to go through conciliation, as discussed above; should an issue remain unresolved after conciliation it may then be referred for investigation. The Industrial Relations Act, 1990, provides that the Labour Court may normally investigate a dispute only in one of the following situations:

- if it receives a report from the Labour Relations Commission that no further efforts on its part will help resolve the dispute;
- if it is notified by the chairperson of the Labour Relations Commission that the LRC has waived its function of conciliation in the dispute.

In either event the parties to the dispute must also request the Labour Court to investigate the dispute. It may also investigate a dispute referred to it under section 20 of the Industrial Relations Act, 1969—

- if it is hearing an appeal in relation to a recommendation of a rights commissioner or of an equality officer;
- if it decides after consultation with the Labour Relations Commission that exceptional circumstances in the case warrant a Labour Court investigation.

In addition, the Labour Court may investigate a dispute at the request of the Minister for Enterprise and Employment.

The Labour Court at present comprises a chairperson, three deputy chairpersons, and nine ordinary members. While all these appointments are made by the minister, ordinary members are nominated for appointment by organisations representative of trade unions and employer interests.

To facilitate speed of operation the Labour Court normally sits by division. A division comprises an independent chairperson (who is the chairperson or deputy chairperson of the Labour Court), an employer representative, and a union representative. Hearings are generally held in private and involve written and oral submissions by the parties and some element of cross-examination.

When the Labour Court feels it has adequately investigated a case it will conclude the hearing and set about issuing a recommendation. The recommendations are generally not legally binding on the parties. However, there are two important instances where decisions are legally binding: (*a*) where the court hears an appeal against the decision of a rights commissioner or an equality officer, and (*b*) where workers or their trade unions refer a dispute for investigation under section 20 (i) of the Industrial Relations Act, 1969 (i.e. where the union refers the dispute on its own and agrees to be bound by the Labour Court's recommendation).

In spite of the generally non-binding nature of its recommendations, the Labour Court has had a very satisfactory record, with over three-quarters of its recommendations accepted by both parties (see, for example, Gunnigle, Morley, and Fitzgerald 1995). Indeed, where recommendations are rejected their terms may often form the basis of a solution on return to local-level negotiations.

The Labour Court was seen to depart from its broad role of promoting collective bargaining and resolving industrial conflict when it was given the role of determinant of disputes by the employment equality legislation, notably the Anti-Discrimination (Pay) Act, 1974, and the Employment Equality Act, 1977 (Fennell and Lynch 1993; Gunnigle, Morley, and Fitzgerald 1995). In such cases a Labour Court determination may be appealed, on points of law only, within six weeks to the High Court. Table 10.13 summarises the extent of Labour Court determinations in the area of employment equality since 1978. (The role of equality officers in promoting employment equality is discussed below.)

Table 10.13: Labour Court determinations, 1978–92

	Employment Equality Act, 1977		Anti-Discrimination (Pay) Act, 1974	
	Number	In favour of claimants	Number	In favour of claimants
1978	2	2	18	8
1979	1	1	23	12
1980	8	3	39	26
1981	6	4	15	9
1982	9	5	10	2
1983	7	2	10	2
1984	4	2	9	3
1985	5	2	11	5
1986	2	1	8	3
1987	2	1	6	5
1988	1	1	7	2
1989	3	2	4	4
1990	4	1	2	2
1991	6	1	8	2
1992	10	4	4	4

Source: Employment Equality Agency, annual reports (various).

RIGHTS COMMISSIONERS

The appointment and functions of rights commissioners were approved by the Industrial Relations Act, 1969. This service was originally attached to the Labour Court. The purpose of the establishment of the service was to reduce the work load of the Labour Court and to provide a speedy service to parties in dispute over the less important industrial relations issues.

The rights commissioner service is now attached to the Labour Relations Commission; however, rights commissioners operate independently in the performance of their functions. They are appointed by the Minister for Enterprise and Employment from a panel submitted by the Labour Relations Commission.

Under the terms of the Industrial Relations Act, 1969, rights commissioners may investigate a trade dispute provided that

- it is not a dispute connected with the rates of pay, hours or times of work or annual holidays of a body of workers;
- it is not a dispute concerning persons who do not have access to the Labour Court;
- a party to the dispute does not object in writing to such an investigation;
- the Labour Court has not made a recommendation about the dispute.

Rights commissioners operate individually. They meet the parties in dispute, provided both agree to such a hearing and agree to accept the commissioner's decision. In practice, rights commissioners mostly investigate disputes concerning individual employees (e.g. discipline or demarcation issues). Hearings are held in private, with the rights commissioner examining each case on its merits and issuing a written recommendation. A great advantage of this service is its flexibility and accessibility, providing a quick and efficient mechanism for dealing with problems that have proved intractable at local level. An objection to an investigation by a rights commissioner must be notified in writing to the commissioner within three weeks of the date of notification by post that a dispute has been referred.

There are at present five rights commissioners. Their role has significantly expanded since 1969 with the enactment of further employment legislation that has given them additional functions. They now have a statutory role in investigating cases under the Unfair Dismissals Act, 1977, the Maternity (Protection of Employees) Act, 1981, and the Payment of Wages Act, 1991.

A recommendation by a rights commissioner is not legally binding, but in practice they tend to be observed by employers and trade unions. However, disputes heard under the Industrial Relations Act, 1969, may be appealed to the Labour Court, resulting in an order that is binding. An appeal against a rights commissioner's recommendation must be notified in writing to the Labour Court within six weeks of the date of the recommendation. Cases in relation to the other Acts under which they have a role can be appealed to the Employment Appeals Tribunal. Similarly, an appeal against the recommendation of a rights commissioner under these Acts must be made within six weeks.

Table 10.14 summarises the work of the rights commissioner service over the period 1979–91. Recommendations appealed to the Labour Court have averaged approximately 16 per cent in recent years. In general the rights commissioner service has been received favourably by all sides of industry (Kelly 1989; Gunnigle, Morley, and Foley 1995).

Table 10.14: Rights commissioner activity, 1979–91

	Disputes dealt with under Industrial Relations Act, 1969	Recommendations issued by Rights Commissioners	Appeals to Labour Court (% in parentheses)	
1979	1,699	506	36	(7.1)
1980	2,025	661	86	(13)
1981	2,057	639	73	(11.4)
1982	1,931	531	63	(11.9)
1983	1,637	583	100	(17.2)
1984	1,445	687	118	(17.2)
1985	1,431	679	109	(16.1)
1986	1,708	603	107	(17.7)
1987	1,732	630	98	(15.6)
1988	1,477	550	76	(13.8)
1989	1,149	455	91	(20)
1990	1,202	434	64	(14.7)
1991	1,521	n.a.	n.a.	

Source: Department of Labour and Labour Court, annual reports.

EQUALITY OFFICERS

Equality officers deal with issues relating to discrimination on the grounds of sex or marital status arising under the terms of the Anti-Discrimination (Pay) Act, 1974, and the Employment Equality Act, 1977. The Anti-Discrimination (Pay) Act entitles women to equal pay for 'like work', while the Employment Equality Act prohibits discrimination against women on the grounds of sex or marital status in non-pay areas such as recruitment, training, promotion, and working conditions. (Further details of these acts are provided in chapter 13.) Employers are obliged to abide by the terms of both Acts. Should a dispute arise, either party can refer it to an equality officer.

Equality officers operate within the scope of the Labour Relations Commission but, like rights commissioners, are independent in the performance of their functions. When a dispute is referred to an equality officer they will carry out an investigation and issue a recommendation based on the merits of the case. During the investigation the equality officer meets the parties and also examines written submissions from both sides. Equality officers are empowered to enter premises, examine records or documents, seek information, and inspect work in progress; to impede an equality officer in their investigation is an offence punishable by a substantial fine. If either party is dissatisfied with the recommendation of an equality officer they may appeal to the Labour Court within forty-two days. The Labour Court's determination in such circumstances is final and legally binding. However, there is a right to appeal the determination of the Labour Court to the High Court on a point of law. Table 10.15 summarises the pattern of equality officer recommendations over the period 1978–92.

Table 10.15: Number of equality officer recommendations, 1978–92

	Employment Equality Act, 1977		Anti-Discrimination (Pay) Act, 1974	
	Number	In favour of claimant	Number	In favour of claimant
1978	5	2	52	n.a.
1979	14	8	52	38
1980	14	9	65	48
1981	20	9	55	42
1982	12	2	27	18
1983	22	11	28	12
1984	28	10	27	7
1985	18	7	17	2
1986	8	3	19	8
1987	11	8	14	7
1988	11	5	16	9
1989	12	8	12	5
1990	35	11	13	5
1991	22	16	8	4
1992	22	12	14	4

Source: Employment Equality Agency, annual reports.

The Employment Equality Act, 1977, also provided for the establishment of the Employment Equality Agency. The EEA is responsible for the promotion of equality of opportunity, the elimination of discrimination between men and women and between married and single in relation to employment, and monitoring the operation of employment equality legislation. It is empowered to offer guidance to claimants who bring a case to the Labour Court. The agency also has the sole right of initiating proceedings in cases of discriminatory advertisements and where there is a general policy of discriminatory practices.

EMPLOYMENT APPEALS TRIBUNAL

The Employment Appeals Tribunal was originally established as the Redundancy Appeals Tribunal under the Redundancy Payments Act, 1967. The Minimum Notice and Terms of Employment Act, 1973, extended the jurisdiction of the EAT to claims brought under that Act by dismissed employees for compensation for loss sustained by them by reason of their employers' failure to give them the statutory period of notice. The agency was renamed the Employment Appeals Tribunal by the Unfair Dismissals Act, 1977, which further extended its work to incorporate claims for redress for unfair dismissals. At present the EAT adjudicates on and interprets a number of other Acts, namely the Maternity (Protection of Employees) Act, 1981, the Protection of Employees (Employers' Insolvency) Acts, 1984 to 1991, the Payment of Wages Act, 1991, and the Worker Protection (Regular Part-Time Employees) Act, 1991. The EAT may also hear appeals from decisions of rights commissioners. Table 10.16 summarises the number and outcome of claims referred to the EAT under these various statutes in 1993.

Table 10.16: Summary of appeals referred in 1993 and outcome of appeals disposed of in 1993

Act	Number of appeals referred*	Allowed	Dismissed	Withdrawn during hearing	Withdrawn before hearing	Total number of appeals disposed of
Redundancy Payments	967	444	202	162	142	950
Minimum Notice and Terms of Employment	3,425	2,609	368	174	329	3,480
Unfair Dismissal (direct claims)	1,145	223	199	239	275	936
Maternity (Protection of Employees)	23	0	8	9	9	26
Protection of Employees (Employers' Insolvency)	100	266	6	1	4	277
Worker Protection (Regular Part-time Employees)	50	3	21	8	9	41
Payment of Wages	0	0	n.a.	n.a.	n.a.	0
Total	**5,710**	**3,545**	**804**	**593**	**768**	**5,710**

*Some appeals disposed of in 1992 were not referred in 1991. Some appeals referred in 1992 are not yet disposed of. Unfair dismissals appeals against the recommendation of rights commissioners are excluded.

Source: Department of Enterprise and Employment (1994).

The EAT comprises a chairperson, who must be a practising barrister or solicitor, and seventeen vice-chairpersons, appointed by the Minister for Enterprise and Employment, and a panel of thirty-eight ordinary members, drawn equally from nominees of employers' associations and the ICTU. The tribunal normally sits in divisions; each division consists of a chairperson or vice-chairperson and one member each from the employer and trade union sides.

Applicants to the EAT may present their case in person or be represented by a barrister or solicitor or by a representative of a trade union or employers' association (Fennell and Lynch 1993). Of the 683 claims and appeals heard under the Unfair Dismissals Acts, 598 employees (87.6 per cent) were represented (96 by trade unions and 502 by solicitor or barrister) and 566 employers (82.9 per cent) were represented (76 by employers' organisations and 490 by solicitor and/or barrister) (Employment Appeals Tribunal, twenty-fifth annual report; Gunnigle, Morley, and Fitzgerald 1995). Employees must observe the time limits specified by the Act under which they apply, otherwise they may lose their right to bring a claim.

The procedures adopted by the EAT follow, to a certain extent, court procedures, but there is a greater degree of informality. Under the various regulations it is possible for parties to a hearing to make an opening statement, call witnesses, cross-examine any witnesses called by any other party, give evidence, and address the tribunal at the close of the evidence. Evidence is normally given under oath. Hearings of the tribunal are usually held in public but may be held in private at the request of either party.

The 'determination' or decision of the tribunal can be given at the close of the hearing but is more usually issued some time later in writing. Should an employer fail to carry out the terms of a determination, proceedings may be taken by the Minister for Enterprise and Employment in the Circuit Court to ensure compliance. EAT determinations are not subject to the principle of precedence as in a court of law. For applicants under the unfair dismissals and maternity legislation the EAT issues determinations that may be appealed to the Circuit Court within six weeks. In the Circuit Court the case is heard *de nova,* i.e. there is a full rehearing of the case. Appeals in relation to the other legislation falling under the jurisdiction of the EAT, such as redundancy, protection of employees, minimum notice, and part-time workers, can only be made to the High Court on a point of law.

The state as employer

Apart from its legislative and facilitatory functions, the state plays a significant role as the country's principal employer. It accounts for approximately one-third of all employees in a range of areas, principally composed of the civil service proper, education, local authorities and health boards, Garda Síochána and Defence Forces, and state-sponsored bodies. The bulk of these employees are represented by trade unions or staff associations. In some areas distinctive employee relations features have developed. However, as the Commission on Industrial Relations (1981) noted, personnel and employee relations issues in the public and private sectors are largely similar, and differences that tend to occur are largely in the area of procedural responses (also see Cox and Hughes 1989).

In relation to the negotiation of pay and conditions of employment, a notable distinction may be drawn between those public sector areas subject to agreed conciliation and arbitration (C&A) schemes and those that come within the scope of the Labour Court and the Labour Relations Commission. C&A schemes date from the nineteen-fifties, and at present schemes operate for such categories as the (non-industrial) civil service, teachers, gardaí, local authorities and health boards, and VECs. A unique feature of the civil service scheme is the network of staff panels that evaluate any claims from recognised unions or staff associations before these are forwarded to conciliation. Conciliation consists of joint councils of management and employee representatives, which consider claims before them and issue an agreed report. The composition and specific role of conciliation councils differ between individual schemes, and only specific issues may be referred to conciliation. These generally include pay, allowances, working hours, overtime, grading, and policy on recruitment, promotion, discipline, pensions, and sickness pay. Most schemes exclude issues relating to individual employees.

The great majority of issues are resolved at conciliation, but those that are not may proceed to arbitration, provided they are arbitrable under the appropriate C&A scheme. An arbitration board normally consists of an agreed chairperson (often legally qualified) and two representatives each from the management and the staff side. Detailed written submissions are made by both sides, and these are supplemented by oral submissions; witnesses may be called as appropriate. The findings of the board are sent to the Minister for Finance and the other appropriate minister, who have one month to either approve the report or submit it to the Government; the Government has the option of accepting the report or moving a Dáil motion to reject or amend it (this latter route is seen as exceptional).

The local authority and health board scheme differs in that both the management and the staff side have the option of rejecting the decision of arbitration. In addition to the specific grades in the public sector, as discussed above, employees in most state-sponsored bodies have access to the Labour Court. Exceptions are An Post and Telecom Éireann, which have a separate C&A scheme.

A notable characteristic of employee relations in the public sector is the special role of the Department of Finance. It acts as the Government's adviser on matters relating to public sector pay and employment-related matters. It critically reviews pay claims, lays down appropriate policy guidelines, and oversees their implementation through direct and indirect negotiations. The department represents the state as employer at the Employer-Labour Conference and is involved in many of the C&A hearings. Another important actor on the management side is the Local Government Staff Negotiations Board (LGSNB), whose role is to assist local authorities and health boards in employee relations. Representatives of the board act on behalf of the management on the appropriate C&A scheme and in major negotiations with non-officer grades.

11

Employer and Management Approaches to Employee Relations

This chapter focuses on the role of employers and managements in employee relations. It first considers employers' objectives in employee relations; the role of employers' organisations is then addressed, with particular emphasis on the Irish situation. Finally, the chapter considers management approaches to employee relations and reviews some contemporary developments.

EMPLOYERS' OBJECTIVES IN EMPLOYEE RELATIONS

The primary concern of organisations operating in a competitive environment is maximising performance and generating satisfactory returns for the owners and stakeholders of the enterprise (Gunnigle et al. 1995). Such returns are often expressed in terms of cost-effectiveness and profitability. The primary goal of the management therefore is to organise the factors of production, including labour, to achieve these objectives. It is difficult to assess the degree to which employers have specific employee relations objectives or adopt related work-place strategies (Thomason 1984; Gunnigle 1995a). Organisations vary greatly, and it is apparent that a particular company's approach will be influenced by a range of external factors, such as historical development and market conditions. Nevertheless it is worth while considering some general beliefs common among employers. Thomason (1984) identifies the following employers' beliefs or objectives in employee relations:

(1) **The preservation and consolidation of the private enterprise system:** This has larger political overtones and relates to the concern of employers to preserve a political and economic environment conducive to achieving business objectives at the enterprise level. They will be particularly concerned that principles such as private ownership, the profit motive and the preservation of managerial authority and control are maintained.

(2) **The achievement of satisfactory returns for the owners:** This relates directly to the organisation's primary business goals. For commercial organisations to survive in the

long term, satisfactory profit levels must be achieved. Consequently, managerial approaches and strategies will always be influenced by this primary concern. Non-profit-making organisations will be equally concerned with cost-effectiveness and quality.

(3) **The effective employment of human resources:** A company's work-force represents a key management resource, and its effective use is central to the management process.

(4) **The maintenance of control and authority in decision-making:** Employers will strive to ensure effective control and authority in executing their management role, particularly in strategic decision-making.

(5) **The establishment and maintenance of satisfactory management-employee relations:** Employers will also strive to maintain good working relations with employees, but this must be achieved within the operational constraints of the enterprise. The scope for agreeing attractive remuneration levels and conditions of employment etc. will vary according to the company's market position and profitability as well as its personnel policy. Good employee relations will be a priority, since they are an important element in ensuring that the company achieves its primary business goals as well as being laudable in itself.

The role of employers' organisations

To help achieve the objectives listed above, it is clear that employers are likely to combine collectively for purposes associated with employment and labour matters. The main impetus for the growth of employers' organisations was the perceived need to react to and deal with the 'new unionism'. This helps in distinguishing between *employers' organisations*, whose purpose was to deal with labour matters, and those where trade and commercial reasons were the main focus and which are normally referred to as *trade associations*. Oechslin (1985) provides a widely accepted definition of employers' organisations as

> formal groups of employers set up to defend, represent or advise affiliated employers and to strengthen their position in society at large with respect to labour matters as distinct from commercial matters.

A particular and traditional reason why employers have formed representative organisations is to prevent harmful economic competition with each other, particularly in relation to pay, and to counter the power of trade unions. Another reason was the increasingly complex nature of collective bargaining and employment legislation. Employers' organisations also provide a forum for the exchange of views among employers (Thomason 1984; Gunnigle et al. 1995). The main role of employers' organisations is to represent employers' views in employee relations; their objectives may be categorised as political, social, economic, and employee relations (see table 11.1).

Table 11.1: Objectives of employers' organisations

1. **Political**: To effectively represent employers' views to the government, the general public and other appropriate bodies so as to preserve and develop a political, economic and social climate in which business objectives can be achieved.
2. **Economic**: To create an economic environment that supports the free enterprise system and ensures that the managerial prerogative in decision-making is protected.
3. **Social**: To ensure that any social or legal changes best represent the interests of affiliated employers.

4. **Employee relations**: To ensure a legislative and procedural environment that supports free collective bargaining, to co-ordinate employers' views and approaches on employee relations matters, and to provide assistance to affiliated employers.

Employers' organisations assume a significant role in representing employers' interests on national issues. They provide a mechanism through which governments can solicit employers' opinions in areas such as labour legislation and are important vehicles for influencing public opinion on more general political matters. This political role of employers' organisations is most clearly associated with the desire to influence broad economic decision-making. Employers' organisations will generally support what could be termed conservative economic policies, which serve to protect the interests of employers and ensure freedom from an excess of state intervention in business. In the area of social policy the approach of employers' organisations will largely be pragmatic. On the one hand they will generally attempt to prevent, or at least lessen, the effects of protective labour or social legislation, such as legal moves towards extending industrial democracy or information disclosure. On the other hand they will accept some degree of social and legislative reform, provided their perceived effects on the interests of business are not adverse. An outline of the objectives of Ireland's largest employers' organisation, the Irish Business and Employers' Confederation (IBEC), is contained in its 'mission statement' (table 11.2).

Table 11.2: Irish Business and Employers' Confederation: 'mission statement'

To influence vigorously the formation of policy at national, European and international levels towards the development of an enterprise culture, the creation of economic and social conditions favourable to the profitable growth and effectiveness of Irish business and employers, and the development of productive employment, whilst having due regard to the interests of the wider community
and
to provide quick-response assistance, information, advice and representation for members in protecting their interests and maximising performance.

The specific role of employers' organisations in employee relations may be categorised into four broad areas, as follows (Gunnigle et al. 1995):

(1) **Exchange of views:** Employers' organisations provide a useful forum for the exchange of opinion and discussion. However, employers may also use employer organisations to develop and agree common policies and strategies in employee relations.

(2) **Representing employers' views to the Government and its agencies:** Employers' organisations provide an important means through which employers may represent their views to the Government. For example, they may seek to influence labour legislation and Government policy generally so that the position of affiliated employers is adequately protected. In Ireland this role is executed principally by the Irish Business and Employers' Confederation (IBEC). It represent employers' opinion on bodies such as the National Economic and Social Council, established by the Government as a forum for the discussion of the principles relating to the economy; the Central Review Committee, which monitors issues arising from centralised agreements; the Employer-Labour Conference, established to allow the various interest groups to deal directly with employee relations issues; and the Employment Equality Agency, the statutory authority with responsibility for the promotion of equality in employment. Employers' organisations also provide representatives for appropriate bipartite or tripartite bodies

such as arbitration councils, Government commissions, and international organisations. IBEC plays the leading role in nominating employers' representatives to such bodies as the Labour Court, the Labour Relations Commission, and the Employment Appeals Tribunal.

(3) **Representing employers' interests to the general public:** Employers' organisations are also involved in representing employers' opinion to the general public on relevant issues, such as impending employment legislation.

(4) **Providing specialised services to members:** An important role of employers' organisations is the provision of a range of employee relations services to their membership. These services include assistance in collective bargaining and advice on labour law. (This role is discussed later in this chapter.)

Employers' organisations in Ireland

As indicated above, employers' organisations can be divided into two categories, employers' organisations and trade associations. While both types are required to register with the Registrar of Friendly Societies, only employers' organisations are involved in employee relations, and they are required to hold a negotiating licence under the terms of the Trade Union Acts, 1941 and 1971. In 1993 there were some thirteen registered employers' organisations as defined above (see table 11.3).

Table 11.3: Employers' organisations in Ireland, 1993

	Membership
Construction Industry Federation	2,188
Cork Master Butchers' Association	42
Dublin Master Victuallers' Association	184
Irish Business and Employers' Confederation	3,279
Irish Commercial Horticultural Association	59
Irish Hotels Federation	514
Irish Master Printers' Association	39
Irish Pharmaceutical Union	1,222
Irish Printing Federation	52
Licensed Vintners' Association	624
Limerick Employers' Association	6
Petroleum Employers' Association	5
Society of the Irish Motor Industry	1,212

Source: Department of Enterprise and Employment (1993).

IRISH BUSINESS AND EMPLOYERS' CONFEDERATION

The Irish Business and Employers' Confederation (IBEC), formed in 1993 by the merger of the Federation of Irish Employers (FIE) and the Confederation of Irish Industry (CII), is the largest employers' organisation in Ireland. IBEC represents business and employers in all matters relating to employee relations, labour, and social affairs. It has a membership of over 3,200 firms, which employ some 300,000 people or approximately 60 per cent of the country's labour force excluding agriculture, the public service, and the self-employed. As the principal representative of business and employers, IBEC seeks to shape national policies and influence decision-making in a way that protects and promotes member-employers' interests.

Unlike its predecessors, IBEC's role is not confined to employee relations: rather, it seeks to represent industry in all matters of economic and social policy. An important role is representing employers' interests to the Government, other 'social partners', and the public. It also provides employers' representatives for various national and international bodies. The organisation structure of IBEC is shown in fig. 11.1.

Fig. 11.1: Irish Business and Employers' Confederation: organisation structure

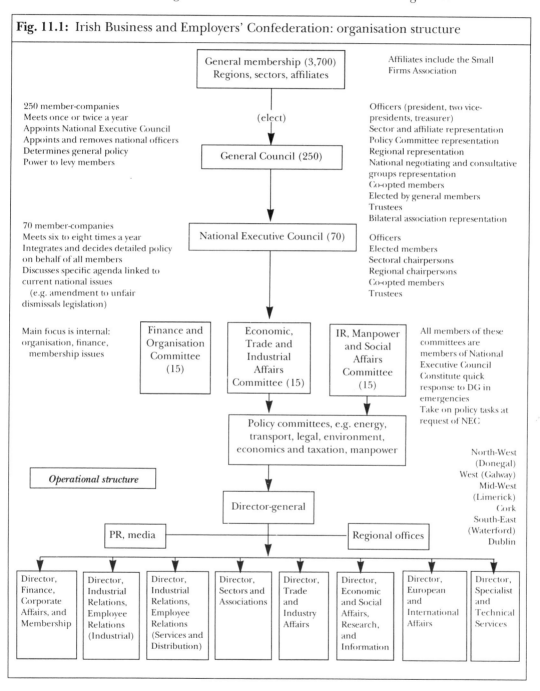

The **Construction Industry Federation** (CIF) is Ireland's second-largest employers' organisation. Unlike IBEC, the CIF is an industry-based organisation, dealing with both trade and employee relations affairs on behalf of employers in the construction industry. It has a membership of over 2,000 firms or some 46 per cent of companies in the construction sector; these firms are estimated to employ approximately 50,000 workers, or 75 per cent of all workers in privately owned construction firms. In the employee relations sphere the main role of the CIF is the negotiation of national registered agreements, representing members at conciliation and arbitration, and providing information and advice to member-companies (Pollock and O'Dwyer 1985).

Most of the other employers' organisations are primarily concerned with trade and commercial issues. However, some also have a strong employee relations dimension. The **Irish Hotels Federation** represents employers' interests on the Hotel Joint Labour Committee and provides general employee relations advice to members; however, it does not involve itself in local bargaining. The **Society of the Irish Motor Industry** provides advice and assistance on personnel and employee relations matters to affiliated members. The **Licensed Vintners' Association** represents Dublin publicans in negotiations on pay and working conditions with the Irish National Union of Vintners', Grocers' and Allied Trades Assistants. It also provides members with a personnel advisory service.

Another interesting employers' organisation is the **Limerick Employers' Federation**, which is a rare example of a regional organisation involved in employee relations. The LEF represents retail and distribution firms in the area. In addition to its trade and commercial role it provides advice and assistance and acts as a forum for the exchange of views on employee relations and personnel matters. The involvement of the remaining employers' organisations in employee relations is minimal.

It is important to note that employers may establish and combine in less formal groupings for purposes associated with employee relations. Such groups are generally used by employers as a forum for the exchange of views and information on employee relations and personnel matters. They may also facilitate the co-ordination of employers' approaches in dealing with particular employee relations issues. Such organisations may be organised by industrial sector (e.g. the Pharmaceutical Sector Personnel Group) or region (e.g. the Limerick-Shannon Personnel Managers' Group) and may meet on a semi-regular basis or only when a significant issue arises. The Institute of Personnel and Development (IPD) in Ireland, the major professional association for personnel management practitioners, may also act as a forum for representing employers' interests in employee relations.

Services of employers' organisations

The earlier discussion alluded to the range of employee relations services provided by employers' organisations in areas such as collective bargaining, research, and advice. These services are discussed below.

Commenting on developments in Britain, Sisson (1983) found that the greatest area of growth in the work of employers' organisations was in the provision of research and advisory services. Such services fall into three broad categories: legal, pay, and specialist consultancy. The growth of labour legislation in Ireland since the nineteen-seventies has led to a significant increase in the demand by employers for specialist legal advice in areas such as dismissal, employment conditions, and employment equality. Many larger employers' organisations provide a specialist legal section to advise and assist member-companies. They may also publish and disseminate guidelines on legislation for their membership.

A more traditional service of employers' organisations is the provision of information and advice to member-firms on wage rates and wage increases. Many employers' organisations conduct surveys of wage levels and fringe benefits for differing occupations, regions, and size of company. Consequently they are able to provide member-firms with up-to-date information on local, regional and national pay trends and to advise such firms on reward issues.

Some employers' organisations also provide members with specialist advice and assistance. These might include performance management, productivity schemes, and recruitment. In a pilot study Butler (1985) found that advisory and consultancy services are seen by members as the most useful function of employers' organisations and that those dealing with legislation, pay and redundancy were most widely used.

COLLECTIVE BARGAINING

Historically, one of the most important services provided by employers' organisations was that of assisting employers in collective bargaining with trade unions. Such bargaining might be of a multi-employer (regional, industry or national) or single-employer nature. Multi-employer bargaining on an industry or, most commonly, national basis has traditionally meant a key role for employers' organisations in conducting negotiations on pay and related matters on behalf of affiliated employers. In Ireland, employers' organisations have been prominent in periods of centralised pay bargaining. IBEC plays a particularly significant role, being the key representative of employers' opinion to the other 'social partners'. However, the Irish experience indicates that even where the location of collective bargaining moves to the enterprise level, employers' organisations still play an important role in advising and assisting managements in the bargaining process. This role may incorporate the co-ordination of policy on pay and employment-related issues; formulating general guidelines for affiliated employers; supplying research data and information for use in negotiations; and providing expert personnel either to conduct the negotiations or to advise and assist the local management (Gunnigle et al. 1995). Such involvement may comprise direct participation in employee relations negotiations but would also cover research and specialist advisory services as well as assistance with the preparation of employment agreements, consultation on particular personnel issues, and the provision of premises and facilities for consultation and negotiation.

A particularly important role for employers' organisations in collective bargaining is that of representing affiliated members in face-to-face negotiations or during third-party referrals. Employers' organisations may represent members in enterprise-level negotiations with trade unions. They may also represent employers' interests in industry or national-level bargaining. An increasingly significant aspect of this representation role applies to mediation and arbitration. Here officials of the employers' organisation may represent affiliates in tribunal hearings, conciliation meetings, and arbitration hearings such as the Labour Court, Labour Relations Commission, and Employment Appeals Tribunal. The extent of such involvement is evident in the summary of IBEC involvement in conciliation, mediation and arbitration shown in table 11.4.

Table 11.4: Irish Business and Employers' Confederation: third-party referrals and negotiations (cases per year)

	1984	1985	1986	1987	1988	1989*	1992
Labour Court investigation	458	420	538	488	386	394	217
Labour Court conciliation	1,176	963	1,470	1,146	874	1,014	684
Employment Appeals Tribunal	241	302	396	190	n.a.	216	258
Rights commissioner	439	312	586	429	n.a.	346	266
Equality officer	16	16	28	35	n.a.	72	18
Consultation with members	7,203	8,155	6,400	6,919	6,726	5,864	4,804
Trade union negotiations	3,590	2,664	2,928	2,842	2,702	2,540	1,286

*Figures for 1990 and 1991 are not available in annual reports.

Source: IBEC, annual reports.

EDUCATION AND TRAINING

An increasingly important service provided by the larger employers' organisations is the provision of education and training programmes for affiliated members. Such programmes are often aimed at keeping member-firms up to date with current developments in employee relations and, particularly, labour law. They may also focus on developing managerial capacity among member-firms by providing training programmes for personnel and employee relations practitioners in areas such as negotiating skills and employment legislation.

Membership of employers' organisations

In analysing the factors influencing membership of employers' organisations, Thomason (1984) notes the impact of *corporate form*. In particular he differentiates between entrepreneurs, who essentially own and run their businesses, and abstract corporate entities, which are run by professional managements. The corporate business form has replaced the older entrepreneurial type of firm as the prevalent type of company in membership of employers' organisations. Thomason argues that this change in composition partly explains the changing role of employers' organisations.

There is also evidence that *country of ownership* may influence membership of employers' organisations. A study of newly established companies in Ireland found that American-owned firms were less likely to join employers' organisations than other foreign-owned companies (Gunnigle 1995b). This may be related to the corporate approach to trade unions and collective bargaining. Where this involves a preference for non-union status, such companies may be reluctant to join an employers' organisation (Purcell and Sisson 1983; Oechslin 1985).

The question of *public sector organisations* becoming members of an employers' organisation is a relatively recent one. While at first it might seem that the status of such bodies is incompatible with membership of an employers' organisation—traditionally a bastion of free enterprise—many have adopted a pragmatic approach by using the services of employers' organisations in certain areas (Oechslin 1985). The Department of Finance and the Local Government Staff Negotiations Board play a role in assisting and advising managements on employee relations issues in many parts of the public sector. However, such bodies, particularly those in the state-sponsored sector, have increasingly taken up membership of employers' organisations.

It has also been argued that *organisation size* is an important factor influencing membership and patterns of use of employers' organisations. It is sometimes suggested that small firms have more to gain by joining employers' organisations, for reasons related to cost and resource considerations (International Labour Office 1975). When a small company reaches the stage where it becomes involved in formalised collective bargaining, joining an employers' organisation may be particularly attractive, as it would not generally be in a position to employ personnel specialists, and the owner or managers of such firms may not have either the necessary time or expertise to effectively handle such matters. Since the cost of joining an association is generally related to the size or profitability (or both), it may be relatively inexpensive for small firms to join. However, despite the apparent validity of this argument there is no conclusive evidence to support the view that small firms are more likely to join employers' organisations (Government Social Survey 1968; Gunnigle 1995); in fact the evidence indicates that employers' organisations are not more frequently used by smaller companies (Brown 1981; Daniel and Millward 1983; Gunnigle 1992). Indeed it seems that larger firms are more likely to join and to make use of the services of employers' organisations and that membership is positively correlated with company size, trade union recognition, and the presence of specialist personnel or employee relations management.

An important influence on company decisions whether or not to join an employers' organisation is the perceived advantages and disadvantages of membership. Clearly such perceptions will be influenced by issues specific to the individual companies, such as the management's desired approach to employee relations. Broader contextual and environmental factors such as industrial sector, size, product market performance and ownership will also be influential (Thomason 1984). Table 11.5 summarises some of the generally perceived advantages and disadvantages of membership of an employers' organisation, although clearly the relative significance of these will vary between companies and between industrial sectors.

Table 11.5: Advantages and disadvantages of membership of employers' organisation

Advantages	Disadvantages
• Collective approaches and uniform policy	• Cost of membership
• Advice on trade union matters	• Loss of autonomy
• Technical advice and information	• Loss of flexibility
• Skilled negotiators	• Comparisons with other firms
• Expert advisory and consultancy services	• Greater acceptance of role for trade unions
• Standardised pay and employment conditions	• Greater formalisation in employee relations
• On par with regional or industry norms	
• Assistance in employee relations difficulties	
• Influence on Government and national affairs	

Source: Gunnigle, McMahon, and Fitzgerald (1995).

The range of employee relations services provided by employers' organisations, considered in the preceding section, correlates closely with the perceived advantages of membership (as outlined in table 11.5). It is appropriate therefore to consider some reasons why companies may choose not to join employers' organisations. A common argument is the potential reduction of *managerial autonomy* in decision-making. As in any formal association, employers' organisations will be keen to ensure that member-firms adhere to commonly agreed polices in areas such as pay and conditions of employment. These policies and related guidelines normally reflect the needs of the general membership; however, it is for the individual company to assess whether such norms are appropriate to its particular needs.

The likelihood of *comparability with other firms* is also an important consideration. By joining an association comprising numerous other companies, a particular firm's pay and conditions will be compared with those pertaining among the general membership. Trade unions often use the terms of collective agreements struck with some member-firms as leverage for securing similar terms with other member-organisations.

Another important consideration influencing membership of an employers' organisation is the impact of a firm's desired *personnel or employee relations style*. As we have seen, the legal definition of employers' organisations means that they are, strictly speaking, trade unions of employers. Traditionally employers' organisations have had a preference for dealing with their employee counterparts, trade unions, through collective bargaining. However, it is also clear that many firms now pursue employee relations 'styles' that seek to avoid trade union recognition (Gunnigle and Brady 1984; McGovern 1989; Gunnigle 1994). Some of these firms place a strong emphasis on dealing with employees on a more individual basis (Gunnigle, Morley, and Turner 1996a). For such firms, membership of an employer's organisation—a trade union of employers—would be totally incompatible with a management approach based on direct relations with individual employees.

A more pragmatic reason for non-membership is the *cost of membership*. Normally firms pay the full cost of membership regardless of services used; this contrasts with the use of management consultants, where firms normally pay only a fee that is related to services provided. Subscriptions to employers' organisation are normally related to company size (number of employees). Using 1993 rates, the following examples reflect the cost of membership of IBEC: 75 employees, £1,406; 300 employees, £5,553; 750 employees, £13,665; 1,500 employees, £22,700.

MANAGEMENT APPROACHES TO EMPLOYEE RELATIONS

While employers' organisations clearly play an important role in employee relations, individual employers are primarily responsible for the development and implementation of employee relations policies and practices within their individual companies and work-places. The remainder of this chapter addresses the role of the management in enterprise-level employee relations and reviews contemporary research on management approaches to employee relations.

Managerial frames of reference

In his seminal work, Fox (1968) argues that management approaches to employee relations are largely determined by the 'frame of reference' adopted by managers. A frame of reference is defined by Thelen and Withall (1979) as 'the main selective influences at work as the perceiver supplements, omits and structures what he notices.' Fox suggests that a manager's frame of reference is important because (*a*) it determines how the management expect people to behave and how they think they should behave (i.e. values and beliefs), (*b*) it determines the management's reactions to actual behaviour (i.e. management practice), and (*c*) it shapes the methods the management choose when they wish to change the behaviour of people at work (e.g. strategies and policies).

Fox identified two alternative frames of reference to help evaluate management approaches to employee relations. These were termed (*a*) the unitarist and (*b*) the pluralist frame of reference. The key features of these two approaches are summarised in table 11.6.

Table 11.6: Unitarist and pluralist frames of reference

Unitarist	Pluralist
Emphasises the dominance of common interests. Everyone—management and employees—should strive to achieve the company's primary business goals, since everyone will benefit.	The company is viewed as composed of different interest groups with different objectives but linked together instrumentally by their common association with the company.
There is only one source of authority—the management—and it must command full loyalty.	The management's role is to achieve some equilibrium satisfying the various interest groups, thus helping to achieve the company's goals.
Anyone who does not share these common interests and does not accept managerial authority is viewed as a dissenter or agitator.	A certain amount of conflict is inevitable, since the objectives of the parties will clash on occasion.
Since dissenters endanger the company's success they must either fall into line, appreciate the overriding importance of corporate goals and accept managerial authority or risk elimination from the company.	The management must expect and plan for conflict so that it can be handled successfully and not endanger the achievement of the company's primary objectives.
	The management should not seek to suppress conflicting interests but rather aim to reconcile them in the company's interests.

Source: Fox (1968).

These contrasting frames of reference represent dominant employee relations orientations that may be adopted by the management. In practice one finds that managers do not strictly adhere to either one of these approaches but may adopt different approaches in different situations or change their approaches over time. Nevertheless the frames of reference approach provides a useful basis for evaluating management approaches to employee relations at the enterprise level. For example, Marchington (1982) considered how management approaches to employee relations might differ depending on the particular frame of reference adopted.

In firstly evaluating management approaches to *trade unions*, Marchington argues that managers holding a unitary perspective would see no role for unions: such managers would see them as 'encroaching on the management's territory,' making unreasonable demands, prohibiting change, flexibility, and, therefore, competitiveness (also see Gunnigle et al. 1995). As a consequence, a trade union would be viewed as an externally imposed force that introduces conflict into the company and prohibits the development of 'good' employee relations. Furthermore, workers associated with the promotion of trade unionism would be seen as 'disloyal', 'agitators', or 'troublemakers'. In contrast, managers adopting a pluralist perspective would see a legitimate role for trade unions in representing and articulating employees' views in the work-place.

A second area where Marchington identified different approaches was in relation to *managerial prerogative*. This refers to areas of decision-making where the management see themselves as having sole authority. Marchington suggests that managers adopting a unitary frame of reference would be unwilling to accept any reduction in management prerogative as a result of trade union organisation. They would see the management as the legitimate decision-making authority. On the other hand, managers adopting a pluralist frame of reference would acknowledge the legitimacy of other interest groups in the company, such as trade unions. They would also accept the need to allow unions a role in decision-making and consequently accept some reduction in managerial prerogative.

The final area where management approaches may differ is in relation to *industrial conflict*. Marchington suggests that managers adopting a unitary frame of reference would view the enterprise very much along 'team' or 'family' lines, with everyone working together to achieve the company's objectives. In this context conflict is seen as something of an aberration, only occurring as a result of a breakdown of communications or the work of troublemakers. By contrast, managers adopting a pluralist frame of reference would accept that some degree of industrial conflict is inevitable, because the interests of management and labour will clash on occasion. Since the pluralist perspective accepts the legitimacy of conflict, managers adopting this frame of reference will tend to plan for it, by, for example, agreeing grievance, disputes and disciplinary procedures.

The concept of management styles

Moving beyond Fox's unitarist-pluralist dichotomy, several commentators have attempted to develop categorisations of management styles in employee relations to explain differences in approach to employee relations. One of the most widely used management styles typologies is that of Purcell and Sisson (1983), who developed a five-fold categorisation of 'ideal-typical' styles of employee relations management, based on differing management approaches to trade unions, collective bargaining, consultation, and communications. This typology is outlined in table 11.7.

Table 11.7: Management styles in employee relations

Management style	Characteristics
Traditionalist	'Orthodox unitarism': Opposes role for unions; little attention to employees' needs.
Sophisticated paternalist	Emphasises employees' needs (training, pay, conditions, etc.); discourages unionisation; demands and facilitates employees' loyalty and commitment.
Sophisticated modern	Accepts trade unions' role in specific areas; emphasises procedures and consultative mechanisms. Two variations: (*a*) *constitutionalists*: emphasise codification of management-union relations through explicit collective agreements;

	(*b*) *consultors*: collective bargaining established but management emphasises personal contact and problem-solving, playing down formal union role at establishment level.
Standard modern	Pragmatic approach: unions' role accepted but no overall policy or strategy developed; 'firefighting' or reactive approach.

Source: Adapted from Purcell and Sisson (1983).

Despite the apparent attractiveness of management style typologies, it appears that in reality it is difficult to categorise companies into neat 'ideal-typical' groupings (Deaton 1995; Gunnigle 1995a). Using data from some 1,400 British companies, Deaton (1985) sought to empirically evaluate the appropriateness of Purcell and Sisson's typology. He first attempted to classify management styles in unionised companies as either 'sophisticated' or 'standard modern'. However, he found it difficult to distinguish between these two types, suggesting that it is rather dubious to classify firms recognising trade unions into either of these groupings. He also attempted to categorise management styles in non-union companies into 'paternalist', 'anti-union', and 'sophisticated paternalist'. Here he found greater evidence of companies conforming to Purcell and Sisson's 'ideal-typical' styles. He found that 'sophisticated paternalist' and 'anti-union' companies emerged as polar opposites, while 'paternalist' companies took the middle ground (having some characteristics common to both 'anti-union' and 'sophisticated paternalist' companies).

Deaton concluded that attempts to classify firms into a small number of ideal styles were problematic and that while the distinction between companies that recognise unions and those that do not is crucial, it may not be possible to sub-divide styles further in companies where unions are recognised. However, Deaton felt that there was a greater tendency in companies that do not recognise unions to adopt the 'identikit' styles suggested above.

Using more anecdotal evidence to examine variations in managerial styles in employee relations, Poole (1986) suggested that the evidence points to the existence of 'a progressively rich array' of hybrid styles rather than any convergence towards particular predominant styles or patterns.

INDIVIDUALISM AND COLLECTIVISM AS DIMENSIONS OF MANAGEMENT STYLES

More recent analyses of management styles in employee relations have tended to focus on key dimensions of management styles rather than on 'ideal-typical' style categorisations. Purcell (1987) provides us with two widely accepted dimensions of styles, namely individualism and collectivism.

Collectivism in employee relations incorporates the extent to which the management acknowledge the right of employees to collective representation and the involvement of the collective in influencing management decision-making (Purcell 1987; Sisson 1994; Storey and Sisson 1994). This dimension deals with both the level of democratic employee representative structures and the extent to which the management legitimise their representational and bargaining role. Thus conceived, the collectivist dimension spans a spectrum from a unitarist perspective incorporating management opposition to employee representation, through a middle ground of adversarial or reluctant collectivism, to a co-operative perspective (Purcell 1987; Marchington and Parker 1990).

High collectivism, therefore, is manifested in the establishment, recognition and incorporation of mechanisms for employee representation, particularly trade unions, as a vehicle in the conduct of enterprise-level employee relations, while at the other extreme low collectivism is manifested in managerial opposition to collective employee representation (see fig. 11.2).

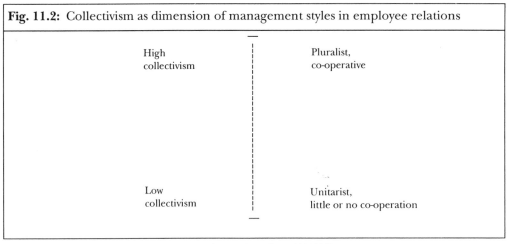

Fig. 11.2: Collectivism as dimension of management styles in employee relations

Source: Adapted from Purcell (1987).

Individualism incorporates the degree to which the management adopt an essentially individualist focus in employee relations management (Purcell and Gray 1986; Purcell 1987; Marchington and Parker 1990). Purcell (1987, 536) describes individualism as

> the extent to which the firm gives credence to the feelings and sentiments of each employee and seeks to develop and encourage each employee's capacity and role at work ... Firms which have individualistically centred policies are thus expected to emphasise employees as a resource and be concerned with developing each person's talents and worth.

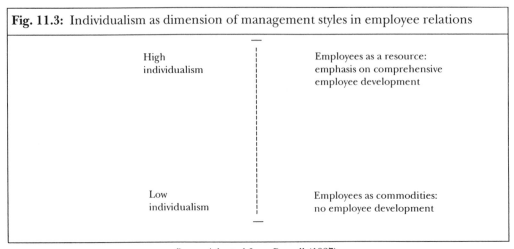

Fig. 11.3: Individualism as dimension of management styles in employee relations

Source: Adapted from Purcell (1987).

Purcell argues that high individualism is characterised by managements recognising the resource value of employees and adopting comprehensive employee development policies. In contrast, low individualism conceives of employees in utility terms within the overriding goal of profit maximisation. Here the management's emphasis is on tight control and the minimisation of labour costs, with little concern for broader human resource issues such as job satisfaction, employment security, and employee commitment (see fig. 11.3).

The contemporary literature identifies an increased management emphasis on the development of an individualist orientation as a significant development in changing patterns of employee relations (Beaumont 1985, 1991; Beaumont and Townley 1985; Kochan, Katz, and McKersie 1986; Guest 1989; Storey 1992; Bacon and Storey 1993). However, we have also seen that high levels of collectivism, and specifically trade union recognition, membership and influence, are integral to the traditional pluralist model considered to be characteristic of employee relations in Ireland (Roche 1989, 1994; Brewster and Hegewisch 1994; Roche and Turner 1994; Hillery 1994; Murphy and Roche 1994). Findings on the levels of collectivism and individualism are seen therefore as critical indicators of change in management styles in employee relations (Beaumont 1985; 1992).

The so-called 'soft' human resource management approach has been associated with a move from collectivism to individualism by means of sophisticated recruitment, rewards and employee development policies (Guest 1987, 1989). However, Purcell (1987) argues that individualism need not necessarily oppose collectivism, so that managements can develop policies to increase individualism while retaining established collectivist structures, including trade union recognition. Marchington and Parker (1990) suggest that this interpretation makes the dimensions of management style more 'dynamic', allowing companies to alter their positions along these dimensions over time.

In a study of recently established companies in Ireland, Gunnigle (1995a) attempted to evaluate management approaches to employee relations on the dimensions of collectivism and individualism. To this end a number of indicators were developed to evaluate the relative management emphasis on individualism and collectivism. These indicators are summarised in table 11.8.

Table 11.8: Indicators of collectivism and individualism

Measures of individualism

1. *Sophistication of the employment and socialisation system:* Measured through an evaluation of the degree of sophistication and relative emphasis on individualism in the management of human resource 'flows'.
2. *Communications:* Based on an analysis of the level, nature and sophistication of management-employee communications.
3. *Performance-related pay:* Measured through an analysis of the incidence of performance-related pay systems and the use made of formal performance appraisals to aid performance-related pay decisions among manual and operative grades.
4. *Employee involvement:* Measured through an analysis of the extent to which the management makes use of explicit techniques to facilitate involvement by employees in decision-making.
5. *Employee autonomy:* Measured through an analysis of the extent to which the management seek to facilitate and promote employee autonomy.

Measures of collectivism

1. *Trade union presence:* Measured through an analysis of levels of trade union recognition and trade union density.
2. *Pattern of trade union organisation:* Measured though an examination of the nature of trade union recognition and the impact of trade unions on work-place employee relations.

3. *Role of trade unions and other employee representative bodies:* Measured through an examination of the role of trade unions and other employee representative bodies in management-employee communications and interactions.
4. *Membership and use made of employers' organisation:* Measured through an examination of the extent to which newly established companies are members of employers' organisations and of the pattern of use of the services of such organisations.

Source: Gunnigle (1995a).

These measures were used to evaluate management styles in a number of Irish companies on the dimensions of collectivism and individualism. While the findings apply only to recently established firms, they provide some interesting insights on management approaches to employee relations in Ireland (see Gunnigle 1995a, 1995b). Probably the most significant finding was the powerful evidence of changing management approaches to collectivism as a means of managing work-place employee relations. Such a trend was evidenced by policies designed to mitigate attempts to achieve trade union recognition or, where unions are recognised, to prescribe tightly their role in work-place employee relations. As noted in the preceding chapter, this evidence points to a severe erosion in levels of trade union recognition and density in newly established firms.

While this differential might be explained by the relative immaturity of newly established companies, it is important to note that pre-production closed-shop agreements have traditionally characterised large industrial start-ups in Ireland (see, for example, O'Hara 1981; Murray 1984; McGovern 1989). It appears that this is no longer so and that such companies are increasingly and consciously choosing the non-union alternative rather than pre-production agreements. The trend emerging indicates a shift from collectivism to individualism. While this development does not mean that collectivist structures are abandoned, it does appear that the strong collectivist tradition characteristic of Irish employee relations is being diluted.

The second critical characteristic identified was a greater emphasis on individualist approaches to employee relations. This study found that most significant indicators of high levels of individualism were performance-based pay systems tied to individual employee appraisals and greater direct communication with employees. An increased management focus on more extensive and direct communication with individual employees was an important feature in many of the companies studied and predominantly so among the non-union companies. In particular, many companies put an especially strong emphasis on communicating information on company performance to employees. In many of these companies such information was used to emphasise issues such as market volatility, intensity of competition, and requirements for high-quality and low-cost production or service. However, it appears that the rationale for such communications was largely based on the utilitarian objectives of facilitating improved employee performance and flexibility, rather than on more altruistic motives such as enhanced employee involvement.

The other critical indicator of individualism identified in the study was the degree of use of performance-related pay systems based on formal appraisals of individual employees' performance (Gunnigle 1995a, 1995b). The study found significant differences between new and longer-established companies in the use of PRP systems based on formal performance appraisals among all employees. The role of appraisal in aiding PRP decisions among non-managerial and white-collar grades is a crucial differentiating factor, since the use of more 'traditional' PRP systems among manual grades is nothing new (see, for example, Clegg 1979; Mooney 1980). However, such PRP systems (e.g. measured day work) were based on quantitative evaluations of employees' performance and were normally the subject of collective bargaining. Quantitative PRP systems were therefore very much integral to the collectivist tradition of Irish employee relations (Mooney 1980; Grafton 1988; Roche 1992b; see also Armstrong and Murliss 1991). By contrast, performance appraisal is essentially an individualist management tool (Beer et al. 1984). By linking performance appraisals to incremental pay decisions, managements in 'newly established' companies are posing a significant challenge to collectivism in employee relations. The collectivist tradition implies that incremental pay decisions are achieved through collective bargaining and, once agreed, apply 'across the board' to all relevant employee categories. In contrast, PRP decisions based on performance appraisal are normally the subject of a management review of individual employees' performance. Consequently, incremental pay decisions are made by the management rather than through collective bargaining and vary according to individual appraisals. Individualism thus replaces collectivism at two critical stages: firstly, the process of appraisal is individualist rather than collectivist (individual appraisal rather than collective bargaining); secondly, the outcome takes the form of varying PRP decisions among individual employees rather than a fixed amount that applies equally to all employees.

Some commentators have suggested that PRP does not necessarily have negative implications for collectivism and specifically for trade unions (Heery 1992). This argument is based on evidence that PRP systems may co-exist alongside collective bargaining on pay (Casey 1992). The evidence from Irish newly established sites does not support this argument. In these companies individualism tends to counterpoise collectivism. Furthermore, the strongest component of individualism in newly established sites is the use of PRP systems based on individual performance appraisals among non-managerial or white-collar grades. The evidence identifies company ownership and trade union recognition as the main factor influencing the adoption of PRP systems based on individual performance appraisals. Such systems were predominantly used in non-union and American-owned companies and were largely absent in unionised companies. As mentioned above, these findings indicate that individualism tends to counterpoise rather than complement collectivism in terms of management styles in employee relations.

Another indicator of increased individualism identified in the literature is the adoption of sophisticated and highly individualist employment systems to effectively manage 'human resource flows', particularly in the areas of selection and employee development (Foulkes 1980; Beer et al. 1984). A further important indicator of high individualism in the current literature is the incidence of extensive mechanisms for facilitating employee autonomy and involvement (Lawler 1978, 1982; Beer et al. 1984). It was interesting that Gunnigle's study of newly established companies did not find widespread evidence of sophisticated employment systems or mechanisms for facilitating employees' involvement or autonomy in the majority of the companies studied (Gunnigle 1995).

In considering these results it can be argued that while individualism appeared to be an important and significant management strategy in employee relations in start-up companies, this did not necessarily imply that the managements in such companies were adopting a 'resource perspective' of employees (see, for example, Purcell 1987). This study found little evidence of a shift from a utility perspective to a resource perspective in newly established companies. The aggregate evidence suggests that while there is a greater emphasis on individualism in newly established companies than in longer-established companies, this does not equate to high levels of individualism. Rather it appears that managements in newly established sites are adopting more individualist approaches in selected aspects of employee relations but are not moving towards a wholly individualist approach equating to the 'soft' HRM model (Beer et al. 1984; Guest 1989; Storey 1989).

12

Employee Relations Practice

This chapter considers key aspects of employee relations practice. Particular emphasis is placed on activities undertaken at the enterprise level, such as collective bargaining, grievance handling, discipline administration, and employee participation.

COLLECTIVE BARGAINING

We have seen that employee relations is primarily concerned with how such issues as pay, conditions of employment, work-place relations and work-place rules are dealt with by employers and employees. An important institution of employee relations is collective bargaining, whereby pay, working conditions and other employment-related issues are regulated between organised employees and the management. Collective bargaining therefore is a mechanism through which divergent employer and worker interests may be reconciled through an orderly process involving negotiation and compromise. An essential feature of collective bargaining is that employees do not negotiate with employers on their own but do so collectively through representatives (normally trade unions, but also through staff associations or employee councils or committees). Some necessary conditions must therefore be fulfilled for collective bargaining to function effectively:

1. Employees must have the freedom to associate, enabling them to join together in trade unions or other organisations that are not in any way under the control or influence of employers.

2. Employers must be prepared to recognise such trade unions or other organisations and to accept the constraints placed on their ability to deal with employees individually.

It should be noted that collective bargaining is not the only method of regulating employment matters. Even in countries where it is widely used, such as Ireland, it usually operates alongside other mechanisms, for example individual bargaining between employer and employees, regulation by the government, the unilateral imposition of terms of employment by the management, or similarly the imposition of terms unilaterally by trade unions. While such methods can represent alternatives to collective bargaining, there is a traditional and widely held view that collective bargaining is the most satisfactory way for employers and employees to regulate conditions of employment (see for example Donovan 1968; International Labour Organisation 1973). The ILO has long argued that collective bargaining offers a number of advantages that make it the most appropriate method of regulating labour issues and that explain its widespread application. These advantages include the following:

1. It is seen as more flexible than other methods (such as statutory control).
2. It helps redress the disparity in bargaining power between the individual employee and their employer.
3. It allows workers an opportunity to participate in decisions on the conditions of employment under which they operate.
4. It provides an orderly mechanism for identifying and handling grievances and differences of opinions through negotiation aimed at securing eventual agreement.

The normal outcome of the collective bargaining process is a collective agreement. However, this objective does not preclude bargaining situations that may break down and result in a strike or other form of industrial action, provided of course there was a genuine attempt to reach agreement.

Collective agreements are frequently regarded as covering two different kinds of arrangements, namely those that deal with substantive issues and those that are procedural in nature. The scope of substantive agreements will obviously vary widely from company to company, but substantive terms incorporate the 'hard' terms of collective agreements, such as those dealing with wage increases, hours of work, and holidays. In contrast, procedural issues are concerned with the ways in which terms and conditions of employment are arrived at and how differences over the application of agreed terms and conditions are settled. Such procedural arrangements normally prescribe how wage claims, disciplinary issues, grievances, disputes and related matters are to be processed or handled by the parties.

Levels of collective bargaining

We have seen that collective bargaining requires collective action on the part of employees. However, employers may engage in collective bargaining on an individual basis or collectively, through, for example, employers' organisations. Trade unions or other representative employee bodies may therefore bargain with one employer, a group of employers, or representatives of an employers' organisation. As a consequence, the location of collective bargaining may vary between companies and over time, and it can occur at a multi-employer or single-employer level. Multi-employer bargaining normally involves the representation of employers' interests by employers' organisations and may take place at the national, regional or industry level. Single-employer bargaining can also take place at a number of levels, depending on the structure of the company. A particular company may be involved in bargaining at the establishment level (generally referred to as work-place bargaining) and at a multi-establishment level (if the company is a multi-site operation). In addition, collective bargaining at the level of the single employer might involve negotiations with an individual union or in a multi-union environment with representatives of a group of unions.

The essential levels at which collective bargaining may take place are summarised in fig. 12.1.

In Ireland the primary location of collective bargaining in recent years has been the national level, involving the Irish Congress of Trade Unions, employers' organisations (such as IBEC), and the Government. Such national-level bargaining normally operates alongside supplementary work-place bargaining on company-level issues such as work practices and productivity.

Fig. 12.1: Levels of collective bargaining

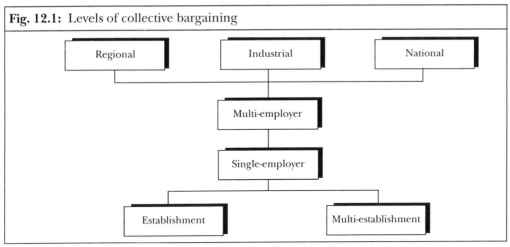

Source: Gunnigle, Garavan, and Fitzgerald (1992).

Several commentators have analysed the pros and cons of bargaining on either a single or multi-employer basis. For example, it is suggested that employers may prefer multi-employer bargaining because it removes the need to deal with annual wage negotiations at the company level and leaves the management team free to devote their time to other aspects of organisational management. It is also suggested that the standardisation of pay levels and working conditions helps to avoid wage competition between employers by regulating an important aspect of the competitive market. It has also been suggested that companies in a comfortable trading position may see multi-employer bargaining as a relatively painless way of dealing with employee relations. On the other hand, multi-employer bargaining may have disadvantages for employers. For example, bargaining on a single-employer (individual) basis may allow the management greater scope to ensure that wage levels and other conditions of employment more closely reflect their competitive position. This may be achieved by linking concessions on wage levels and working conditions to union or worker commitments to increase productivity or contribute to other cost reductions in a way that may be more difficult to achieve through multi-employer bargaining.

Collective bargaining in Ireland

In Ireland the scope of collective bargaining is extensive, with the terms of collective agreements becoming implied terms of the individual employee's contract of employment. Collective bargaining has traditionally been the main area of activity of personnel management practitioners and a major consideration for most larger companies (Shivanath 1987). The Irish system of collective bargaining is essentially voluntary in nature, relying on the moral commitment of the participants to adhere to agreements achieved through the bargaining process. An important characteristic of collective bargaining is a tendency towards high levels of centralisation in the level of bargaining.

As noted above, centralised bargaining essentially describes institutionalised negotiations between representatives of trade union federations and employers' organisations about wages and other issues. It is clear that centralised wage agreements have been an important and distinctive feature of Irish employee relations. Although the first attempts at centralised pay bargaining took place in 1948 and led to a series of 'wage rounds', it was not until the nineteen-seventies that the first National Wage Agreement (of seven) was negotiated. In addition to dealing with basic wage increases, these agreements included arrangements for moving towards equal pay for equal work, for special anomaly claims, for incentive schemes and productivity bargaining, and for procedures for resolving disputes.

These early national agreements did not involve direct Government participation as a separate party to the negotiations (however, the Government was involved in its role as an employer). Towards the end of the seventies, as it became clear that national pay bargaining was closely linked to the Government's economic and social policy, it became directly involved in negotiations in its own right and not simply as an employer. The result was the more ambitious National Understandings, of which two were negotiated, in 1979 and 1980. These agreements embraced policies not just on employment and pay but also on issues such as tax, education, health, and social welfare.

The sequence of centralised agreements ceased at the expiry of the second National Understanding in 1982. The years 1982–86 witnessed a short period of decentralised bargaining, during which it appeared that company viability and economic performance became a key criterion in shaping levels of wage increases. Settlement levels varied widely between industries and industry sectors, with little convergence towards a wage round norm (see McGinley 1989a, 1989b). The Government at times sought to impose a norm through pay guidelines, but these were largely ignored by private sector negotiators and, as von Prondzynski (1985) argues, were best seen as the Government's opening position in public sector pay negotiations. A notable feature of this period was the reduction over the rounds in the number and range of supplementary cost-increasing claims. Wage costs rose by only 7 per cent between 1980 and 1985, compared with an average of 37 per cent in competing countries (Hardiman 1988).

The most important factor in the return to centralised bargaining in 1987 was undoubtedly the growing crisis in the public finances. The national debt represented 148 per cent of GNP in 1986, while unemployment had risen dramatically and contributed to an apparently disastrous economic outlook. A critical Government concern was the need to control the public sector pay bill. The newly elected Government led by Fianna Fáil announced a number of measures to improve the public finances, including restrictions on public sector pay. The Government also indicated its interest in attaining a three-year pay agreement. The ICTU and some prominent union leaders also indicated interest in discussing a national plan for growth and economic recovery. Negotiations for a new agreement eventually concluded towards the end of 1987, with the adoption of the terms of the Programme for National Recovery (1987–90). Since then two further such agreements were negotiated, the Programme for Social and Economic Progress (1991–93) and the Programme for Competitiveness and Work (1994–97).

The sequence of centralised wage agreements since 1970 is summarised in table 12.1, while table 12.2 sets out the detailed provisions of the most recent Programme for Competitiveness and Work.

Table 12.1: Centralised wage agreements, 1970–97

First National Wage Agreement	1970
Second National Wage Agreement	1972
Third National Wage Agreement	1974
Fourth National Wage Agreement	1975
Fifth National Wage Agreement	1976
Sixth National Wage Agreement	1977
Seventh National Wage Agreement	1978
First National Understanding	1979
Second National Understanding	1980
Programme for National Recovery	1987–90
Programme for Economic and Social Progress	1990–93
Programme for Competitiveness and Work	1994–96

Note: There were no centralised agreements in the period 1982–87.

Table 12.2: Pay terms of Programme for Competitiveness and Work, 1994

Category	1994	1995	1996	1994–97
Private sector employees, basic increases*	2% for 12 months on basic pay from 1 Jan.	2.5% for 12 months on basic pay from 1 Jan.	2.5% for first 6 months; extra 1% in second 6 months	Increase of 8% in basic pay over 3 years
Building sector, basic increases	5-month pause, then 2% for 12 months	2% for 12 months from 1 June	2% for 4 months; 1% for next 3 months; 1% for final 3 months	5-month pause, then 8% increase over 33 months; deal lasts 39 months
Public service employees, basic increases	Freeze to 1 June, then 2% for 12 months	2% for 12 months from 1 June	1.5% from 1 June; 1.5% from 1 Oct.; 1% from 1 Jan. 1997; deal expires June 1997	5-month pause, then 8% rise in basic pay over 3 years to June 1997
Public service, local or special awards	1% rise payable from 1 Apr. as down-payment before completed negotiation	0.75% rise payable from 1 Jun. after negotiation	0.75% rise payable from 1 Jun. after negotiation; final 0.5% payable from 1 Jun. 1997	Maximum of 3% rise in pay for productivity increases under this carry-over from PESP

*Excluding building and construction sector.

Source: Tansey (1994).

This most recent period of centralised bargaining is widely characterised as representing a shift towards a more corporatist approach to collective bargaining and employee relations in Ireland (see, for example, Roche 1994c; Teague 1995; O'Donnell and O'Reardon 1996). Corporatist arrangements are characterised by (*a*) government intervention in collective bargaining so that negotiations become tripartite, (*b*) a debate over broader issues, such as macro-economic concerns, and (*c*) the existence of consensus in the national interest. As evidence of this corporatist experimentation, pay determination since 1970 has predominantly been negotiated with reference to some centrally bargained wage agreement between the 'social partners' (particularly employers' organisations and trade unions), with varying degrees of Government involvement, up to and including direct negotiations, as evidenced by the Programme for National Recovery, the Programme for Economic and Social Progress, and the Programme for Competitiveness and Work.

However, as Roche (1995) comments, the Irish model of 'social partnership' is somewhat narrow, involving only the top levels of the unions and employers' bodies. He argues that centralised agreements in Ireland have not 'directly sought to impact in any significant way' on developments or changes in work-place employee relations and describes the Irish model as 'truncated social partnership'. Undoubtedly the pros and cons of centralised agreements will be the subject of extensive debate as the possibility and nature of further agreements are evaluated.

NEGOTIATING IN EMPLOYEE RELATIONS

The fundamental constituent of collective bargaining is the negotiations process. Negotiation in employee relations involves discussions and interactions between representatives of employers and employees over some divisive issues with the object of reaching agreement. For the unionised company, management-union negotiations represent the main vehicle for reaching agreement over a broad range of employee relations issues, such as pay and conditions of employment. Such negotiations are normally termed 'distributive bargaining', since they involve bargaining or haggling over issues where a favourable settlement for one party means an element of loss for the other. This 'win-lose' approach represents an adversarial model of collective bargaining, where each party pursues its own specific objectives and hopes to make minimal concessions to the other side. It is most obvious in pay negotiations, where concessions by the management inevitably represent both a quantifiable cost and a reduction in profits or dividends. On the other hand, negotiations can have a joint problem-solving approach, sometimes referred to as 'integrative' or 'co-operative' bargaining, where both parties are concerned with finding a jointly acceptable solution resulting in benefits for both sides (often referred to as a 'win-win' approach). Inevitably, employee relations negotiations will involve some combination of both approaches.

Phases in the negotiation process

Formal employee relations negotiations normally involve one party submitting a claim to the other party and subsequently entering discussions on this claim or issue. Such negotiations may conclude either in agreement on the issues raised or, possibly, in failure to agree, resulting in a breakdown of the negotiation. Such an impasse may be addressed through further negotiation, the use of third-party mediation, or the instigation of industrial action. It should be noted that employee relations negotiations may also occur at a more informal level, involving the line management and employees and/or their representatives. Such negotiations normally involve less important or individual issues, such as employee grievances or minor disciplinary issues.

The negotiating process itself will generally follow a number of predictable phases. These may be categorised as (*a*) preparation for negotiations, (*b*) bargaining, and (*c*) follow-up action, as outlined in table 12.3.

Table 12.3: Phases in negotiation process

Phase	Activities
1. Preparation	Agree objectives and mandate
	Research
	Choose negotiating team
	Assess bargaining power
2. Bargaining	Discover positions
	Expectation structuring
	Compromise and movement
3. Post-negotiation	Document agreement or disagreement
	Clarify
	Agree action plans
	Communicate
	Implement action plans
	Review

Source: Gunnigle, McMahon, and Fitzgerald (1995).

PREPARATION

As with all types of managerial activity, careful preparation is an important prerequisite of success in employee relations negotiations. Parties to the negotiations should be familiar with the details of the issue in hand and have a clear understanding of their objectives and mandate before entering the bargaining arena. This normally involves establishing a bargaining range, including the limits within which each party is prepared to reach agreement. In practice this often means establishing an *ideal settlement point,* a *realistic settlement point,* and a *fall-back position,* beyond which a party is not prepared to enter agreement. These positions are illustrated in fig. 12.2 in the context of hypothetical negotiations between a trade union and employer on wage increases.

An important aspect of effective preparations for employee relations negotiations is adequate research. Effective preparation also involves ensuring that appropriate administrative arrangements are made in relation to timing, location, and support

Fig. 12.2: Management-union bargaining range (example of pay negotiations)

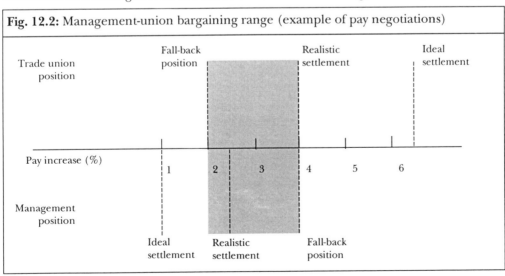

Source: Gunnigle, Garavan, and Fitzgerald (1992).

facilities. The size and composition of the negotiating team largely depends on the issue for negotiation; it is generally suggested that, with the exception of minor issues, a negotiating team should comprise a minimum of two people to facilitate the preparation of the case, record-keeping, and evaluation of progress (Nierenberg 1968). In larger organisations the personnel manager will normally represent the management; however, line managers may often handle smaller issues or assist the personnel manager during major negotiations.

Fig. 12.3: Stages in bargaining process

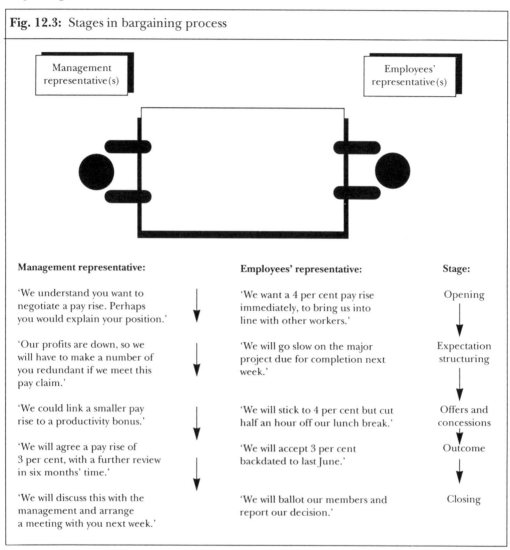

Management representative:	Employees' representative:	Stage:
'We understand you want to negotiate a pay rise. Perhaps you would explain your position.'	'We want a 4 per cent pay rise immediately, to bring us into line with other workers.'	Opening
'Our profits are down, so we will have to make a number of you redundant if we meet this pay claim.'	'We will go slow on the major project due for completion next week.'	Expectation structuring
'We could link a smaller pay rise to a productivity bonus.'	'We will stick to 4 per cent but cut half an hour off our lunch break.'	Offers and concessions
'We will agree a pay rise of 3 per cent, with a further review in six months' time.'	'We will accept 3 per cent backdated to last June.'	Outcome
'We will discuss this with the management and arrange a meeting with you next week.'	'We will ballot our members and report our decision.'	Closing

Source: Gunnigle, Garavan, and Fitzgerald (1992).

BARGAINING

Fig. 12.3 outlines the typical phases in the actual bargaining process, namely (*a*) opening, (*b*) expectation structuring, (*c*) offer, concession, movement, (*d*) agreement or disagreement, and (*e*) close.

The opening phase normally involves both parties articulating their positions. At this stage both parties normally attempt to find out more about each other's positions and assess the degree to which movement and concession are possible. The next phase often involves what is termed 'expectation structuring', where each party attempts to convince the other of the logic of their position and their depth of commitment to that position.

The parties may also emphasise what are seen as deficiencies in the other side's position. Each party to the negotiation thus attempts to structure or influence the other party's expectations and tries to convince them to accept whatever concessions are offered. For example, during pay negotiations employers often refer to factors such as increased competition or the need for re-investment in an attempt to reduce employee or union expectations. The 'offer, concession, movement' phase generally follows the process of expectation structuring. This stage involves some initial offers and concessions by either party. During this phase adjournments are often used to allow the parties to evaluate their options and progress so far.

After some time both parties will be in a position to evaluate the likelihood of reaching agreement or, possibly, the extent and implications of a breakdown in the negotiations. Both parties will normally recognise and anticipate the closing phase in the bargaining process. This normally involves completing the agreement, issues for further negotiation, procedures for interpretation of the agreement, or details of breakdown.

POST-NEGOTIATION PHASE

At the end of the negotiations the parties will normally report back on the outcome, the employee or union side reporting back to the workers they represent and the management team reporting back to the senior and, possibly, line management. This post-negotiation phase normally involves reviewing the implementation of any agreement reached and possibly a general evaluation of the implications of the negotiations and agreement.

INDUSTRIAL CONFLICT

Given the potential differences of interest that can arise on employment matters, it is not surprising that some degree of conflict is likely in employee relations. There are numerous explanations for why industrial conflict occurs.

In the preceding chapter the 'pluralist' and 'unitarist' framework was suggested as a useful model for explaining employee relations interactions and industrial conflict (Fox 1968, 1974; Marchington 1982). In the pluralist framework, companies are seen as comprising a range of people and groups with different interests and priorities. This model suggests that the interaction of these competing interests and groups necessitates the development of institutional arrangements that help manage these competing interests and achieve a level of 'bargained compromise' that allows the company to conduct its normal business. The pluralist framework therefore accepts that conflict in companies is inevitable, because the needs and objectives of various interest groups will clash on occasion. The unitarist framework provides a different explanation for industrial conflict. This approach is based on the premise that companies are essentially cohesive and harmonious units and that all members of the company (management and employees) should share common goals. Within the unitarist framework there is only one source of authority, namely the management (Fox 1968, 1974; Marchington 1982). The management and the employees are seen as having the same interests, with conflict occurring only as a result of misunderstandings or the efforts of troublemakers. Within the unitarist model, therefore, industrial conflict is not seen as inevitable and consequently there is no perceived need for institutional arrangements for dealing with it.

In practice it would seem that some degree of conflict is inherent in employee relations and that differences will arise between the management and workers. These differences are not necessarily harmful and need not necessarily lead to industrial conflict. In some instances such conflicts can have decidedly positive effects, by, for example, leading to positive changes in management practice.

Industrial conflict is normally categorised into two broad forms: (*a*) explicit and organised industrial conflict and (*b*) unorganised and more implicit industrial conflict (Bean 1976). Explicit, overt forms of industrial conflict are organised and systematic responses and include strikes, go-slows, and overtime bans. Implicit reactions include absenteeism, labour turnover and poor performance and may often reflect low levels of employee satisfaction and morale.

Fig. 12.4: Strike activities in Ireland: strike frequency, 1922–91

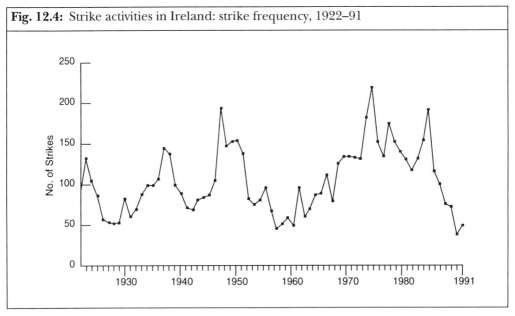

Source: UCD data-base of strike statistics (Kelly and Brannick 1990).

Strike activity in Ireland

The most visible way in which workers can demonstrate industrial conflict is to go on strike. Strike action can take different forms and can arise for a variety of reasons.

'Official' strikes are defined as those that have been fully sanctioned by the union executive. Such strikes normally occur after negotiations have failed to resolve the issue and when all due procedures have been exhausted (Gunnigle et al. 1995). In contrast, 'unofficial' strikes are those that have not been sanctioned by the trade union. Such strikes tend to be quite reactive in nature and are often sparked off by a particular event or incident at the work-place level, such as the dismissal or suspension of a worker.

Unless subsequently granted official approval by the trade union, unofficial strikes normally last for a shorter time and involve fewer workers than official strikes (Wallace and O'Shea 1987; Wallace 1988a, 1988b).

Fig. 12.5: Strike activities in Ireland: number of workers involved, 1922–91

Source: UCD data-base of strike statistics (Kelly and Brannick 1990).

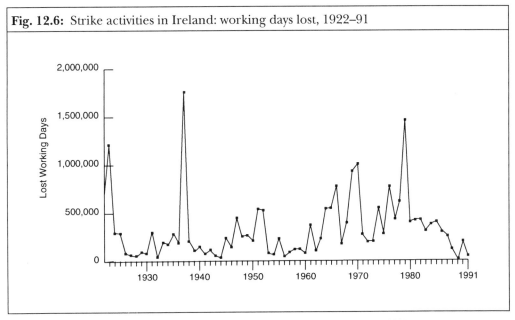

Fig. 12.6: Strike activities in Ireland: working days lost, 1922–91

Source: UCD data-base of strike statistics (Kelly and Brannick 1990).

Three important measures are normally used in evaluating the extent of strike activity, namely (*a*) strike frequency (the number of strikes), (*b*) the number of workers involved, and (*c*) the number of working days lost. Using these indicators, figs. 12.4–12.6 summarise the pattern of strike activity in Ireland over the period 1922–91. (This outline of strike activity is based on data from University College, Dublin—see, for example, Kelly and Brannick 1983, 1986, 1989a, 1990; Brannick and Doyle 1994—and the Department of Enterprise and Employment.) This evidence shows a clear upward trend in strike activity during the nineteen-sixties and seventies, followed by a significant decline for much of the eighties and into the nineties.

In evaluating the pattern of strike activity, Kelly and Brannick (1983) identify two key trends: (*a*) the disproportionate effect of a few large strikes on strike statistics and (*b*) the different patterns of strike activity between the public and private sectors. In relation to the former, Kelly and Brannick note that over the period 1960–79 forty-three strikes (2 per cent of the total in this period) accounted for 57 per cent of all days lost through strikes, and they comment:

> Clearly, the Irish strike pattern is extremely sensitive to this comparatively small number of large strikes and it has been an enduring feature over the 20 year period. Indeed should these be removed from the Irish strike quantum the result would be a record which would show a comparatively strike-free nation in terms of workers involved and total man-days lost.

In evaluating patterns of strike activity in the public and private sectors, Kelly and Brannick found that the private sector was the most strike-prone sector in the period 1960–86. However, their study indicated that the proportion of strike activity accounted for by the private sector was greatest during the nineteen-sixties but has been declining since then. This development has paralleled a marked increase in the proportion of strike activity accounted for by the public sector over the period (see table 12.4). Kelly and Brannick found that much of the strike activity in the public sector has been concentrated among a relatively small number of organisations. They identified nine organisations that accounted for 62 per cent of all strikes, 85 per cent of the numbers involved, and 86 per cent of the days lost in the period 1960–84.

Table 12.4: Strike activity in public and private sectors, 1960–92

	Strike frequency		*Workers involved*		*Working days lost*	
	Public sector	Private sector	Public sector	Private sector	Public sector	Private sector
1960–69	17.9	82.1	36.5	63.5	24.2	75.8
1970–79	18.3	81.7	22.6	67.4	37.9	62.1
1980–89	29.1	70.9	68.9	31.1	37.7	62.3
1990–92	47.5	52.5	67.1	32.9	31.9	68.1

Source: Brannick and Doyle (1994).

A number of critical factors affecting the level and pattern of strike activity have been identified, such as the level of economic activity (business cycle), unemployment (tightness or looseness of the labour market), industrial development, inflation (earnings), and unionisation (see, for example, Brannick and Doyle 1994). The decline in strike activity during the nineteen-eighties is generally explained by the deep recession and rising unemployment (see Gunnigle et al. 1995). However, management strategies and practice also influence levels of industrial conflict and strike activity.

The impact of a range of factors that may influence strike patterns is illustrated in Kelly and Brannick's analysis of strikes among multinational companies in Ireland (Kelly and Brannick 1988a, 1988b, 1988c, 1989b, 1991). They found that American companies were the most strike-prone during the nineteen-sixties. However, this declined dramatically from the seventies, to a stage where American multinationals now have a low incidence of strike activity. In contrast, the strike record of British companies deteriorated dramatically over the period. Kelly and Brannick attribute this increase to product market difficulties encountered by British-owned companies in Ireland resulting from increased competition. In evaluating the improvement of the strike record of American companies, Kelly and Brannick offer two reasons: (1) the changed industrial composition of American multinationals: most are now high-technology companies in the 'newer' industrial sectors, particularly electronics and chemicals (as opposed to labour-intensive companies producing standardised products in the nineteen-sixties); and (2) American multinationals are predominantly in the electronics sector, which has been to the forefront in developing what are seen as innovative and proactive employee relations or HR strategies and policies.

The relative impact of official and unofficial strikes is another important issue affecting patterns of strike activity. In their study of unofficial strikes, Wallace and O'Shea (1987) found a dramatic reduction in the number of unofficial strikes since the middle nineteen-seventies (see table 12.5). Since 1982 approximately 40 per cent of strikes have been unofficial, compared with an average of 66 per cent in the mid-seventies. As unofficial strikes are normally shorter and involve fewer employees, this has meant that unofficial strikes now account for a very small proportion of working days lost through strike activity (Wallace and O'Shea 1987; Wallace 1988a, 1988b).

Table 12.5: Official and unofficial strikes: frequency and working days lost, 1980–91

	Unofficial strikes	Official strikes	Working days lost, unofficial strikes	Working days lost, official strikes
1980	81	51	184,000	219,500
1981	61	56	131,000	305,000
1982	55	76	74,000	363,000
1983	58	93	58,000	253,000
1984	75	116	51,000	313,000
1985	45	70	43,000	394,000
1986	38	62	20,500	295,500
1987	22	54	25,000	235,000
1988	26	46	6,500	123,500
1989	13	28	11,600	29,800
1990	16	35	6,800	196,900
1991	13	39	9,300	73,600

Source: Department of Labour (1992).

Other forms of industrial action
Other forms of action, such as overtime bans and working to rule (i.e. working to the

letter of written terms and conditions of employment), are often more common than strikes themselves. These other forms of overt action can provide an effective means of achieving bargaining goals while not entailing the potential hardships of strike action. In particular, actions such as go-slows and overtime bans can place considerable pressure on employers to move towards resolution while not jeopardising employees' income or job security to as great a degree as might be the case as a result of a strike (Gunnigle et al. 1995).

A far less obvious result of poor employee relations is a lack of commitment to the company and lack of trust in the management, which can have far-reaching long-term effects. Changes in work practices, for example, may be bitterly resisted; if other jobs are available, labour turnover may be high; recruitment may be difficult; productivity may fall; and absence may be high. It is important that managements are aware of such long-term consequences and have a clear and fair policy on employee relations.

Finally, it is important to note that employers may also instigate industrial action. The principal form of industrial action undertaken by managements is a lock-out, which involves preventing the work-force from attending at work and is the equivalent of strike action by an employer.

CONFLICT RESOLUTION: DEALING WITH DISPUTES IN EMPLOYEE RELATIONS

At the level of the enterprise, all parties involved in employee relations have an important role to play in the handling and resolution of conflict. The senior management have overall responsibility for the development of effective policies and procedures for handling employee relations and industrial conflict. Where a specialist personnel function exists it will normally have responsibility for advising the top management on optimal employee relations strategies and developing appropriate procedures and practices. It may also provide training, advice and guidance to the line management in handling work-place issues. Line managers and shop stewards have a key role in handling disputes and grievances that arise at the shop-floor level. Trade unions undertake a similar role on the employee side.

As already mentioned, industrial conflict should not be viewed as having a necessarily negative impact on employee relations. Industrial conflict can have certain positive effects, allowing employees to draw attention to and pursue issues of concern and so facilitating change and development in the nature of employee relations.

Possibly the most widespread response to conflict in the work-place has been the development of joint mechanisms for discussing and resolving issues of difference (Gunnigle et al. 1995). Such institutionalisation of conflict is primarily characterised by the development of procedures for facilitating conflict resolution. This institutionalisation of conflict reflects an implicit acceptance that issues of conflict will arise and is characteristic of the pluralist approach to employee relations discussed earlier (see Fox 1966, 1974; Marchington 1982). In creating institutions (such as collective bargaining) and procedures for handling employee relations and industrial conflict, the parties seek to create a framework through which they can interact, argue, disagree and agree while allowing for the continuing operation of the business (Jackson 1982; Gunnigle et al. 1995).

Grievance, disputes and disciplinary procedures are a characteristic feature of Irish employee relations and represent an important means of dealing with employee relations and industrial conflict at the level of the enterprise (see, for example, Wallace 1989).

GRIEVANCE HANDLING

In employee relations the term 'grievance' is normally used to describe a formal expression of employee dissatisfaction. Given the nature of industrial organisation, it is inevitable that employees, either individually or in groups, will have grievances that they want the management to address. The great majority of such grievances normally involve minor complaints related to the immediate work environment. These grievances therefore can normally be handled at the shop-floor level by the line management and employees or employee representatives. It is suggested that managers should pay particular attention to effective grievance handling and its contribution to the promotion of good employee relations in the work-place. It is also suggested that managements should handle employee grievances promptly, since the non-handling of grievances may give rise to frustration, which can permeate through to other employees and promote an uneasy working environment in which disputes and poor employee relations can arise (Gunnigle et al. 1995). Some basic guidelines for managers involved in grievance handling are listed in table 12.6.

Table 12.6: Management check-list for grievance handling

- The management should make every effort to understand the nature of, and the reasons for, disputes and grievances.
- All levels of the management should be aware of the important influence that grievance handling has on industrial and company performance generally.
- The management should establish a policy that sets out an orderly and effective framework for handling disputes and grievances.
- The line management, particularly first-level supervision, must be aware of their central role in effective grievance handling.

An important aspect of grievance handling is the establishment and application of grievance procedures (Thomason 1984). Such a procedure normally lays down the stages and the approaches to be followed in handling grievances in the work-place. The main advantages of such procedures include (*a*) increased clarity in employee relations interactions, (*b*) the prevention of misunderstandings and arguments over interpretation, (*c*) ease of communication, and (*d*) increased fairness and consistency in application (Hawkins 1979; also see Wallace 1989, Gunnigle et al. 1995).

The main aim of grievance procedures is to ensure that issues raised by employees are handled adequately and settled fairly and as near as possible to their point of origin. Such aims are based on the premise that, operated effectively, grievance procedures include a strong preventive dimension in helping to avoid the development of grievance issues into more serious industrial disputes.

Most problems or complaints raised by employees should ideally be handled by the immediate supervisor, without recourse to a formal grievance procedure. However, issues that warrant more thorough consideration may be more appropriately handled through a formal agreed procedure. Grievance procedures should normally be in writing, should be simple and easy to operate, and should aim to handle disputes and grievances fairly and consistently. Formal procedures generally follow an upward path from one organisational level to the next. A sample grievance procedure in a unionised company is outlined in table 12.7.

Since it is not always possible to resolve all grievances at the enterprise level, it is generally necessary to make provision for the referring of issues to an independent third party for mediation or arbitration. (The main third-party agencies were outlined in chapter 10.) Grievance procedures normally contain a provision that no form of industrial action will be taken by either party until all stages of the procedure have been exhausted and an agreed period of notice has expired. Effectively operated, this ensures that both parties have ample opportunity to settle issues either through direct discussion or by opting for third-party referral.

Table 12.7: Sample grievance procedure

	Procedural level	
	Management	Employee/trade union
1. Issue involving local rules or employment conditions affecting an individual or small work group	Immediate supervisor	Employee(s) concerned
2. (*a*) Any issue that has remained unresolved at stage 1	Department manager (with relevant supervisor as appropriate)	Employee(s) concerned and shop steward or employee representative
(*b*) Grievance or claim where the issue has direct implications for a group of workers on a departmental or section basis		
3. (*a*) Any issue that has remained unresolved from stage 2	Personnel manager and line manager(s)	Employee(s) concerned and/or shop steward or employee representatives (including union official)
(*b*) Grievance or claim with company-wide implications		
4. An unresolved issue that has been through the appropriate lower stages and remains unresolved	Third-party investigation: rights commissioner; Labour Relations Commission	
5. Any issue that remains unresolved after stage 4	Labour Court investigation; Employment Appeals Tribunal	

HANDLING DISCIPLINARY ISSUES

Inevitably, situations will arise in organisations where the management seek to take disciplinary action against employees who fail to conform to the established rules or norms. Most organisations will seek to establish and maintain what they consider acceptable standards or norms in areas such as performance, attendance, and conduct at work. Should employees breach these standards, the management will normally seek to take some form of disciplinary action. This may range from relatively minor rebukes to more serious sanctions such as formal warnings, suspension, or dismissal.

An important aspect of discipline administration is the establishment of acceptable rules and standards and the use of disciplinary procedures to deal with breaches of such rules. Disciplinary rules set out the standards of acceptable behaviour expected from employees and the consequences of not meeting these standards, while disciplinary procedures constitute the administrative machinery for applying these rules and carrying out any resulting action.

A critical concern in the area of discipline administration is the legal context within which discipline should be administered. For example, the common law concept of natural justice requires that

(1) there should be a basic understanding of what constitutes a transgression: company rules or standards should therefore be clearly outlined and communicated;

(2) the consequences of breaching such rules or standards should be clear;

(3) employees not achieving the required standard should be so informed and given the opportunity to improve where possible;

(4) employees alleged to have breached discipline are entitled to fair and consistent treatment, including an opportunity to state their case, to have access to representation, and to appeal to a higher authority.

These principles, combined with the legislative framework surrounding discipline administration, suggest that companies should have some formal disciplinary procedure, should ensure that employees are familiar with its contents, and should apply this procedure in a reasonable way.

The legal context for discipline administration is outlined in chapter 13.[1] The most significant legislative developments affecting discipline administration are the Unfair Dismissals Acts, 1977 and 1993, which provide guidelines on what constitutes fair and unfair dismissal and a mechanism for dealing with claims of unfair dismissal and for deciding on redress for those found to be unfairly dismissed.

A disciplinary procedure is an important aspect of effective discipline administration. Disciplinary procedures serve to establish an explicit method for bringing alleged offences to the notice of employees, to allow employees an opportunity to respond to such charges, and to facilitate the imposing of disciplinary action as necessary.

A critical initial step in establishing a disciplinary procedure is to outline company rules and standards and the form of disciplinary action associated with breaches of these rules or standards. The establishment of explicit work-place rules helps to ensure consistency in the treatment of employees. Such an outline should identify (*a*) those rules and standards whose breach may lead to dismissal in the first instance (e.g. theft or violence at work) and (*b*) those rules and standards whose breach would lead to the operation of a standard disciplinary procedure (e.g. lateness, absenteeism, inadequate work performance). To facilitate the effective administration of disciplinary procedures the golden rule would seem to be that such procedures be (*a*) agreed between the management and employees, (*b*) understood by the management and employees, (*c*) fair, and (*d*) applied consistently. A sample disciplinary procedure is presented in table 12.8.

Table 12.8: Sample disciplinary procedure

Preamble

The following disciplinary procedure will be used to deal with all breaches of company rules and standards, except where the offences or transgression constitute gross misconduct.

The primary aim of this procedure is to help employees whose conduct or performance falls below company requirements to achieve the necessary improvement. This is desirable in contributing both to the company's success and to the fair treatment of employees. It is company policy to apply this procedure as reasonably as possible and to ensure consistency and order in its application. It will apply to all breaches of company rules or standards not constituting gross misconduct, including, but not limited to, the following:
- bad timekeeping
- unauthorised absence
- lack of co-operation
- unacceptable work performance
- poor attendance
- breaches of safety regulations

Disciplinary procedure

1. In the first instance, the employee concerned will be asked to attend a *counselling interview* by their supervisor, where their transgression will be made clear, the standard of performance required outlined, and the employee verbally reprimanded.
2. In the second instance the employee will receive a *verbal warning* at a formal meeting with their supervisor and department manager, where details of the misdemeanour and the consequences of further offences will be explained.
3. In the third instance the employee will receive a *final written warning* from the personnel manager at a meeting with the department manager and, if appropriate, the supervisor, where the employee will be informed of the details of the offence and future performance standards required and informed that further offences will lead to suspension or dismissal.
4. In the last instance the employee will either be *suspended without pay* or *dismissed* (depending on the offence), notice of which will be given to the employee at a meeting with the general manager, where the offence will be explained both verbally and in writing and the employee advised of their right of appeal.

Gross misconduct

Gross misconduct is conduct of such a serious nature that the company could not tolerate keeping the employee in employment, and it is hoped that such instances will not occur. However, for the mutual protection of the company and its work-force, any employee found guilty of gross misconduct may be dismissed summarily. Examples of gross misconduct include
- violation of a criminal law
- consumption or possession of alcohol or illegal drugs
- acts or threats of physical violence
- theft from another employee or from the company
- malicious damage to company property
- falsifying company records (including clock cards)

Before any action is taken, the company will thoroughly investigate the case, during which time the employee will be suspended. After such investigation the employee will attend a meeting with the company management, where they will have an opportunity to state their case and be advised of their right of appeal. Should the company still feel that the employee was guilty of gross misconduct, they will be dismissed and given a letter explaining the nature of the offence and the reasons for their dismissal.

An important element in ensuring procedural fairness and equity in discipline administration is the employee's right to adequate representation (either by a fellow-employee or a trade union representative). The management should also ensure that accurate records are maintained in disciplinary cases.

It is important to note that the unfair dismissals legislation places the burden of proof primarily on the employer. Consequently the management must be able to substantiate their case with adequate documentary evidence. Much of this work will be the responsibility of the specialist personnel function. In disciplinary cases the onus is on the management to thoroughly investigate the circumstances and establish the facts of the case. If, after a thorough investigation, it is decided that disciplinary action may be necessary, a meeting is normally arranged with the employee (or employees) concerned. The purpose of such interviews is to assess culpability, decide on appropriate action, and attempt to effect the desired change in the employee's behaviour. The disciplinary interview also provides employees with an opportunity to present their point of view.

Only after a thorough investigation and disciplinary meeting are the management in a position to decide on appropriate action. Should the investigation and disciplinary meeting point to a need for disciplinary action, the management's position should be explained to the employee, who should be made fully aware of their shortcomings and the management's concern. The precise nature of any improvement required and the means of achieving it should be explained, as should the consequences of future transgressions.

There is an onus on the management to ensure that employees fully understand the discipline imposed and the right of appeal. After the interview the details should be accurately recorded and a copy given to the employee concerned (and their representative, as necessary). Any commitments entered into should be carried out promptly.

In the longer term the total process should be monitored from a number of viewpoints, such as the impact on employees' behaviour, trends in disciplinary incidents, and the effectiveness of various forms of discipline. The area of discipline administration should be approached by the management in a positive vein, the overall objective being to change employee behaviour. The personnel function has an important role to play in establishing disciplinary policy and related procedures and in monitoring their application throughout the company. Two essential factors that need to be kept in mind are the need for reasonableness and consistency in undertaking disciplinary action.

TOWARDS A 'NEW MODEL': PARTNERSHIP v. ADVERSARIALISM

Much of employee relations practice, and particularly that concerning collective bargaining, is grounded in what is characterised as 'adversarialism'. The adversarial system, based on the premise that the interests of management and labour conflict, relies primarily on bargaining interactions between these parties to achieve 'mutually acceptable compromises'.

As noted earlier, employee relations in Ireland is characterised by a strong adversarial tradition. This system has come in for increasing criticism in recent years, both in Ireland and abroad. A general criticism has been the perceived dominance of distributive bargaining, with its emphasis on dividing limited resources (Fisher and Ury 1986). It is argued that this approach leads the parties to develop adversarial positions, believing that any gains can only be made by inflicting losses on the other side. Distributive bargaining reflects the very essence of the traditional pluralist-adversarial employee relations model: claims, offers, bluff, threats, compromise, movement, agreement, or conflict. It is suggested that approaches based on more integrative or co-operative bargaining represent a more attractive alternative, with the emphasis on a collaborative approach, exploring common ground, and seeking solutions of benefit to both parties.

The so-called 'partnership approach' to employee relations is grounded in such thinking, suggesting that employers, workers and their representative organisations should seek to jointly address employee relations problems and develop mutually beneficial solutions (see, for example, Kochan and Osterman 1994; Beaumont 1995).

Based on recent analyses of industrial change, it is widely argued that there is a need for a new 'partnership' model of employee relations that incorporates a strong trade union role (see, for example, Kochan and Osterman 1994). This need emerges from the argued weakness of a traditional employee relations system based on adversarial collective bargaining. It is further argued that this new model allows both sides to break out of the traditional adversarial relationship through the adoption of a 'new employee relations' model based on 'mutual gains' principles. The essence is that employers and unions enter into a set of mutual commitments as follows:

1. Employers recognise and facilitate workers' rights to information, consultation, and involvement.

2. Workers and trade unions commit themselves actively to productivity improvements.

3. The gains of productivity improvements are shared between employers and workers.

4. Productivity improvements do not result in redundancies: instead, employers actively seek new markets to keep workers gainfully employed.

In essence the 'mutual gains' argument is that workers and trade unions actively pursue with the management solutions to business problems and appropriate work reorganisation in return for greater involvement in business decisions and in the process of work reorganisation.

In evaluating the merits of developing such a new relationship with workers and their trade unions, it appears that both sides face a fundamental choice on the nature of management-employee relations. Should the involvement of workers and unions be confined to joint consultation or extended to joint regulation? From a worker and union perspective, joint consultation initiatives run the risk of remaining essentially 'symbolic', whereby workers or unions have no real influence but become associated with decisions regarding which they possess no right of veto. Employers may be equally reticent to enter into joint regulation initiatives, as they may lead to a slowing in the decision-making process.

Some of the difficulties in developing partnership approaches in enterprise-level employee relations are apparent in recent debates. As noted earlier, a criticism of patterns of social partnership in Ireland is that its operation is restricted to the most senior levels of employer and trade union interests, with little diffusion into enterprise-level employee relations (see Roche 1995). At the enterprise level, a critical aspect of the partnership debate is that concerning employee participation.

Employee participation

Partnership approaches to employee relations are invariably associated with initiatives designed to facilitate greater employee participation. Employee participation may be broadly interpreted as any mechanisms designed to increase employees' contribution to managerial decision-making. Increased employee participation is an important aspect of many recent initiatives in the area of work organisation (see, for example, Marchington and Parker 1990; ICTU 1993; Kochan, Katz, and McKersie 1986; Kochan and Osterman 1994). Employee participation can take numerous forms and can range from the relatively superficial, such as the management informing employees of decisions that affect them, to consultation with employees on certain decisions or to joint participation in the decision-making process itself. Such initiatives may result in a variety of institutional arrangements, such as suggestion schemes, joint consultative committees, works councils, quality circles, and board-level participation. Employee participation can also be facilitated through collective bargaining, which attempts to lessen the sphere of managerial prerogative and make more issues subject to joint negotiation and agreement.

It is possible to identify four different forms of participation, varying in both the level and the nature of participation: (*a*) representative participation, (*b*) equity participation, (*c*) task participation, and (*d*) participation through collective bargaining (Gunnigle et al. 1995) (see table 12.9). Variations in approaches to employee participation may stem from a variety of reasons, such as the structure and development of collective bargaining, the attitude of trade unions, and the political philosophy of the Government. The variety of institutional arrangements adopted in different countries and by different organisations may also reflect different policies and approaches to employee participation. Participation may be supported by the law or may be established through collective agreements, and may be minimal or extensive.

Table 12.9: Forms of employee participation

Task participation: This encompasses various initiatives to design jobs and work systems that allow for greater employee involvement in decisions affecting employees' jobs and immediate work environment. Such initiatives can take a variety of forms, such as autonomous work groups, quality circles, and consultative meetings or committees.

Equity participation: This involves the adoption of mechanisms through which employees can gain an equity share in their companies through various profit-sharing and share-ownership schemes. Some such schemes may have the broad objective of increasing employees' loyalty, commitment and morale through the closer identification of their interests with those of the company. However, equity participation by itself will not normally allow for a substantial increase in employee influence, as employees will generally represent a minority of the shareholders. Companies such as the John Lewis Partnership in Britain and Donnelly Mirrors in Ireland have long been known for their policy of sharing profits with employees, and many companies now offer share options or some other form of profit-sharing.

Representative participation: This has been the focus of most attention and applies to institutionalised arrangements that give employees access to management decision-making, sometimes with statutory support. The most obvious example is the provision for the election of worker-directors to the boards of management. It also applies to lower-level participation, such as joint consultative committees and works councils. The Worker Participation (State Enterprises) Act, 1977, introduced board-level participation to seven state-sponsored bodies, which was extended to a number of other state organisations under the terms of the Worker Participation (State Enterprises) Act, 1988. However, board-level representation has largely been confined to the state-sponsored bodies covered by the legislation.

Participation through collective bargaining: This has been the most traditional approach to achieving higher levels of employee participation. The growth of work-place bargaining has greatly facilitated this process, with trade unions being the key mechanism for representing and extending employees' rights at the work-place level. However, this approach is seen as essentially adversarial in nature and therefore has incurred the criticism that it is not an effective means of promoting a joint problem-solving approach to employee relations issues.

A vital aspect of the debate on employee participation is the role of trade unions. Traditionally the Irish trade union movement did not seem particularly committed to representative forms of employee participation, such as worker-directors or works councils (Morrissey 1989). Reactions to participation though equity participation have been mixed, and no discernible trend is evident. Indeed, apart from support for greater disclosure of information, the traditional trade union approach to employee participation has been marked by a considerable degree of apathy. Such apathy has strong links with the doubts many trade unionists harbour about the implications of representative participation for the union's role in collective bargaining.

However, the trade union position seems to have altered in recent years. The ICTU policy documents *New Forms of Work Organisation* and *Managing Change* suggest that unions need to take a more proactive role in influencing the planning and implementation of new work-force management strategies (ICTU 1993, 1995). These reports place a particular emphasis on task participation at the enterprise level. They note the importance for trade unions of developing, and actively participating in, employee involvement initiatives in the work-place. They also identify important aspects of employee participation that unions need to address, particularly the joint monitoring of participation initiatives in the work-place, the involvement of unions in the internal communications processes of companies, access to and understanding of business information, and involvement in high-level business decision-making.

It is often suggested that all parties in employee relations can benefit from increased employee participation (Beer et al. 1984). For example, it is suggested that employers need a flexible and committed work-force that will respond to change and perform at high levels of productivity with minimum levels of supervision and that this can be achieved through employee involvement or participation initiatives. From the employees' perspective it is suggested that the achievement of a say in decisions that affect their working lives is a legitimate goal, allowing them greater control and discretion in their jobs (Hackman and Oldham 1980). Even at the macro-level, the state and the community at large may benefit from positive work-place relations based on trust, open communication, and employee satisfaction (Beer et al. 1984).

However, the achievement of real and effective participation in organisations remains problematic (Marchington and Parker 1990; Salamon 1992). Employers' organisations may for example argue that business confidence and discretion in decision-making must be maintained to encourage investment and expansion, while at the same time suggesting that barriers to workers' involvement must be removed and employees given a worthwhile say in decision-making. This perspective is commonly used to encourage employees' involvement in shop-floor issues while legitimising the retention of the management prerogative in higher-level decision-making (Gunnigle and Morley 1992).

Indeed it might be suggested that the four forms of participation described above can be viewed as options in a participative mix, any combination of which might suit a particular organisation. The imposition of particular models might prove problematic, and it seems important that any legislative measures should allow for flexibility in the modes of participation to be adopted. As much as anything, it would appear that effective participation requires a high level of commitment and positive engagement from employers, employers' organisations, employees, and trade unions. Trust has been identified as an essential element in facilitating effective communications and information disclosure or exchange (Whelan 1982). Indeed it would appear that the existence of high-trust relations is more important than the actual participative form or mechanism adopted.

Task participation and the teamworking debate

Possibly the most widely debated contemporary participation form is task participation, and particularly the issue of 'teamworking'. Geary (1994a) defines task participation as

> opportunities which management provides at workplace level for consultation with and/or delegation of responsibilities and authority for decision making to its subordinates either as individuals or as groups of employees relating to the immediate work task and/or working conditions.

Task participation therefore involves the devolution to employees of greater control over work-related decisions: workers' involvement in contributing opinions and solving problems is actively facilitated. Workers are thus required to concern themselves with broader enterprise objectives, such as improving productivity, controlling costs, etc.

Two key forms of task participation can be identified (Sisson 1994):

- *consultative participation*, whereby workers are given the opportunity to become involved in decisions and to make their views known; however, the management retains the prerogative to make final decisions;
- *delegative participation*, whereby workers are empowered to make key decisions without the need for management approval.

Within the broad outlines of the debate on task participation, the growth of interest in teamworking emerges as a significant element, with far-reaching implications for employee relations and personnel or human resource management (HRM). Teamworking is seen as an advanced form of delegative participation whereby workers make key decisions such as those concerning the selection of team leaders, team members, roles, etc. (Geary 1994a, 1994b). The concept of teamworking has its roots in traditional notions of improving the quality of working life. While these early developments met with some support in the United States and Scandinavia, they had little impact in Ireland. In recent years there has been a significant increase in employers' interest in work reorganisation and teamworking. It now appears that employers are now the key instigators of teamworking (Beaumont 1995). This contrasts with earlier initiatives in teamworking, which were worker or union-driven and were designed to improve the quality of working life of employees.

Since there is little empirical evidence on the diffusion of teamworking in Ireland, a useful basis for considering its extent and nature is John Geary's review of work reorganisation and teamworking in Europe (Geary 1995a; also see Geary 1994b, 1995b). Geary notes that teamworking is more evident on the Continent than in Ireland or Britain. In Ireland such initiatives appear to be few in number and are largely efficiency-driven rather than quality-driven or people-driven. Geary further notes that Irish developments have largely involved 'tinkering at the margins' of existing work practices and are confined to a handful of foreign-owned companies.

While the progress of teamworking on the Continent also appears modest, some significant developments appear to have taken place in the automotive sector, especially in Germany (Roth 1993; also see Womack, Jones, and Roos 1990). In evaluating the Continental experience in teamworking, Geary identifies five crucial areas:

1. *The regulation of teamwork:* Geary notes that the introduction of teamworking has been achieved more through agreement with employees' representatives than by unilateral imposition. This is attributed to the strength of collective employee

representation (especially works councils and the trade union involvement in industry bargaining) in countries such as Germany and Sweden, which have led the way in the introduction of teamworking.

2. *The objectives of teamworking:* Geary identifies achieving a balance between managerial goals of improved economic efficiency, and workers' goals of improved quality of work life, as a critical issue in facilitating the successful introduction of teamworking. In particular, it appears that trade unions are more willing to engage in teamworking when it is not used solely, or primarily, to achieve managerial aims.

3. *Impact on working lives:* Geary's analysis of the Continental experience indicates that teamworking has favoured skilled workers and that the 'sex divide' has been left relatively untouched (a significant division remains, with limited opportunities for women). However, specialist categories, such as engineers and accountants, have been transferred to line positions. Geary further notes that employers have not relied solely on persuasion to introduce teamworking but that 'more traditional forms' of management control have also been used, such as increased employee surveillance and more intense work schedules, and that in general increased levels of skill and of effort have been a common outcome of teamworking. However, Geary also identifies potential positive changes associated with teamworking, such as improved working conditions and job security, which can lead to productive efficiencies and encourage workers' acceptance of teamworking.

4. *Teamwork and management support:* Geary suggests that the Continental experience indicates that management commitment and support is an absolute prerequisite for the effective introduction of teamworking. He suggests that if teamworking is introduced as an 'island solution' it has little chance of success and identifies the 'indifference and resistance' of the line management as a significant impediment to the effective introduction of teamworking.

5. *Integrating teamworking with other aspects of P/HRM:* Finally, Geary suggests that the evidence from the Continent indicates that teamworking is likely to be more successful where it is integrated with complementary changes in other aspects of personnel or HR policy. In particular, a number of essential policy changes are identified: (*a*) a shift from individual-based pay to team-based pay, (*b*) significant investment in training and development, and (*c*) the maintenance of job security commitments.

IMPLICATIONS FOR THE INTRODUCTION OF TEAMWORKING: THE TRADE UNION DIMENSION

Based on the Continental experience, Geary (1994a) suggests that a critical issue in teamworking is the development of strategies for dealing with employee representatives and trade unions. Employers commonly object to the involvement of unions in work reorganisation and teamworking, on the grounds that it is too time-consuming and serves to slow the process of organisational change. However, Geary points to the offsetting benefits of union involvement, based on the Continental experience: firstly, unions and employee representatives will have expertise that can benefit the process, and, secondly, they can legitimise the 'necessity of proposed change' to their membership. An additional benefit is that such involvement forces the management to integrate personnel considerations more centrally in their decision-making than might otherwise be the case.

On this theme, Geary raises the critical question of how to involve employee representatives and trade unions in the introduction of work reorganisation initiatives such as teamworking. Since in Ireland such changes are normally discussed in the traditional collective bargaining arena, Geary questions whether new institutional arrangements need to be developed. In particular, it is noted that in many of the countries that have experimented with teamworking there is an institutional separation whereby traditional collective bargaining issues are the remit of union-employer bargaining at the industry level, while working arrangements are normally dealt with within the enterprise through works councils (especially in Germany and France). Turning specifically to Ireland, Geary poses a number of questions on this dilemma:

- Can the introduction of teamworking be productively discussed through traditional 'adversarial' collective bargaining arrangements?
- Is there a need for arrangements of the works council type?
- Are Irish managers ready for this type of joint decision-making?
- Is it better if the structures used for informing employees are employee-based and not strictly union-based?

A final and critical concern for companies is how they can effectively facilitate such change. Geary's analysis identifies the effective 'managing of managers' as the key to successful teamworking (Geary 1994a, 1995a, 1995b). He argues that employers must move beyond their traditional concern of 'getting the goods out the door and reducing costs': instead he suggests that there is a need to reconcile the management of managers with the objectives of employee involvement. In particular he argues that the reward and appraisal system for managers should reward managers who facilitate effective teamworking. Finally, it should be noted that increased employee participation and teamworking will not mean an end to 'adversarial' collective bargaining. As Geary points out, pay issues and 'significant changes' in work organisation may still be channelled through 'traditional' collective bargaining.

13

Employment
Law

This final chapter explores the legal framework within which personnel management takes place.[1] Two particular aspects of employment or labour law concern us here:

(1) individual labour law, which concentrates on the relationship between the individual worker and the employer, and

(2) collective labour law, which is concerned with regulating the relationship between employers and collectivities of employees—normally trade unions.

Earlier, in chapter 10, much of the discussion focused on elements of collective labour law, and it is recommended that the reader review that chapter in tandem with this one. The main emphasis in this chapter is on documenting the various legislative provisions that have particular relevance to the practice of personnel management in Ireland. We begin with a brief introduction to the sources of law that have implications for the employment relationship. The formation of a contract of employment is then examined, and various statutes affecting employment are discussed. The chapter concludes with a brief discussion on the reform of collective labour law in the Industrial Relations Act, 1990.

SOURCES OF IRISH LAW
The Irish legal system comprises a number of sources of law, namely the Constitution, statute law, and common law.

- The *Constitution* is essentially divided into two parts: firstly, that which sets down fundamental personal rights that are guaranteed to every Irish citizen and that the state is obliged to protect, and, secondly, that which directs the structures and establishment of various institutions, such as the Oireachtas, Government, and judiciary.
- *Statute law* consists of the various Acts that have been passed over the years, collectively referred to as legislation. After the Constitution, statute law is the most important source of law. It can be broadly classified according to its subject matter: thus we have family law, company law, land law, criminal law, labour law, and so forth. A number of pertinent employment statutes are reviewed later in this chapter.

- *Common law* is an unwritten system that has evolved over the centuries. Often called 'judge-made law', it consists of the decisions made by the judiciary when cases are decided. In practice this means that judges refer to similar cases when making their decisions; this is commonly known as following a precedent, and it provides for some element of consistency in the interpretation of the law. Common law implies a number of duties into the contract of employment. Employers' duties specify that all employers must reimburse employees for legitimate expenses and must provide a duty of care, a safe place of work, a safe system of work, safe machinery, and competent co-workers. As the employment relationship is a contract for personal services, it is implied that employees will perform their work personally, work co-operatively, obey all reasonable instructions, give fidelity to the employer, employ reasonable care and skill, and avoid conflicts of interest.

FORMATION OF A CONTRACT OF EMPLOYMENT

The contract of employment is the legal basis of the employment relationship and is central to the interpretation and application of statutory rights (Gunnigle et al. 1995). As with the basic law of contract, it requires that there be 'offer and acceptance', the offer being made by the employer and the acceptance by the employee when he or she agrees to work for the employer. There must also be 'consideration', or remuneration from the employer for work done; and both parties must intend to create legal relations, that is, both parties must recognise that they have particular rights and obligations that must be observed. The contract of employment may be made either orally or in writing.

Common law attempts to distinguish between a *contract of service* and a *contract for service.* An employee is someone who is employed under a contract of service; this is distinct from an independent contractor, who is employed under a contract for service. The distinction is a vital one, for a variety of reasons, not least of which is that only employees can benefit from much of the modern employment legislation granted to workers (Fennell and Lynch 1992).

Three tests have been developed to differentiate between contracts of and for service:

(1) **The control test:** This is based on the principle that the employer has the right to control how the work is done. In other words, the employer not only tells the employee what to do but how to do it. However, this test is difficult to administer in practice, particularly where many contracts of service (employees) have considerable discretion over the work they do.

(2) **The integration test:** This is based on the view that an employee is a person whose work is integrated into the business, whereas independent contractors merely work *for* the business. This test is also difficult to apply today, since it fails to take account of work practices such as home working that can give the appearance of self-employment and thus might be construed as contracts for service.

(3) **The multiple or economic reality test:** Under this test, the entire arrangement between employer and worker is reviewed in determining whether the worker is an employee or an independent contractor. Thus the court would seek information concerning

— whether wages, sickness and holiday pay are provided and who pays them;

— whether income tax and social welfare are deducted under the PAYE and PRSI schemes by the company;

— whether the worker shares in the profits or losses of the company;

—whether tools and equipment for the job are provided by the company;
—whether there are specific provisions relating to termination of employment; and finally
—whether the company is entitled to exclusive service.

If the person is free to work for other companies, provides his or her own equipment, sets his or her own work pace and can sub-contract the work to others, then it would generally be assumed that he or she is an independent contractor.

Nevertheless, despite the variety of issues that can be examined in dealing with this question, Fennell and Lynch (1992) suggest that a certain amount of confusion exists about what test should be applied. Table 13.1 outlines the key differences that can exist between a contract of service and a contract for service.

Table 13.1: Differences between contract of service and contract for service

Contract of service	Contract for service
Employer-employee relationship	Employer-contractor relationship
Usually a continuous relationship	A relationship based on a one-off piece of work
Duty of care owed to employees	Duty of care arising from occupier's liability
Generally liable for the vicarious acts of employees, e.g. any wrong or injury done by an employee while in the course of his or her work	Generally not liable for the vicarious acts of independent contractors
Protective legislation applies to contract	Protective legislation does not apply (apart from Safety, Health and Welfare at Work Act, 1989)
Wage or salary payment	Fee payment
Subject of contract is to carry on continuous work	Subject of contract is once-off

Source: Gunnigle, Garavan, and Fitzgerald (1992).

EMPLOYMENT LEGISLATION

There is a considerable body of employment legislation that provides a basic floor of rights for individual employees. This legislation is marked by several inconsistencies, particularly with respect to the differing periods of service required to qualify and the different adjudicating mechanisms employed (refer to chapter 10 for full details). Several important Acts have been passed since the nineteen-seventies that have increased the number of rights employees can expect from the employment relationship. A summary of employment legislation and its main provisions is given in table 13.2.

Table 13.2: Summary of employment legislation

Terms and conditions of employment

Conditions of Employment Acts, 1936 and 1944	Hours of work, overtime, shift work, breaks
Holidays (Employees) Act, 1973	Annual leave; public holidays
Protection of Young Persons (Employment) Act, 1977	Conditions for employing young people
Terms of Employment (Information) Act, 1994	Provision of a written statement to employees setting out particulars of their conditions of employment
Payment of Wages Acts, 1979–91	Payment by cheque; deductions from pay
Worker Protection (Regular Part-Time Employees) Act, 1991	Extends benefits of employment legislation to part-time workers
Pensions Act, 1990	Rights in relation to pensions

Employment equality

Anti-Discrimination (Pay) Act, 1974	Equal pay for like work
Employment Equality Act, 1977	Equality in working conditions, recruitment, training, and promotion
Maternity (Protection of Employees) Acts, 1981 and 1994	Maternity pay and job security, right to health and safety, and paternal leave in certain circumstances
Adoptive Leave Act, 1995	Rights of an adopting mother or a sole male adopter
Paternity Leave Act	Just becoming law at the time of writing

Termination of employment

Redundancy Payments Acts, 1967–91	Payment of lump sum on redundancy
Unfair Dismissals Act, 1977	Protection against unfair dismissal
Protection of Employment Act, 1977	Consultation before group redundancies

Health, safety, and welfare

Office Premises Act, 1958	Minimum health and safety standards for offices
Safety, Health and Welfare at Work Act, 1989	Duties on employers, employees, and others
Safety, Heath and Welfare at Work Regulations, 1993	Specific procedures and regulations for employers

It is important to note that certain categories of employees are excluded from the protection of employment legislation; examples include the Garda Síochána and Defence Forces, FÁS trainees, those working for a close relative in the home, certain public sector categories, and anyone engaging in illegal employment. It is important to consult the particular Act for precise details in relation to excluded categories.

Individual rights of employees

The following is a brief summary of the main individual rights of employees. Most of the statutory rights (i.e. those granted under the various Acts) are available only to those who have had a specific period of continuous employment with their company or organisation. Legally this is known as the 'qualifying period', but unfortunately there is little consistency from one right to another, as differing periods of service apply.

Terms and conditions of employment

WRITTEN PARTICULARS OF TERMS OF EMPLOYMENT

A contract of employment comes into force as soon as a job offer is made and accepted, whether orally or in writing, and the appropriate conditions related to the formation of a contract are adhered to. The Terms of Employment (Information) Act, 1994, implements an EU directive that requires employers to provide a written statement setting out particulars of the employee's terms of employment within twenty-eight days or to refer employees to where they can find details of their employment. The Act also repeals sections 9 and 10 of the Minimum Notice and Terms of Employment Act, 1973, as these are overtaken by the provisions of this Act.

Information to be included in the written statement includes:
- the full names of the employer and employee;
- the address of the employer or principal place of business, or the registered address of the employer as registered in the Companies Registration Office;
- the place of work or, where there is no main place of work, a statement that the employee is required or permitted to work at various places;
- the job title or nature of the work;
- the date of the beginning of the employment;
- if the contract is temporary, the expected duration of the employment;
- if the contract is for a fixed term, the date on which the contract expires;
- the rate of remuneration or method of calculating remuneration;
- whether remuneration is paid weekly, monthly, or otherwise;
- terms or conditions relating to hours of work (including overtime);
- terms or conditions relating to paid leave (other than paid sickness leave);
- terms or conditions relating to incapacity for work through sickness or injury;
- terms or conditions relating to pensions and pension schemes;
- periods of notice the employee is entitled to receive and is required to give on the termination of employment; where this cannot be indicated when the written statement is given, the written statement must give the method for determining the period of notice;
- a reference to any collective agreements that affect the terms of employment; where the employer is not a party to the agreement, the written statement must indicate the bodies or organisations that made the agreement.

PAY

The Payment of Wages Act, 1979, provides that no deductions can be made without the explicit consent of the employee and that the employer must give employees an itemised pay statement setting out any deductions from their salary or wages and explaining the nature and amount of the deductions. This procedure has to be complied with unless the payment is by credit transfer, in which case it must be given as soon as possible. This applies to all employees, whatever capacity or sector they may be employed in.

HOLIDAYS

The entitlement of employees to holidays and leave is governed by the Holidays (Employees) Acts, 1973–91. Under these Acts all but a few categories of employees are entitled to a specified number of annual public holidays and a specified period of annual leave.

Section 4 of the Act deals with public holidays, on which all employees are entitled to a paid day's leave *or* an extra day's pay. At present there are nine public holidays:

New Year's Day (1 January)
St Patrick's Day (17 March)
Easter Monday
May Public Holiday (first Monday in May)
June Public Holiday (first Monday in June)
August Public Holiday (first Monday in August)
October Public Holiday (last Monday in October)
Christmas Day (25 December)
St Stephen's Day (26 December)

Section 3 deals with annual leave. It specifies that employees who work at least 120 hours a month are entitled to fifteen days' leave after one year. Two weeks of this leave normally run consecutively, and employees are paid before taking their holidays. Regular part-time employees are entitled to six hours' leave per hundred hours worked.

Under section 6 of the Act the exact timing of the annual leave is determined by the employer, but they must consult the employee to make him or her aware of the matter. Where the employee has eight months' service or more in the year they must get an unbroken period equivalent to two working weeks of annual leave.

NOTICE OF TERMINATION

Both the employer and the employee are normally entitled to a minimum period of notice, although either employer or employee may accept pay in lieu of notice. Under section 4 (1) of the Minimum Notice and Terms of Employment Acts, 1973 and 1994, any employee who has thirteen weeks' continuous service is entitled to a statutory minimum notice. Section 4 (2) of the Act sets out the periods of minimum notice to which employees covered by the Act are entitled, as follows:

Continuous service of employee	Minimum notice
Less than 2 years	1 week
More than 2 years but less than 5	2 weeks
More than 5 years but less than 10	4 weeks
More than 10 years but less than 15	6 weeks
15 years or more	8 weeks

These are *minimum* periods: if a contract of employment gives an entitlement to a longer period, the longer period will apply.

Under section 6 the employer in turn is entitled to a period of notice of not less than one week from an employee who has been in continuous employment for thirteen weeks or more. This period does not increase in line with the length of service; however, the contract of employment may specify a period of notice that is required by the employer.

The Employment Appeals Tribunal has stated that the notice given by the employer must be sufficiently certain and precise, leaving no room for ambiguity or uncertainty. The precise expiry date must be specified. Employees to whom these provisions apply are entitled to the same rights during the minimum notice period as they would enjoy but for the notice.

If the employer fails to give the employee the proper period of notice, the employee may claim breach of contract through the courts (common law remedy) or, if they are covered by the Minimum Notice and Terms of Employment Act, through an action to the Employment Appeals Tribunal. Categories of workers not covered by these provisions include the Garda Síochána and Defence Forces, local authority employees, and civil servants.

However, where the employer terminates the contract, it is also important that they give notice correctly, as this could affect the effective date of dismissal and therefore the eligibility of an employee's claim of unfair dismissal to be heard by the Employment Appeals Tribunal. The effective date of dismissal should be made very clear (in writing) to the employee, and any period of notice given must not be less than the minimum statutory period or the formal contractual period of notice.

The Worker Protection (Regular Part-Time Employees) Act, 1991, extends the benefit of the protective employment legislation to regular part-time employees, i.e. those who are in continuous employment for at least thirteen weeks with the same employer and who normally work at least eight hours per week.

Employment of young people

The Protection of Young Persons (Employment) Act, 1977, lays down a number of restrictions on the employment of young people.

The Act imposes a minimum age of fourteen for employment. A person between the ages of fourteen and sixteen may work a normal week of 37½ hours and a maximum of 40 hours; they are entitled to overtime for the extra 2½ hours. For employees over sixteen the figures are 40 hours and a maximum of 45 hours. There are also overtime and night work restrictions on young people, i.e. those under eighteen years of age.

EMPLOYMENT EQUALITY

Maternity protection and maternity leave

The Maternity Protection Act, 1994, applies to all women who work at least eight hours per week and who are insurable for the purposes of the social welfare code. The main purpose of the Act is to provide protection for all pregnant employees and those who have recently given birth or who are breast-feeding. It does this by giving them certain legal rights, the main ones being

- the right to fourteen weeks' paid maternity leave;
- the right to up to four weeks' additional unpaid maternity leave;
- the right to return to work;
- the right to take time off from work without loss of pay to attend antenatal and post-natal care medical appointments;
- the right to health and safety leave in certain circumstances;
- the right to protection of their job during maternity leave, additional maternity leave, father's leave, and health and safety leave, and time off for antenatal or postnatal care;

- the right not to be dismissed for any pregnancy-related reason, from the beginning of pregnancy until the end of maternity leave;
- the right of an employed father to leave where the death of the mother occurs within fourteen weeks of the birth.

The Act entitles female employees to a period of maternity leave of at least fourteen weeks if notice is given to the employer in writing at least four weeks before the expected date of birth, together with a medical certificate establishing the fact of pregnancy. There is no qualifying service in order to secure the right. The exact dates of the maternity leave can be chosen by the employee, but they must cover the four weeks before and the four weeks after the birth.

During the period of maternity leave there is no break in the continuity of the employee's service. She is entitled to return to her job after the birth, provided she notifies the employer in writing of her intention at least four working weeks before the expected date of return. Strict compliance with these requirements is essential.

FATHER'S ENTITLEMENT TO LEAVE

In the event of the death of the mother within fourteen weeks of the birth of a living child, the father of the child has certain leave entitlements, referred to as 'leave to which the father is entitled' and 'further leave to which the father is entitled'. Where leave to which the father is entitled has been taken, he may choose to take a further period of four weeks' leave. Notice to take the further leave may be given at the same time as the original notification or, if it is later, not later than four weeks before he is due to resume work having taken his original leave entitlement.

Anti-discrimination legislation

The Anti-Discrimination (Pay) Act, 1974, gives women an entitlement to equal pay for 'like work'. This is interpreted as meaning the same work under the same or similar conditions, or similar work where differences are small and occur infrequently, or work of equal value that demands similar effort. Many women in recent years have successfully claimed that the work they do is the same as or broadly similar to that done by a man and that any differences that do exist are not of practical importance in relation to their terms and conditions of employment.

Under section 17 of the Employment Equality Act, 1977, there are a number of grounds on which discrimination is permitted. These include:
- grounds of physiology, e.g. a model;
- grounds of authenticity for the purpose of a form of entertainment, e.g. an actor;
- where people of both sexes are required for personal services, e.g. toilet attendants;
- where the work takes place in countries where only members of one sex would be able to carry out the duties, e.g. in those cultures that would not accept a woman in a position of authority.

Employees wishing to bring a claim under the Anti-Discrimination (Pay) Act must submit it to an equality officer, who will investigate the dispute and issue a recommendation. Disputes under the Act are referred to the Labour Court, which can refer the application to an industrial relations officer or an equality officer. Equality officers work in the Labour Court and are appointed by the Minister for Labour.

Employment Equality Act, 1977

This Act prohibits discrimination on the grounds of sex or marital status. Discrimination is prohibited in the following areas:

- recruitment;
- conditions of employment other than pay;
- provision of training or work experience;
- promotion.

Discrimination can be direct (where women 'need not apply') or indirect (where a non-essential criterion is used in filling the vacancy and a substantially higher proportion of people of one sex or of one marital status would be able to satisfy that criterion, for example a requirement that applicants for the job of postman or postwoman be at least 6 feet tall). While not specifically mentioned in the Act, sexual harassment is also covered.

Cases of discrimination are dealt with by equality officers. The Employment Equality Agency was set up under the Act to promote equality of opportunity and to monitor the operation of equal pay legislation.

'Positive discrimination' is not unlawful, provided the employer is attempting to redress an existing imbalance in a particular grade or type of work.

Adoptive leave

Under the Adoptive Leave Act, 1995, an adopting mother or a sole male adopter who is in employment is entitled to

- a minimum of ten consecutive weeks' leave from work, beginning on the day of placement of the child, and
- up to four weeks' additional leave.

The ten-week period of adoptive leave will qualify for a social welfare benefit in the majority of cases.

TERMINATION OF EMPLOYMENT

Section 14 (1) of the Unfair Dismissals Act, 1977, provides that, within twenty-eight days of offering employment, an employer must give the employee a notice in writing setting out the procedure the employer will observe before and for the purpose of dismissing the employee. If an employee is dismissed, the employer must give them a written statement of the reasons why, within two weeks of the date of dismissal.

It is wise to send all such statements by recorded delivery and, where related previous correspondence exists—such as warning letters—to include copies of these as well. Although all such earlier incidents or warnings should have been properly recorded and the employee given copies at the time they occurred, it is advisable to include copies and refer to them again in the final written reasons for dismissal. An employee may take a case before the Employment Appeals Tribunal if written reasons are refused or if the reasons are perceived to be inadequate.

Unfair dismissal

Under the Unfair Dismissals Act, 1977, once an employee has been continuously employed for one year he or she has a right of action if he or she is unfairly dismissed. If an employee has been dismissed and he or she perceives it as being unfair, he or she can bring a case to the Employment Appeals Tribunal or a rights commissioner within six months of the date of dismissal. This is the date when his or her proper notice would have terminated even if he or she were not given proper notice in the first instance. (The Employment Appeals Tribunal and rights commissioners are discussed in chapter 10.)

The following categories of employees are *not* entitled to submit a claim for unfair dismissal:

- employees who have less than one year's continuous service with the same employer (if it is shown that a dismissal resulted wholly or mainly from the employee's membership or proposed membership of a trade union or from their activities on behalf of a trade union the requirement of one year's continuous service does not apply; a woman who claims she was dismissed because of pregnancy may bring her unfair dismissal claim even though she does not have a year's continuous service with her employer);
- those over the normal retiring age;
- close relatives of the employer who are members of his or her household and work in a private dwelling-house;
- members of the Garda Síochána and Defence Forces;
- those employed by or under the state;
- those serving an apprenticeship with FÁS;
- officers of a local authority, health board, or vocational education committee.

Dismissal is automatically unfair where it is shown that it resulted wholly or mainly from any of the following causes:

- the employee's trade union membership or activities;
- religious or political opinion;
- involvement in legal proceedings against the employer;
- the race or colour of the employee;
- the sexual orientation of the employee;
- the pregnancy of the employee;
- unfair selection for redundancy.

The onus of proving that a dismissal was in fact fair rests on the employer, except in the case of constructive dismissal, that is, where an employee leaves the company because conditions within the company make it impossible for him or her to stay, for example where his or her authority was removed, or where he or she could no longer contribute to organisational decision-making.

The decision to dismiss must be taken carefully, as the penalties that may be incurred if the dismissal is ruled as unfair by the Employment Appeals Tribunal are severe. It is important, therefore, to know the conditions under which an employee may be fairly dismissed.

Dismissal for misconduct

The issue of reasonableness has great significance in the context of dismissal for misconduct. The Employment Appeals Tribunal will consider general industrial standards. There is no absolute definition of reasonableness, since it depends on individual circumstances within the company. The EAT has emphasised that misconduct must be measured in the context of the employee's actions and not just the consequences or potential consequences of that behaviour to the employer. It has further decided that in misconduct cases the employer must, before taking the decision to dismiss, consider whether there were mitigating circumstances, such as a record of good service, personal difficulties experienced by the employee, the fact that this was the first instance, etc.

In the case of minor misconduct—such as persistent lateness—an employer must show that they had followed all the stages in the disciplinary procedure and, having exhausted these, had given written warning that further infringements would lead to dismissal. To prove that the employer had acted properly they would need to have kept a written record of all the procedures they had gone through in the case.

If the misconduct was more serious—such as fighting, breaking a work rule, or sleeping on duty—going through every stage of the procedure might be unnecessary. However, the employer would need to observe the rules of natural justice:

- the employee has a right to be told the facts of the case against him or her;
- the employee has the right to a hearing (to tell his or her side of the story);
- the employee has the right to representation of his or her choice;
- the employee has the right to appeal to a higher level of his or her choice within the company.

Failure to comply with the rules of natural justice may render a dismissal unfair.

An employer should also

- enquire into the matter to find out what really happened; if fact-finding is going to take some time it may be necessary to suspend the employee on full pay;
- interview the employee to get his or her side of the story, advising him or her of his or her right to be represented if appropriate;
- decide on the basis of the information what action is reasonable in the circumstances (Did the employee know the rule that was broken? Was he or she aware of its significance? Would a clearly stated warning of dismissal for repetition be more reasonable than dismissal for a first offence? How have similar cases been treated in the past?—i.e. is the employer being consistent with previous 'custom and practice'?);
- make clear to the employee what action is to be taken and how he or she can appeal against the decision if the procedure allows this.

Capability, competence, or qualifications

Section 6 (4) (*a*) of the Unfair Dismissals Act provides that a fair basis for dismissal relates to the capability, competence or qualifications of the employee for performing work of the kind he or she were employed by the employer to do. While it may be fair to dismiss someone for incapability, if a complaint were made an employer would need to convince a tribunal that they had a valid reason for dismissing the person and that they had acted reasonably in treating that reason as a sufficient cause for dismissing the person.

Capability as determined by the Employment Appeals Tribunal usually relates to dismissals arising from illness, injury, or similar inadequacy. The question whether the employee was to blame for the illness or incapacity is irrelevant. In the case of capability the tribunal has introduced a number of exceptions:

1. Where an employee who is incapacitated by injury or illness could be given lighter work that he or she would have been able to perform, the dismissal may be unfair.
2. Where an employee is absent it is up to the employer to try to find out why: it is not reasonable to assume without further investigation that the absence is due to illness that might justify dismissal.

INCAPABILITY BECAUSE OF ILL-HEALTH

One example to demonstrate incapability through ill health is an actual case of an employee who had had substantial periods of absence from work because of illness over the four years that he had been employed, averaging some fifty days a year. In the summer of his fourth year of employment he was absent for 10½ weeks with flu. When he returned to work he was seen by the production director in the presence of his shop steward and was dismissed with pay in lieu of notice. The reason given for his dismissal was his cumulative periods of absence, which could no longer be tolerated.

He appealed to the Employment Appeals Tribunal on the grounds that it was not his fault that he had been ill and that his dismissal was therefore unfair. The tribunal held that the dismissal was indeed unfair, primarily because the employer had taken no steps to investigate his many absences and had not undertaken any previous formal review of his medical history.

In any such case an employer needs to ask how reasonable it is to dismiss an employee who has been off work for an extended period. Reasonable action would again consist of being seen to follow fair procedures and securing the fullest possible information. Fair procedure might include

- visiting the employee (perhaps on more than one occasion) to find out how likely it is that they will be returning to work and to make clear to them how long the company can wait;
- if the company cannot wait any longer, obtaining an independent medical report, which would be a useful element in making a decision;
- considering whether alternative work could be made available;
- informing the employee of the decision.

INCAPABILITY BECAUSE OF INCOMPETENCE

Competence issues arise where an employee is alleged to have demonstrated a poor work performance, for example failure to meet reasonable targets set by the employer. To act fairly in dismissing someone for this reason an employer must detail evidence of the alleged incompetence and must have discussed this with the employee. An employer would also need to establish that they did not contribute to the incompetence by failing to make requirements clear, or by not providing the necessary facilities to allow the job to be done competently.

A warning might be appropriate. If so, it should clearly state what is required of the employee and within what time limits. Particularly with a long-serving employee, it might be more reasonable to consider whether a less arduous job could be found.

As with misconduct, warnings are not necessary if an employer believes they serve no purpose, but the employer might have to convince a tribunal of this. A case will obviously be much easier to make if an employee has been given warnings and a chance to improve, with as much reasonable help from the employer as possible.

INCAPABILITY BECAUSE OF QUALIFICATIONS

This concept refers primarily to the absence of formal qualifications that are essential to the job, which is another fair basis for dismissal under certain circumstances. This category might include the case of an accountant losing their professional qualification, or the case of an employee who misled an employer into thinking they had certain qualifications or experience on joining but in fact had not. It might also arise where the employee did not have the qualifications on joining but agreed to take steps to obtain them but who seems unable to obtain them despite repeated attempts and every assistance from the company.

Reasonable dismissal in this category would depend on how critical the qualification was to the job and the duties of the employee in question and how long the situation was likely to continue. As in other cases, an employer would need to consider whether an alternative job could be offered for which the person was qualified.

BREAKING ANOTHER STATUTE

It is fair for an employer to dismiss an employee who could not continue to work without breaking another law. The sales representative who loses their driving licence is a clear example. As usual, however, the employer would need to consider alternatives to dismissal. Could the employer offer alternative work? Could other arrangements be made for the period?

INDUSTRIAL ACTION

Section 5 (1) of the Unfair Dismissals Act provides that the dismissal of an employee by way of lock-out is not unfair if the employee is offered reinstatement or re-engagement from the date of resumption of work. Section 5 (2) provides that dismissal for taking part in a strike or other industrial action is unfair if any other employee or employees who took part in the strike were reinstated or re-engaged. Where an employer dismissed all the employees who took part, the onus is still on them to prove that they had fair grounds under one of the previous headings or on other substantial grounds. If they cannot do so the dismissal will be unfair.

OTHER SUBSTANTIAL GROUNDS

An employer may succeed even if a dismissal does not fall under any of the previous headings where they can claim that it qualifies on 'other substantial grounds'. This heading has not been used very often, and furthermore there is little consistency in the decisions of the Employment Appeals Tribunal.

An example might be where an employee's behaviour while off the job might be having an effect on the employer's business, as was argued in the case of *Flynn v. Sisters of the Holy Faith* UD 235/1983, HC Costello J. [1985] ILRM 336, or where there is a conflict of interest between the employee and employer, for example if a sales representative owns a 50 per cent share in the employer's closest competitor.

Redundancy

Section 6 (4) (*c*) of the Redundancy Payments Act, 1991, provides that a dismissal resulting from the redundancy of an employee is not unfair. Redundancy is basically defined as dismissal caused by the fact that the employer has ceased their business, or that they no longer require the work carried out by the particular employee, or they are reducing the scope of their work-force. The onus is on the employer to prove the existence of redundancy. They cannot simply claim that a situation of redundancy exists: they must produce substantial evidence.

Even where there is genuine redundancy, not all dismissals will necessarily be fair. A number of qualifications have been introduced:
1. Where an employee was selected in contravention of a procedure that has been

agreed between the employer and the employee or trade union or that was established by custom and practice, and no special reasons are produced for departing from this procedure, then the dismissal will be unfair.

2. If the employer had an ulterior motive in selecting the particular employee, then the dismissal will be unfair, even if there was genuine redundancy.

An employer should not use arbitrary criteria in selecting employees for redundancy. The Employment Appeals Tribunal examines all aspects of an employee's conduct, including the observance of statutory obligations such as the Protection of Employment Act, 1977 (this allows for consultation and information relating to mass redundancies). Not only must an employer use proper criteria but these criteria must be applied in a fair manner.

REDUNDANCY PAYMENTS

Under the Redundancy Payments Acts, 1967–91, employees who have had at least two years' continuous service and who work at least eight hours a week and have not reached retirement age are entitled to a redundancy payment in the event of being made redundant. This payment is calculated as follows:

- a sum equivalent to the employee's normal weekly working remuneration, plus
- half of their normal weekly remuneration for each year of their continuous employment between their sixteenth birthday and their forty-first birthday (or up to the termination of the contract of employment), plus
- their full weekly remuneration for each year of continuous employment from their forty-first birthday until the dismissal, i.e. up to the termination of the contract.

Employees are not entitled to redundancy payment if they unreasonably refuse an offer of suitable alternative employment with their own employer or with another company in the same group where continuity of employment can be maintained, provided the alternative employment does not involve a significant reduction in status or conditions.

LEGAL REGULATION FOR REDUNDANCY

Redundancy legislation is very complex, containing many detailed provisions and rules. As a general classification, the Acts fall into two categories:

- legislation dealing with collective redundancies; this lays down procedural regulations to be observed by employers and bestows a number of rights on trade unions;
- legislation on what constitutes redundancy, the right to redundancy payments, and the calculation of continuous service.

The Protection of Employment Act, 1977, lays down procedural obligations in the case of collective redundancies. There are a number of specific provisions that a manager will need to be aware of:

1. The Act applies to a situation where in a period of thirty days a number of employees are dismissed for redundancy. The minimum number varies, depending on the total size of the work-force.

2. The main obligation on employers is consultation and notification. If a company has a collective redundancy, the Minister for Enterprise and Employment must be notified at least thirty days before the final dismissal. The employer must also send a copy of this notice to the employees' representatives.

3. At least thirty days before the dismissal, the employer must enter into consultation

with the employees' representatives with a view to reaching agreement on such issues as the numbers to be made redundant, alternative courses of action, and the way the redundancies are to be implemented. The Act does not specify what happens in the event of agreement not being reached.

4. Employers are also obliged to provide employees with certain information relating to the redundancy. Examples include the reasons for the redundancy, the number of employees affected, and the period during which it is to take place.

5. Employers are also obliged to keep adequate records of the situation.

In the event of redundancy taking place, the individual employee's situation is governed by the Redundancy Payments Acts, 1967–91. Under section 7 of the 1967 Act, as amended, 'an employee who is dismissed shall be taken to be dismissed by reason of redundancy if the dismissal is attributable wholly or mainly to one of the following':

- where the employer has ceased or intends to cease to carry on the business for the purpose of which the employee was employed;
- where the requirements of the business do not require the particular type of work that the employee has to offer;
- where the employer decides to carry on the business with fewer employees;
- where the employer decides that the work the employee does is to be done in a different manner;
- where the employer decides that the work done by the particular employee should from now on be done by a person who is capable of doing other work that the employee is not sufficiently qualified to do.

Once the employee fits one of the redundancy categories, it is then necessary to examine whether they meet the additional requirements set out in the Acts. The main requirements are that the employee (*a*) must have a minimum of 104 weeks' continuous employment and (*b*) must be aged between sixteen and sixty-five. Other important provisions include the following:

1. The entitlement to a redundancy payment cannot be waived, and any term in a contract of employment that purports to do so is invalid.

2. The employer must give notice in writing to the employee of the proposed dismissal and must send a copy to the Minister for Enterprise and Employment thirty days in advance. The employer must also furnish the employee with a redundancy certificate.

3. The employer is entitled to offer the redundant employee suitable alternative employment if it exists. The job offered must be on the same or similar terms. If the employee unreasonably refuses this alternative offer they may lose their entitlement to a redundancy payment.

4. The Acts allow the employee time off to try out the alternative job to test its suitability. The employee has four weeks to test its suitability.

5. Employees eligible for redundancy pay are entitled to reasonable time off work, with pay, to look for another job. In such circumstances the employer may seek evidence that the employee is really using the time off in the intended manner. If the employer refuses to allow time off, the employee may bring the matter to the Employment Appeals Tribunal.

6. An employee who is under notice does not have to work this notice if it is agreed that they should receive any due payment in lieu.

HEALTH AND SAFETY AT WORK

Both common law and statute law lay down a number of provisions concerning health and safety in the work-place. A useful classification of the relevant statutes is as follows:

- those that deal exclusively with the safety and health of workers;
- those concerned with the regulation of hours of work;
- those not designed exclusively as workers' protection measures but nevertheless providing varying degrees of protection;
- those on the borderline between issues of general environmental pollution and occupational health and safety.

Common law

Outside all the legislation that exists on health and safety at work, an employer may incur liability at common law. The position here is that an employer is legally responsible for any injuries or diseases that occur on the job. Case law has clearly laid down that an employer must exercise reasonable care towards employees and must guard them against any likely injury or disease. If an employer fails to live up to this obligation, liability for negligence will occur if an employee is injured. However, it is important to remember that liability will only arise when an employer's negligence actually caused an employee's injury or disease. Furthermore, the incident that occurs must be reasonably foreseeable. The reason for this is simple: the common law is not concerned with anticipating damages or setting standards of good behaviour in order to prevent accidents. The common law only comes into play after the event, and its main function is to compensate employees for any injuries they receive while at work.

As well as laying down a general principle of employers' liability for injuries, the courts have gone further and have specified different elements of the employer's duty. This is directly relevant and provides a useful framework within which to evaluate a company's safety effort. The four duties are worth considering in detail.

1. SAFE PLANT AND EQUIPMENT

This duty covers machinery, raw materials, tools, etc. However, employers will not incur liability if they obtain supplies from a reputable company and had no reason to suspect that they were faulty.

Employers must also keep up to date on the potential dangers of new processes and machinery. They will have observed their duty of care if they keep up to date with information that is already known to exist: no liability will arise against a hazard that scientific knowledge is not yet aware of.

2. COMPETENT FELLOW-WORKERS

Employers are expected to take reasonable steps to ensure that employees are able to do their jobs. This involves clarifying the personal qualities and skills required to do the particular job, ensuring that there is a systematic recruitment and selection procedure, and providing the necessary training to do the job, including providing special remedial training where necessary.

For an employee to succeed in an action under this heading he or she would have to show two things:
(1) that the other worker was unsuitable for the job;
(2) that the employer had not been sufficiently careful in appointing or retraining the other worker.

If an employee undertakes quite unpredictable behaviour that causes injury to a fellow-employee, the employer will not be held responsible.

3. PROVISION OF SAFETY EQUIPMENT AND EFFECTIVE SUPERVISION

Employers are under an obligation to provide employees with the necessary protective equipment and clothing required to do the job without exposing them to risk or injury. Proper instructions should also be issued. The courts have also clearly stated that it is not enough for the employer to inform the employee that the equipment is available: they must take reasonable measures to see that the employee uses it.

4. SAFE PREMISES AND SYSTEM OF WORK

Employers must take great care in the way work is laid out and organised. They must not expose employees to risks that could easily be avoided by more careful organisation. They are also expected to maintain their premises in a reasonable state.

The courts have held that this duty extends to a customer's premises. If an employee is injured while working on a customer's premises, they may have a claim against the employer. The employer's responsibility will be less, however, than if it was on their own premises. Employers will be liable to their employees for injuries that arise out of defects in the customer's premises that would have been apparent and that the employer should have taken reasonable precautions against.

Employers will not be liable as a general rule for employees' safety on their way to and from work. However, if the employer provides a company bus for transporting staff, they must have a competent driver and must ensure that the bus is properly maintained. Furthermore, if an employer allows employees onto the premises outside working hours, reasonable steps must be taken to ensure that the premises are safe. The law further holds that employers are vicariously liable for any damage or injury caused by their employees while in the course of their employment.

The Safety, Health and Welfare at Work Act, 1989

This Act, which applies to all places of work, establishes regulations and codes of practice for dealing with specialist areas of safety, health and welfare at work. The Act established the National Authority for Occupational Safety and Health, which has a chairperson and ten ordinary members (three nominated by employees' organisations, three nominated by employers' organisations, and four representatives of Government departments, state agencies, and other relevant bodies). The authority has a number of particular duties:

• enforcement of the Act;
• the provision of advisory services;
• the promotion of a 'safety culture';
• research into work practices.

In addition, the authority, with the assistance of specialist advisory committees, develops regulations and codes of practice for different work activities as the need arises.

DUTIES IMPOSED BY THE LEGISLATION—EMPLOYERS

1. To ensure the health, safety and welfare at work of all employees (section 6). The Act gives examples of some areas that must be considered:

(*a*) the design, provision and maintenance of the place of work;

(*b*) safe means of access to and exit from the place of work;

(*c*) the provision and maintenance of machinery without risk;

(*d*) safe systems of work;

(*e*) the provision of information, instruction, training, and supervision;

(*f*) where hazards exist that cannot be controlled or eliminated, the provision and maintenance of suitable protective equipment;

(*g*) adequate and current emergency plans;

(*h*) ensuring safety with regard to articles or substances in use;

(*i*) the provision and maintenance of welfare facilities;

(*j*) the use of specialist services to provide for the health, safety and welfare of the work-force.

2. To ensure that those not in their employment who may be affected are not exposed to risks to their safety or health (section 7).

3. To prepare a **safety statement** (section 12). The safety statement must
   —specify the manner in which health, safety and welfare will be secured;
   —be based on an identification of hazards and an assessment of risks;
   —include arrangements made and resources provided;
   —specify the co-operation required from employees;
   —specify the names of the people responsible.
   The safety statement must be brought to the attention of all those who are affected by it.

4. To consult employees. Under the Act, employers must consult their employees so that they can make and maintain effective measures; they can co-operate in promoting and developing measures to ensure health and safety and so that the effectiveness of their arrangements can be ascertained.

5. To take account of employees' views (section 13). Not alone must there be consultation but employers must take account of representations made by the work-force.

DUTIES IMPOSED BY THE LEGISLATION—EMPLOYEES

Section 9 details the general duties of employees while at work.

1. They must take reasonable care for their own safety and that of any other person who may be affected.

2. They must co-operate to such an extent that all relevant statutory provisions are complied with.

3. They must use the equipment provided in a safe manner.

4. They must report any problems they become aware of that might have an effect on safety, health, or welfare.

In addition to imposing duties on various categories of participants, the Act confers quite specific *rights* on employees. They have the right to make representations to and to consult their employers on matters of safety, health and welfare in their place of work. The *safety representative*—

(1) must make representations to the employer;

(2) must investigate accidents and dangerous occurrences;

(3) must talk or write to inspectors;

(4) must receive advice and information from inspectors;

(5) must carry out inspections;

(6) must investigate potential hazards;

(7) must accompany an inspector on normal tours of inspection;

(8) must have paid time off to acquire required skills;

(9) must have paid time off to discharge their functions;

(10) must not be placed at any personal disadvantage.

COLLECTIVE LEGISLATION

Collective labour law establishes the legal framework for employee or industrial relations and is distinguished from individual labour law in that it is concerned with regulating the relationship between employers and collectivities of employees—normally trade unions (Gunnigle et al. 1995). (Readers should refer to chapter 10 on the role of trade unions and collective issues that have application for personnel management.)

The Industrial Relations Act, 1990, became law in July 1990 and is now the definitive legislation governing relations between employers and employees and their representatives. The Act represents the most comprehensive revision of the law governing trade unions, trade disputes and employee relations generally in the eighty-four years since the adoption of the Trade Disputes Act, 1906 (Gunnigle et al. 1995).

The purpose of the 1990 Act, as outlined by the then Minister for Labour, Bertie Ahern (1991), is 'to put in place an improved framework for the conduct of industrial relations [with the] overall aim of maintaining a stable industrial relations climate.'

The provisions of the Act can be broadly divided between trade union law and industrial relations legislation.

Trade union law

TRADE DISPUTES

The approach adopted in the area of trade disputes law was to repeal the Trade Disputes Acts, 1906 and 1982, and to reintroduce the main provisions of these Acts with amendments. The main features of the provision relating to trade disputes are as follows:

1. *Individual disputes:* The Act withdraws immunity from one-person disputes where agreed procedures have not been followed.
2. *Secondary action:* This is now restricted unless the union can show that the secondary employer directly sought to frustrate the aims of the dispute.
3. *Picketing:* Workers may now picket only their own employer at the employer's place of work.
4. *Immunities:* The Act places limitations on the blanket immunity that existed under section 4 of the Trade Disputes Act, 1906, in respect of tortious acts (acts for which a civil action for damages could be brought). This immunity now exists only for acts 'committed in contemplation or in furtherance of a trade dispute.'
5. *Worker v. worker disputes:* These no longer fall within the definition of a trade dispute.
6. *Injunctions* (an instruction or order issued by a court to a party to an action to refrain from some act): In trade disputes where a secret ballot has been held and one week's notice given, the granting of injunctions to employers, especially *ex parte* injunctions, is restricted.

SECRET BALLOTS

From 18 July 1992, union rules must contain provisions for the holding of a secret ballot before any form of industrial action can be taken. No injunction will be granted to an employer in the event of a secret ballot having been held.

TRADE UNION RATIONALISATION

The Act makes a number of amendments to existing trade union law designed to encourage mergers and to discourage the formation of new or breakaway unions. The Act essentially increases the minimum membership required for trade unions to secure a negotiating licence (to 1,000) and the sum of money required to be held on deposit with the High Court (varying according to the size of the union but with a minimum of £20,000). The Act also amends the Trade Union Act, 1975, by offering grants towards the expenses incurred in a two-year period before a merger attempt, even if the attempt fails.

Industrial relations law

The 1990 Act provides for the establishment of the Labour Relations Commission and divides functions between it and the Labour Court. Previously the Labour Court had two primary functions—a conciliation and an investigative function—along with a number of secondary functions, such as those of joint industrial councils, joint labour committees, rights commissioners, etc. Under the 1990 Act all functions of the Labour Court, with the exception of its investigative function, have been taken over by the Labour Relations Commission (see chapter 10; see also Gunnigle et al. 1995).

At this stage the impact of the Act on employee relations is unclear. Wallace (1991), for example, argues that a continuation of the strict judicial interpretation of the Act would mean that employers may have the opportunity to use the law in a wide range of circumstances. He also suggests a more fundamental uncertainty about the extent to which employers will use the law, even if the opportunities arise, considering the traditional voluntarist nature of our system.

Notes

Chapter 2 (p. 41)

1. This section on human resource management draws primarily on material in P. Gunnigle, G. McMahon and G. Fitzgerald, *Industrial Relations in Ireland: Theory and Practice*, Dublin: Gill & Macmillan 1995.

Chapter 3 (p. 61)

1. The Price Waterhouse Cranfield Project on International Strategic Human Resource Management was established in 1989 to analyse the nature of HRM practices at company level in Europe. The second survey, conducted in 1992, involved an analysis of HRM practices in twelve European countries. The project is co-ordinated by Prof. Chris Brewster and Ariane Hegewisch at Cranfield School of Management, Bedford. Ireland participated in the survey for the first time in 1992. For a review of the overall data emanating from the project see Brewster and Hegewisch (1994). Gunnigle, Flood, Morley and Turner (1994) provide a treatise on HRM in Ireland.

Chapter 10 (p. 215)

1. For a critical review of the impact of centralised agreements in Ireland since 1987 see, for example, Teague (1995), O'Donnell and O'Reardon (1995).

Chapter 12 (p. 261)

1. This section provides an overview of the legal context of discipline administration and is not a legal interpretation thereof. Readers requiring more comprehensive information on the legal context of discipline administration might refer to Fennel and Lynch (1993) or von Prondzynski (1989).

Chapter 13 (p. 270)

1. This chapter provides an overview of Irish employment law but is not a legal interpretation thereof. For detailed information readers should refer to the particular Act or write to the Department of Enterprise and Employment. Those requiring a more detailed treatment on Irish employment law should refer to, for example, Fennell and Lynch (1992) or Meenan (1994).

Bibliography

Adams, J. (1965), 'Inequity in social exchange' in L. Berkowitz (ed.), *Advances in Experimental Social Psychology, vol. 2,* London: Academic Press.

Ahern, B. (1991), 'The Industrial Relations Act, 1990' (speech by the Minister for Labour at a seminar organised by Irish Society for Labour Law, 13 July 1991).

Aldag, R., and Brief, A. (1979), *Task Design and Employee Motivation,* New York: Scott, Foreman.

Alderfer, C. (1972), *Existence, Relatedness and Growth,* New York: Free Press.

Alexander, L. (1985), 'Successfully implementing strategic decisions', *Long-Range Planning,* vol. 18, no. 3, 91–7.

Anastasi, A. (1982), *Psychological Testing,* London: Macmillan.

Anderson, N. (1992), 'Eight decades of employment interview research: a retrospective meta-review and prospective commentary', *European Work and Organisational Psychologist,* 2, 1–32.

Anderson, N., and Shackleton, V. (1986), 'Recruitment and selection: a review of developments in the 1980s', *Personnel Review,* vol. 15, no. 4.

Anderson, N., and Shackleton, V. (1993), *Successful Selection Interviewing,* Oxford: Blackwell.

Appelbaum, S., and Shapiro, B. (1991), 'Pay for performance: implementation of individual and group plans', *Journal of Management Development,* vol. 10, no. 7.

Arment, L. (1990), 'Learning and training: a matter of style', *Industrial and Commercial Training,* vol. 22, no. 3, 16–21.

Armstrong, M. (1987), 'Human resource management: a case of the emperor's new clothes', *Personnel Management,* vol. 19, no. 8, 30–5.

Armstrong, M. (1995), *A Handbook of Personnel Management Practice* (5th ed.), London: Kogan Page.

Armstrong, M., and Baron, A. (1995), *The Job Evaluation Handbook,* London: Institute of Personnel and Development.

Armstrong, M., and Murlis, H. (1988), *Reward Management: a Handbook of Salary Administration,* London: Kogan Page.

Armstrong, M., and Murlis, H. (1991), *Reward Management: a Handbook of Remuneration Strategy and Practice,* London: Kogan Page.

Armstrong, P. (1988), 'The personnel profession in the age of management accountancy', *Personnel Review,* vol. 17, no. 1, 25–31.

Armstrong, P. (1994), 'Accountancy and HRM' in J. Storey (ed.), *Human Resource Management: a Critical Text,* London: Routledge.

Arnold, J., Cooper, C., and Robertson, I. (1995), *Work Psychology: Understanding Human Behaviour in the Workplace* (2nd ed.), London: Pitman.

Ashton, D. (1986), 'Current issues in line/staff relationships', *Management Education and Development,* 10, 2, 105–18.

Atkinson, A. (1984), *Flexible Manning: the Way Ahead,* London: Institute of Manpower Studies.

Atkinson, J. (1984), 'Human resource strategies for flexible organisations', *Personnel Management,* Aug. 1984, 28–31.

Atkinson, J., and Meager, N. (1986), 'Is flexibility just a flash in the pan?', *Personnel Management,* Sep. 1986, 26–9.

Attley, William (1994), 'The new organisation: the trade union perspective', paper presented to annual conference of Irish Institute of Training and Development, Waterford.

Attwood, M. (1989), *Personnel Management,* London: Macmillan.

Avery, R., Miller, H., Gould, R., and Burch, P. (1987), 'Interview validity for selecting sales clerks', *Personnel Psychology,* 40, 1–12.

Bacon, N., and Storey, J. (1993), 'Individualization of the employment relationship and the implications for trade unions', *Employee Relations,* vol. 15, no. 1, 5–17.

Bain, G. (1970), *The Growth of White Collar Unionism,* Oxford: Clarendon.

Balkin, D., and Gomez-Mejia, L. (1987), *New Perspectives on Compensation,* Englewood Cliffs: Prentice-Hall.

Bandura, A. (1986), *Social Foundations of Thought and Action,* Englewood Cliffs: Prentice-Hall.

Barrow, M., and Loughlin, H. (1992), 'Towards a learning organisation, 1: The rationale', *Industrial and Commercial Training,* 24, 1, 3–7.

Bean, R. (1976), 'Industrial reactions' in E. Cohen and G. Studdard (eds.), *The Bargaining Context,* London: Arrow.

Beardwell, I., and Holden, L. (1994), *Human Resource Management: a Contemporary Perspective,* London: Pitman.

Beaumont, P. (1980), 'The success of white collar recognition claims', *Employee Relations,* vol. 2, no. 4.

Beaumont, P. (1985), 'New plant work practices', *Personnel Review,* vol. 14, no. 5, 15–19.

Beaumont, P. (1991), 'Trade unions and HRM', *Industrial Relations Journal,* vol. 22, no. 4, 300–8.

Beaumont, P. (1993), *Human Resource Management: Key Concepts and Skills,* London: Sage.

Beaumont, P. (1995a), *The Future of Employment Relations,* London: Sage.

Beaumont, P. (1995b), 'The European Union and developments in industrial relations' in P. Gunnigle and W. Roche (eds.), *New Challenges to Irish Industrial Relations,* Dublin: Oak Tree, in association with Labour Relations Commission.

Beaumont, P., and Townley, B. (1985), 'Greenfield sites, new plants and work practices' in V. Hammond (ed.), *Current Research in Management,* London: Frances Pinter.

Beer, M., Spector, B., Lawrence, P., Mills, D., and Walton, R. (1985), *Human Resource Management: a General Manager's Perspective,* New York: Free Press.

Beer, M., Spector, B., Lawrence, P., Quinn-Mills, D., and Walton, R. (1984), *Managing Human Assets: the Groundbreaking Harvard Business School Program,* New York: Free Press/Macmillan.

Beeridge, J. (1992), 'Human resource management in Britain', *Employee Relations,* vol. 14, no. 5, 62–92.

Bell, D. (1974), *Planning Corporate Human Resource,* London: Longman.

Benge, E. (1944), *Job Evaluation and Merit Rating,* Washington: US National Foreman's Institute.

Bennet, R. (1991), *Management,* London: Pitman.

Berg, A. (1989), 'Part-time employment: a response to economic crisis', in S. Rosenberg (ed.), *The State of the Labor Market,* New York: Plenum.

Bevan, S., and Thompson, M. (1992), 'How are companies interpreting performance management?', *Personnel Management,* Nov. 1992.

Biddle, D., and Evenden, R. (1989), *Human Aspects of Management,* London: Institute of Personnel Management.

Birchall, A. (1975), *Job Design: Planning and Implementation Guide for Managers,* London: Gower.

Blackwell, J. (1990), 'The changing role of part-time work in Ireland and its implications', *Labour Market Review,* no. 1, June 1990.

Blennerhassett, E. (1983), *Work Motivation and Personnel Practices: a Study of Civil Service Executive Staff,* Dublin: Institute of Public Administration.

Blennerhassett, E., and Gorman, P. (1986), *Absenteeism in the Public Service: Information Systems and Control Strategies,* Dublin: Institute of Public Administration.

Block, P. (1990), *The Empowered Manager,* San Francisco: Jossey Bass.

Blyton, P., and Morris, J. (eds.) (1991), *A Flexible Future: Prospects for Employment and Organisation,* Berlin: De Gruyter.

Blyton, P., and Morris, J. (1992), 'HRM and the limits of flexibility', in P. Blyton and P. Turnbull (eds.), *Reassessing Human Resource Management,* London: Sage.

Blyton, P., and Turnbull, P. (eds.) (1992), *Reassessing Human Resource Management,* London: Sage.

Blyton, P., and Turnbull, P. (1994), *The Dynamics of Employee Relations,* London: Macmillan.

Boerlijst, G., and Meijboom, G. (1989), 'Matching the individual and the organisation', in P. Herriot (ed.), *Assessment and Selection in Organisations: Methods and Practice for Recruitment and Appraisal,* Chichester: Wiley.

Bowey, A. (1974), *A Guide to Human Resource Planning,* London: Macmillan.

Bowey, A., and Thorpe, R. (1986), *Payment Systems and Productivity,* London: Macmillan.

Boyd, A. (1972), *The Rise of Irish Trade Unions, 1729–1970,* Tralee: Anvil.

Boydell, T. (1983), *A Guide to Job Analysis,* London: BACIE.

Boyer, R. (ed.) (1988), *The Search for Labour Market Flexibility,* Oxford: Clarendon.

Bramham, J. (1988), *Practical Human Resource Planning,* London: Institute of Personnel Management.

Brannick, T., and Doyle, L. (1994), 'Industrial conflict', in T. Murphy and W. Roche (eds.), *Irish Industrial Relations in Practice,* Dublin: Oak Tree.

Braverman, H. (1974), *Labour and Monopoly Capital: the Degradation of Work in the Twentieth Century,* London: Monthly Review Press.

Breen, R., Hannon, D., Rottman, D., and Whelan, C. (1990), *Understanding Contemporary Ireland: State, Class and Development in the Republic of Ireland,* Dublin: Gill & Macmillan.

Brewster, C. (1990), 'Flexible Working and Strategic HRM in Europe: Research Data', MCE Industrial Relations Conference, Brussels, Nov. 1990.

Brewster, C., and Hegewisch, A. (eds.) (1994), *Policy and Practice in European Human Resource Management (Price Waterhouse Cranfield Survey)*, London: Routledge.

Brewster, C., Hegewisch, A., Lockhart, T., and Mayne, L. (1993), 'Flexible working patterns in Europe', *Issues in People Management*, no. 6.

Brown, J. (1994), *The Juridification of the Employment Relationship*, Aldershot: Aylesbury.

Brown, W. (1981), *The Changing Contours of British Industrial Relations*, Oxford: Blackwell.

Buchanan, D. (1979), *The Development of Job Design Theories and Techniques*, London: Saxon House.

Buchanan, D., and McCalman, J. (1989), *High Performance Work Systems: the Digital Experience*, London: Routledge.

Buckley, R., and Caple, J. (1992), *The Theory and Practice of Training*, London: Kogan Page.

Buller, P., and Napier, N. (1993), 'Strategy and human resource management: integration in fast growth versus other mid-sized firms', *British Journal of Management*, vol. 4, no. 2, 77–90.

Butler, P. (1995), 'Employer Organisations: a Study', BBS project, University of Limerick.

Byrne, T. (1988), 'IPM in Ireland, 1937–1987', *IPM News*, vol. 3, no. 2.

Cairns, N., and Thompson, J. (1988), 'Human resource planning in Northern Ireland', *Journal of Irish Business and Administrative Research*, vol. 9.

Calvert, G., Mobley, S., and Marshall, L. (1994), 'Grasping the learning organisation', *Training and Development*, June 1994.

Carey, A. (1967), 'The Hawthorne Studies: a radical criticism', *American Sociological Review*, June 1967.

Cascio, W. (1986), *Managing Human Resources: Productivity, Quality of Work Life, Profits*, New York: McGraw-Hill.

Casey, B., Lakey, J., and White, M. (1992), *Payment Systems: a Look at Current Practice* (Research Series, no. 5), London: Policy Studies Institute, Department of Employment.

Chandler, A. (1962), *Strategy and Structure: Chapters in the History of the Industrial Enterprise*, Cambridge (Mass.): MIT Press.

Cherns, A., and Davis, L. (1975), *The Quality of Working Life*, London: Macmillan.

Chubb, B. (ed.) (1992), *FIE: Federation of Irish Employers, 1942–1992*, Dublin: Gill & Macmillan.

Clarke, P. (1989), 'Payment by result schemes: a review of trends', *Industrial Relations News*, no. 8, 23.

Clegg, H. (1979), *The Changing System of Industrial Relations in Great Britain*, Oxford: Blackwell.

Cole, G. (1988), *Personnel Management: Theory and Practice*, London: DP Publications.

Commission on Industrial Relations (1972), *Employers' Organisations and Industrial Relations* (Study no. 1), London: HMSO.

Confederation of Irish Industry (1981), *Jobs and the Workforce* (Business Report no. 11), Dublin: CII.

Cox, B., and Hughes, J. (1989), 'Industrial Relations in the Public Sector' in *Industrial Relations in Ireland: Contemporary Issues and Developments*, Dublin: University College.

Cradden, T. (1992), 'Trade unionism and HRM: the incompatibles', *Irish Business and Administrative Research*, vol. 13, 37–48.

Culliton, J. (1992), *A Time for Change: Industrial Policy for the 1990s* (Report of the Industrial Policy Review Group), Dublin: Stationery Office.

Curson, C. (1986), *Flexible Patterns of Work*, London: Institute of Personnel Management.

Dale, M. (1995), *Successful Recruitment and Selection: a Practical Guide for Managers*, London: Kogan Page.

Daniel, W., and Millward, N. (1983), *Workplace Industrial Relations in Britain: the DE/PSI/ESRC Study*, London: Heinemann.

Dastmalachian, A., Blyton, P., and Adamson, R. (1991), *The Climate of Workplace Relations*, London: Routledge.

Davis, L. (1966), 'The design of jobs', *Industrial Relations*, vol. 6, no. 1.

Deaton, D. (1985), 'Management style and large scale survey evidence', *Industrial Relations Journal*, vol. 16, no. 2, 67–71.

Department of Enterprise and Employment (1993), *Duties and Responsibilities of Employee Representatives and the Protection and Facilities to be Afforded Them by Their Employer*, Dublin: Stationery Office.

Dineen, D. (1987), 'Employment Development in the Irish Economy since 1979', paper presented to International Conference on the Changing Nature of Employment: New Forms and New Areas, Paris: BIPE.

Dineen, D. (1988), *Changing Employment Patterns in Ireland: Recent Trends and Future Prospects*, Limerick: University of Limerick.

Dineen, D. (1992), 'Atypical work patterns in Ireland: short term adjustments or fundamental changes', *Administration*, vol. 40, no. 3, autumn 1992.

Dineen, D. (1993), 'Employment Trends and Labour Market Issues in the 1990s', paper presented to conference, Employment Programmes in a Changing Labour Market, Dublin, 15–16 Nov. 1993.

Dobson, P. (1989), 'Reference reports' in P. Herriot (ed.), *Assessment and Selection in Organisations*, New York: Wiley.

Doeringer, P., and Piore, M. (1971), *Internal Labor Markets and Manpower Analysis*, New York: Lexington.

Donnelly, E. (1987), 'The training model: a time for change?', *Industrial and Commercial Training*, May–June 1987, 3–6.

Downes, D. (1986), 'Human Resource Planning in Ireland: a Survey of Current Practice in the Mid-West Region', BBS project, NIHE, Limerick.

Driver, M. (1982), 'Career concepts: a new approach to career research' in R. Katz (ed.), *Career Issues in Human Resource Management*, Englewood Cliffs: Prentice-Hall.

Du Brin, A. (1978), *Human Relations: a Job Oriented Approach*, Virginia: Reston.

Duffy, K. (1993), 'Training: why we lag behind our Euro partners', *Irish Independent*, Business and Recruitment Supplement, 18 Mar. 1993, 3.

Easterby-Smith, M. (1986), *Evaluation of Management, Training and Development*, Aldershot: Gower.

Edwards, M., Ewen, A., and O'Neal, S. (1995), 'Using multisource assessment to pay people not jobs', *ACA Journal*, summer 1995, 4–17.

Ehrenberg, R., and Smith, S. (1991), *Modern Labour Economics: Theory and Public Policy*, New York: Harper-Collins.

Elger, T. (1991), 'Flexible futures?: new technology and the contemporary transformation of work', *Work, Employment and Society,* vol. 1, no. 4.

Elliott, R. (1990), *Labour Economics: a Comparative Text,* Maidenhead: McGraw-Hill.

Evenden, R., and Anderson, G. (1992), *Management Skills: Making the Most of People,* Wokingham: Addison-Wesley.

Farnham, D. (1984), *Personnel in Context,* London: Institute of Personnel Management.

Farnham, D., and Pimlott, J. (1990), *Understanding Industrial Relations,* London: Cassell.

Fennel, C., and Lynch, I. (1993), *Labour Law in Ireland,* Dublin: Gill & Macmillan.

Fisher, R., and Ury, W. (1986), *Getting to Yes,* London: Hutchinson.

Fitzgerald, T. (1971), 'Why motivation theory doesn't work', *Harvard Business Review,* July–Aug. 1971, 12–19.

Flanders, A. (1968), *Trade Unions,* London: Hutchinson.

Fletcher, C., and Williams, R. (1985), *Performance Appraisal and Career Development,* London: Hutchinson.

Flood, P. (1989), 'Human Resource Management: Promise, Possibility and Limitations', research paper, University of Limerick.

Flood, P. (1990), 'Atypical employment: core-periphery human resource strategies: the implications for corporate culture', *Industrial Relations News,* no. 9–10.

Foley, A. (1990), 'Indigenous manufacturing' in A. Foley and M. Mulreany (eds.), *The Single European Market and the Irish Economy,* Dublin: Institute of Public Administration.

Foley, K., and Gunnigle, P. (1994), 'The personnel/human resource function and employee relations' in P. Gunnigle, P. Flood, M. Morley and T. Turner, *Continuity and Change in Irish Employee Relations,* Dublin: Oak Tree.

Foley, K., and Gunnigle, P. (1995), 'The personnel function: change or continuity' in T. Turner and M. Morley, *Industrial Relations and the New Order,* Dublin: Oak Tree.

Foley, K., Gunnigle, P., and Morley, M. (1994), 'Financial rewards and company ownership: an examination of reward practices in the Republic of Ireland', *International Executive,* vol. 36, no. 5, 575–99.

Fombrun, C. (1986), 'Environmental trends create new pressures on human resources' in S. Rynes and G. Milkovich (eds.), *Current Issues in Human Resource Management: Commentary and Readings,* Plasco (Texas): Business Publications.

Fombrun, C., Tichy, N., and Devanna, M. (1984) *Strategic Human Resource Management,* New York: Wiley.

Foulkes, F. (1980), *Effective Personnel Policies: a Study of Larger Non-Union Enterprises,* Englewood Cliffs: Prentice-Hall.

Fowler, A. (1988), 'New directions in performance pay', *Personnel Management,* Nov. 1988, 30–4.

Fowler, A. (1991), 'Performance related pay', *Personnel Management Plus,* June 1991.

Fowler, A. (1996), ' How to pick a job evaluation system', *Personnel Management,* 8 Feb. 1996, 42–3.

Fox, A. (1966), 'Management ideology and labour relations', *British Journal of Industrial Relations,* 4.

Fox, A. (1968), *Industrial Sociology and Industrial Relations* (Royal Commission on Trade Unions and Employers' Associations, Research Paper no. 3), London: HMSO.

Fox, A. (1974), *Beyond Contract: Work, Power and Trust Relations,* London: Faber.

Fox, R. (1987), *Training of the Employed: Statistics for Ireland,* Dublin: AnCO.

Fox, R., and O'Reilly, A. (1979), *Corporate Human Resource Planning in Ireland*, Dublin: AnCO.

Galbraith, J., and Nathanson, D. (1978), *Strategic Implementation: the Role of Structure and Process*, St Paul: West Publishing.

Galvin, P. (1988), *Managers for Ireland: the Case for Development of Irish Managers*, Dublin: Advisory Committee on Management Training, Department of Labour.

Garavan, G., Costine, P., and Heraty, N. (1995), *Training and Development in Ireland: Context, Policy and Practice*, Dublin: Oak Tree.

Garavan, T. (1991), 'Strategic human resource development', *Journal of European Industrial Training*, vol. 15, no. 1, 17–31.

Garavan, T., Morley, M., and Flynn, M. (1997), '360 degree feedback: its role in employee development', *Journal of Management Development*, 23, 1.

Geary, J. (1994a), 'Task participation: employee's participation: enabled or constrained' in K. Sisson (ed.), *Personnel Management: a Comprehensive Guide to Theory and Practice in Britain*, Oxford: Blackwell.

Geary, J. (1994b), *New Forms of Work Organisation: Implications for Employers, Trade Unions and Employees* (Working Paper no. 9), Dublin: Graduate School of Business, University College.

Geary, J. (1995a), *Working at Teamwork: Lessons from Europe* (Working Paper), Dublin: Graduate School of Business, University College.

Geary, J. (1995b), 'World class manufacturing and the implications for industrial relations' in P. Gunnigle and W. Roche (eds.), *New Challenges to Irish Industrial Relations*, Dublin: Oak Tree, in association with Labour Relations Commission.

Gladstone, A. (1984), 'Employers' associations in comparative perspective: functions and activities' in J. Windmuller and A. Gladstone (eds.), *Employers' Associations and Industrial Relations: a Comparative Study*, Oxford: Clarendon.

Goffee, R., and Scase, R. (1986), 'Are the rewards worth the effort?: changing managerial values in the 1980s', *Personnel Review*, vol. 15, no. 4.

Government Social Survey (1968), *Workplace Industrial Relations*, London: HMSO.

Grafton, D. (1988), 'Performance-related pay: securing employee trust', *Industrial Relations News*, no. 44, 17 Nov. 1988, 11–12.

Green, F., Krahn, H., and Sung, J. (1993), 'Non-standard work in Canada and the United Kingdom', *International Journal of Human Resource*, vol. 14, no. 5, 70–86.

Guest, D. (1983), 'Personnel management strategies, procedures and techniques' in D. Guest and J. Kenny, *A Textbook of Techniques and Strategies in Personnel Management*, London: Institute of Personnel Management.

Guest, D. (1987), 'Human resource management and industrial relations', *Journal of Management Studies*, vol. 24, no. 5, 503–21.

Guest, D. (1989), 'Human resource management: its implications for industrial relations and trade unions' in J. Storey (ed.), *New Perspectives on Human Resource Management*, London: Routledge.

Guest, D. (1990), 'Human resource management and the American dream', *Journal of Management Studies*, vol. 27, no. 4. 377–97.

Guest, D. (1992), 'Right enough to be dangerously wrong: an analysis of the "in search of excellence" phenomenon' in G. Salamon (ed.), *Human Resource Strategies*, London: Sage/Open University Press.

Guest, D., and Hoque, K. (1994), 'Yes, personnel does make a difference', *Personnel Management*, Nov. 1994, 40–4.

Gunnigle, P. (1989), 'Management approaches to industrial relations in the small firm' in *Industrial Relations in Ireland: Contemporary Issues and Developments*, Dublin: University College.

Gunnigle, P. (1991), 'Determinants and nature of personnel policy choice: the context for human resource development', *Journal of European Industrial Training*, vol. 15, no. 3, 22–31.

Gunnigle, P. (1992a), 'Changing management approaches to employee relations in Ireland', *Employee Relations*, vol. 14, no. 5, 40–51.

Gunnigle, P. (1992b), 'Human resource management in Ireland', *Employee Relations*, vol. 14, no. 5, 5–22.

Gunnigle, P. (1992c), 'Ireland' in C. Brewster, A. Hegewisch, L. Holden and T. Lockhart (eds.), *The European Human Resource Management Guide*, London: Academic Press.

Gunnigle, P. (1993), 'Multinational Companies and Labour Relations: a Perspective on the Experience of the Republic of Ireland', paper presented to OECD/Hungarian Ministry of Labour seminar, Labour-Management Relations in Foreign Enterprises in Hungary, Budapest, June 1993.

Gunnigle, P. (1995a), 'Management styles in employee relations in greenfield sites: challenging a collectivist tradition', PhD thesis, Cranfield School of Management, Bedford.

Gunnigle, P. (1995b), 'Collectivism and the management of industrial relations in greenfield sites', *Human Resource Management Journal*, vol. 5, no. 4.

Gunnigle, P., and Brady, T. (1984), 'The management of industrial relations in the small firm', *Employee Relations*, vol. 6, no. 5.

Gunnigle, P., and Daly, A. (1992), 'Craft integration and flexible work practices: training implications', *Industrial and Commercial Training*, vol. 24, no. 10, 10–18.

Gunnigle, P., and Flood, P. (1990), *Personnel Management in Ireland: Practices, Trends and Developments*, Dublin: Gill & Macmillan.

Gunnigle, P., Flood, P., Morley, M., and Turner, T. (1994), *Continuity and Change in Irish Employee Relations*, Dublin: Oak Tree.

Gunnigle, P., Foley, K., and Morley, M. (1994), 'A review of organisational reward practices' in P. Gunnigle, P. Flood, M. Morley and T. Turner, *Continuity and Change in Irish Employee Relations*, Dublin, Oak Tree.

Gunnigle, P., Garavan, T., and Fitzgerald, G. (1992), *Employee Relations and Employment Law in Ireland*, Limerick: Plassey Management and Technology Centre, University of Limerick.

Gunnigle, P., McMahon, G., and Fitzgerald, G. (1995), *Industrial Relations in Ireland: Theory and Practice.* Dublin: Gill & Macmillan.

Gunnigle, P., and Moore, S. (1994), 'Linking business strategy and human resource management: issues and implications', *Personnel Review*, vol. 23, no. 1, 63–84.

Gunnigle, P., and Morley, M. (1993), 'Something old, something new: a perspective on industrial relations in the Republic of Ireland', *Review of Employment Topics*, vol. 1, no. 1, 114–43.

Gunnigle, P., Morley, M., and Foley, K. (1995), 'Human resource management in Ireland' in I. Brunstein (ed.), *Human Resource Management in Western Europe*, Berlin: De Gruyter.

Gunnigle, P., Morley, M., and Turner, T. (1994), 'Developments in industrial relations and HRM in the Republic of Ireland', *Irish Business and Administrative Research*, vol. 15, 76–92.

Gunnigle, P., Morley, M., and Turner, T. (1996a), *Challenging Collectivist Traditions: Individualism and the Management of Industrial Relations in Greenfield Sites* paper presented to first conference of Irish Academy of Management, Cork, Sept. 1996.

Gunnigle, P., Morley, M., and Turner, T. (1996b), *Strategic Integration and Industrial Relations: the Impact of Managerial Styles* (Working Paper), Limerick: Department of Personnel and Employment Relations, University of Limerick.

Gunnigle, P., and Roche, W. (eds.) (1995), *New Challenges to Irish Industrial Relations*, Dublin: Oak Tree and Labour Relations Commission.

Hackman, J., and Oldham, G. (1976), 'Motivation through the design of work: test of a theory', *Organisational Behaviour and Human Performance*, vol. 16.

Hackman, J., and Oldham, G. (1980), *Work Redesign*, New York: Addison-Wesley.

Hakim, K. (1991), 'Cross national comparative research on the European Community: the EC labour force surveys', *Work, Employment and Society*, vol. 5, no. 1, 101–17.

Hamblin, A. (1974), *Evaluation and Control of Training*, Maidenhead: McGraw-Hill.

Hannaway, C. (1987), 'New style collective agreements: an Irish approach', *Industrial Relations News*, no. 13, 16–22.

Hannaway, C. (1992), 'Why Irish eyes are smiling', *Personnel Management*, May 1992, 38–41.

Hardiman, N. (1988), *Pay, Politics and Economic Performance in Ireland, 1970–1987*, Oxford: Clarendon.

Harrison, R. (1992), *Employee Development*, London: Institute of Personnel Management.

Hawkins, K. (1979), *A Handbook of Industrial Relations Practice*, London: Kogan Page.

Heery, E. (1992), 'Divided We Fall?: Trade Unions and Performance-Related Pay', paper presented to London School of Economics and TUC seminar, London School of Economics, 19 Mar. 1992.

Hegewisch, A., and Bruegel, I. (1992), 'Flexibilisation and Part-Time Work in Europe', BSA 92 Conference, Canterbury, Apr. 1992.

Heraty, N. (1992), 'Training and Development: a Study of Practices in Irish Based Companies', MBS thesis, University of Limerick.

Heraty, N., and Morley, M. (1994), 'Human resource development in Ireland: position, practices and power', *Administration*, 42, 3, 299–319.

Herriot, P. (1989), *Recruitment in the 90s*, London: Institute of Personnel Management.

Herzberg, F. (1966), *Work and the Nature of Man*, New York: Staples.

Herzberg, F. (1968), 'One more time: how do you motivate employees?', *Harvard Business Review*, Jan.–Feb. 1968, 115–25.

Higgins, C. (1992), 'Executive search: an essential requirement for the 1990s', *Industrial Relations News*, 38, 8 Oct. 1992.

Hill, J., and Trist, E. (1955), 'Changes in accidents and other absences with length of service', *Human Relations*, 8 May 1955.

Hillery, B. (1989), 'An overview of Irish industrial relations' in *Industrial Relations in Ireland: Contemporary Issues and Developments*, Dublin: University College.

Hillery, B. (1994), 'The institutions of industrial relations' in T. Murphy and W. Roche (eds.), *Irish Industrial Relations in Practice*, Dublin: Oak Tree.

Hoevemeyer, V. (1989), 'Performance based compensation: miracle or waste', *Personnel Journal*, July 1989.

Hofer, C., and Schendel, D. (1978), *Strategy Formulation: Analytical Concepts*, St Paul: West Publishing.

Hourihan, F. (1994), 'The European Union and industrial relations' in T. Murphy and W. Roche (eds.), *Irish Industrial Relations in Practice*, Dublin: Oak Tree.

Hunter, J., and Hunter, R. (1984), 'Validity and utility of alternative predictors of job performance', *Psychological Bulletin*, 96, 72–98.

Hunter, L., and McInnes, J. (1992), 'Employers and labour flexibility: the evidence from case studies', *Employment Gazette*, June 1992, 307–15.

Huseman, R., Hatfield, J., and Miles, E. (1987), 'A new perspective on equity theory: the equity sensitivity construct', *Academy of Management Review*, vol. 12, 222–34.

Iles, P. (1994), 'Developing learning environments: challenges for theory, research and practice', *Journal of European Industrial Training*, vol. 18, no. 3.

Iles, P., and Mabey, M. (1993), *Strategic Human Resource Management*, London: Blackwell.

International Labour Organisation (1975), *Collective Bargaining in Industrialised Market Economies*, Geneva: ILO.

Irish Business and Employers' Confederation (1993), *An Introduction*, Dublin: IBEC.

Irish Congress of Trade Unions (1993), *New Forms of Work Organisation: Options for Unions*, Dublin: ICTU.

Irish Congress of Trade Unions (1995), *Managing Change*, Dublin: ICTU.

Irish Industrial Relations Review (1993), 'Trade union organisation in the Republic', vol. 2, no. 7, July 1993.

Jackson, M. (1982), *Industrial Relations: a Textbook*, London: Kogan Page.

Johnson, G., and Scholes, K. (1993), *Exploring Corporate Strategy*, London: Prentice-Hall.

Kakabadse, A. (1990), 'Top People, Top Teams', paper presented to annual conference of Irish Institute of Training and Development, Limerick.

Keenan, J., and Thom, A. (1988), 'The future through the keyhole: some thoughts on employment patterns', *Personnel Review*, vol. 17, no. 1, 20–4.

Keenoy, T. (1990), 'HRM: a case of the wolf in sheep's clothing?', *Personnel Review*, vol. 19, no. 2, 3–9.

Kelly, A. (1975), 'Changes in the occupational structure and industrial relations in Ireland', *Management*, no. 2.

Kelly, A. (1989), 'The worker director in Irish industrial relations' in *Industrial Relations in Ireland: Contemporary Issues and Developments*, Dublin: University College.

Kelly, A., and Brannick, T. (1983), 'The pattern of strike activity in Ireland, 1960–1979: some preliminary observations', *Irish Business and Administrative Research*, vol. 5, no. 1, 65–77.

Kelly, A., and Brannick, T. (1985), 'The strike-proneness of public sector organisations', *Economic and Social Review*, vol. 16, no. 4, 251–71.

Kelly, A., and Brannick, T. (1986), 'The changing contours of Irish strike patterns, 1960–1984', *Irish Business and Administrative Research*, vol. 8 no. 1, 77–88.

Kelly, A., and Brannick, T. (1988a), 'Explaining the strike proneness of British companies in Ireland', *British Journal of Industrial Relations*, vol. 26, no. 1, 37–57.

Kelly, A., and Brannick, T. (1988b), 'The management of human resources: new trends and the challenge to trade unions', *Arena: Journal of the Irish Institute of Training and Development*, Aug. 1988, 11–15.

Kelly, A., and Brannick, T. (1988c), 'Strike trends in the Irish private sector', *Journal of Irish Business and Administrative Research*, vol. 9, 87–98.

Kelly, A., and Brannick, T. (1989), 'Strikes in Ireland: measurement, indices and trends' in *Industrial Relations in Ireland: Contemporary Issues and Developments*, Dublin: University College.

Kelly, A., and Brannick, T. (1991), 'The Impact of New Human Resource Management Policies on US MNC Strike Patterns', Dublin: Department of Business Administration, University College.

Kelly, J. (1980), 'The costs of job redesign: a preliminary analysis', *Industrial Relations Journal*, vol. 11, no. 3.

Kelly, J., and Clegg, C. (1982), *Autonomy and Control at the Workplace: Context for Job Redesign*, London: Croom Helm.

Kerr, A., and Whyte, G. (1985), *Irish Trade Union Law*, Abingdon: Professional Books.

Keynes, J. M. (1936), *The General Theory of Employment, Interest and Money*, London: Macmillan.

Kirkpatrick, D. (1959), 'Techniques for evaluating programmes', *Journal of the American Society for Training Directors*, 13.

Klein, J. (1989), 'The human cost of manufacturing reform', *Harvard Business Review*, Mar.–Apr. 1989.

Kochan, T., Katz, H., and McKersie, R. (1986), *The Transformation of American Industrial Relations*, New York: Basic Books.

Kochan, T., and Osterman, P. (1994), *The Mutual Gains Enterprise*, Cambridge (Mass.): Harvard Business School Press.

Kohn, A. (1993), 'Why incentive plans cannot work', *Harvard Business Review*, Sep.–Oct. 1993, 54–63.

Labour Relations Commission (1992), *Annual Report*, Dublin: Stationery Office.

Laffan, B. (1984), *The Youth Employment Scheme in Ireland* (Strathclyde Papers), Strathclyde Business School.

Lane, C. (1988), 'Industrial change in Europe: the pursuit of flexible specialisation in Britain and West Germany', *Work, Employment and Society*, vol. 12, no. 2, 141–68.

Latham, G. (1988), 'Human resource training and development', *Annual Review of Psychology*, no. 39, 545–82.

Latham, G., and Crandall, S. (1991), 'Organisational and social influences affecting training effectiveness' in J. Morrison (ed.), *Training for Performance*, Chichester: Wiley.

Lawler, E. (1977), 'Reward systems' in J. Hackman and J. Suttle (eds.), *Improving Life at Work: Behavioral Science Approaches to Organisational Change*, New York: Goodyear.

Lawler, E. (1978), 'The new plant revolution', *Organisational Dynamics*, winter 1978, 3–12.

Lawler, E. (1982), 'Increasing worker involvement to enhance organisational effectiveness' in P. Goodman (ed.), *Change in Organisations*, San Francisco: Jossey Bass.

Lawler, E. (1986), *High Involvement Management*, San Francisco: Jossey Bass.

Leddin, T., and Walsh, B. (1994), *The Macro Economy of Ireland*, Dublin: Gill & Macmillan.

Legge, K. (1989), 'Human resource management: a critical analysis' in J. Storey (ed.), *New Perspectives on Human Resource Management*, London, Routledge.

Lewis, C. (1984), 'What's new in selection?', *Personnel Management,* Jan. 1984.

Litwin, G., and Stringer, R. (1968), *Motivation and Organizational Climate,* Boston: Harvard University Press.

Lockett, J. (1992), *Effective Performance Management: a Strategic Guide to Getting the Best from People,* London: Kogan Page.

Long, P. (1988), 'A Review of Approved Profit Sharing (Trust) Schemes in Ireland and the UK', dissertation, Dublin Institute of Technology.

Lundy, O., and Cowling, A. (1996), *Strategic Human Resource Management,* London: Routledge.

Lupton, T. (1976), 'Best fit in the design of organisations' in E. Miller (ed.), *Task and Organisation,* New York: Wiley.

Mabey, M., and Salamon, G. (1995), *Strategic Human Resource Management,* Oxford: Blackwell.

McBeath, G., and Rands, N. (1989), *Salary Administration* (4th ed.), London: Gower.

McCarthy, C. (1977), 'A review of the objectives of the national pay agreements, 1970–1977', *Administration,* vol. 25, no. 1.

McCarthy, W., O'Brien, J., and Dowd, V. (1975), *Wage Inflation and Wage Leadership,* Dublin: Economic and Social Research Institute.

McClelland, D. (1961), *The Achieving Society,* New York: Van Nostrand.

McClelland, D., and Boyatzis, R. (1982), 'Leadership motive pattern and long term success in management', *Journal of Applied Psychology,* vol. 67, no. 2.

McEwan, N., Carmichael, C., Short, D., and Steel, A. (1988), 'Managing organisational change: a strategic approach', *Long-Range Planning,* 21, 6, 71–8.

McGinley, M. (1989a), 'Pay increases in the 1980s: the issue of control', *Industrial Relations News,* no. 30, Aug. 1989.

McGinley, M. (1989b), 'Pay increases between 1981 and 1987' in *Personnel and Industrial Relations Directory,* Dublin: Institute of Public Administration.

McGovern, P. (1988), 'Increasing opposition to unionisation in the 1980s', *Industrial Relations News,* no. 45, 24 Nov. 1988, 15–18.

McGovern, P. (1989a), 'Union recognition and union avoidance in the 1980s' in *Industrial Relations in Ireland: Contemporary Issues and Developments,* Dublin: University College.

McGovern, P. (1989b), 'Trade union recognition: five case studies', *Industrial Relations News,* no. 6, 9 Feb. 1989, 12–16.

McGregor, A., and Sproull, A. (1992), 'Employers and the flexible workforce', *Employment Gazette,* May 1992, 225–34.

McGregor, D. (1960), *The Human Side of Enterprise,* New York: McGraw-Hill.

McInnes, J. (1988), 'The question of flexibility', *Personnel Review,* vol. 17, no. 3, 12–15.

Mackay, L., and Torrington, D. (1986), *The Changing Nature of the Personnel Management,* London: Institute of Personnel Management.

McLagan, P. (1989), 'Models for HRD practice', *Training and Development Journal,* Sep. 1989, 49–59.

McMahon, G. (1988), 'Personnel selection in Ireland: scientific prediction or crystal ball gazing?', *IRM News,* vol. 3, no. 3, 20–3.

McMahon, G. (1989), 'The Joint Labour Committee system' in *Industrial Relations in Ireland: Contemporary Issues and Developments,* Dublin: University College.

McMahon, G., and Gunnigle, P. (1994), *Performance Appraisal: How to Get it Right*, Dublin: Productive Personnel Ltd in association with IPM (Ireland).

McMahon, G. (1988), 'Personnel selection in Ireland: scientific prediction or crystal ball gazing?', *IRM News*, vol. 3, no. 8, 20–3.

McMahon, J. (1994), 'Employee relations in small firms' in P. Gunnigle, P. Flood, M. Morley and T. Turner, *Continuity and Change in Irish Employee Relations*, Dublin: Oak Tree.

McNamara, G., Williams, K., and West, D. (1988), *Understanding Trade Unions: Yesterday and Today*, Dublin: O'Brien Educational.

Macon, T., and Dipboye, R. (1988), 'The effects of interviewers' initial impressions on information gathering', *Organisational Behaviour and Human Decision Processes*, 42, 364–87.

Makin, P., and Robertson, I. (1986), 'Selecting the best selection technique', *Personnel Management*, Nov. 1986.

Marchington, M. (1982), *Managing Industrial Relations*, London: McGraw-Hill.

Marchington, M. (1990), 'Analysing the links between product markets and the management of employee relations', *Journal of Management Studies*, vol. 27, no. 2, 111–32.

Marchington, M., and Parker, P. (1990), *Changing Patterns of Employee Relations*, Hemel Hempstead: Harvester Wheatsheaf.

Marginson, P. (1991), 'Continuity and change in the employment structure of large firms' in A. Pollert (ed.), *Farewell to Flexibility*, Oxford: Blackwell.

Marsden, D. (1986), *The End of Economic Man?: Custom and Competition in Labor Markets*, New York: St Martin's Press.

Marsh, A. (1973), *Managers and Shop Stewards*, London: Institute of Personnel Management.

Marshall, A. (1928), *Principles of Economics* (8th ed.), London: Macmillan.

Maslow, A. (1943), 'A theory of human motivation', *Psychological Review*, vol. 50, no. 4.

Mathis, R., and Jackson, J. (1994), *Human Resource Management* (7th ed.), St Paul: West Publishing.

Mayo, A. (1991), *Managing Careers: Strategies for Organisations*, Wimbledon: IPM.

Meulders, P., and Tytgat, B. (1989), 'The emergence of atypical employment in the European Community' in G. Rodgers and J. Rodgers (eds.), *Precarious Jobs in Labour Market Regulation: the Growth of Atypical Employment in Western Europe*, Geneva: ILO.

Miles, R., and Snow, C. (1978), *Organizational Strategy, Structure and Process*, New York: McGraw-Hill.

Miles, R., and Snow, C. (1984), 'Designing strategic human resources systems', *Organisational Dynamics*, spring 1984, 36–52.

Mintzberg, H. (1978), 'Patterns in strategy formulation', *Management Science*, vol. 24, May 1978, 934–48.

Mintzberg, H. (1988), 'Opening up the definition of strategy' in J. Quinn, H. Mintzberg and R. Rames (eds.), *The Strategy Process: Concepts, Contexts and Cases*, Englewood Cliffs: Prentice-Hall.

Mintzberg, M. (1973), *The Nature of Managerial Work*, New York: Harper and Row.

Mondy, R., and Noe, R. (1984), *Personnel: the Management of Human Resources*, London: Allyn and Bacon.

Monks, K. (1992), 'Personnel management practices: uniformity or diversity?: evidence from some Irish organisations', *Irish Business and Administrative Research*, vol. 13.

Mooney, P. (1980), *An Inquiry into Wage Payment Systems in Ireland,* Dublin: Economic and Social Research Institute/European Foundation for the Improvement of Living and Working Conditions.

Mooney, P. (1988), 'From Industrial Relations to Employee Relations in Ireland', PhD thesis, Trinity College, Dublin.

Moorhead, G., and Griffin, R. (1989), *Organizational Behavior,* New York: Houghton Mifflin.

Morley, M., and Garavan, T. (1993), 'The New Organisation: Its Implications for Training and Development', paper presented to national conference of Irish Institute of Training and Development, Galway, Apr. 1993.

Morley, M., and Gunnigle, P. (1993), 'Trends in flexible working patterns in Ireland' in P. Gunnigle, P. Flood, M. Morley and T. Turner, *Continuity and Change in Irish Employee Relations,* Limerick: University of Limerick.

Morrissey, T. (1989), 'Employee participation at sub-board level' in *Industrial Relations in Ireland: Contemporary Issues and Developments,* Dublin: University College.

Moss Kanter, R. (1983), *The Change Masters,* London: Unwin Hyman.

Mowday, R. (1987), 'Equity theory predictions of behaviour in organisations' in R. Steers and L. Porter, *Motivation and Work Behavior,* New York: McGraw-Hill.

Mowday, R., Porter, L., and Steers, R. (1982), *Employee-Organization Linkages: the Psychology of Commitment, Absenteeism and Turnover,* New York: Academic Press.

Muchinski, P. (1986), 'Personnel selection methods' in C. Cooper and I. Robertson (eds.), *International Review of Industrial and Organisational Psychology,* New York: Wiley.

Mumford, A. (1986), 'Learning to learn for managers', *Journal of European Industrial Training,* 10, 2, 1–22.

Munns, V. (1966), 'The functions and organisation of employers' associations in selected industries' in *Employers' Associations* (Royal Commission on Trade Unions and Employers' Associations, Research Paper no. 7), London: HMSO.

Munro Fraser, J. (1966), *Employment Interviewing,* London: MacDonald and Evans.

Murphy, T., and Roche, W. (eds.) (1994), *Irish Industrial Relations in Practice,* Dublin: Oak Tree.

Murray, S. (1984), *Employee Relations in Irish Private Sector Manufacturing Industry,* Dublin: Industrial Development Authority.

Murray, S. (1984), *Industrial Relations in Irish Private Sector Manufacturing Industry,* Dublin: Industrial Development Authority.

Nevin, E. (1963), *Wages in Ireland,* Dublin: Economic and Social Research Institute.

Nicholson, N., and Arnold, J. (1989), 'Graduate early experience in a multinational corporation', *Personnel Review,* 18, 4, 3–14.

Nicholson, N., and West, M. (1988), *Managerial Job Changes: Men and Women in Transition,* Cambridge: Cambridge University Press.

Nierenberg, G. (1968), *The Art of Negotiating,* New York: Cornerstone.

Niven, M. (1967), *Personnel Management, 1913–1963,* London: Institute of Personnel Management.

O'Brien, J. (1981), *A Study of National Wage Agreements in Ireland* (paper no. 104), Dublin: Economic and Social Research Institute.

O'Brien, J. (1989), 'Pay determination in Ireland' in *Industrial Relations in Ireland: Contemporary Issues and Developments,* Dublin: University College.

O'Connor, E. (1995), 'World class manufacturing in a semi-state environment' in P. Gunnigle and W. Roche (eds.), *New Challenges to Irish Industrial Relations,* Dublin: Oak Tree, in association with Labour Relations Commission.

O'Connor, K. (1982), 'The impact of the Unfair Dismissals Act, 1977, on personnel management and industrial relations', *Irish Business and Administrative Research,* vol. 5, no. 2.

Oechslin, J. (1985), 'Employers' organisations' in R. Blanpain (ed.), *Labour Law and Industrial Relations,* Deventer: Kluwer.

O'Hara, B. (1981), *The Evolution of Irish Industrial Relations: Law and Practice,* Dublin: Folens.

O'Mahony, D. (1958) *Industrial Relations in Ireland,* Dublin: Economic and Social Research Institute.

O'Malley, E. (1983), 'Late Industrialisation under Outward Looking Policies: the Experience and Prospects of the Republic of Ireland', PhD thesis, University of Sussex.

O'Neill, G., and Lander, D. (1994), 'Linking employee skills to pay: a framework for skill-based pay plans', *ACA Journal,* winter 1994, 14–27.

Organisation for Economic Co-operation and Development (1990), *Education in OECD Countries, 1987–1988,* Paris: OECD.

Ost, E. (1990), 'Team-based pay: new wave incentives', *Sloan Management Review,* spring 1990.

O'Sullivan, C. (1996), 'Time ripe for the Irish annual hours contract?', *IR Data Bank,* vol. 14, Feb. 1996, 21–3.

Ouchi, W. (1981), *Theory Z: How American Business Can Meet the Japanese Challenge,* Reading (Mass.): Addison-Wesley.

Pearse, J. (1987), 'Why merit pay doesn't work: implications for organisations theory', in D. Balkin and L. Gomez-Mejia (eds.), *New Perspectives on Compensation,* Englewood Cliffs: Prentice-Hall.

Pedler, M., Boydell, T., and Burgoyne, J. (1989), 'Towards the learning company', *Education and Development,* vol. 20, part 1.

Perry, B. (1984), *Einfield: a High Performance System,* DEC Educational Services Development and Publishing.

Personnel Standards Lead Body (1993), *A Perspective on Personnel,* London: Personnel Standards Lead Body.

Peters, T., and Waterman, R. (1982), *In Search of Excellence: Lessons from America's Best Run Companies,* New York: Harper and Row.

Pettigrew, P., Hendry, C., and Sparrow, P. (1988), *Linking Strategic Change, Competitive Performance and Human Resource Management: Results of a UK Based Empirical Study,* Coventry: University of Warwick.

Pettinger, R. (1994), *Introduction to Management,* London: Macmillan.

Phelps-Brown, H. (1986), *The Origins of Trade Union Power,* Oxford: Oxford University Press.

Philpott, L., and Sheppard, L. (1993), *Managing for Improved Performance,* London: Kogan Page.

Plumbley, P. (1985), *Recruitment and Selection,* London: Institute of Personnel Management.

Pollert, A. (1988), 'The flexible firm: fact or fixation?', *Work, Employment and Society*, vol. 2, 3, 281–316.

Pollert, A. (ed.) (1991), *Farewell to Flexibility*, Oxford: Blackwell.

Pollock, H., and O'Dwyer, L. (1985), *We Can Work It Out: Relationships in the Workplace*, Dublin: O'Brien Educational.

Pont, J. (1991), *Developing Effective Training Skills*, Maidenhead: McGraw-Hill.

Poole, M. (1986), 'Managerial strategies and styles in industrial relations: a comparative analysis', *Journal of General Management*, vol. 12, no. 1, 40–53.

Porter, M. (1980), *Competitive Strategy: Techniques for Analysing Industries and Competitors*, New York, Free Press.

Porter, M. (1985), *Competitive Advantage: Creating and Sustaining Superior Performance*, New York: Free Press.

Porter, M. (1987), 'From competitive advantage to corporate strategy', *Harvard Business Review*, May–June 1987, 43–59.

Porter, M. (1990), *The Competitive Advantage of Nations*, New York: Free Press.

Purcell, J. (1987), 'Mapping management styles in employee relations', *Journal of Management Studies*, vol. 24, no. 5, 533–48.

Purcell, J. (1989), 'The impact of corporate strategy on human resource management' in J. Storey (ed.), *New Perspectives on Human Resource Management*, London: Routledge.

Purcell, J., and Gray, A. (1986), 'Corporate personnel departments and the management of industrial relations: two case studies in ambiguity', *Journal of Management Studies*, vol. 23, no. 2, 205–23.

Purcell, J., and Sisson, K. (1983), 'Strategies and practice in the management of industrial relations' in G. Bain (ed.), *Industrial Relations in Britain*, Oxford: Blackwell.

Quinn Mills, D. (1991), *Rebirth of the Corporation*, New York: Wiley.

Randell, G. (1994), *Performance Appraisal in Personnel Management: a Comprehensive Guide to Theory and Practice in Britain*, Oxford: Blackwell.

Reid, M., Barrington, M., and Kenney, J. (1992), *Training Interventions: Managing Employee Development*, London: Institute of Personnel Management.

Reilly, R., and Chao, G. (1982), 'Validity and fairness of some alternative selection procedures', *Personnel Psychology*, 35.

Revans, R. (1982), 'Action learning: the skills of diagnosis', *Management Decision*, 21, 2, 46–52.

Reynaud, J. (1978), *Problems and Prospects for Collective Bargaining in the EEC Member States* (document no. V/394/78-EN), Brussels: European Community.

Ridgely, P. (1988), 'How relevant is the FUE?', *Irish Business*, Feb. 1988.

Robertson, I., and Makin, P. (1986), 'Management selection in Britain: a survey and critique', *Journal of Occupational Psychology*, 59.

Roche, W. (1988), 'Ireland: trade unions in Ireland in the 1980s', *European Industrial Relations Review*, no. 176.

Roche, W. (1989), 'State strategies and the politics of industrial relations in Ireland since 1945' in *Industrial Relations in Ireland: Contemporary Issues and Developments*, Dublin: University College.

Roche, W. (1990), 'Industrial Relations Research in Ireland and the Trade Union Interest', paper presented to ICTU conference, Joint Research between Trade Unions, Universities, Third-Level Colleges and Research Institutes, Dublin.

Roche, W. (1992), 'Modelling trade union growth and decline in the Republic of Ireland', *Irish Journal of Business and Administrative Research*, vol. 14, no. 1, 87–103.

Roche, W. (1994a), 'Pay determination, the state and the politics of industrial relations' in W. Roche and T. Murphy (eds.), *Irish Industrial Relations in Practice*, Dublin: Oak Tree.

Roche, W. (1994b), 'The trend of unionisation' in W. Roche and T. Murphy (eds.), *Irish Industrial Relations in Practice*, Dublin: Oak Tree.

Roche, W. (1995), 'The New Competitive Order and Employee Relations in Ireland: Challenges and Prospects', paper presented to IBEC conference, Human Resources in the Global Market, Dublin, Nov. 1995.

Roche, W., and Geary, J. (1994), *The Attenuation of Host-Country Effects?: Multinationals, Industrial Relations and Collective Bargaining in Ireland* (Business Research Programme Working Paper), Dublin: Smurfit Graduate School of Business, University College.

Roche, W., and Gunnigle, P. (1995), 'Competition and the new industrial relations agenda' in P. Gunnigle and W. Roche (eds.), *New Challenges to Irish Industrial Relations*, Dublin: Oak Tree.

Roche, W., and Larragy, J. (1989), 'The trend of unionisation in the Irish Republic' in *Industrial Relations in Ireland: Contemporary Issues and Developments*, Dublin: University College.

Roche, W., and Tansey, P. (1992), *Industrial Training in Ireland: Report Submitted to Industrial Policy Review Group*, Dublin: Department of Industry and Trade.

Roche, W., and Turner, T. (1994), 'Testing alternative models of human resource policy effects on trade union recognition in the Republic of Ireland', *International Journal of Human Resource Management*, vol. 5, no. 3, 721–53.

Rodger, A. (1952), *The Seven-Point Plan*, London: National Institute of Industrial Psychology.

Roethlisberger, F., and Dickson, W. (1939), *Management and the Worker*, Cambridge (Mass.): Harvard University Press.

Ross, J. (1981), 'A definition of HRM', *Personnel Journal*, 60, 10, 781–83.

Roth, S. (1993), 'Lean production in German motor manufacturing', *European Participation Monitor*, no. 5, 35–9.

Royal Commission on Trade Unions and Employers' Associations (1968), *Royal Commission on Trade Unions and Employers' Associations, 1965–1968* (Donovan Report) (Cmnd 3623), London: HMSO.

Salamon, G. (1992), *Human Resource Strategies*, London, Sage/Open University Press.

Salamon, M. (1992), *Industrial Relations: Theory and Practice*, Hemel Hempstead: Prentice-Hall.

Sanfilippo, F., and Weigman, G. (1991), 'A compensation strategy for the 1990s', *Human Resource Professional*, vol. 4, no. 1, fall 1991.

Sargeant, A. (1990), *Turning People On: the Motivation Challenge*, London: Institute of Personnel Management.

Schneider, B., and Schmitt, N. (1986), *Staffing Organisations*, Illinois: Waveland.

Schuler, R. (1987), 'Personnel and human resource management choices and organizational strategy', *Human Resource Planning*, vol. 10, no. 1, 1–17.

Schuler, R. (1989), 'Strategic human resource management', *Human Relations*, vol. 42, no. 2, 157–84.

Schuler, R. (1992), 'Strategic human resource management: linking the people with the strategic needs of the business', *Organisational Dynamics,* vol. 21, no. 1, 18–31.

Schuler, R. (1995), *Managing Human Resources* (5th ed.), St Paul: West Publishing.

Schuler, R., Galante, S., and Jackson, S. (1987), 'Matching effective HR practices with competitive strategy', *Personnel,* Sep. 1987, 18–27.

Schuler, R., and Jackson, S. (1987a), 'Linking competitive strategies with human resource management practices', *Academy of Management Executive,* vol. 1, no. 3, Aug. 1987, 209–13.

Schuler, R., and Jackson, S. (1987b), 'Organizational strategy and organizational level as determinants of human resource management practices', *Human Resource Planning,* vol. 10, no. 3. 125–41.

Senge, P. (1990), The Fifth Discipline, New York: Doubleday.

Shivanath, G. (1987), 'Personnel Practitioners, 1986: Their Role and Status in Irish Industry', MBS thesis, NIHE, Limerick.

Sisson, K. (1983), 'Employers' Organisations' in G. Bain (ed.), *Industrial Relations in Britain,* Oxford: Blackwell.

Sisson, K. (1989), *Personnel Management in Britain,* Oxford: Blackwell.

Sisson, K. (1994), 'Workplace Europe: Direct Participation in Organisational Change: Introducing the EPOC Project', paper presented to International Industrial Relations Association Fourth European Regional Congress, Transformation of European Industrial Relations: Consequences of Integration and Disintegration, Helsinki.

Smith, A. (1776), *The Wealth of Nations,* reprinted London: Pelican 1970.

Smith, M., Gregg, M., and Andrews, D. (1989), *Selection and Assessment: a New Appraisal,* Pitman, London.

Smith, M., and Robertson, I. (1993), *The Theory and Practice of Systematic Staff Selection,* London: Macmillan.

Sparrow, P., and Bognanno, M. (1993), 'Competency requirements forecasting: issues for international selection and assessment', *International Journal of Selection and Assessment,* vol. 1, no. 1, 50–8.

Sparrow, P., and Hiltrop, J. (1994), *European Human Resource Management in Transition,* London: Prentice-Hall.

Stata, R. (1989), 'Organisational learning: the key to management innovation', *Sloan Management Review,* vol. 30, no. 3, Spring 1989.

Steers, R., and Mowday, R. (1987), 'Employee turnover in organisations' in R. Steers and L. Porter (eds.), *Motivation and Work Behavior,* New York: McGraw-Hill.

Steers, R., and Porter, L. (1987), *Motivation and Work Behavior,* New York: McGraw-Hill.

Steers, R., and Rhodes, S. (1978), 'Major influences on employee attendance: a process model,' *Journal of Applied Psychology,* 63, 391–407.

Stewart, A. (1991), 'Performance appraisal' in J. Prior (ed.), *Handbook of Training and Development* (2nd ed.), Aldershot: Gower.

Stewart, R. (1976), *Contrast in Management: a Study of Different Types of Managers' Jobs, their Demands and Choices,* Maidenhead: McGraw-Hill.

Storey, J. (ed.) (1989), *New Perspectives on Human Resource Management,* London: Routledge.

Storey, J. (1992), *Developments in the Management of Human Resources,* Oxford: Blackwell.

Storey, J. (1995), *Human Resource Management: a Critical Text,* London: Routledge.

Strauss, G., and Sayle, L. (1972), *Personnel: the Human Problems of Management,* Englewood Cliffs: Prentice-Hall.

Sugarman, L. (1986), *Life Span Development,* London: Methuen.

Suttle, S. (1988), 'Labour market flexibility', *Industrial Relations News,* vol. 38, 6, 13–16.

Taylor, F. (1911), *The Principles of Scientific Management,* New York: Harper.

Taylor, F. (1947), *Scientific Management,* London: Harper and Row.

Thelen, H., and Withall, J. (1979), 'Three frames of reference: the description of climate', *Human Relations,* vol. 2, no. 2, 159–76.

Thomason, G. (1984), *A Textbook of Industrial Relations Management,* London: Institute of Personnel Management.

Thompson, P. (1983), *The Nature of Work: an Introduction to Debates on the Labour Process,* London: Macmillan.

Thurley, K., and Wood, S. (1983), *Industrial Relations and Management Strategy,* Cambridge: Cambridge University Press.

Tiernan, S., Morley, M., and Foley, E. (1996), *Modern Management: Theory and Practice for Irish Students,* Dublin: Gill & Macmillan.

Turner, H. (1962), *Trade Union Growth, Structure and Policy,* London: Allen and Unwin.

Turner, T. (1994), 'Unionisation and human resource management in Irish companies', *Industrial Relations Journal,* 25.1, 39–51.

Turner, T., and Morley, M. (1995), *Industrial Relations and the New Order,* Dublin: Oak Tree.

Tyson, S. (1985), 'Is this the very model of the modern personnel manager?', *Personnel Management,* May 1985.

Tyson, S. (1987), 'The management of the personnel function', *Journal of Management Studies,* Sep. 1987.

Tyson, S. (1992), 'Business and human resource strategy', *Irish Business and Administrative Research,* vol. 13, no. 1, 1–5.

Tyson, S., and Fell, A. (1986), *Evaluating the Personnel Function,* London: Hutchinson.

Tyson, S., Witcher, M., and Doherty, N. (1994), *Different Routes to Excellence,* Bedford: Human Resource Research Centre, Cranfield School of Management.

Umstot, D. (1988), *Understanding Organisational Behaviour* (2nd ed.), St Paul: West Publishing.

University of Limerick (1992), *Price Waterhouse Cranfield Project (Ireland),* Limerick: University of Limerick.

Vaill, P. (1982), 'The purposing of high performing systems,' *Organizational Dynamics,* autumn 1982.

Visser, J. (1991), 'Trends in union membership', *OECD Outlook,* July 1991.

von Prondzynski, F. (1985), 'The death of the pay round', *Industrial Relations News,* no. 43, Nov. 1985.

von Prondzynski, F., and McCarthy, C. (1984), *Employment Law in Ireland,* London: Sweet and Maxwell.

Vroom, V. (1964), *Work and Motivation,* New York: Wiley.

Wagner, R. (1949), 'The employment interview: a critical summary', *Personnel Psychology,* 2, 17–46.

Walker, C., and Guest, R. (1952), *The Man on the Assembly Line,* Boston: Harvard University Press.

Walker, J. (1980), *Human Resource Planning*, New York: McGraw-Hill.

Wall, T. (1982), 'Perspectives on job redesign' in J. Kelly and C. Clegg (eds.), *Autonomy and Control at the Workplace: Context for Job Redesign,* London: Croom Helm.

Wallace, J. (1988a), 'Unofficial strikes in Ireland', *Industrial Relations News,* no. 8, 15 Feb. 1988.

Wallace, J. (1988b), 'Workplace aspects of unofficial strikes', *Industrial Relations News,* no. 9, 3 Mar, 1988.

Wallace, J. (1989), 'Procedure agreements and their place in workplace industrial relations' in *Industrial Relations in Ireland: Contemporary Issues and Developments,* Dublin: University College.

Wallace, J. (1991), 'The Industrial Relations Act, 1990, and Other Developments in Labour Law', paper presented to Mid-West Chapter, Institute of Personnel Management, University of Limerick.

Wallace, J., and O'Shea, F. (1987), *A Study of Unofficial Strikes in Ireland,* Dublin: Stationery Office.

Walsh, J. (1996), 'Internationally Mobile Managers: Some Linkages to Human Resource Strategy and Creativity', paper presented to Irish Academy of Management conference, Management Research in Ireland: the Way Forward, 12–13 Sep. 1996.

Walton, R. (1985), 'From control to commitment in the workplace', *Harvard Business Review,* Mar.–Apr. 1985, 77–84.

Walton, R., and Lawrence, P. (1985), *Human Resource Management: Trends and Challenges,* Cambridge (Mass.): Harvard Business School Press.

Ward, P. (1995), 'A 360 degree turn for the better', *People Management,* Feb. 1995, 20–2.

Wareing, R., and Stockdale, J. (1987), 'Decision making in the promotion interview: an empirical study', *Personnel Review,* 16, 4.

Webb, S., and Webb, B. (1920), *The History of Trade Unionism,* London: Longman.

Webster, B. (1990), Beyond the mechanics of HRD, *Personnel Management,* 22, 3, 44–7.

Webster, E. (1964), *Decision Making in the Employment Interview,* Québec: Eagle Publishing.

West, P. (1994), 'The learning organisation: losing the luggage in transit?', *Journal of European Industrial Training,* vol. 18, no. 11.

Wexley, K., and Latham, G. (1991), *Developing and Training Human Resources in Organisations,* New York: Harper-Collins.

Whelan, C. (1982), *Worker Priorities, Trust in Management and Prospects for Worker Participation* (paper no. 111), Dublin: Economic and Social Research Institute.

Wickham, J. (1993), *New Forms of Work in Ireland: an Analysis of the 'New Forms of Work and Activity' Data Set* (Working Paper no. WP/93/31/EN), Dublin: European Foundation for the Improvement of Living and Working Conditions.

Wiesner, W., and Cronshaw, S. (1988), 'A meta-analytic investigation of the impact of interview format and degree of structure on the validity of the employment interview', *Journal of Occupational Psychology,* 61, 275–90.

Williamson, O. (1978), *Markets and Hierarchies: Analysis and Anti-Trust Implications,* Glencoe (NY): Free Press.

Windmuller, J. (1984), 'Employers' associations in comparative perspective: organisation, structure and administration' in J. Windmuller and A. Gladstone (eds.), *Employers' Associations and Industrial Relations: a Comparative Study,* Oxford: Clarendon.

Womack, J., Jones, D., and Roos, D. (1982), *The Machine that Changed the World,* New York: Rawson Associates.

Wright, V., and Brading, L. (1992), 'A balanced performance', *Total Quality Magazine,* Oct. 1992.

Index

industrial relations, 7, 39–40, 47. *see also* employee relations
    as personnel activity, 4–6
    and public policy, 16–17
    trade disputes, 288–9
    traditional, 48
Industrial Relations Act, 1990, 202, 206, 215–23, 270, 288–9
industrial relations officer (IRO), 217
Industrial Revolution, 1–2
Industrial Training Act, 1967, 163–4
Industrial Training in Ireland (Roche and Tansey), 170–72
information technology, 174
Institute of Personnel and Development (IPD), 168, 232
Institute of Public Administration (IPA), 168
integration test, 271
internal flow, 20–21
internal labour market, 54, 92
International Labour Organisation (ILO), 163, 246
International Monetary Fund (IMF), 162
interviews, 86–90
    appraisal interview, 152–4
Irish Bank Officials' Association (IBOA), 204
Irish Business and Employers' Confederation (IBEC), 229–30, 247
    analysis of industrial training, 169–70
    description of, 230–31
Irish Congress of Trade Unions (ICTU), 170, 203, 246, 266
    description of, 207
Irish Distributive and Administrative Trades Union (IDATU), 204
Irish Hotels Federation, 232
Irish Institute of Training and Development (IITD), 167, 171
Irish Management Institute (IMI), 168
Irish Municipal, Public and Civil Trade Union (IMPACT), 204
Irish National Teachers' Organisation (INTO), 204
Irish National Union of Vintners', Grocers' and Allied Trades Assistants (INUVGATA), 204, 232
Irish Nurses' Organisation (INO), 204
Irish Transport and General Workers' Union (ITGWU), 4, 204, 209

Jacob's, 2
JIT, 174
job analysis, 74–5

job classification, 124
job description, 76
job enrichment, 19
job evaluation
    choosing scheme, 129
    competence-based, 127–8
    criticisms of, 128–9
    Hay method, 126, 127
    job classification, 124
    job ranking, 123–4
    paired comparison, 125
    points rating, 125–6
job ranking, 123–4
joint industrial councils (JICs), 219
joint labour committees (JLCs), 219

Labour, Department of, 162, 277, 288
Labour Court, 211, 216–17, 223, 225, 226, 230, 233, 277, 289
    appeals, 222
    role of, 219–21
labour market, 20–21, 50–63
    flexibility, 54–6
    forecasting demand, 68–73
    internal v. external, 31
    Irish profile, 58–63
        demography, 58–9
        education, 61
        employment and unemployment, 59–61
        flexibility, 61–3
    operation of labour markets, 53–4
    theories of, 50–53, 56–8
        competitive model, 51–2, 57
        institutional model, 52, 57–8
        radical model, 52–3, 58
Labour Markets, White Paper on, 171
Labour Relations Commission, 215–19, 221, 223, 225, 230, 233, 289
Labour Services Act, 1987, 165–6, 169, 171
labour stability index, 69–70
Larkin, Jim, 4, 204
law. *see* employment law
learning organisation, 191–3
learning transfer, 180–81
Lemass, Seán, 162
Licensed Vintners' Association, 232
Limerick Employers' Federation, 232
Limerick-Shannon Personnel Managers' Group, 232
Local Government Staff Negotiations Board (LGSNB), 226, 235
lock-outs, 258